Forging a Sustainable Southwest

Forging a Sustainable Southwest

The Power of Collaborative Conservation

The Power of Collaborative Conservation

STEPHEN E. STROM

THE UNIVERSITY OF
ARIZONA PRESS
TUCSON

The University of Arizona Press
www.uapress.arizona.edu

We respectfully acknowledge the University of Arizona is on the land and territories of Indigenous peoples. Today, Arizona is home to twenty-two federally recognized tribes, with Tucson being home to the O'odham and the Yaqui. Committed to diversity and inclusion, the University strives to build sustainable relationships with sovereign Native Nations and Indigenous communities through education offerings, partnerships, and community service.

ISBN-13: 978-0-8165-5368-6 (paperback)
ISBN-13: 978-0-8165-5369-3 (ebook)

Cover design by Leigh McDonald
Cover photo by Tahnee Robertson
Designed and typeset by Sara Thaxton in 10/14 Warnock Pro with Arno Pro, Else NPL Std, and Acumin Pro Condensed

Library of Congress Cataloging-in-Publication Data
Names: Strom, Stephen, author.
Title: Forging a sustainable Southwest : the power of collaborative conservation / Stephen E. Strom.
Description: Tucson : University of Arizona Press, 2024. | Includes bibliographical references and index.
Identifiers: LCCN 2024005278 (print) | LCCN 2024005279 (ebook) | ISBN 9780816553686 (paperback) | ISBN 9780816553693 (ebook)
Subjects: LCSH: Nature conservation—Southwest, New. | Community-based conservation—Southwest, New.
Classification: LCC QH76.5.S695 S77 2024 (print) | LCC QH76.5.S695 (ebook) | DDC 333.78/2160979—dc23/eng/20240326
LC record available at https://lccn.loc.gov/2024005278
LC ebook record available at https://lccn.loc.gov/2024005279

Printed in the United States of America
♾ This paper meets the requirements of ANSI/NISO Z39.48-1992 (Permanence of Paper).

CONTENTS

Forging a Sustainable Southwest

Introduction

When you talk long enough and listen enough, and dare to open up your mind enough, you realize that most people and sides are making ethical and moral arguments that deserve high respect. Yes: achieving a vibrant community economic footing is a worthy—and moral—objective. Likewise, embedding communities in healthy, lasting landscapes is a moral imperative. If we pause to listen and honestly reflect, most of us believe that community and the land are both sacred, that both must be honored.

—CHARLES WILKINSON, IN *STITCHING THE WEST BACK TOGETHER*

A Defining Event

The first nine months of 1983 were unusually wet in Arizona. By late September a combination of a wet winter and abundant summer monsoon rains left the ground fully saturated throughout much of the state. From September 28 to October 4 it rained continuously—a deluge triggered by Pacific Tropical Storm Octave. Torrents of rain from Octave and its offshoot weather systems soaked the lands throughout a region extending from south of Flagstaff to the Mexican border and from western New Mexico to the California line—part of a seventy-thousand-square-mile area encompassing much of what hydrologists call the Lower Colorado watershed.

Rain, streams, and rivers in the watershed followed paths determined by gravity and the region's topography, descending from mountains to desert, hills to valleys. Waters rushed southward from heights of the Mogollon Rim past Prescott, flowing downward along the Agua Fria and Verde Rivers, until torrents of water reached the Gila and Salt Rivers to the east and west of Phoenix. The San Francisco River propelled water from the teeming rains falling on the White Mountains westward to the already swollen Gila. From near

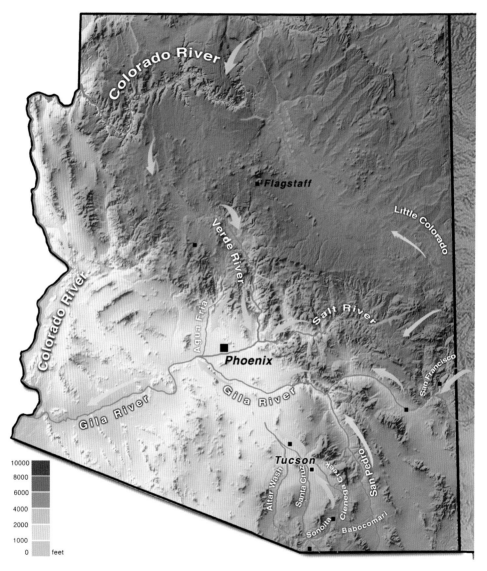

FIGURE 0.1 Major rivers and streams in the Lower Colorado River watershed. Flow directions are indicated by the turquoise arrows. (Map by Stephen Strom.)

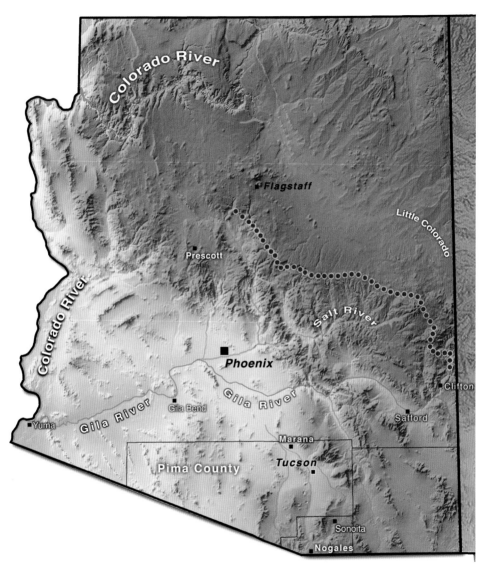

FIGURE 0.2 Arizona cities mentioned in the text, along with county boundary lines for Pima County (which includes Tucson and Marana), Santa Cruz County (which includes Sonoita and Nogales), and Cochise County (east of the Pima and Santa Cruz County boundary lines). The Mogollon Rim is indicated by the highlighted dots. (Map by Stephen Strom.)

FIGURE 0.3 Bridge over the Rillito River, severed during the 1983 flood triggered by rains from Tropical Storm Octave. (Photo by Peter Kresan.)

the Mexican border, the San Pedro and Santa Cruz Rivers and Cienega Creek, bloated by rain cascading down from the Canelo Hills, the Huachuca, Whetstone, and Santa Rita Mountains, carried their voluminous floodwaters northward, joining the Gila south and east of Phoenix. And then the Gila, overflowing with waters from its tributaries, reached its junction with the Colorado River west of Yuma, inundating agricultural fields, the flood's fury finally dissipating as its waters spread out over the flatlands at the mouth of the Gulf of California.[1]

The weeklong rains from Octave caused major floods along the Gila, San Pedro, San Francisco, and Santa Cruz Rivers. Parts of the town of Clifton were inundated by waters from the San Francisco River, while the Gila River engulfed parts of Safford. A portion of Interstate 10 south of Phoenix was submerged by the Gila, severing the main artery linking Phoenix with Tucson. North of Tucson, the Santa Cruz River flooded acres of farmland and forced residents of the town of Marana to evacuate, while to the city's south, the river inundated parts of Nogales.

In Tucson itself, flooding was particularly severe along the Santa Cruz and along its tributaries—the Pantano and Rillito washes fed in turn by waters flowing northwestward along Cienega Creek. At the height of the flood on October 3, only one of the eighteen bridges over the normally dry Santa Cruz River was open. The Rillito was transformed from a dry wash into a broad river. At one point, the Rillito so far overflowed its nominal banks that it flooded nearby residences and caused an office building to collapse into its raging waters.

FIGURE 0.4 Santa Cruz River raging near Saint Mary's Road in Tucson during the 1983 flood. (Photo by Peter Kresan.)

FIGURE 0.5 The Gila River flooding agricultural fields and severing a bridge southwest of Gila Bend. (Photo by Peter Kresan.)

The flood caused hundreds of millions of dollars in damage and was responsible for fourteen deaths and nearly a thousand injuries. The tragic effects were a result of a rare combination of meteorological events and manmade damages to stream and river environments over the preceding century: pumping groundwater to support agriculture and urban growth and loss of riparian areas due to groundwater depletion and overgrazing. The result: rivers confined to narrow channels, their waters unable to spread out and be absorbed along stream banks, and onrushing floodwaters coursing through barren riparian areas lacking the vegetation that otherwise would have slowed the surge.

While losses of life and property were horrendous, the 1983 disaster catalyzed a series of actions aimed not only at minimizing the effects of future floods but at forging a community commitment to shared stewardship of land and water in Pima County—at 9,200 square miles, a county larger than the combined areas of Connecticut, Rhode Island, and Delaware. The county is home to Tucson and Marana, where the surging Santa Cruz River and the waters below the convergence of Cienega Creek, Pantano Wash, and the Rillito River wreaked havoc on property and infrastructure.[2]

A Large-Landscape Perspective

In the immediate aftermath of the flood, the Pima County Board of Supervisors and the Regional Flood Control District developed plans to both repair the damage inflicted by the flood and invest in efforts to mitigate the effects of future Octave-like events. County citizens approved a bond issue that provided funding to replace damaged infrastructure; to purchase and remove homes located in floodplains, thus providing a wide buffer area for the waters from future floods to spread out harmlessly; and to protect the banks along the newly widened river courses.

At this point, county leadership could well have been satisfied with their response to a devastating but historically rare event. Instead, they approached hydrologists and other experts and asked what would happen if an Octave-scale event were to occur in the future, as the Tucson metro area continued to grow rapidly, with its population projected to double in twenty-five years.

Their answer was sobering: as homes, streets, and highways extended outward from the city center into the surrounding desert, floodwaters from the next Octave could prove even more damaging as they flowed toward

Tucson, rushing over concrete and asphalt rather than being absorbed by soil and vegetation. Experts urged county leadership to look beyond local flood-mitigation investments and develop plans for strategic investments in the health of the watersheds surrounding the metro area.

In response, the supervisors first chose to purchase land along lower Cienega Creek in order to create the Cienega Creek Natural Preserve and thereby protect a natural floodplain. Located approximately 25 miles southeast of downtown Tucson, the preserve encompasses a 4,000-acre corridor spanning 12 miles of Cienega Creek. By isolating the corridor from development and protecting vegetation adjacent to the creek, county leaders aimed to ensure that the land within the preserve would continue to perform its historic natural functions: slowing and absorbing onrushing floodwaters, and as an added environmental benefit, supporting a rich biological community.[3]

The county next looked to protect the entire Cienega Creek watershed: a region extending from the creek's headwaters more than 60 miles southeast of Tucson in the Canelo Hills to the newly acquired natural preserve. In 1986 the 35,000-acre Empire Ranch located about 15 miles south of the preserve and spanning a significant part of the Cienega watershed, became available for purchase. The county administration hoped to acquire both the Empire Ranch and nearby land owned by the State of Arizona, and to connect the Empire and adjacent lands in the Sonoita Valley with federally administered national forest land. Their plan would not only have protected the Cienega watershed from development but would as well have created a 100-mile-long corridor from the Mexican border to Oracle, Arizona, northwest of Tucson: a landscape comprising forested mountains, riparian areas, and some of the last remaining tracts of native grasslands in the Southwest—habitat for rich and diverse populations of mammalian, avian, reptilian, and aquatic species.[4]

Though this plan didn't fully achieve its ambitious goals, the county's efforts at landscape-scale conservation eventually set in motion a series of land swaps that enabled the Bureau of Land Management to take ownership of the Empire Ranch—a first step toward future congressional designation of Las Cienegas National Conservation Area (NCA) and the Sonoita Valley Acquisition Planning District (SVAPD).[5] With the Empire Ranch at its core, the conservation area and SVAPD spans 140,000 acres (220 square miles). If all lands within the SVAPD could be incorporated into conservation area, the goal of protecting a most of the Cienega watershed would finally be achieved

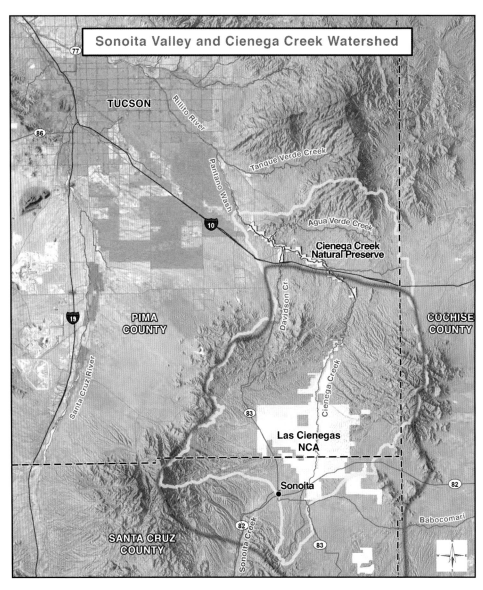

FIGURE 0.6 Approximate boundaries of the Cienega Creek watershed (light green) and the Sonoita Valley (purple). The Cienega Creek Natural Preserve is shaded yellow, while Las Cienegas National Conservation Area is shaded in light ivory. Rivers and creeks are labeled in blue. The Sonoita Valley Acquisition Planning Map is outlined in white. (Map prepared for the Cienega Watershed Partnership and modified by Stephen Strom.)

(see chapter 2 for a discussion of the challenges of acquiring or otherwise protecting those lands).

Landscape-Scale Conservation and Land Stewardship

Pima County's creation of the Cienega Creek Natural Preserve, coupled with the citizen-based effort to create Las Cienegas NCA catalyzed a multiyear effort that culminated in the adoption of one of the largest landscape-scale conservation and land stewardship plans in the nation: the Sonoran Desert Conservation Plan (SDCP).

The SDCP represents a pragmatic solution to problems that have vexed the West for more than a century: providing a context for supporting growth and a vigorous economy while preserving the health of Pima County's waters, rangelands, and forests. The county's approach made creative use of the Endangered Species Act (ESA) to inform and regulate new home construction and to guide preparation of a county-wide land-use plan. In return for accepting formula-based requirements to set aside biologically critical lands, home developers would no longer face the uncertainties of ESA-based litigation resulting from incidental taking of habitat critical to endangered species.

The genius of the SDCP planning effort lay in the choice of Pima County leadership to avoid a narrow conservation-versus-development debate, instead engaging county citizens in discussions aimed at developing an overarching vision for the county's future. Following more than six hundred public meetings and guided by input from two hundred technical reports, the county proposed the framework for a plan that allowed for growth while preserving critical species habitats; creating and protecting corridors to enable wildlife to move between habitat patches; sustaining healthy riparian areas; creating mountain parks; preserving historical and cultural sites; and recognizing the value of sustainably operated working ranches.[6]

The framework was approved in 1999, and over the next four years, citizens and experts used it to develop a comprehensive plan. In 2003 the county began implementing elements of the plan through land acquisitions and management arrangements, through land use and infrastructure planning, and by enacting development regulations. County citizens demonstrated their strong support for the SDCP at the ballot box by approving two open-space bond initiatives that enabled the county to invest more than $200 million to meet plan objectives.

Over the ensuing years, the county has used these funds to develop urban parks, to preserve or restore multiple cultural sites, to create or upgrade hiking, biking, and equestrian trails, and to purchase or negotiate protections for 230,000 acres of conservation lands. Many of the latter are working ranches, managed to protect or restore watersheds and to ensure that the land continues to support a rich and diverse mix of native plants, animals and aquatic life. The county's North Star continues to be a firm commitment to balancing the protection of its cultural and natural resource heritage with maintaining an economically vigorous, growing community.

The citizens who worked for almost two decades to set the stage for creating Las Cienegas NCA and the Sonoran Desert Conservation Plan either implicitly or explicitly recognized the interdependence of human, plant, and animal communities and their environment. Ecologists might use different phrasing: "thinking and acting to protect ecosystem functions on an ecoregional scale." To translate: ecosystems are a dynamic biological community of interacting organisms—including humans—and their physical environment, while ecoregions are relatively large areas of land or water containing geographically distinct assemblages of ecosystems; adjacent ecoregions contain significantly different ecosystem mixes.[7]

Managing Human Influences

As the fallout from Octave vividly demonstrated, humans and what they build and do can play a critical role in affecting ecosystems and ecoregions. Past choices to deplete groundwater—and as a consequence to eradicate riparian areas—led to far more severe flooding than would otherwise have taken place had lands in the watersheds surrounding Tucson been stewarded more prudently. The reckoning for humans resulting from short-sighted development and careless land use in the past was loss of life and property. The toll for plants and animals was loss of critical habitat.

The rapid growth of the West continues to fragment landscapes, threaten watersheds, and undermine the complex interactions among plants, animals, and people, disrupting the natural functions and equilibria of ecosystems and ecoregions. In the 170 years since gold was found in Sutter's Creek, more than 165,000 square miles of the West's "wide open spaces" have been lost to development: an area larger than that of the entire state of California. At present, the growth of suburban and exurban subdivisions, oil and gas fields, agricultural operations, and the roads that link them consume lands at a rate of 4,300 square miles per decade.[8]

The consequent loss and fragmentation of open space has undermined the health of forests, grasslands, and watersheds, with resulting detrimental effects on wildlife, species diversity, and water supply. Ecosystems that could otherwise store carbon have been lost or disrupted, and the unquantifiable values of scenic beauty and solitude have been diminished.

Climate change threatens to exacerbate the magnitude of these threats and to compress the time available for ecosystems to restore balance and function. Over the past two decades, the West has experienced historic droughts, along with more frequent and destructive wildfires. Streams are contaminated by the ash from forest fires, and the flow of the Colorado River has decreased so much that the water levels in Lake Powell and Lake Mead reservoirs are critically low. Fish and wildlife have suffered as they have been forced to find new habitats in response to rising temperatures. In places where suitable new habitat is unavailable, species numbers have decreased, sometimes to the point of local extinction.[9]

Overarching Questions

What lands should we conserve or protect in order to foster functioning ecosystems? How do we conserve them? Is it possible to restore some of the damage already inflicted on lands and water? And how do we meet the shared goals of sustainable land stewardship and economic vitality in a context where cities, suburbs, and exurbs continue to grow in response to increasing population?

However we answer these questions, we need to recognize that the majority of lands critical to addressing current environmental challenges are held in private hands. How can we motivate landholders to engage in discussions focused on landscape-scale protection and stewardship? What role should county, state, and federal agencies play in those discussions, and when should they become involved?

Some History as We Begin This Exploration

Until recently, land conservation and environmental protection in the United States has been based largely on two strategic approaches: setting aside lands of outstanding aesthetic, scientific, or cultural value, and regulating activities that affect air and water quality and species habitat.

Beginning with the establishment of Yellowstone National Park in 1872, U.S. citizens and their representatives have preserved more than 300 million acres for public use: national parks, forests, monuments, and wilderness areas that are the envy of the world.[10] In the mid-twentieth century, conservation-minded citizens advocated for passage of legislation aimed at setting aside in perpetuity areas of outstanding environmental importance where "the earth and its community of life are untrammeled by man, where man himself is a visitor who does not remain."[11] Since the enabling legislation for the Wilderness Act was enacted in 1964, the U.S. Congress has established more than 800 wilderness areas, their land totaling nearly 120 million acres (almost 200,000 square miles).

Following the end of World War II, rapid population and industrial growth led to dramatic changes in the American natural and social landscape. Growth brought with it not only transformative progress but, in its wake, scarred lands and polluted air and water. Increasing concerns about extant and potential environmental damage led in the 1970s to creation of the Environmental Protection Agency (EPA) and passage of landmark legislation aimed at protecting and restoring biologically sensitive habitat and ecosystems (the Endangered Species Act) and the nation's water and air quality (the Clean Air and Clean Water Acts).[12]

However, lands protected as national parks, monuments, forests, or wilderness areas typically represent only a fraction of the much larger mosaics of federal, state, and private lands needed to preserve the integrity and healthy function of critical environmental resources. Although the Endangered Species, Clean Air, and Clean Water Acts provide essential regulatory tools, meeting the conservation challenges we face today requires not only regulating how and whether land and resources can be used but developing landscape-scale strategies to protect and steward lands to sustain and restore healthy forests, grasslands, and watersheds; minimize further habitat loss; and store carbon to mitigate the effects of global warming.[13]

FIGURE 0.7 Lake Mead, upriver from Hoover Dam. The "bathtub ring" (white) illustrates the extent to which water levels in the lake have dropped during the decades-long drought in the Southwest. As of this writing, the water levels in both Lake Mead and Lake Powell have reached critical points, threatening the dams' ability to continue production of hydroelectric power. Current climate models based on the present rate of global warming predict that the American Southwest will become both drier and hotter over the next century. (Mjponso, Wikimedia Commons, CC-BY-SA-3.0.)

The Structure of the Book

Forging a Sustainable Southwest introduces readers to four landscape-scale conservation efforts that provide insight into how diverse groups of citizens are confronting these issues. Through the voices of individuals involved in these efforts, we learn what motivated them to initiate conversations about land use; the approaches they took to develop collaborative plans for protecting, restoring, and stewarding lands sustainably; the management and funding tools they used; and their perception of both successes and the challenges that remain.

In chapter 1, we first provide an overview of the physical, climatic, and biological environments for the regions in southeastern Arizona and southwestern New Mexico that encompass the four large-landscape conservation efforts discussed in chapters 2 through 6. Chapter 1 next examines the role humans have played in shaping ecological functions in these regions: altering watershed function and fire regimes; introducing invasive species; frag-

menting landscapes and habitat for plants and animals; and altering climate conditions at a rate that exceeds the ability of many ecosystems and their inhabitants to adapt.

Chapter 2 focuses on the Sonoita Valley, where valley residents came together to forge a vision for how best to balance economic needs, cultural values, and conservation of public lands. Their years-long efforts led to the creation of Las Cienegas National Conservation Area and, later, the formation of a broadly based stakeholder group that has guided stewardship of the NCA and surrounding public land for much of the past two decades.

In chapter 3, we turn to the development of the Sonoran Desert Conservation Plan. Here, those intimately involved with formulating the SDCP describe how the plan took shape; what sustained their efforts during the two-decade journey from 1983, when Octave's floodwaters inundated the metro Tucson area, to the plan's adoption in 2003; their successes in preserving and restoring biologically sensitive lands; and how the SDCP continues to provide a robust framework for meeting an ever-changing political and environmental landscape.

FIGURE 0.8 Arizona State Route 83, snaking through the Sonoita Valley, facing north. The foothills of the Santa Rita Mountains are on the left; the Empire Mountains to the right. The Rincon and Catalina Mountains are near the center left and center right, respectively. (Aerial photo by Stephen Strom.)

The creation of Las Cienegas NCA and the SDCP provide examples of landscape-scale conservation efforts shaped by large, broadly based, and ideologically diverse stakeholder groups.

Chapter 4 examines an effort initiated instead by a small group of cattle ranchers who banded together in 1993 to form the Malpai Borderlands Group. Initially, their goal was to protect grasslands spanning more than eight hundred thousand acres located in the Mexican borderland region of southwestern New Mexico from fragmentation by encroaching exurban home developments. Over the past three decades, the group has achieved that goal by raising funds to place ranches under permanent conservation easement, thereby precluding development. During that period, they have also forged collaborative programs with federal agencies and NGOs to manage naturally caused fires in a manner that keeps the grasslands productive, to restore damaged rangeland, and to preserve habitat and movement corridors for rich and diverse wildlife populations.

In chapter 5 we discuss the efforts of a single rancher, Josiah Austin, to restore watershed function and grassland health on Cienega Ranch, located

FIGURE 0.9 Cienega Creek, wending its way westward toward the Cienega Creek Natural Preserve and its junction with the Pantano Wash near Vail, Arizona. The cottonwoods, just turning in late fall, define the path of the creek. An extensive mesquite bosque surrounds the cottonwoods. (Aerial photo by Stephen Strom.)

FIGURE 0.10 Grasslands adjacent to Sonoita Creek, a tributary of the Santa Cruz River, near Patagonia Lake State Park. The hills are covered with Arizona poppies that emerged after the onset of monsoon rains. (Aerial photo by Stephen Strom.)

on the eastern slopes of the Dos Cabezas and Chiricahua Mountains above the Sulphur Springs Valley. Over forty years, Austin has raised private and public funds to install more than forty thousand rock structures and check dams with the goal of arresting soil erosion and slowly filling in gullies formed during a century of negligent stewardship. The land Austin manages also benefits from his participation in annual meetings of the Malpai Borderlands Group (MBG), where ranchers and rangeland experts discuss how best to assess and improve grassland health.

Together, the MBG and Josiah Austin provide examples of how a small number of like-minded private landholders can carry out conservation on a landscape scale. Finding incentives to encourage similar efforts will be crucial in meeting the national need to protect and steward lands to the benefit of both landholders and the public.

In chapter 6, we summarize and discuss the potential of multiple options for protecting, restoring, and stewarding land, along with various options for incentivizing individuals and communities to invest in the partnerships needed to achieve landscape-scale conservation goals.

If we are indeed to find and follow paths toward an environmentally healthy West, we might well reflect on the words of Aldo Leopold, who urged us to recall that we are "members of a community of interdependent parts. A land ethic simply enlarges the boundaries of the community to include soils, waters, plants, and animals. . . . A land ethic changes the role of *Homo sapiens* from conqueror of the land community to plain member and citizen of it. It implies respect for his fellow members, and also respect for the community as such. It is inconceivable to me that an ethical relation to land can exist without love, respect, and admiration for land."[14]

CHAPTER 1

Geological, Hydrological, Biological, and Anthropogenic Context

Arizona Today

Arizona today consists of three well-defined regions, each having distinct geomorphology (or physiography).[1]

The first is the Colorado Plateau. The plateau is elevated between five thousand and seven thousand feet above sea level and is centered on the shared boundaries of Arizona, New Mexico, Colorado, and Utah. Its geological history is revealed in the ordered layers of rock strata carved by the Colorado River, manifest most dramatically in the Grand Canyon.

The second is the Basin and Range region, which occupies the southern part of Arizona.[2] Here, linear ranges of mountains extending along a mostly north–south axis alternate with broad valleys. The Basin and Range topography extends from northwestern Mexico through New Mexico, Arizona, and western Utah, with its character most dramatically revealed in Nevada. In the southeast corner of Arizona, the high mountain ranges of the Basin and Range system are referred to as "sky islands" rising above desert and grassland "seas."

The third is known as the Transition Zone, a relatively narrow region of rugged mountains and valleys located between the 5,000-to-7,000-foot-high Colorado Plateau and the 1,000-to-5,000-foot-elevation valleys of the Basin and Range region.[3]

Each of these regions, or physiographic provinces as they are sometimes known, are youthful in the geological sense, having gestated during the past 100 million years or so and come to term only 6–10 million years ago.

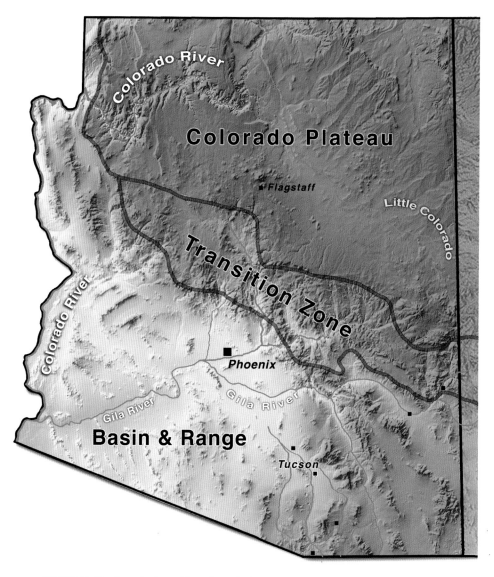

FIGURE 1.1 The three physiographic regions of Arizona: Colorado Plateau, Basin and Range, and Transition Zone. (Map by Stephen Strom.)

FIGURE 1.2 A color-enhanced satellite relief map of the western United States in which green regions are low elevation; yellow, intermediate; and brown, high. The map illustrates the pattern of parallel, roughly north–south chains of mountains and valleys in the Basin and Range system. The pattern is particularly well illustrated in the state of Nevada (*center left*). Note the prevalence of snow on the west-facing sides of the mountains: a result of the combined effects of moisture-laden air driven eastward by prevailing winds being lifted toward mountain peaks, where the air temperature is cooler and water vapor condenses to form snow. Most of the snow is deposited on the west side of mountains. The land east of the mountains falls in a snow or rain shadow. (Alexrk2, Wikimedia Commons, CC-BY-SA-3.0.)

A Living, Evolving Landscape: Rocks, Water, and Soil

While the basic topography of today's Arizona was set around six million years ago, the land continues to change. Given enough time, even the hardest rocks will break down or dissolve in response to changing temperatures and interactions with water, ice, salts, acids, and growing plants. Once broken, wind and water carry rock fragments away, eroding underlying mountains and depositing weathered fragments along mountain sides as alluvial fans, or in valleys below.[4] To dramatize the power of weathering and erosion: in the course of just six million years, the Colorado River, which once meandered on the nearly flat surface of the eponymous forming plateau, incised a mile-deep canyon (the Grand Canyon), cutting through sandstone, limestone, and shale until it reached hard igneous rocks (formed as molten rock cooled, then solidified) below.

Whether on top of a mountain, in a valley, along an alluvial fan, or at the bottom of the Grand Canyon, surface and deposited material reflects a complex ensemble of past physical, chemical, and biological processes. Add in time and pressure, and soils take form, establishing a context essential to supporting today's diverse life forms. The character of those soils plays a major role in controlling how the water that sustains all life flows and seeps into the ground. Along with sunlight, temperature, and precipitation are the other ingredients that determine where and whether species can adapt and survive. In Arizona and the West, topography—shaped over the past one hundred million years—plays an essential role in regulating or mediating both local and area-wide climatic conditions.

Creating Different Environmental Conditions: Topography, Temperature, and Precipitation

On most days, air suffused with water vapor evaporating from the surface of the Pacific Ocean is carried eastward over California by prevailing westerly winds. When moist air encounters the Sierra Nevada mountain range, it is forced upward into the much cooler atmosphere above the Sierras. As colder air is unable to hold as much water in vapor form as warmer air, the vapor condenses into water droplets (or if cold enough, into snowflakes). When the droplets become large and heavy enough, they fall as rain on the western slopes of the Sierras. Cold air, now dried by release of water over the Sierra,

FIGURE 1.3 A photograph of the Grand Canyon, illustrating the coherent layered strata revealed as the Colorado River incised the Colorado Plateau over the past six million years. Note the top white layer, which is composed of limestone produced by an accumulation of shells or shell fragments at a time when the Colorado Plateau was covered by a warm, shallow sea. The layers directly below are composed of shale, a sedimentary rock formed by mud altered by a combination of chemical, physical, and biological processes. (Murray Foubister, Wikimedia Commons, CC-BY-SA-2.0.)

slides down the east side of the mountains and continues on its eastward journey.[5]

The snow-capped Sierras are a delight to the eye and a source of water for residents of California's booming cities. But to the east, little water remains to slake the thirst of plants and animals in the Mojave and Sonoran Deserts, both largely shielded from Pacific moisture by the rain shadow provided by the Sierras. In a typical year, the western slopes of the Sierras might receive eighty inches of precipitation, while regions in the Mojave Desert to the east receive but two to ten inches. Precipitation in the western parts of the Sonoran Desert are similar, while the eastern regions receive more rain thanks to summer precipitation resulting from southwestward flows of moist air from the Gulf of Mexico (fig. 1.2).

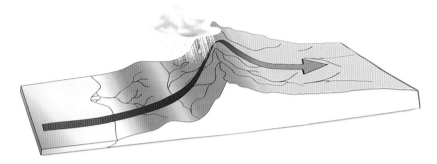

FIGURE 1.4 An illustration of how moist air, driven eastward by winds from the west encounters the Sierra Nevada, is lifted to higher, cooler elevations where water condenses into liquid (rain) or solid (snow or ice) form. Rain or snow falls on the west side or on the peaks of the Sierras, while air, now devoid of significant water vapor, descends the eastern slope of the mountains, warms, and flows over the Mojave and Sonoran Deserts. Warm air is color-coded red; cool air is coded blue. (Figure modified from an image prepared by Theblologyprimer, Wikimedia Commons, CC0.)

FIGURE 1.5 A more detailed examination of the relationship between elevation (*left*, in feet), temperature (*right*, in degrees Fahrenheit), and relative humidity (*left*, in percentages illustrated by moisture-laden air bubbles; relative humidity increases from 28 percent near the desert floor to 100 percent at an elevation of 10,000 feet). Note that temperature decreases with increasing elevation, and as a result, relative humidity increases. The temperatures and relative humidity values adopted for this figure are typical of those in the Sonoran Desert near Tucson during the early summer, when monsoon rains first appear. Note as well the change in vegetation from the cactus and shrub mix on the desert floor to the pine forests on mountaintops. (Base figure by the Sky Island Alliance.)

On a more local scale, when the occasional influx of moist air encounters a mountain in southeast Arizona, on average more precipitation falls near a mountain peak than along its slopes or on the valley floor. For example, the top of 9,200-foot-high Mount Lemmon north of Tucson receives 30 inches in a typical year, while the 2,500-foot-high desert floor below receives only 11 inches. This difference arises from the decrease in air temperature and the resulting increase of relative humidity as elevation increases. The relative humidity on the hot (95-degree) desert floor might be 30 percent on a summer day, compared to the 100 percent humidity at the cool (60-degree) top of the mountain. As such, a given volume of air at the hot, dry desert floor can hold considerably more water vapor than the cooler top of the mountain, which at the same time on that same day may have conditions ripe for rain.

The increase in precipitation and decrease in temperature with increasing elevation provides—along with altitude-dependent soil content—hospitable conditions for a wide range of life forms. Cacti and other shrubs cover the desert floors, while pine forests populate the top of Mount Lemmon. The mix of aquatic, avian, and mammalian species are adapted to changes in vegetation, temperature, precipitation, soil, and water.[6]

Cycling Water Through a Watershed: Topography and Soils

Topography and soil are essential as well to the flow and storage of water. In the introduction, we saw how Octave's deluge of water followed the topographic contours of the land: always flowing downslope and, in Arizona, inexorably toward the Colorado River, near the border of Arizona and Mexico southwest of Yuma. The land that collected precipitation from Octave—from the Mogollon Rim to the north, to the New Mexico mountains to the east, to the Catalina, Rincon, and Santa Rita Mountains to the southeast—and drained all its over-filled streams and rivers into the Colorado provides a vivid example of a regional-scale watershed, in this case the Lower Colorado watershed.[7]

What happens as rain falls on a watershed? Some of it flows, as Octave so dramatically demonstrated, in streams running over the surface of the ground (surface water). However, some of the water soaks into or infiltrates the soil and gradually moves downhill through a shallow soil layer

FIGURE 1.6 The flow of water in a watershed: from rain clouds to mountain- or hillsides, to tributaries, to streams, and ultimately into a lake. Note that water not only flows on the surface but infiltrates the soil into the ground below. Groundwater, too, slowly makes its way to the lake. (Government Accountability Office / Environmental Protection Agency.)

into a stream. Some may seep much deeper into the ground, where it can be stored for long periods of time (thousands or tens of thousands of years in some cases) in underground aquifers, until it ever-so-slowly makes its way to a stream.

How much and how deeply water seeps into the ground and begins to flow as groundwater depends on the type of soil covering the land. For example, tightly packed clays are far less permeable than sandy or other porous soils. Rain falling on ground already wet from prior precipitation events or containing soils like clay cannot infiltrate the ground efficiently and will for the most part run off directly into streams.

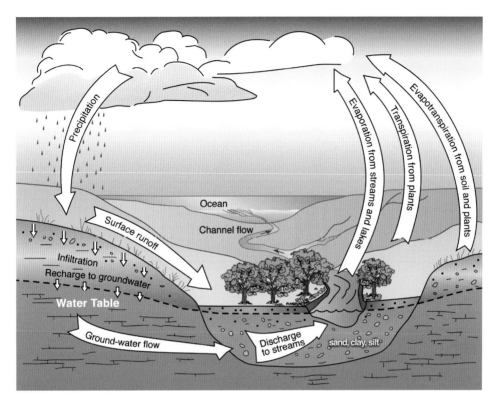

FIGURE 1.7 The hydrologic cycle. Rain falls on the ground. Part flows downward along mountains or hills, while part seeps or infiltrates through the soil into the ground. The highest level of the groundwater supply is the water table. Both surface water and groundwater flow to lower-lying streams or rivers. Water from streams, rivers, and lakes evaporates, water absorbed by plants is eventually returned to the atmosphere as it evaporates from their leaves, and moist soil, too, returns water to the atmosphere where the cycle begins anew. (Modified from an illustration produced by University of Kansas.)

Wherever water that falls as rain or snow travels, it will eventually evaporate and return to the atmosphere. How fast that happens in any given region depends on the local temperature, relative humidity of the surrounding air, soil content, and a host of other factors. Vegetation returns water to the atmosphere as well, as roots absorb rain-moistened soil and transport water to plant leaves from which water escapes to the air in vapor form (transpiration).

The cycle of evaporation from ocean waters into the atmosphere, to precipitation in the form of rain and snow, to surface runoff, groundwater infiltration, evaporation, or plant transpiration back into the air is called the hydrologic or water cycle.[8]

Flowing Waters: Rivers, Streams, and Riparian Areas

With this overview of watersheds in hand, we can look more closely at the processes that influence the flow of water in streams and rivers as well as the vegetation that takes hold along a stream bank.

Some surface water may be ephemeral, appearing only after a steady rainfall or an event similar to Tropical Storm Octave. Perennial flows, where surface water is visible throughout the year, are typically *gaining streams,* in which surface water is constantly renewed from below by groundwater, the top reaches of which define the uppermost part of the water table.

Streams that flow intermittently throughout the year are typically *losing streams,* in which the water table lies below the land surface and water on the surface drains into the ground. Surface water from these streams can appear seasonally if the water table rises sufficiently close to the land surface. In some cases, parts of a stream may be intermittent and in other parts perennial as the underlying soil and geological conditions cause the water table to rise or fall. Dry streambeds are those in which the water table lies well below the land surface.[9]

Lands adjacent to rivers and perennial and some intermittent streams are called riparian areas. The presence of surface and groundwater along stream banks and broader river floodplains creates environmental conditions conducive to rich communities of plants, avian and mammalian life, and food and shade for aquatic organisms.[10]

Vegetation in riparian areas typically differs significantly from adjacent uplands. In the Sonoran Desert, sedges and rushes in a healthy riparian area might be found closest to the stream, with willows and cottonwoods populating regions further away, while cacti, ocotillo, and other desert plants occupy the uplands.

Ecosystems and Ecoregions

The broad range in topography, climate, soil, and water—both surface and groundwater—within the Lower Colorado River watershed provide natural environments or habitat for an impressively wide variety of flora and fauna.

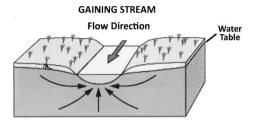

GAINING STREAM

Flow Direction

Water Table

LOSING STREAM

Flow Direction

Water Table

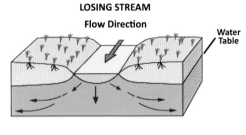

LOSING STREAM DISCONNECTED FROM THE WATER TABLE

Flow Direction

Water Table

A

FIGURE 1.8 (*a*) A gaining stream (*top*); losing stream (*center*); and dry streambed (*bottom*). (U.S. Geological Society.) (*b*) A riparian area typical of those found in the Sonoita Valley (elevation 4,000–5,000 feet), with sedges and rushes occupying a region closest to the streambed and large deciduous trees sinking their roots into the water table, while further upland, grass brush and oak predominate. (Illustration by Stephen E. Strom.)

B

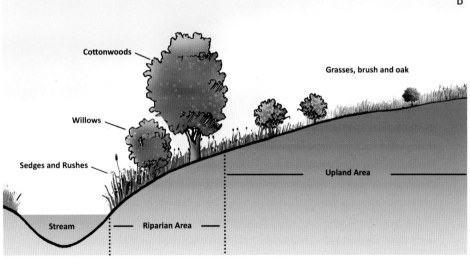

Cottonwoods

Grasses, brush and oak

Willows

Sedges and Rushes

Upland Area

Stream

Riparian Area

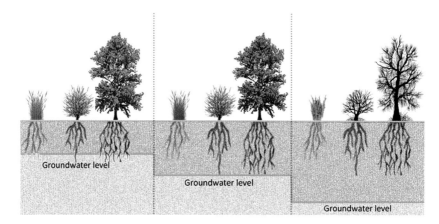

FIGURE 1.9 An illustration of what occurs when groundwater in a riparian ecosystem is disrupted. The leftmost panel illustrates a healthy riparian area, in which the roots of sedges and brush, willows, and cottonwoods can reach the top of the water table. In the center panel, the root systems of sedges and brush can no longer reach groundwater level, and they die off, while willows and cottonwoods are barely hanging on. In the rightmost panel, the groundwater level has dropped so much that no native species can survive (Water Science School, "Groundwater Decline and Depletion," U.S. Geological Survey, 2018, https://www.usgs.gov/special-topics/water-science-school/science/groundwater-decline-and-depletion). However, invasive trees having deep root systems, such as tamarisk, can survive and over time replace native species. Many riparian areas in Arizona have been degraded or destroyed by pumping groundwater to excess (Mellissa M. Rohde, Ray Froend, and Jeanette Howard, "A Global Synthesis of Managing Groundwater Dependent Ecosystems Under Sustainable Groundwater Policy," *Groundwater* 55, no. 3 [2017], https://ngwa.onlinelibrary.wiley.com/doi/epdf/10.1111/gwat.12511). (Illustration by Stephen E. Strom.)

Some are well adapted to the extreme summer heat and winter cold of arid desert floors and find all the resources they need for survival and reproduction in that habitat. Others are best suited to the tops of mountains, where winter temperatures reach into the single digits and rain and snow are abundant.

This range in physical conditions gives rise to multiple ecosystems, each comprising areas where plants, animals, and other organisms interact with one another to create a stable, life-supporting complex. Ecosystems comprise both living parts (biotic)—plants and animals—and non-living parts (abiotic)—climate, soil, and water. Each component of an ecosystem takes and returns something from its environment to sustain a system in equilibrium that supports the continued health of all living constituents. If a single factor—say the depth of the water table in a riparian ecosystem—changes,

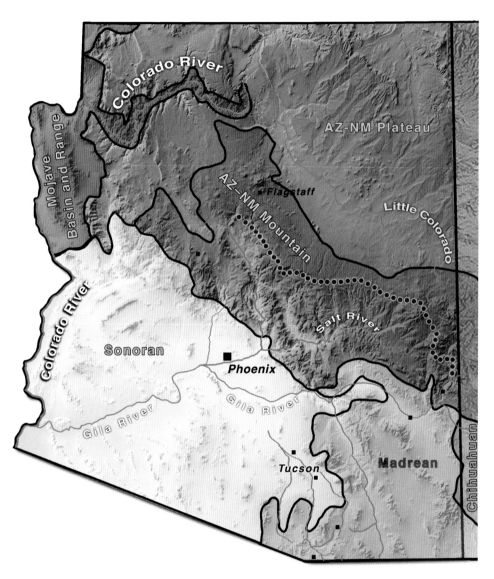

FIGURE 1.10 The six ecoregions found in Arizona. The Sonoran Desert Basin and Range, Madrean Archipelago, and Chihuahuan Desert ecoregions are located in the southern third of the state (*left to right*), from the Colorado River to the New Mexico border. The Mojave Basin and Range, Arizona–New Mexico Plateau, and Arizona–New Mexico Mountains are located in the northern part of the state (*left to right*) from the Colorado River to the New Mexico border. The outline of the Mogollon Rim is shown as a brown and white dotted line. (Map by Stephen Strom.)

it will disrupt the system equilibrium by affecting which plants can survive by extending root systems to reach the water table and whether the animals that depend on the remaining vegetation for shelter and food can continue to thrive.

Ecosystems come in all sizes. For example, a grassland ecosystem in southeast Arizona where pronghorn antelope roam feeding on grasses, forbs, and sage and Botteri's sparrows nestle in plains of sacaton grass may cover tens of thousands of acres. By contrast, absent external disturbances, a small pool or even a single log can support its own stable ecosystem.

Over the past several decades, ecologists have studied the diversity of ecosystems throughout the continental United States and defined a set of thirty ecoregions where the mosaic of ecosystem components—biotic, abiotic, terrestrial, and aquatic—are similar. While adjacent ecoregions may share some ecosystems in common, the differences in ecosystem character outweigh the commonalities.[11]

The areas discussed in subsequent chapters—Las Cienegas NCA, Pima County, the Malpai Borderlands, and the Cienega Ranch—are contained within the Madrean Archipelago, the Sonoran Desert, and the Chihuahuan Desert ecoregions. The following sections summarize the physical and climatic conditions characterizing each of these ecoregions and provide examples of the rich diversity of plant and animal life they support.[12]

Madrean Archipelago

The Madrean Archipelago ecoregion is typified by Basin and Range topography comprising 25 "island" mountain ranges in the United States and 15 in Mexico, each surrounded by desert "seas." The mountain ranges trend southeast to northwest, with several peaks reaching an elevation of 9,000 feet above sea level, and the highest, Mount Graham, peaking at nearly 11,000 feet. The valleys range in elevation from 2,500 to 5,000 feet. In recognition of its distinctive physiography, the Madrean Archipelago is sometimes referred to as the Sky Island region.

The archipelago of mountain ranges within the ecoregion lies between two major cordilleras (extensive mountain ranges characterized by a series of parallel mountain chains)—the Sierra Madre Occidental to the south in Mexico and the Rocky Mountains to the north—and two great deserts—the Chihuahuan on the east and the Sonoran on the west.[13]

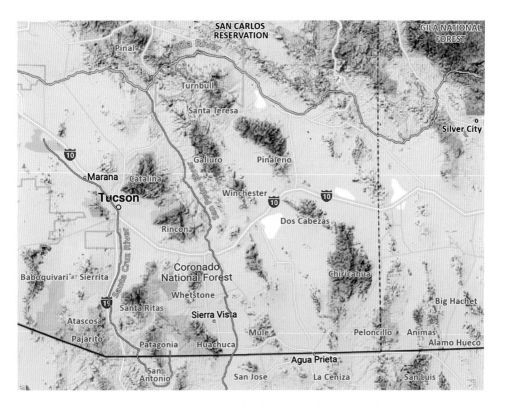

FIGURE 1.11 An elevation map of the Sky Island region of the Madrean Archipelago ecoregion with mountain ranges identified. Note the alternating mountain ranges and valley floors typical of the Basin and Range province. (Adapted from Google Maps by Stephen Strom.)

The climate in the region varies widely, as might be expected given its varied topography. Precipitation ranges from 5 to 10 inches at the lowest elevations, from 15 to 20 inches in regions lying between 4,000 and 6,000 feet, and from 25 to 35 inches on mountains peaks. Half or more of the precipitation occurs during the summer monsoons, while the remainder comes from Pacific storms that pass through the region between November and March. There is little spring rainfall.

The location of the Madrean Archipelago between two cordilleras provides plants and animals connected pathways or stepping-stones to disperse to and from the Sierra Madre and Rocky Mountains, while its proximity to the Chihuahuan and Sonoran Basin and Range regions allows for east–west movement of species.[14]

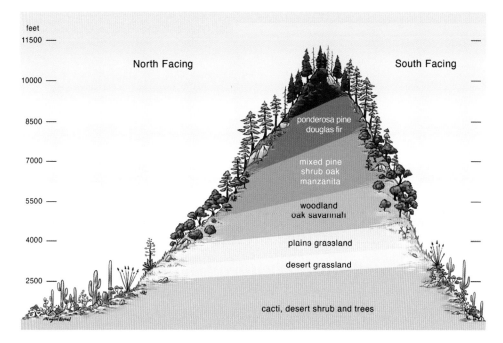

feet
11500 —

North Facing

South Facing

10000 —

8500 —

ponderosa pine
douglas fir

7000 —

mixed pine
shrub oak
manzanita

5500 —

woodland
oak savannah

4000 —

plains grassland

desert grassland

2500 —

cacti, desert shrub and trees

FIGURE 1.12 An illustration of life zones in the Madrean Archipelago. An elevation scale is provided on the left- and right-hand sides of the figure. Note that the life zones on south-facing slopes of mountains are shifted upward, as the temperature averaged over the seasons is higher on those slopes. (Adapted from a figure prepared by Meagan Bethel for the Sky Island Alliance.)

Moreover, the elevation range between valley floors and mountain peaks provides a wide range of environments for both endemic and transient species.[15] An ecologist with a poetic bent might note that the Madrean Archipelago is a place where deserts meet mountains, jaguars meet black bears, and cacti meet cottonwood trees.

More prosaically, the Madrean Archipelago is a biodiversity hotspot, a region hosting an exceptional number of plants and animals. Consider the range of vegetation: at the base of the mountain islands are arid deserts where cacti and shrubs predominate; in somewhat cooler and wetter areas at three thousand to six thousand feet elevation, desert and plains grasslands take over; and in those regions above the grasslands where precipitation is higher and temperatures lower, oak savanna, mixed pine, and ponderosa pine and Douglas fir are the defining flora in zones of ever-increasing elevation. The intact springs, streams, cienegas, wetlands, and marshes in the

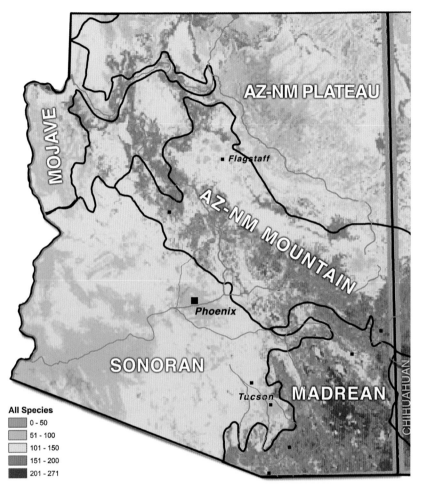

FIGURE 1.13 A map depicting species richness in each of the six ecoregions in Arizona. The scale (*left*) provides a relative measure of species richness. Note the especially high richness in the Madrean Archipelago and northern Chihuahuan Desert ecoregions. The former is noted as a biodiversity hotspot in recognition of the diversity and richness of species in the region. The range in elevations and the presence of a number of healthy riparian areas are responsible in good measure for species richness and diversity. The species count data come from K. G. Boykin et al., "A National Approach for Mapping and Quantifying Habitat-Based Biodiversity Metrics Across Multiple Spatial Scales," *Ecological Indicators* 33 (2013): 139–47, https://www.epa.gov/sites/default /files/2015-09/documents/boykin_et_al_2013_mapping_biodiversity_metrics.pdf.

region support water-dependent species such as sedges, rushes, willows, sycamores, and cottonwoods.

The range of vegetation, climate, and water resources in the Sky Islands supports more than 80 mammalian species, including the northern jaguar and the Mexican gray wolf, ocelots, black bears, beavers, bats, and coatimundi; 14 species of native fish, including the Gila chub; and more than 100 species of resident birds, including subtropical species such as the elegant trogon. Coursing through the Madrean ecoregion, the San Pedro River, Cienega Creek, and the Santa Cruz River are important flyways for migratory birds and butterflies. Perhaps as many as half of the bird species in the United States depend in some way on the resources available in the rivers, creeks, and uplands in the Madrean ecoregion.[16]

The topography of the region allows fauna to move from lower to higher altitudes within a given sky island mountain chain in response to climate and other environmental changes and, when needed, to move from one chain to another. Moreover, human use patterns have to date not fragmented the Madrean landscape significantly. That in turn ensures for the present that species have access to multiple habitat patches and can migrate from one patch to another without significant impediment.

As climate warms, regions like the Madrean offer the possibility of migration of vegetation and dependent mammalian species to higher elevations or more northerly latitudes. In that sense, they are relatively resilient in the face of future climate change. The rub: with increasing elevation, the area that can serve as habitat for species survival generally becomes smaller.

Sonoran Desert Basin and Range

The eastern part of the region exhibits characteristic Basin and Range structure manifest in a series of high valleys and mountain ranges. Mountaintops range from up to 10,000 feet in the easternmost extent of the region to 3,000 feet in the west. The elevations of basin valleys rise from sea level near Yuma to 3,000 feet in southeast Arizona.

The Sonoran Basin and Range climate is warm and dry. In winter, daytime temperatures average between 65 and 70 degrees Fahrenheit, while overnight temperatures can sometimes drop below freezing, as the dry conditions lead to large day-night temperature swings. In summer months, temperatures in desert valleys climb well over 100 degrees Fahrenheit during the day.

Annual precipitation averages 3 inches to 20 inches in the basin regions, while higher-elevation valleys enjoy more rain as well as occasional snow. Mountaintop precipitation can reach 40 inches annually.

The precipitation pattern is bimodal, as winter weather systems carry moisture from west to east while in the summer, southwest flows from the Gulf of Mexico bring monsoon rains. The western part of the ecoregion receives most of its precipitation in winter and little from the monsoon, while the pattern reverses in the east.[17]

The bimodal precipitation pattern supports two flowering season each year, with some plants blooming in spring following winter rains and others flowering in summer following monsoon precipitation. By contrast, vegetation in the Mojave Desert ecoregion to the west depends largely on winter rains, while in the Chihuahuan ecoregion to the east, summer rains provide most of the moisture.

Vegetation in the Sonoran Basin and Range differs from both the Mojave and Chihuahuan Desert ecoregions in that the signature creosotes of the Mojave and the grasslands and shrubs dominant in the Chihuahuan give way to palo verde trees and the iconic saguaro cactus in the Sonoran.

Other plants typical of the Sonoran region include ocotillo, brittlebush, ironwood, mesquite, and a panoply of cacti: buckhorn cholla, cane cholla, jumping cholla, night-blooming cereus, desert Christmas cactus, barrel cactus, fishhook cactus, and organ pipe cactus.

Mammals of note found in the Sonoran ecoregion include pronghorn antelope, bighorn sheep, coatimundi, cougar, coyote, black-tailed jackrabbit, and desert kangaroo rat.

Well-known birds among the rich Sonoran population of avian species include the Gila woodpecker, whose nest-holes serve as birdhouses for other birds; the iconic roadrunner sometimes found speeding across the desert in search of snakes or rodents; wrens, including the state bird of Arizona, the cactus wren; and owls both large and small, with the elf owl often found peeking out of a hole in a saguaro cactus being perhaps the most photogenic.[18]

Chihuahuan Desert

The Chihuahuan Desert spans a region between southeast Arizona to the Edwards Plateau in south central Texas and extends five hundred miles southward into Mexico. Only its northwest portion falls within the Lower Colorado watershed.

The topography of the region reflects its origin in the Basin and Range stretching event. The area receives between six and sixteen inches of precipitation depending on elevation, with most falling as rain during a summer monsoon season. The summers are hot, and the winters cool to cold.

At lower elevations, seas of desert grassland and shrub cover the land, accompanied by yucca, agave, and a remarkable diversity of cacti. Oak, juniper, and pinyon pine woodlands populate higher-elevation regions.

The Chihuahuan Desert is home to mule deer, pronghorn, jaguar, javelina, and gray fox along with the largest remaining black-tailed prairie dog complex in North America. It is also the only place where the Mexican prairie dog can be found.

Along with the Sonoran Basin and Range ecoregion, the Chihuahuan Desert is one of the richest ecoregions in the U.S. and northern Mexico for migratory birds, as its desert grasslands serve as wintering grounds for a large proportion of North American Great Plains birds.[19]

The Role of Humans in Ecosystems

Thus far, we have discussed topography, temperature, precipitation, and soil as key abiotic components of ecosystems, along with the wide range of flora and fauna that have over millennia adapted to these conditions and established stable, synergistic relationships with one another. We have not yet discussed a critical element of these ecosystem: ourselves.

For much of the ten thousand to fifteen thousand years before the arrival of the first European settlers, the Southwest was relatively lightly populated by Indigenous people who, while they interacted with and altered environmental conditions, did so in a manner and at a pace that did little to disrupt ecosystem equilibria on a large scale. That changed in major way in the nineteenth century, particularly after the end of the Civil War, when Americans headed West in great numbers. When they arrived in Arizona, they saw opportunity and potential wealth in the state's expansive grasslands, bountiful forests, and mineral deposits.

By the end of the century, more than 1.5 million cattle grazed on lands throughout the state, far more than the number that could be supported even in times of plentiful rainfall—a disaster waiting to happen in times of drought. Major timber operations were launched in northern Arizona, while silver, gold, lead, molybdenum, copper, and coal mining fueled the growing economy.[20]

On public land overseen by the U.S. Forest Service, forests were logged extensively, old growth replaced with new. But in service of protecting logging interests and nearby communities, the Forest Service required that every effort be made to immediately extinguish fires of either natural or man-induced origin. Motivated by seemingly benevolent impulses, the Forest Service interrupted the natural cycle of frequent, low-intensity burns that clear out underbrush and thin new growth. As a consequence, many of the state's forests are now tinderboxes, crowded with new-growth trees and carpeted with highly flammable undergrowth. The result: mega fires fueled by undergrowth, leaping to the tops of remaining old growth and creating fast-moving crown infernos.[21]

Mining thrived in the state—celebrated in Arizona's branding itself as "the Copper State"—and provided gainful employment and tax monies that have helped the state thrive. But with little regulation, runoff from tailings often polluted streams and, over time, infiltrated groundwater and aquifers.[22]

At one time, Arizona's grasslands seemed as limitless as those in the Great Plains. But in less than 150 years, much of this grassland has morphed into shrubland as a consequence of overgrazing. As grasslands were trampled under the hooves of cattle and further degraded during droughts in the 1920s and 1930s, the federal government imported fast-growing, drought-tolerant grasses from Africa to provide forage for the remaining herds and to stabilize topsoil. While mostly successful in meeting these immediate objectives, African grasses have rapidly replaced native grasses, and mammalian and avian species that once depended on those native grasses are disappearing.[23]

In an otherwise arid land, free-flowing rivers—the Colorado, Little Colorado, Verde, Gila, Salt, San Pedro, and Santa Cruz—seemed to promise an endless source of water for agriculture. Indeed, in centuries past, Indigenous peoples built extensive irrigation systems to support thriving agricultural communities.[24]

The new arrivals wanted not only water for their fields and orchards but water whose flow they could regulate so that it would be available at the right times in the right seasons. Rather than depending on local canal systems for irrigation, they built dams to store water in reservoirs and release it when needed and also to control flooding and supply hydroelectric power to a growing population. The Roosevelt Dam on the Salt, the Coolidge Dam on the Gila, the Bartlett Dam on the Verde, and the Hoover and Glen Canyon

Dams on the Colorado are but a few of those built to harness the rivers of Arizona to their needs. While providing a timely water source for farms along with carbon-free electricity, dams altered the natural flow of water and in so doing undermined aquatic life, along with the web of organisms that depend on well-functioning riparian areas.[25]

Following the end of World War II, what had for more than a century been a steady flow of migrants to the Southwest turned into a flood. In 1958, 1.2 million people called Arizona home. By 2022 the number reached more than 7 million, a sixfold increase. By contrast, the U.S. population rose by just under a factor of two during that time: from 174 million to 335 million.[26]

The booming population required one resource above all others: water. By the late 1960s, it became clear that the needs of Arizona's growing population could not be supplied by rivers entirely within its boundaries. As a result, homes and farms began to depend increasingly on drilling wells and pumping groundwater, some of which had been stored in underground aquifers for tens of thousands of years.

Farming in Arizona provides food for families throughout the United States, but agriculture, including cultivation of water-intensive crops such as cotton or pecans, uses almost 75 percent of the water in the state. What was, and is, a miracle—turning a desert into a bounteous land—stressed supplies of ground- and surface water to a near breaking point.[27]

The mismatch between projected increases in population and available ground- and surface water supply became so daunting that Arizona's congressional delegation lobbied for authority and funding to build a massive canal system—built as part of the Central Arizona Project—to carry water from the Colorado River in western Arizona to the cotton fields near Gila Bend, to the thirsty citizens of Phoenix, past the world's largest irrigated pecan orchard near Picacho Peak north of Tucson, and finally to Tucson and Green Valley. The project was completed in 1993 at a cost of $4 billion ($8 billion in 2022).[28]

As Arizona's cities have grown and new suburbs and exurbs proliferated, a web of roads have been built to connect them with one another and with cities and markets throughout the country. Many are marvels of engineering, conquering the most rugged of mountainous terrain. But those same roads that enable ready transport of goods and people present impediments to wildlife whose need for food, shelter, and genetic diversity depends on access to linked habitat patches, now fragmented by humans.[29]

With the knowledge we have today, past decisions may seem short-sighted. It is helpful to remember, though, that most were made by people and their governing institutions in service of providing safe, secure, and prosperous lives for citizens and communities. What people and their representatives failed to do, in most cases, was to consider on equal footing the future of all elements of environment—water, plants, animals—with which we share this earth. Reflecting on past decisions regarding human impacts on the environment without considering the state of ecological knowledge and immediate needs of the time or assigning blame to perceived bad actors seems unproductive given the challenges we face today and those that lie ahead.

Instead, we might be better served to look at the current state of ecosystems and, guided by our best current understanding of the role of all variables affecting their health, develop policies and take actions to better balance our needs with the panoply of species with whom we share this space and on whom we very much depend. As opposed to any other biotic element in an ecosystem, humans have the ability to make choices in how we interact with our environment—choices that can allow us to live in better harmony with our environment while enjoying its benefits.

Anthropogenic Changes

In this section we examine the role of five anthropogenic change agents and their effects on ecosystems: water use; alteration of natural fire regimes; introduction of invasive species; fragmentation of the landscape by roads, farms, and cities, and more recently the border wall, which prevents wildlife movement between habitat in the United States and Mexico; and rapid alteration of climate arising from greenhouse gas emissions. My goal is to illustrate how these change agents alter the nature of ecosystems, and to do so objectively, as if I were examining how any abiotic variable—say, soil or topography—influences ecosystem behavior.

Water Use

The demands of human-driven water consumption have resulted in a dramatic change in the character of rivers and streams. According to the Bureau of Land Management's Rapid Ecological Assessment for the Sonoran Basin and Range Ecoregion, more than 70 percent of stream length in the

THE SANTA CRUZ RIVER

The Santa Cruz River starts in the grasslands of the San Rafael Valley of Arizona, and first heads south into Mexico, then turns northward, crossing the border once again and heading past Nogales, Tubac, Green Valley, and Tucson before blending into agricultural fields north of Marana. The river at one time flowed perennially through much of its 210-mile course, but demands for water have lowered the water table in the course of decades of groundwater pumping. Today, the river is dry except during storm events or in areas fed by treated effluent from sewage plants in Nogales and Tucson.

The stretch of natural river flow in the San Rafael Valley, along with the riparian areas restored by treated effluent provide important habitats and migration corridors for migratory birds as well as home for threatened or endangered species such as the Gila topminnow and lesser long-nosed bat, a pollinator essential to the survival of a number of iconic desert plants.

region that was once catalogued as perennial is now observed to be either ephemeral or intermittent.[30] By midway through the twentieth century, the region's demands for water already exceeded supply from surface waters by a factor of three, with the result that groundwater became a major source for human consumption, agriculture, and mining. What people failed to take into account was that groundwater pumping to support agriculture or serve the needs of a growing population would have major effects not only where it is pumped but miles downstream as well.

In many regions of Arizona, the rate of groundwater depletion far surpasses the natural replenishment process of rainfall followed by gradual infiltration. A substantial portion of underground water reserves originally derived from rainfall that occurred hundreds or even thousands of years ago. Once this water is used, restoring it becomes a challenging task. Depleting groundwater and lowering water table turns gaining streams into losing streams and losing streams into ephemeral streams or dry washes as surface water loses connection to groundwater altogether.[31]

In turn, depleting groundwater and altering flow regimes has a profound effect on the health of riparian areas and the panoply of diverse species that depend on them. Groundwater pumping has resulted in the loss of more than 90 percent of Arizona's wetlands and riparian woodlands. When pumping lowers the water table sufficiently, the roots of native trees—willows and cottonwoods, for example—can no longer reach a water source. Gaining streams become losing streams, and some lose connection to groundwater altogether (fig. 1.8).

The loss of perennial streams has a devastating effect not only on riparian vegetation but on aquatic, mammalian, and avian species as well. For example, birds endemic to a region depend on riparian corridors for food and shelter, and migratory birds count on these areas as important stopovers for rest and refueling for their northward or southward journeys. Wildlife movement is affected too, as lack of cover and water forces species to seek other paths through more hospitable environments.[32]

Lowering water tables through excessive groundwater pumping puts native species at risk for another reason: creating conditions for highly invasive tamarisk trees, whose roots can reach more deeply than those of native cottonwoods, willows, and mesquite. Birds, mammals, and amphibians that depend on native vegetation are forced to migrate elsewhere—if there is an elsewhere. Moreover, dominance of tamarisks increases soil salinity over time—another factor in reducing the diversity of vegetation in these regions.

Loss of riparian areas affects humans as well. By removing the ecological "sponge" once provided by vegetation in riparian zones, floodwaters are no longer slowed. Instead, they rush through narrowed channels produced over time by erosion of soil no longer bonded together by healthy plant communities. Reduced vegetation on streambanks also diminishes the role riparian areas play in filtering flowing water and maintaining water quality.

Groundwater pumping is not the only threat to the health of rivers and streams. Water courses are, after all, only one part of a much larger watershed. What happens elsewhere in the watershed, from mountains to forests to uplands to streamsides, can significantly alter the flow and purity of water. Sediments from charred forests or fertilizer from farms carried downward to rivers and streams can drastically affect riparian ecosystems and aquatic life, and rendering these waters suitable for human use in turn can require expensive treatment.[33]

Flow regulation from dams changes the frequency, timing, and velocity of flows, thereby altering the conditions to which aquatic and amphibious life have adapted. Dams keep sediment from coursing downstream and building banks, sandbars, and quiet pools that many fish require for habitat, nutrients, or spawning. Temperatures downstream from the dam no longer fully reflect the seasonal changes to which native fish are adapted. Vegetation is affected as well. For example, the reproductive cycles of willows and cottonwoods are adapted to the rhythms of seasonal flooding that predated dams. While cottonwoods and willows produce seeds in synchrony with spring floods of the past, flooding is now modulated by dams. But invasive tamarisks produce seeds throughout a much broader growing season and, given a longer time to spread those seeds, slowly but surely outcompete native vegetation.[34]

Fire

Fire occurs naturally in all of Arizona's ecoregions. As a result, species are adapted to a natural rhythm of fire events. Indigenous communities used fire as a tool to periodically reduce fuel loads in forests and to keep grasslands relatively free of brush and trees. However, over much of the past century, fire has been suppressed in forests and grasslands: a result of both federal and state policy, and in some cases local practice.

The increase in understory growth in forests has provided fuel for fires that now burn at higher temperatures and spread rapidly. If hot enough, fires can alter soil composition, rendering soils hydrophobic. In such cases, water no longer seeps into the soil but runs off, sending sediment and debris pouring into springs and streams. During significant rain events, stormflows of historic levels have followed major forest fires.[35]

In the past, frequent low-intensity fires thinned out dense stands of smaller trees. By choosing to suppress fire, competition from these smaller trees robs older, larger trees of water and makes them less resistant to drought. Smaller trees also act as fire ladders, leading flames that otherwise would propagate on or near forest floors to the tops of taller trees, sometimes igniting crown fires. Exactly that happened in the Arizona–New Mexico ecoregion in 2002 and 2013 during the Rodeo-Chediski and the tragic Yarnell Fires, respectively.[36]

In Arizona's grasslands, naturally caused fires take place on seven-to-ten-year timescales. Left to this natural rhythm, both grass and young shrubs and mesquites burn. The grass, however, is well adapted to this cycle and rejuvenates, while the brush and mesquite are killed off. By suppressing fire, shrubs and mesquite are able to gain a foothold and over time take over grassland ecosystems.

Invasive Species

Introduction of nonnative species can ofttimes have a significant effect on ecoregions. In some cases, such species can outcompete natives for re-sources and negatively affect the viability of the mix of plants and animals that established equilibrium relationships pre-invasion.

One such species of particular danger to the Sonoran Basin and Range ecoregion is buffelgrass. The grass, native to Africa, Asia, and the Middle East, was imported during the 1930s during a period of extreme drought in the Southwest. Its high drought tolerance and deep root system appeared to make it an ideal plant to stabilize areas suffering from ongoing water erosion. Moreover, it grows quickly, propagates profusely, and serves as forage for cattle in regions starved of native grasses.[37]

Today, the presence of buffelgrass in the Sonoran Basin and Range ecoregion represents a serious threat to the cactus–palo verde ecosystem in the lower parts of the Sonoran Desert. That ecosystem, perhaps best typified by the iconic saguaro cactus, evolved in a regime of infrequent (once per several hundred years), low-intensity fires. The introduction of buffelgrass renders the cactus–palo verde system susceptible to far more frequent and far more intense fire—fires that burn at 1,400 degrees Fahrenheit, three times the temperature at which native vegetation burns. After a fire, buffelgrass can recover more quickly than native species, seed more profusely, and outcompete plant species attuned to infrequent, lower-temperature fires. The downstream effects of significantly altering or eventually extirpating the cactus–palo verde ecosystem are significant, and illustrative of how seemingly well-intentioned changes in an ecosystem can have profound effects.[38]

Fragmentation

The natural environment of any species is its habitat—a home where it can find food and shelter and reproduce. Habitat can be as small as a single pool or as large as a grassland savanna. When we speak of "preserving habitat," we are talking about a natural system specific to a particular plant or animal. "Preserving habitat" sometimes evokes the notion of providing a single reserve of sufficient size for a particular species to survive. But setting aside a single habitat patch isn't sufficient for species to survive and thrive.[39]

Wildlife need to range from one habitat patch to another. Say, for example, one such patch is impacted by fire, flood, or invasion by exotic species. Animals will need access to other habitat patches as well as the ability to move from their old home to a new environment. If species are unable to move freely within and among natural environments, they become more susceptible both to environmental stressors and disease and show greater rates of extinction.[40]

BUFFELGRASS

Buffelgrass (*Pennisetum ciliare*, a.k.a. *Cenchrus ciliaris*) is a drought-tolerant, perennial bunchgrass native to Africa, Asia, and the Middle East. Beginning in the 1930s (and continuing through the early 1980s), buffelgrass was intentionally propagated throughout warm, arid portions of the United States, including the Sonoran Desert of Arizona, to control erosion and provide forage for cattle.

Buffelgrass is native to a very different plant and animal community. African savannas are far less diverse than our Sonoran Desert, generally consisting of densely packed fields of grasses sparsely dotted with trees. Unlike the Sonoran Desert, savannas have evolved a natural fire regime. Native plants there are dense and highly flammable. Trees and shrubs in the savannas are adapted to survive hot fires; after a fire, they reseed and regenerate quickly. It is an ecosystem dominated by frequent, very high-intensity fires (1,300–1,600 degrees Fahrenheit) with flames that can reach up to twenty-five feet in height.

By contrast, the Sonoran Desert ecosystem is one of the most diverse in the world. The Sonoran is also virtually free of wildfires. Wide spacing between individual plants limits fuel to feed a fire, and fires generally burn themselves out before destroying a significant amount of habitat. Native plants flourish during times of rain but typically die back significantly in the dry season, limiting the amount of fuel available for fires. Because a consistent fire regime has not evolved in the Sonoran Desert, native plants typically cannot reseed or regenerate after a fire. Fires in the Sonoran Desert are infrequent, isolated, and very low intensity (burning at temperatures of about six hundred degrees Fahrenheit).

The introduction of buffelgrass into the Sonoran Desert ecosystem packs a one-two punch: the double threat of competition for space and addition of fire has the capability to transform the landscape irrevocably. Buffelgrass propagates quickly, filling in natural open spaces. Native Sonoran Desert wildlife species like tortoises and mule deer do not eat buffelgrass. Without a natural control source, buffelgrass grows unchecked, crowding out native plants that serve as food sources for native wildlife by robbing them of moisture, nutrients, and sunlight.

Buffelgrass alters the fire regime of an area, establishing a positive feedback loop. It negatively impacts the diversity of vegetation and threatens desert ecosystems. Native species are edged out and destroyed. Loss of plant diversity directly impacts animal diversity. The increase in fire occurrence and intensity may lead to extirpations of long-lived species like the saguaro, palo verde, ironwood, creosote, and desert tortoise.

The iconic saguaro, which occurs naturally only in the Sonoran Desert, is extremely well adapted to thrive in its hot, arid climate, but it is not at all adapted to fire. Neither the cactus nor its seeds can survive an intense buffelgrass fire. The population of slow-growing saguaros has little chance to recover following a fire. Even those individual cacti that escape the destruction of the fire itself would have little chance to reestablish in areas overrun by buffelgrass and are vulnerable to the inevitable next fire. Meanwhile, with every fire, buffelgrass becomes a larger and larger proportion of the plant life, leading to more intense fires, and so on, with ever-increasing damage to the ecosystem.

Removal of the saguaros, a keystone species, would have a cascading effect on the rest of the ecosystem. Native solitary bees, migratory white-winged doves (saguaro specialists that rely on saguaros almost entirely for nutrients and water during their breeding season), and migratory nectar-feeding bats such as lesser long-nosed and Mexican long-tongued bats, among others, rely on the flowers of the saguaro for food. Saguaro fruit is an important energy-rich (flesh), protein-rich (seeds), moisture-rich food source for the aforementioned animals as well as for javelinas, desert tortoises, coyotes, foxes, desert rodents, millipedes, an array of birds, and Native peoples. This food (and associated moisture) is available at a time, mid-June, when there is not much else in the desert to eat. Birds, big and small, use the saguaro for nesting—hawks and great horned owls build and use nests in the crook of its arms, while woodpeckers, kestrels, purple martins, screech owls, elf owls, pygmy owls, and others nest within woodpecker-excavated cavities inside the saguaro.

Cavity-nesting birds have few nesting choices in the Sonoran Desert. The cactus ferruginous pygmy owl, currently proposed for relisting under the Endangered Species Act, relies almost exclusively on saguaro as a nesting site.

The resulting removal of some species and reduction of others would in turn impact what they eat and what eats them, would leave seeds un-spread, flowers un-pollinated, soil un-aerated—each of which would in turn impact other plants and animals down the line. Over time, one of the most biodiverse areas in the world would be transformed into a virtual monoculture.

—JULIE STROM, PIMA COUNTY NATURAL RESOURCES, PARKS AND RECREATION

FIGURE 1.14 (a) Cactus ferruginous pygmy owl. (b) Lesser long-nosed bat. (Photos by Bruce Taubert.)

However, development of Arizona and its infrastructure has affected not only the size and quality of habitat patches but the ability of species to move from one patch to another. Humans have severely fragmented once contiguous habitat by building what is effectively a labyrinth of obstacles: agricultural fields, homes, factories, roads, and fences.

Doing so has not only threatened particular species but has undermined the regulation of ecosystems by predators.[41] In Arizona, top-down or apex predators are jaguars, mountain lions, Mexican wolves, grizzly bears, and black bears. Absent a sufficient number of these predators, populations of herbivores such as deer explode.[42] The increased demand for vegetation to feed larger and larger numbers of deer can denude a landscape. In riparian areas, an overpopulation of deer can rapidly consume streamside vegetation, with consequent catastrophic effects on mammalian and aquatic life, as well as on the areas' ability to ameliorate flooding.[43]

FIGURE 1.15 Saguaro cactus and desert brush landscape, west side of Tucson Mountain Park. The saguaros are widely separated, and the brush between them is relatively sparse. Were buffelgrass to replace native brush and grass species, a fire could destroy the saguaro-based ecosystem. (Aerial photo by Stephen Strom.)

Apex carnivores typically require large, connected habitat spaces. Habitat fragmentation and hunting have led to the decline of these species and, in some areas, to their total absence from ecosystems.

Climate Change

As geological forces shaped the Arizona we know today, climate changed from arid to tropical and back again. The ecosystems of the day continuously adapted to changing topography, soil conditions, temperature, precipitation, and the advance and retreat of inland seas and waterways. The ecosystems in which humans now live are just the latest in a long chain of temporally interlinked systems (on a geological timescale), each suited to a particular time and place, and each dependent on the legacy of ecosystems past. A humbling thought.

You, reader, might ask, "In view of these dramatic changes in climate and ecosystems over the millennia, why should humans be concerned by temperatures rising by a few degrees over the next fifty years or perhaps five degrees over the next century?" The answer: Past ecosystems generally had thousands of years to adapt to changing conditions, while we are at present warming the earth at a rate far greater than that faced by ecosystems in the past. Species in those ecosystems had time to adapt to change. Today, most do not.

The literature on the potential impacts of global warming and consequent changes in climate patterns has grown exponentially over the past decades, and threats to ecosystems from coral reefs to tundra have been well documented and publicized. At times, in order to raise awareness of the very real long-term threats of climate change, rhetoric can approach "the end is nigh" levels—understandable when trying to counter a barrage of misinformation arising from those whose short-term interests or political agendas benefit from climate change denial. It has become all too common as well to attribute a single unusual weather event to the effects of climate change, thereby providing climate deniers with ample opportunity to cite past singular events as counterargument.

However, if we are going to increase support for the behavioral changes and economic investments needed to slow or reverse global warming, it seems best to stick strictly to the facts as we know them, explain the reasons for concern, and provide practical examples of how climate change is affecting ecosystems today.

In that spirit, I've chosen two perhaps parochial examples relevant to the Madrean Archipelago and Arizona–New Mexico ecoregions to demonstrate that even relatively trivial-seeming changes in temperature can cascade rapidly, disrupting delicate equilibria established over centuries or millennia.

Current models of climate change, based on the warming expected from anthropogenically driven carbon emissions, are all in qualitative agreement in predicting an increase in temperature and a decrease in precipitation over the next century in each of Arizona's six ecoregions. Indeed, over the past fifty years, average monthly temperatures in southern Arizona have increased by about one degree Fahrenheit, and for the past twenty years, the region has witnessed significant drought. Both trends are consistent with climatologists' models.[44]

In the Madrean Archipelago ecoregion, that seemingly minor one-degree increase in average temperature is apparently already having significant effects on growing seasons in the region. Plants, including grasses, which in the past used to begin growing in April, start to push up from the ground in March. And rather than dying off October, their growing season now runs through November.

When plants green up earlier in the spring, they begin to consume soil moisture from winter rains earlier. But springs in the Madrean ecoregion are typically dry; rains don't usually arrive again until the beginning of monsoon season, in July. As a result, plants run out of water earlier in the spring than they did before and die in June, before the summer rains arrive. By extending the growing season by a month in the fall, moisture from rainfall that arrives in late October and November is now used by plants that are still growing, still have green leaves, and are still transpiring, rather than being stored in the soil through winter for use during the spring growing season.

That modest one degree of temperature rise has thus already begun to stress the grassland ecosystem and has raised the possibility of undermining the advantage to cattle ranchers in parts of the Madrean ecoregion: having two healthy grass-growing seasons where adequate forage is available for spring and fall calving.[45]

If temperatures continue to rise, grasses will need more water. With increasing drought and change in seasonal growth patterns, the rich grasslands of the region will eventually morph into shrubland, with only the most drought-tolerant grass species surviving.

Changes in plant growing cycles—the study of which is called *phenology*— affect the lives of wildlife species was well. The undisturbed riparian areas in the Madrean ecoregion provide key corridors and stopovers for birds that migrate south to Mexico and Central America in the winter. Their migration patterns have long been adapted to the growth cycles of vegetation in the Madrean. If temperatures continue to rise and rainfall decreases, these birds will no longer be able to find the food, tree canopy, and ground cover that they have depended on for millennia.[46]

In northern Arizona, in the forests of the Arizona–New Mexico ecoregion, the modest one-to-two-degree temperature increase over the past fifty years has led to a proliferation of bark beetles, which have already begun

to devastate the region's woodlands. With increasing temperatures, bark beetles are now able to produce two generations of offspring during the growing season of the spruce-fir woodlands that populate the higher elevations of the ecoregion. Combined with higher temperatures, which increase transpiration, and drought, these magnificent trees become stressed and susceptible to the onslaught of not one but two generations of bark beetles. Dead and dying trees become accelerants in forest fires, threatening not only surviving trees but the entire ecosystem of the region, including its human inhabitants.[47]

Concluding Thoughts and a Look Ahead

Ecosystems have evolved over time in response to changes in abiotic conditions—temperature, precipitation, topography, soil—as well as to biotically driven modifications. The latter might include introduction of nonnative species by birds spreading seeds during cross-continental avian migrations or the appearance of a new species such as upright walking mammals—us.

Changes of all types can place stressors on an ecosystem. In some cases, the system is resilient and can, over time, adjust gracefully. In others, change

FIGURE 1.16 Grasslands on the Appleton-Whittell Research Ranch of the National Audubon Society, part burned by a naturally caused low-intensity fire (*left*) and part unaffected by the blaze (*right*). Fire is a natural and critical part of a grassland ecosystem. Absent fire, brush and mesquite gradually replace native grasses. The Santa Rita Mountains appear in the distance at the center of the image, while the Mustang Mountains appear on the far right. (Aerial photo by Stephen Strom.)

agents can have effects that cascade through a system so quickly and with such negative consequences that the system degrades or collapses. Over the past two centuries in particular, the rapid growth of human populations and advancements in technology have reached a point where the environment has been impacted on all scales: from local ecosystems like ponds and streams to larger areas such as grasslands, forests, watersheds, and ecoregions and ultimately to the planet itself. For humans to avoid catastrophic breakdowns in the very ecosystems of which they are a part requires approaches to environmental stewardship that acknowledge and address challenges across all these scales.[48]

Over the past several decades, those who understand the urgency of establishing harmonious and sustainable relationships with our environment have begun to approach the urgent need for local and regional stewardship by engaging citizens in conversation, identifying shared goals for shaping the future of the lands around them, developing plans that enjoy community-wide support, implementing those plans, monitoring successes and failures, and adapting plans to new realities. Doing so takes time, but in the doing, a community begins to take collective responsibility for what all its members share in common. And reestablishing community and restoring a sense of "the commons" is perhaps one of the most daunting and important challenges faced by the nation today.[49]

The following chapters provide an overview of four efforts to achieve large-landscape conservation goals. Based on lessons learned from those endeavors—as well as discussions with ranchers, NGOs, environmentalists, conservation biologists, policy makers, and leadership and staff of federal agencies—we summarize tools and incentives available to individuals and communities to protect, restore, and steward lands sustainably.

CHAPTER 2

Establishing Las Cienegas National Conservation Area

The Natural Setting

The focus of this chapter—Las Cienegas National Conservation Area—lies at the heart of the Sonoita Valley, a six-hundred-square-mile basin of rolling grasslands and oak-studded savannas surrounded by a ring of mountain ranges: the Canelo Hills and the Santa Rita, Empire, Rincon, Whetstone, and Mustang Mountains.[1] Three major streams—the Babocomari River, Sonoita Creek, and Cienega Creek—each begin near the town of Sonoita and the nearby Canelo Hills. From their headwaters in the valley, the Babocomari River courses southeast, Sonoita Creek courses southwest, and Cienega Creek courses north through the valley toward Tucson. Each hosts species-rich riparian corridors.[2]

Two-thirds of the land in the Sonoita Valley is Forest Service, Bureau of Land Management (BLM), or state trust land, while the remainder is held largely by ranching families and individual homeowners. Two unincorporated towns, Sonoita (home to 803 people in 2020) and Elgin (home to 168), are the only significant population centers.[3]

In the past, the valley's mineral-rich mountains and bounteous grasslands supported a number of mining and extensive ranching operations.[4] Today, ranches remain a vital part of the region's culture and economy and are critical to preserving large tracts of connected species habitat in the face of a steady influx of urban emigrants and a growing number of vintners.

The range of life zones in the Sonoita Valley, from riparian areas at valley floors (elevation 3,000–4,000 feet) to pine forests on the mountain peaks

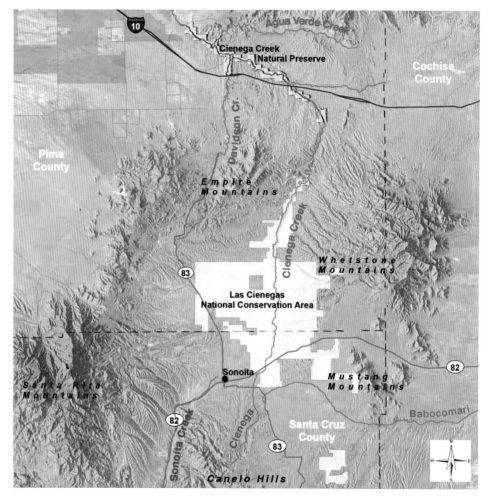

FIGURE 2.1 Map of the Sonoita Valley. (Prepared for the Cienega Watershed Partnership and modified by Stephen Strom.)

(6,000–9,000 feet), provides dramatically different environments suited to a wide variety of plant, mammalian, amphibian, aquatic, and avian species: typical of the Sky Islands of the Madrean Archipelago ecoregion.[5] Species richness results as well from the horizontal dispersal of plant and animal life to and from the Chihuahuan and Sonoran Deserts and neotropical areas in Mexico, along with the ability of fauna to migrate vertically in response to seasonal changes in temperature.[6]

Despite its proximity to the rapidly growing cities of Tucson and Sierra Vista, the Sonoita Valley landscape remains relatively unfragmented by de-

FIGURE 2.2 Canelo Hills oak woodland landscape. (Aerial photo by Stephen Strom.)

velopment. As a result, predators such as the northern jaguar, Mexican gray wolf, and ocelots that require large home ranges can and still do move freely among the woodlands and grasslands of the valley. However, construction of the U.S.-Mexico border wall during the Trump administration now precludes movement of these and other mammals along five-hundred-mile-long mountain and desert corridors where they once roamed freely.[7]

Of the multiple natural environments supported in the Sonoita Valley, three are among the rarest in the American Southwest: desert grasslands, riparian areas, and cienegas.[8]

The grasslands, perhaps the most visually compelling and largest component of the region by area, support habitat for a large number of species well adapted to the mix of native vegetation populating this landscape. Signature avian species such as Botteri's and Rufous-winged sparrows and scaled quail depend on tall grass for cover and nesting, while Swainson's hawks and other raptors look to grasslands for their main food sources: rodents, reptiles, and rabbits.[9]

The black-tailed prairie dog, coyote, gray fox, bobcat, coatimundi, javelina, and iconic pronghorn are among notable mammalian grassland denizens. A large number of herpetofauna—Sonoran spotted whiptail, Chihuahuan earless lizard, Madrean alligator lizard, desert grassland whiptail, desert kingsnake, and both the western diamondback and Mohave rattlesnakes—also find amenable habitat in the grasslands.

At the center of Sonoita Valley and spanning its entire length is its main life-sustaining artery: Cienega Creek. Its headwaters lie at the southern ex-

FIGURE 2.3 Whetstone Mountains, looking east toward Sonoita Valley (*left*), with Santa Rita Mountains in the background. (Aerial photo by Stephen Strom.)

FIGURE 2.4 Mustang Mountains grassland near Rose Tree Ranch. (Aerial photo by Stephen Strom.)

FIGURE 2.5 Oak savanna in the foothills of the Santa Rita Mountains. (Aerial photo by Stephen Strom.)

tent of the valley in the pine-oak woodlands of the Canelo Hills. From there, the creek flows northward, passing by the Mustang Mountains and the towns of Elgin and Sonoita before entering Las Cienegas NCA as it crosses Arizona State Route 82.[10]

As Cienega Creek proceeds northward through the NCA, it continues to be fed by surface flows and groundwater seeping downward from the surrounding mountains: the Santa Rita and Empire Mountains on the west and the Whetstone Mountains on the east. For about half its fifty-mile journey toward Vail and Tucson, the bedrock underlying the NCA lies close

to the surface, lifts the water table, and enables perennial flows that support one of the richest riparian areas in southeast Arizona. At a place called the Narrows, the bedrock level sinks, and except for heavy rain events, the Cienega Creek channel north of the Narrows remains dry until it crosses Interstate 10, turns westward, and enters land protected by Pima County as the Cienega Creek Natural Preserve. There, the bedrock level rises, the surface flow becomes perennial once again, and a cottonwood-willow forest and an extensive mesquite bosque flourish along its banks. Waters from the creek eventually empty into Pantano Wash, which feeds the Rillito and ultimately the Santa Cruz Rivers.[11]

FIGURE 2.6 Empire Mountains. (Aerial photo by Stephen Strom.)

FIGURE 2.7 Agua Verde Creek, a tributary of Cienega Creek, with Rincon Mountains in background. Vegetation is cactus and desert scrub. (Aerial photo by Stephen Strom.)

FIGURE 2.8 Cienega Creek passing through Las Cienegas NCA. Note the cottonwoods turning in late fall, surrounded by a mesquite bosque. (Aerial photo by Stephen Strom.)

FIGURE 2.9 Cottonwoods in fall along Cienega Creek, just south of the Narrows. (Aerial photo by Stephen Strom.)

FIGURE 2.10 Riparian area in fall, Cienega Creek. (Photo by Stephen Strom.)

In 1987 the Pima County Board of Supervisors prepared a proposal to the Arizona Department of Environmental Quality (ADEQ) asking the department to designate the portion of Cienega Creek north of I-10 as a "Unique Water of the State of Arizona."[12] In their nomination, the board noted that the water quality of the stream is consistently better than state standards and that it provides a rare ecological and recreational resource within the Tucson metropolitan area. ADEQ agreed and named Cienega Creek one of Arizona's Outstanding Waters.

In all, Cienega Creek supports nearly twenty miles of marshland and riparian forest, and in some areas, broad and thick mesquite bosques, or increasingly rare sacaton grass flats and meadows. These habitats serve as home to an impressive array of endemic and transient avian species, including the endangered southwestern willow flycatcher, black hawk, and gray hawk, along with emblematic birds such as the great blue heron and yellow-billed cuckoo. The creek also supports a diverse populations of reptiles and amphibians, the threatened Mexican garter snake and Chiricahua leopard frog noteworthy among them.[13]

Cultural History
Indigenous Peoples in and Around the Sonoita Valley

Humans have occupied areas around the Sonoita Valley and Sky Island region for at least twelve thousand years. Between about 12000 BCE and 8000 BCE, archaeological evidence indicates that denizens of the valley—Paleoindians—lived in small, mobile groups of hunter-gatherers. In the cooler climate that characterized the beginning of this period, woodlands, grasslands, and marshes extended to lower elevations that today support vegetation adapted to desert heat and aridity. Mammoths and other now-extinct large mammals roamed the valley and provided a key source of nourishment for Paleoindian groups. Large kill sites containing the remains of mammoths and other large mammals have been found in the nearby San Pedro River Valley: testimony to the efficiency of Paleoindian hunting strategies.

By 8000 BCE, the big game animals that had sustained Paleoindians disappeared, perhaps because of overhunting, a change from cooler and wetter climate to hotter and more arid conditions, or both. As a result, survival required a change in food sources. Native Americans of the time began to hunt smaller game and to add more plants to their diets, collecting amaranth and other grains in the grasslands and walnuts and acorns in the uplands. Waters of Cienega and Sonoita Creeks and their surrounding riparian areas provided both opportunities for hunting and fishing, and a hospitable base for gathering plants.

There is evidence that cultivation of corn in the area may have begun as early as 5700 BCE. By 4000 BCE the region's occupants began to rely more and more on agriculture, transitioning from primary dependence on gathering to cultivating crops. The floodplains surrounding Cienega Creek, its tributaries and other waters in the valley provided good soil for their burgeoning agricultural efforts. Greater dependence on crops and the need to tend them led to near-permanent occupation along the creek starting around 800 BCE.[14]

There is clear archaeological evidence of permanent villages along Cienega Creek dating back to 750 CE. Larger villages built ceremonial centers and ball courts. Crops were grown on terraces adjacent to the creek. The uplands and woodlands provided wild supplements to maize, melons, squash, and beans, among other cultivated crops. The multiple plant life zones around the creek supplied wild sorrel greens and tubers in late winter; agave hearts and yucca flowers in May; sotol flowers in June; amaranth after the onset of the summer monsoons; and during the fall, walnuts, pinyon nuts, and juniper berries. Rabbits and other small game, along with deer and antelope, served as protein sources.[15]

Village life along the creek persisted for another seven hundred years, until 1400–1450 CE, when the large settlements in the river valley were abandoned.[16] During the same time period, dramatic changes affected

migration patterns and Native populations throughout the Southwest. Climate change, changes in religious practices, and conflict among tribal groups have all been suggested as possible causes.[17] However, the reasons for this rapid disintegration of Native societies have not yet been identified with certainty. Following the mid-fifteenth-century collapse of Native villages in the region, archaeological evidence suggest that robust homes built before 1400–1450 were replaced by simpler wood and brush structures. Large villages were replaced by small encampments.

The Spanish Colonial Period

Fewer than one hundred years after the collapse of village life along Cienega Creek, the first Europeans arrived in the Southwest. In 1539 CE a Spanish explorer, Fray Marcos de Niza, traveled northward across today's border with Mexico, perhaps near the town of Lochiel, and into the San Rafael grass-

FIGURE 2.11 Floodplains adjacent to Sonoita Creek provided a place for Native peoples to cultivate crops. Note the modern fields left of the creek in this fall landscape. (Aerial photo by Stephen Strom.)

FIGURE 2.12 (a) Sotol stalk with flowers; (b) agave heart; (c) sotol flowers close-up. (Photos by Stephen Strom.)

lands, just south of Sonoita Valley. There is some contradictory evidence indicating that he may instead have continued northeastward and followed the course of the San Pedro River.

After his return to Mexico City, Marcos de Niza spread stories of Native cities housing great treasures. In 1540 Francisco Vázquez de Coronado set out to find the rumored "cities of gold." Historians examining the records of the Coronado expedition believe that Coronado may have come close to passing through or perhaps a few tens of miles east of the Sonoita Valley as he and his men ultimately journeyed northward from Mexico along the San Pedro River.[18]

Jesuit Padre Eusebio Francisco Kino arrived in what is today southeast Arizona and upper Sonora, Mexico, in 1687, nearly 150 years after Marcos de Niza and Coronado first entered the region. His assignment was to establish missions in New Spain's northwestern frontier. As Kino wrote, he served two majesties—the church and the crown. For the church, missions saved souls and spread the Christian faith. For the crown, they served as training grounds for Native people to accept their role as subjects of the king and citizens of a growing New Spain. In Kino's mind, missions would secure salvation for their people, along with economic growth, safety, and the expansion of Spanish culture.

Father Kino traveled through upper Sonora, Mexico, and southeast Arizona for twenty-four years, establishing missions, and in the course of forty expeditions into Arizona and northern New Mexico produced the first reliable maps of northern Sonora and southern Arizona.[19] In all, Kino established 11 missions, 7 in Sonora and 4 in Arizona—Mission Los Santos Ángeles de Guevavi (near Beyerville, about four miles north of Nogales), Mission San Cayetano de Calabazas (Rio Rico), Mission San José de Tumacácori (Tubac), and Mission San Xavier del Bac (Tucson).[20] The restored Tumacácori mission is now a national historic park, and the reconstructed Mission San Xavier is located within the Tohono O'odham Nation.

In 1698 Father Kino made his way from the San Pedro River into the Sonoita Valley. In his reports, he noted contacts with bands of Native Americans living along Sonoita Creek. Three years after his first visit to the valley, Kino built a *visita* near present-day Sonoita for use as a resting place during travels between missions.

The settlements Kino documented in the course of his 1698 expedition were occupied by Sobaipuri O'odham peoples, who took advantage of the

FIGURE 2.13 Tumacácori Mission, one of the four such missions built in Arizona by Father Kino. It is strategically located adjacent to the Santa Cruz River, whose path is revealed by the golden fall colors of cottonwood trees, with the Santa Rita Mountains in the distance. (Aerial photo by Stephen Strom.)

floodplains to cultivate crops along Cienega Creek and its tributaries emerging from the Santa Rita, Empire, and Whetstone Mountains. The Sobaipuri were related to two tribes living to the west: the Tohono O'odham and Hia-Ced O'odham peoples.[21]

Kino reported that the O'odham peoples had already incorporated Spanish crops, cattle, and horses into their daily lives—testimony to the indirect impact of Coronado's and subsequent Spanish expeditions to Mexico and the Southwest. As Kino saw it, he was called not only to share the teachings of Christ with Indigenous peoples but to improve their daily lives. In service of that goal, Kino arranged to bring herds of cattle and horses to each of his missions and introduced new crops, among them wheat.

As wheat is more frost tolerant than native grasses, it provided a new and important food source for the O'odham, one that could be harvested during the winter months. By contrast, their staple crop for millennia, corn, is a summer crop gathered during early fall. Having a winter crop available represented a significant supplement to the O'odham diet. (It is worth emphasizing that the exchange was hardly one-way, as the Spanish brought back Native American crops—corn and potatoes in particular—to Europe.)

Compared to other missionaries of the time, Kino was broadly tolerant of Indigenous culture, learned their languages, and was a voluble opponent of the practice of enslaving Native peoples to work in the regions' mines and ranches. He was himself a highly successful rancher and used the fruits of his labors to supply cattle, sheep, and goats to each of his missions.

Unfortunately, the Spanish brought more than horses, livestock, and seeds to the region: they introduced diseases. Native peoples had never encountered smallpox, measles, and influenza. Because Indigenous peoples initially lacked antibodies capable of targeting these diseases, epidemics swept through and devastated Native populations.

Another threat to the O'odham, as well as other southern Arizona tribes and the Spanish settlers themselves, came from Apache Indians. The horses introduced by the Spanish provided the Apaches—once a far less combative hunter-gatherer culture—with the mobility needed to raid nearby settlements. Evidence suggests that the Sobaipuri were driven from Cienega and Sonoita Creeks during the 1770s and moved to greater safety to the west along the Santa Cruz River. Conflict between the Apaches, local Native groups, Spanish settlers, and later Euro-Americans continued in the Sonoita Valley and environs until the 1880s.[22]

Today, the O'odham, whose ties to vast lands in northern Mexico and throughout southeast Arizona date back more than eight hundred years, call a much smaller reservation home. Established in 1917, Tohono O'odham lands now span a 4,460-square-mile area (about the size of the state of Connecticut) of the Sonoran Desert, from Sasabe, Arizona, on the south to near Casa Grande on the north, and from Three Points on the east to Why on the west. Since the advent of strict border enforcement, exchange between O'odham families in Mexico and the United States has become challenging, inhibiting not only visits but the gathering of culturally significant plants and access to ceremonial sites on both sides of the international line.

The O'odham still look to the Sonoita Valley as a source of traditional plant and animal resources as well as a spiritual center. They come to the valley to collect yucca leaves and bear grass in the grasslands to support an ongoing, and remunerative basket-making tradition.

O'odham ancestors are buried in the Sonoita Valley, and their burial grounds as well as life-giving springs are considered sacred sites. Ceremonies and vision quests continue in the valley, along with ongoing efforts to pass on to their children vibrant O'odham cultural traditions linked to the Sonoita Valley.[23]

Transition from the Spanish Colonial to the American Era

During the seventeenth and eighteenth centuries, governors in Sonora and what became southern Arizona—a region known as the Pimería Alta—looked to the centralized authority of New Spain in Mexico City for guidance. After a decade-long war, Mexico gained independence from Spain in 1821. Given the demands of organizing governance and economic arrangements in a newly independent country, the remote Pimería Alta region received relatively little attention from the authorities in Mexico City. Mexican citizens living in the region began to look northward to the rapidly growing United States as their primary trading partner, and to develop an independent economic base—activities that were strictly prohibited during the Spanish colonial period.[24]

Soon after Mexican independence, settlers petitioned the Mexican government for grants of land large enough to support livestock raising and agriculture in the arid lands of the Pimería Alta. In the hope of encouraging larger, more permanent settlements on its northern frontier, the Mexican government approved vast land grants; a typical parcel was 20,000 acres (around 30 square miles) in size.[25] Two grants were made in today's Sonoita Valley: San Ignacio del Babocomari, which spanned 35,000 acres along the Babocomari River, and San José de Sonoita, a 5,100-acre grant of land along Sonoita Creek. The former is still largely intact and operated today as a successful cattle-ranching operation by members of the Brophy family.

FIGURE 2.14 The Babocomari River flowing westward past the present-day headquarters of the Babocomari Ranch. (Aerial photo by Stephen Strom.)

The lands granted by the Mexican government were of course not unoccupied. The Tohono O'odham and their ancestors had lived in and among the lands and waters of the

Pimería Alta for millennia. In their cultures, land wasn't owned but rather was considered territory traditionally held in common by a group of people. By contrast, both Hispanics and Americans abided by the principle of private property. Land was owned for the benefit of an individual, not a group, and the "right" of private ownership was guaranteed by the governments in either Mexico City or Washington. The increasing encroachment of settlers claiming ownership of Indigenous lands unsurprisingly led to clashes with Hispanic settlers and undermined the long, largely constructive relationships between Native peoples and the missions. The land grant period ended in the 1830s as Apache raids threatened areas outside the reach of Mexican military outposts (presidios).

By the mid-1840s, expansionists led by President John Tyler and his successor, James Polk, set their eyes on incorporating Texas and the Oregon territory into the United States. Polk was able to negotiate a "compromise" with Britain that established the boundary between the Oregon territory and Canada near its present location between Washington and British Columbia. In the case of Texas, Polk chose in 1845 to recognize the Republic of Texas. Texas had claimed independence from Mexico in 1836 after the victory at the Battle of San Jacinto by Texan Americans led by Sam Houston over the army led by General Antonio López de Santa Anna. The newly declared republic petitioned for statehood in the United States, and following fraught discussions in the U.S. Congress, Texas was admitted to the Union in late 1845.[26]

The United States argued that the Rio Grande should be the legal border between Texas and Mexico, while the Mexican government claimed that the border properly belonged further north, along the Rio Nueces. Polk sent an administration representative to Mexico City charged not only with settling the border dispute in Texas but with arranging to purchase Mexican holdings further west: in New Mexico Territory and California. The president of Mexico refused to meet with Polk's envoy. Following the report from his plenipotentiary, Polk chose to interpret this diplomatic slight as a casus belli and ordered General Zachary Taylor to occupy the area between the Nueces and the Rio Grande in January 1846. In May Taylor was informed that Mexican troops had crossed the Rio Grande and attacked his troops. In the ensuing clash, sixteen of Taylor's soldiers were killed. In response, the U.S. Congress declared war on Mexico.

After the Mexican soldiers' incursion into south Texas, U.S. troops quickly occupied New Mexico Territory and California and achieved a string of victories in northern Mexico. Polk grew impatient with a war effort aimed at subduing Mexico from the north and sent General Winfield Scott to Veracruz to capture the port and march inland to place Mexico City under siege. The capital fell to U.S. forces in September 1847.

In February 1848 a newly formed Mexican government signed the Treaty of Guadalupe Hidalgo which ceded territory now part of the states of New Mexico, Arizona, western Colorado, Utah, Nevada, and California. In return, the Mexican government received $15 million ($550 million in 2022). At the time, the Mexican-American War was met by passionate objections in Congress led by then House of Representatives member Abraham Lincoln, along with those of northern abolitionists concerned that slavery would spread to the newly acquired territories. In a country that then firmly believed in Manifest Destiny, Lincoln's admonitions were ignored, and Taylor became a national hero and succeeded Polk as president.

The United States' appetite for land acquisition in the Southwest was not yet sated. Spurred by advocates for a southern cross-continental railroad route, President Franklin Pierce appointed James Gadsden as ambassador to Mexico and charged him with acquiring additional lands from Mexico. Gadsden successfully negotiated purchase of twenty-nine thousand square miles of land spanning the bootheel of New Mexico, and all of current-day Arizona south of the Gila River. The price: $10 million dollars (about $330 million in 2022).[27]

Settlers were at first slow to arrive in southern Arizona after the Gadsden Purchase. The three key drivers of the Arizona economy of the nineteenth and twentieth century—mining, farming, and ranching—were still developing at a relatively slow pace, not significantly dissimilar to that of the late Spanish and Mexican colonial periods.[28]

That changed soon after the Civil War, when the Southern Pacific Railroad was granted land acquired as part of the Gadsden Purchase and began construction on tracks that would eventually extend from San Diego to El Paso. The first Southern Pacific train reached Tucson from the west in March 1880, and the final link to El Paso was completed in May 1881. Upon its completion, the rail line linked Arizona to markets throughout the United States, spurring dramatic changes in three economic engines that

FIGURE 2.15 Davidson Creek flowing northward under a railroad bridge built by the Southern Pacific Railroad (now part of the Union Pacific system) on land acquired in the Gadsden Purchase. (Aerial photo by Stephen Strom.)

fueled the Arizona economy from the late nineteenth to the mid-twentieth century.

Mining

Silver and lead mines began to flourish in and around the Sonoita Valley. Boom towns sprung up—Harshaw, Mowry, Washington Camp, and Duquesne—to support extraction of silver and lead. The discovery of a large silver deposit in Tombstone in 1878 led to industrial-scale mining that quickly drew ten thousand people to the town. Regional railroads financed by wealthy mining interests were built to service mines throughout the region. The New Mexico and Arizona Railroad connected the Sonoita Valley with Sonora, Mexico, in 1882, and the Benson to Nogales railroad linked to the Southern Pacific line. Silver, gold, lead, and copper rode the rails to national markets and carried provisions to two new villages: Sonoita and Elgin.

The community of Greaterville arose following discovery of gold in 1874, and after easily mined surface veins were exhausted, a hydraulic mining operation was set up in nearby Kentucky Camp. The town of Rosemont was built around a copper mine in the Santa Rita Mountains, and in response to the need for copper wire essential to electrifying the nation, copper mining operations expanded in Rosemont and nearby Helvetia. Copper demand peaked during World War I, declined dramatically during the 1930s, and rose again during World War II. As we will discover in later sections, attempts to develop the Rosemont copper deposits played a major role in catalyzing the establishment of Las Cienegas NCA. Today, those efforts threaten the waters of Cienega Creek and its tributaries despite the protections afforded by the NCA.[29]

Agriculture

Indigenous peoples had farmed successfully for many centuries before Europeans arrived. In the Sonoita Valley, crops were cultivated on floodplains, while in the warmer and more arid Santa Cruz River valley to the west, the O'odham developed canal systems to carry water from the river to their fields. Spanish farmers in the Pimería Alta adopted similar irrigation techniques, excavating acequias (canals) to lead water from an earthen diversion dam to an agricultural parcel.

Both the O'odham and Spanish settlers considered water a communal resource. The Spanish developed a legal system in which a water user's as-

FIGURE 2.16 The Santa Rita Mountains, not far from the community of Greaterville. (Aerial photo by Stephen Strom.)

sociation (*común de agua*) and a judge (*juez de agua*) elected by the association decided how best to ensure equitable distribution of a scarce and unpredictably available resource. Despite the challenges of farming in a desert that receives annual rainfall of ten inches or less, cultivated fields along the Santa Cruz River supported productive fields of barley, wheat, and a variety of vegetables. Farmers in New Spain succeeded by recognizing that in a land where water is scarce, cooperation regarding its use was essential. By treating water as a communal resource, many individual farmers were able to irrigate their fields and sustain viable crop yields.

After the Civil War and the coming of rail transport to southern Arizona, the arrival of American settlers accelerated. Some sought riches in mines, others in raising cattle. Still others saw farming as a path to success and began to intensify agricultural uses along the Santa Cruz and Rillito Rivers. As for the Spanish and O'odham before them, successful farming required

irrigation. But unlike their predecessors in the region, who treated water as a resource held in common, individual farmers each drew as much as they wanted (or could) from the rivers.[30]

Hero of the Civil War, explorer of the Southwest, and pioneering scientist John Wesley Powell, who knew the West perhaps better than any American of his time, tried to alert politicians to the realities of farming in the arid lands:

> In western Europe, where our civilization was born, a farmer might carry on his work in his own way, on his own soil . . . and he could himself enjoy the products of his labor. Out of this grew modern agriculture where the farmer owns his land, cultivates the soil with his own hands, and reaps the reward of his own toil. The farming of the arid region cannot be carried on in this manner. Individual farmers with small holdings cannot sustain themselves as individual men.

Powell urged prudence in distributing newly acquired western lands to settlers, using an approach that drew on the centuries-long experiences of Indigenous, Hispanic, and Mexican farmers. Powell lobbied decision makers in Washington to adopt a policy by which "the waters are to be divided among the people so that each man may have the amount necessary to fertilize his farm, each hamlet, town, and city the amount necessary for domestic purposes, and that every thirsty garden may quaff from the crystal waters that come from the mountains."[31] But politicians, developers, entrepreneurs, and individuals, eschewing restraint and a respect for limits, were all unreceptive to Powell's entreaties.

With an "every man for himself" mentality, other new arrivals chopped wood from riparian-area trees for homes and enterprises, while aspiring ranchers grazed cattle near rivers and streams. An irreplaceable resource—water—was under siege from multiple directions. Surface water soon proved insufficient to meet the needs of farmers and the growing number of enterprises that sought water from the Santa Cruz and its tributaries (including lower Cienega Creek). They began to pump groundwater, and, combined with the destruction of riparian areas by woodcutting and overgrazing, the result was predictable: the river system became susceptible to flooding and

erosion, the river channel incised, and deep arroyos developed along irrigation channels. What once were perennial waters surrounded by sedges, cottonwoods, willows, and mesquite bosques became treeless, intermittent streams flowing in channels well below their original banks.[32]

Today, stark evidence of groundwater depletion in the area is sometimes manifest in ground subsidence and, occasionally, sinkholes, each of which trigger fissures in the earth's surface with consequent damage to roads and pipes.[33] Fortunately, as we'll see in chapter 3, citizens of Pima County have recognized many of the errors of the past and are working together to plan a more sustainable future. By treating the natural environment as a shared resource, they hope to reverse some of the environmental harms inflicted by early settlers and their descendants who in times past eschewed the need for cooperation and planning in the face of scarcity.

Ranching

Ranching in the Sonoita Valley and environs had its origin with Father Kino's introduction of cattle, sheep, and goat herds to his mission communities. Both the O'odham people and Hispanic settlers ranched successfully in what had been abundant grasslands in southern Arizona. Large land grants made

FIGURE 2.17 Grasslands surrounding the Rose Tree Ranch near Elgin, Arizona, after monsoon rains. (Aerial photo by Stephen Strom.)

first by the Spanish during the colonial period and then by the Mexican government during the 1820s provided the grazing acreage needed to support larger operations.[34]

Cattle grazing in the area was, however, limited and eventually curtailed by Apache raids until 1870, when General George Crook began a decade-long series of campaigns to remove the Apaches. When Crook arrived, contemporary reports indicate there were fewer than two thousand cattle in all of present-day Arizona south of the Gila River.

During the 1870s, more U.S. settlers began to take advantage of the Homestead Act of 1862, which provided that any adult citizen could lay claim to 160 acres of surveyed government land. In return, they were required to live on and cultivate the land for five years, after which they would receive unencumbered title. The goal was to turn land acquired by treaty or purchase into private parcels, which would then be either cultivated or grazed by cattle or sheep. While appropriate for less arid regions, a typical 160-acre plot could sustain neither agriculture nor stock raising in lands west of the one-hundredth meridian.

Again, John Wesley Powell implored political leaders to adjust their land distribution policies to the realities of ranching in the arid west: "Though the grasses of the pasturage lands of the West are nutritious, they are not abundant, as in the humid valleys of the East. Yet they have an important value. To be utilized they must be carefully protected and grazed only in proper seasons and within prescribed limits. Ten, twenty, fifty acres are necessary for the pasturage of a [single] steer; so the grasses can be utilized only in large bodies [of land]."[35]

Congress eventually passed the Desert Land Act of 1877, which amended the Homestead Act to grant 640 acres to citizens who would agree to irrigate parcels in arid lands. As Powell had warned, the reality was that much larger tracts—comparable in size (more than ten thousand acres) to the Mexican land grants of the 1820s—were needed to support either ranching or agriculture.

Although he hoped for better, Powell knew the minds of his fellow citizens as well as he knew the canyons and mesas of the west. He noted presciently that "the people of the West are entering upon an era of unparalleled speculation, which will result in the aggregation of the lands and waters in the hands of a comparatively few persons," but added "let us hope that there is wisdom enough in the statesmen of America to avert the impending evil."[36]

FIGURE 2.18 Average annual rainfall in the lower forty-eight states. With the exception of the West Coast, rainfall west of the one-hundredth meridian drops off dramatically from that characterizing the eastern half of the country. (Map courtesy Department of the Interior.)

Doomed by the realities of farming or ranching on small tracts in a region of limited rainfall, most homesteaders failed, and often sold their land to wealthy individuals who had the capital needed to acquire both land and livestock. Less scrupulous individuals used "homesteaders" as front men for amassing lands sufficient in size for a viable cattle operation. By the 1880s, large herds of cattle filled the grasslands and riverbanks, and each rancher grazed as many cattle as he could. Once again, individuals assumed that resources, however obtained, were infinite in supply, and theirs to use and consume as they wished.

Their comeuppance arrived in the 1890s with its multiple years of severe drought. The once-rich grasslands were laid bare by starving cattle. Cattle died by the thousands, and most of the surviving herds had to be sold. Many ranching operations failed, but though some owners survived to live another day, the grasslands did not. An area once thought to rival the Great Plains in pasturage was completely transformed.

Grasses and forbs most suitable for livestock forage were destroyed. As a consequence, naturally caused fires that burned through grasslands every ten years or so lack sufficient fuel. Shrubs and mesquite took over the grasslands, rendering them unsuitable for grazing. To compound this environmental catastrophe, years of drought were interspersed by periods of heavy winter rains triggered by the El Niño effect. Soil no longer held together by grasses and forbs was easily eroded, and once rolling hills covered with thick grass were stripped of topsoil and intruded by deep arroyos.[37]

Even in the face of region-wide environmental devastation, a few ranches in and around the Sonoita Valley managed to survive and flourish. In the grasslands of the San Rafael Valley, just south of the Canelo Hills, rancher Colin Campbell was able to develop a major cattle-raising enterprise. His secret: matching the number of cows to available forage.[38]

Another highly successful ranch was started in 1876, when Nova Scotia emigrant Walter Vail acquired a 160-acre homestead parcel near Cienega Creek that he dubbed the Empire Ranch. Calling his quarter-square-mile property along the creek a ranch was indicative of both his optimism and ambition. Along with two British partners, Vail eventually acquired 100,000 acres of land surrounding the original Empire Ranch parcel, and at its peak, the Empire supported 50,000 head of cattle. Vail's influence on the area, as a rancher, mining entrepreneur, local politician, and founding member of Arizona Stock Growers Association, is memorialized in the naming of the town of Vail, located east of Tucson adjacent to lower Cienega Creek.[39]

Over the better part of a century, the Empire Ranch changed hands a number of times. But it was its final disposition that played a central role

FIGURE 2.19 Grasslands of the San Rafael Valley. The cottonwoods in their fall colors trace the path of the Santa Cruz River. (Aerial photo by Stephen Strom.)

in the next part of our story: the establishment of Las Cienegas National Conservation Area.

The 1983 Flood

The loss of life and property damage from Tropical Storm Octave described in the introduction, while tragic, provided the impetus for sober reflection on the elements that led to the multiple catastrophic events of late September and early October 1983. That somber task became the primary responsibility of the Pima County Regional Flood Control District and its thirty-three-year-old director, Chuck Huckelberry. Huckelberry faced not only the immediate need to repair damaged infrastructure but a much larger challenge: developing strategies to prevent future damaging floods. With the help of a young and creative staff, he looked critically at all the factors that affected the flow of water in the Tucson basin and developed a multipronged strategy. To support rebuilding and future flood-mitigation efforts, the residents of Pima County in 1984 passed the first of what would become multiple bond issues supporting forward-looking land-use policies.[40]

Julia Fonseca, a young hydrologist working with Huckelberry, recalls,

> The rapidity of the response to the 1983 flood was stunning. The 1984 bond issue included monies for flood-prone land acquisition. Mainly those funds went to buy out people who were in the floodplain, to remove poorly planned subdivisions, people in trailers and so forth, out of the floodplain, so they wouldn't get harmed again. It was a very compassionate response too, because there was no federal funding for that kind of thing that could come in rapidly enough at that time to deal with people's problems. Pima County gave them the value of their homes [as assessed] before the flood—which was very compassionate—so that these people could find alternative housing.

The next steps involved redirecting water flows from paved roadways into detention basins and exploring alternatives for reinforcing riverbanks so that water would flow safely within bank-protected channels.

But perhaps most consequential was a decision not only to look at water flow within the Tucson basin, but to understand how water sources upstream from the floodplains of the Rillito River and the Pantano Wash contributed to the intensity of the 1983 flood. That meant turning the flood control district's attention to Cienega Creek. Chuck Huckelberry recalls,

> We had learned a pretty valuable lesson back in October of '83 that said if you can preserve upper watersheds you have a better ability to withstand future flooding. So the real driving force initially with regard to protection along the Cienega basin was all related to reducing future flood losses in the urban area. [Why? Because] Cienega Creek connects to the Pantano Wash which connects to the Rillito which connected to the Santa Cruz River.

A key element to slowing flow along Cienega Creek involved protecting and, where needed, restoring riparian areas. With this goal in mind, Huckelberry connected with a conservation-minded rancher, Walter Armer, who shared his interest in protecting land around Cienega Creek. In 1986 flood control district funds were used to purchase a twelve-mile stretch of the lower creek. The sale agreement with Armer stipulated that no buildings, motorways, or cars would be permitted on the newly acquired land and that any activity would be in service of maintaining and protecting riparian areas in what became the Cienega Creek Natural Preserve.[41]

Julia Fonseca was charged with implementing policies that would achieve the goals of the land acquisition: "Chuck said [to me], 'do everything you can to protect this place.' His vision and our vision was to protect the watershed function, especially as the creek moved through [Pima County near and north of I-10]. [Cienega Creek is] one of the last perennial streams in southern Arizona, the Santa Cruz River having been dried up. This was like a little precious remnant, where there was some water still." Chuck Huckelberry reinforces Fonseca's thoughts regarding the significance of the acquisition: "I think we were all enthusiastic because the Cienega Creek was the last low-level perennial stream in southern Arizona."

One of the first steps taken in managing the preserve was restricting access to riparian areas by cattle. Julia Fonseca recalls,

> The cows were eating all the vegetation. The cottonwoods couldn't get any higher than a few inches because they would be eaten down by the livestock. There were native grasses there, but they were [only] several inches high [as a result of cattle grazing]. But when they [the grasses] were allowed to grow higher, we started to see pools forming. I said to some of the cowhands work-

FIGURE 2.20 (*a*) Chuck Huckelberry, Pima County administrator, now retired. (Pima County Communications Office.) (*b*) Julia Fonseca (*left*), former senior planning manager for the Pima County Office of Sustainability and Conservation, and Shela McFarlin (*right*), retired from the BLM Tucson Field Office. (Courtesy of Karen Simms.)

ing the area, "Did you ever see pools before?" and they said, "No. We've been here since 1974. We've never seen pools. We've never seen cattails."

By restoring riparian areas to their natural function, they became better "sponges" for floodwaters, as well as providing more favorable habitat for mammalian, avian and amphibian species.

Looking Upstream from the Cienega Creek Natural Preserve

Huckelberry and Fonseca were deeply concerned that the flood mitigation afforded by riparian areas in the preserve would prove meaningless if large-scale residential development were to take place upstream from the preserve along Cienega Creek.

Central to their concern was the fate of the Empire Ranch, as Cienega Creek flows through the center of the forty-two-thousand-acre Empire, located twenty miles south of the Cienega Creek Natural Preserve.

The original owner of the Empire, pioneering rancher and entrepreneur Walter Vail, sold the ranch in 1928 to the Chiricahua Ranches Company, a consortium headed by three brothers of the Boice family. In 1969 the Boices sold the ranch to Gulf America Corporation, which initially planned a satellite city comprising fifty-eight thousand residential units. While the corporation's plans for the development began to take form, the Boice family continued ranching on the Empire.[42]

After reviewing Gulf America's proposal, the Pima County Planning and Zoning Commission approved a plan in 1972 that would have restricted the development to thirty thousand homes initially but allowed for rezoning to enable additional development in the future. The late Tom Meixner, head of the Department of Hydrology and Atmospheric Sciences at the University of Arizona, notes, "If that land had been developed, the size of floods along Pantano Wash and the Rillito River would be much larger. Moreover, a portion of the region's renewable groundwater, drinking water, comes from that watershed." That groundwater would have needed to be pumped to supply Gulf America's proposed satellite city.

Gulf America Corporation's plans faltered as its stock prices plummeted, and they were forced to sell the land. In 1974 Anamax mining company purchased the land with the goal of eventually using water from Cienega Creek to support a copper mining venture in the nearby Santa Rita Mountains. Julia Fonseca captures their intention in this pithy comment: "They were going to make a billion dollars sucking the upper Cienega dry to supply water to the Rosemont Mine."

While waiting for their plans to develop the mine to crystallize, Anamax discontinued the Boice grazing leases on the Empire and instead leased those rights to John Donaldson in 1975.[43]

This time, Cienega Creek was threatened not only by depletion of the surface and groundwater from the creek to service the proposed Anamax mine but by possible contamination of creek tributaries such as the stream that runs through nearby Davidson Canyon. However, fortune once again smiled on the Cienega Creek watershed and Pima County. Starting in the early 1980s, the price of copper declined, and in 1985 Anamax abandoned its plans to develop the Rosemont Mine and decided to sell the Empire Ranch.

Chuck Huckelberry and Julia Fonseca worked with their staff to develop a proposal to purchase the Empire Ranch using funds from the flood control

FIGURE 2.21 Artist conception of a portion of Gulf America Corporation's proposed plan for a thirty-thousand-unit development. (Courtesy Empire Ranch Foundation.)

district. The Pima County supervisors approved a resolution for Huckelberry to negotiate with Anamax.[44] "It was so daring of Chuck and the [Pima County] Board [of Supervisors], but Chuck especially, to propose using the flood control district tax levy to buy the Empire Ranch when it was put on the market. That was an astonishing act of leadership," recalls Julia Fonseca.

Although Pima County's efforts to purchase the ranch ultimately were not successful, Huckelberry and the county refused to abandon plans to protect the upper Cienega watershed. Instead, they approached the late congressman Jim Kolbe (Republican U.S. representative from Arizona, 1985–2007), who grew up in the Sonoita Valley grasslands, and two individuals who would change the face not only of the valley but of the state of Arizona.

Acquisition of the Historic Empire Ranch

The first of those individuals who changed the face of the valley was Dean Bibles, appointed Arizona state director of the BLM in 1982. The second was Bruce Babbitt, who served as governor of Arizona from 1978 to 1987, and later as secretary of interior from 1993 to 2001. Bibles and Babbitt had already undertaken a series of mutually beneficial land exchanges, swapping

FIGURE 2.22 (a) Former Arizona governor and secretary of interior Bruce Babbitt. (Gage Skidmore, Wikimedia Commons.) (b) Former Arizona state director of the BLM Dean Bibles. (Conservation Lands Foundation.)

TEXT PORTRAIT: DEAN BIBLES

Dean Bibles joined the BLM after graduating from Texas A&M in 1957 with a degree in range man-
agement. He retired as assistant to the secretary of the interior in 1997 after helping to develop
policies for acquiring environmentally sensitive lands and working with the Department of State
as chairman of the United States National Committee for the Man in the Biosphere Program. In
the intervening years, Bibles served as BLM state director for Arizona from 1982 to 1989, later as
state director for Oregon and Washington, and in several positions in the Department of Interior
in Washington, D.C.

Under his leadership in Arizona, the BLM acquired nearly 2.5 million acres of state, federal, and
private lands through a variety of land exchanges. Bibles used these exchanges to acquire crucial
ecosystems, wildlife habitat, and sites of archaeological value. These exchanges led to the eventual
establishment of Las Cienegas National Conservation Area, the San Pedro Riparian National Con-
servation Area, the Ironwood National Forest, and the Agua Fria Monument.

Bibles received Distinguished Executive awards from President Ronald Reagan and President
Bill Clinton, the Meritorious Executive award from President George H. W. Bush, and the Secretary
of Interior's Meritorious and Distinguished Service awards. He currently serves on the National
Committee of the National Parks Conservation Association and the Public Lands Foundation.

I was born on a ranch up in the Hill Country of Texas. Because I was the number four child, I
had the good fortune of staying on a ranch with my grandparents a lot. My grandfather was well
read and very conservation minded.

I finished high school at age sixteen and got a job working on aircraft gunnery radars for
B-36 bombers. At the time, the Korean War had just started, and my dad said, "Dean, you ought to
consider going through the military as an officer. Why don't you go to Texas A&M?"

I took his advice, went to A&M, and with permission from the military got a degree in range
management. While working a summer job with the Soil Conservation Service, I was part of a team
sent to Great Falls, Montana, for a range management meeting. During that meeting, I connected
with some folks in the Wyoming BLM office who offered me a job in Lander, Wyoming.

The day I graduated from A&M and was commissioned, I had my little Chevy loaded and
headed to Wyoming. After serving six months of active duty in Virginia, I was assigned to reserve
duty in Wyoming. Soon after, I met my wife, a wheat farmer's daughter from Kansas, on a Hal-
loween evening. We celebrated sixty-two years together just this past Monday (March 8, 2021).

As for the next stages of my life, I would say that several things fell into place. The first was my
great-grandfather's being a land surveyor. For some reason I've just always had a natural feeling
for land descriptions, land survey methods. I am usually able to take a fairly quick look at a piece
of land, and to determine whether it's important for conservation purposes.

I also got on very well with folks in the livestock industry because I was raised on a ranch and
I could rope and brand calves, break horses and read a horse. I can recall a fellow in Wyoming
who had chased a number of BLM people off his land. I went out there one day and found this

guy wrestling with a yearling heifer. It was hard to see who had who down. I just bailed over the fence, grabbed that heifer's tail, and hooked its back leg and pulled it through and held it down while he finished branding it.

We went ahead and branded six more before we stopped and introduced ourselves. He was stunned that I was BLM. From that moment on, we got along fine. He agreed to the stocking plans and everything I asked him to do. My boss just couldn't believe that I went out there by myself without protection.

I've always encouraged our employees that were trying to deal with ranchers or loggers to *listen*. Let folks talk. If you get out there and a rancher wants to talk about his prize bull or his grandkids, let him talk it out. You'll eventually get around to what you're here for. Don't just rush in and say, "I've got a college education and I'm here to tell you how to run this ranch." You'll be run off. To me that's the key, being willing to listen. You don't just go busting into somebody's house and say, "I'm here to do this and I'm in a rush, do It my way." It's not going to work.

When I became state director in Arizona, Bruce Babbitt was governor. Bruce and I would sit down regularly and go over statewide issues, trying to see how we might make landownership adjustments that would produce income for the state trust while protecting watersheds, critical habitat, and so forth. Bruce and I described it as "repositioning lands in Arizona."

In those days [1982–89, when Bibles served as BLM state director], we had a delegation that really worked together. In today's world it would be unheard of. I could either call Barry Goldwater [Republican U.S. senator, 1953–65 and 1969–87] or Morris Udall [Democratic U.S. representative, 1961–91] and say, "I need to talk about some land exchanges to the delegation." So they'd say, "Let's work on it." I'd get a call back and they'd ask, "Can you be back here in D.C. at 7 p.m. on Thursday next week?"

When I got there, the entire Arizona delegation would be in either Barry's or Mo's office. I'd make a presentation, and they would then ask for my advice and recommendations. The delegation would talk it over and we'd discuss some adjustments if need be. Just before the meeting was adjourned, either Barry or Mo would go around the room and make sure that everybody in the delegation was behind moving legislation to enable a land exchange. When they agreed, they all worked together to make it happen. There was absolutely no discussion about whether it was Republican, Democrat, or independent. It was just, if this was what's good for the nation and for Arizona, they made it happen.

During the time I was in Arizona, we exchanged 2.5 million acres of state trust and BLM lands. We'd have a team of state people and BLM people that would look at tracts of land and ask, "Does this land have conservation, recreation, or other values that should warrant its being in the public interest to stay in public ownership, or should it be transferred to the State Land Department where they can use it to make the money for the school trust?" We did that statewide, helping the state get lands that were income producing and, in return, valuable conservation lands. I'm very proud of what we did in Arizona. We had a statewide map, and we said, "This is what we want this state to look like eventually."

BLM and state trust lands.[45] The result was a win-win: conservation lands for the BLM and economically valuable lands for the state trust.

According to Bruce Babbitt, "Dean Bibles was really absolutely key because prior to that time, I'm not sure that BLM had ever had much interest in land exchanges or that much attention had been given to it. We really went on a tear. We started off with the San Pedro Riparian National Conservation Area," a thirty-mile-long strip of land protecting riparian areas along the San Pedro River, from the Mexican border to just south of Benson, Arizona.[46] John Leshy, who served under Babbitt in the Department of Interior from 1993 to 2001 comments, "Bibles and Babbitt really kind of remade the map of the state of Arizona in some ways in the 1980s by primarily exchanging rural isolated scattered parcels of state land for developable BLM land. They did it all administratively."

Keenly aware of the BLM's receptivity to land exchanges, Chuck Huckelberry approached Jim Kolbe, Bruce Babbitt, and Dean Bibles on behalf of Pima County to assess whether the BLM might be able to acquire the Empire Ranch from Anamax. Since the BLM lacked the funds or authority to purchase the Empire outright, acquiring the ranch would require a

FIGURE 2.23 The San Pedro River coursing through the San Pedro Riparian National Conservation Area. (Aerial photo by Stephen Strom.)

complex exchange involving Anamax, the federal government, and a third (private) party.

Fortunately, Dean Bibles had already met a similar challenge in acquiring land for the San Pedro Riparian National Conservation Area in 1986. There, the parties involved were Tenneco, Inc., the BLM, and a Phoenix-based land developer. In the exchange, the developer purchased the Tenneco property along the San Pedro River and then transferred ownership to the BLM. In exchange, Tenneco received low-conservation-value but developable BLM land west of Phoenix.

At the time of the San Pedro and other BLM land exchanges in Arizona, the national director of the BLM was Robert Burford. As Dean Bibles remembers,

> My boss was Bob Burford, and Burford was very close to the [Reagan] White House on everything. As we were doing quite a number of these exchanges, it got to the point that many environmental groups were writing really nice letters to Burford congratulating him on all the great things we were doing, which was putting me in deep trouble! He did not like [the exchanges] at all so

he finally just pretty well put his foot down and said, "This thing of just going out and acquiring entire ranches, I'm not in favor of that anymore."

I looked [at the factors that would be involved in an exchange involving the Empire] and thought, "I've got to get the administration's approval because I am catching too much flak from our director about exchanges, and this is one that he's not going to like." So then Jim Kolbe went to Bob and said, "Would you let me have Dean bring the maps in and us go over this thing with you?" Burford said, "Yeah, I'll do that." So they had me come back to D.C., and Jim and I met with him over at Interior, and he still said no to the exchange. So Jim said, "Well, at least come out and let us show you the Empire and what we want to do." And he said okay.

We went [to the Empire Ranch] and Jim opened the gates. Of course, Bob thought that was funny having a congressman opening the gates for us, but we went down and met with John Donaldson, who was running [cattle on the Empire]. It turned out that Burford and John had known each other from cattle-trading days. Bob was a rancher from the Western Slope of Colorado, over around Fruita. So John convinces Burford that the best thing that could ever happen was to have BLM acquire the Empire, continue some livestock grazing, and not let it go into all of the development of homes. So Bob finally said, "Okay. I'll give you permission, but I won't raise my little finger to help you if you get in trouble." Without Jim Kolbe, the Empire exchange would have never happened because my director was adamantly opposed.

With Director Burford's approval in hand, Bibles arranged for a Phoenix land developer to purchase the Empire Ranch from Anamax, deed it to the BLM, and transfer ownership of BLM land near Phoenix to the developer.[47] As one of the conditions negotiated in the exchange, the BLM received all water rights on the Empire. With this three-step dance complete, the threat of development along the upper Cienega watershed lifted.

The late Henri Bisson, who in his role as district manager of the BLM's Phoenix office worked closely with Dean Bibles during this period, captures the importance of the Empire Land exchange:

> The exchange prevented all of that habitat from being disturbed. When we acquired the Anamax holdings on the Empire Ranch, we got the water rights that went with the land. It's ironic that so many years later [beginning in 2001] there would be a big battle with HudBay Minerals over development of the

FIGURE 2.24 (*a*) The late Henri Bisson (courtesy BLM); (*b*) Jesse Juen, BLM (courtesy Jesse Juen); (*c*) Peter Warren, The Nature Conservancy (courtesy Christine Conte, The Nature Conservancy).

Rosemont copper mine. It would have been a hell of a lot worse if we had never done what we did in terms of conserving that piece of country, because otherwise HudBay might well have gained access to water from Cienega Creek for the mine.

The Nature Conservancy staff member Peter Warren, who spent his career in New Mexico and Arizona facilitating arrangements to protect grasslands, commented,

Acquiring the Empire is a good example to me of how so much revolves around basically dumb luck and coincidence and just being ready. But the reason it was possible was because the price of copper crashed, and we had a guy [Dean Bibles] who had the administrative guts to do a really big innovative exchange project. The exchange represented a confluence of kind of lucky events which kind of worked out because there were enough people ready to act when the stars aligned.

The late congressman Jim Kolbe echoed Warren's praise for Bibles's efforts: "Bibles was really kind of the driving force behind it. He saw this as a great opportunity to acquire the Empire at no cost and at fair trade market value."

Through a combination of vision, persistence, political leadership, and a good deal of serendipity, the Empire was now safe from development and under BLM management. Still in question, though, was how the BLM intended to manage the land.

Developing a Community-Based Vision for the Future of the Empire Ranch

All Bureau of Land Management lands are managed according to a resource management plan (RMP): "blueprints to keep public landscapes healthy and productive." At a top level, an RMP comprises two major components: desired outcomes and permitted land use. When the BLM acquired the Empire Ranch, the agency was required to develop an RMP for the property. This task eventually fell to Jesse Juen, who had been appointed manager of a newly created Tucson Field Office in 1994.

Juen's predecessors had followed what was standard practice at the BLM: prepare a plan internally; seek public comment; make revisions; and seek further comment. Juen recalls, "When I got there, the staff was working on a management plan. They had done a good job of inventorying the land and assessing what was out there. They were finding rare species, listed species, native intact systems of aquatics, and so on. John Donaldson and his family, Mac and others, had been out there ranching for several years and were doing a great job. But we kept stalling out."

Juen relates a story that captures the difficulties faced by the staff:

The staff took me to two community meetings. We explained what the planning process was, how we would engage the public and how we wanted their feedback. At the first meeting, a prominent environmentalist stands up and says, "Well, we really appreciate all of this but it's a big waste of time. I just wanted to let you know that if you have any intent of allowing cattle to con-

TEXT PORTRAIT: JESSE JUEN

Jesse Juen was raised in El Paso, Texas, and began his career with the U.S. Forest Service before joining the BLM as a wildlife biologist in New Mexico's Roswell area office. He has served as an assistant area manager in Kingman, Arizona; field manager for the Tucson Field Office; associate state director for New Mexico, Oklahoma, Texas, and Kansas; manager for national conservation areas and national monuments within the National Landscape Conservation System; and state director of the BLM in New Mexico. He retired from the BLM in 2015. Juen played a critical role in catalyzing the community-based discussions that led to establishment of Las Cienegas NCA and has worked throughout the west with land users, local communities, and other partners in managing the BLM's public land.

I was born and raised in Texas, where there is little concept of BLM, Forest Service, or other public lands. So when I was young, my perception was that you either had to know somebody who owned land or have enough money to recreate in the outdoors. You might be able to go to a city park or a state park, but that was it.

I went to Texas A&M for my undergrad work, and then I went up to Texas Tech University because my wife-to-be was enrolled there. I took a job in Lubbock, and just for the fun of it I took a graduate-level class at the university. During that time, I was approached by a professor who said, "You need to be doing master's level work." At his urging, I enrolled in graduate school and later received degrees in wildlife and fisheries and then wildlife and range. My first postgraduate job was with a Forest Service research lab based at Texas Tech.

I next came over to the BLM in 1981 and started to work on BLM-held rangeland leased by ranchers. I would get up in the morning, take off, go out to meet with one of the ranchers, stop by and have coffee with them, introduce myself, and try to learn who they were as people and how they managed their ranch. I'd then say, "Hey, I'm planning to go out and do these studies or look for wildlife or do whatever, would you want to come with me?"

Sometimes they would, sometimes they wouldn't. But almost every one of them would say, "We'd love to hear what you find. Will you come on back by and have dinner with us and tell us what you found?" So I did that for several weeks until my manager finally came to me and said, "So you're leaving about 6:30 in the morning and you're getting back about 6:30 in the evening. What's going on?" I just kind of shrugged my shoulders and said, "This is what I'm doing. Is this wrong?" He looked at me and he smiled and said, "Nope. You're doing everything right."

That work helped me understand people that are out on public lands making a living. It's no different in terms of their operation if they're using their privately held land or leased BLM land. They're trying to figure out how to manage the whole ranch (private plus leased land) just as if it were all private and trying to make a living for themselves and their family. So that really influenced how I approached management on a day-to-day basis within the BLM.

My passion is wildlife and wildlife habitat, but I've evolved over time and it's really helping people out that gets me jazzed. I often find myself in the role of bringing people and organizations together with folks that they don't know and introducing them to resources and opportunities that they might not otherwise hear about or be able to access. In approaching each of these problems I go back to the advice I got from [facilitator] Carlos Nagel when we started discussions with the Sonoita Valley Planning Partnership: "We can solve so many problems if people are willing to engage with the issues, understand what they are, and then come up with a common set of facts, and be open enough to be creative about what solutions might be."

Since retiring from the BLM, I've been working as an adviser with a few nonprofits—the Western Landholders Alliance and the New Mexico Association of Conservation Districts—and with other groups focused on land-use planning, management, and restoration of land health.

FIGURE 2.25 At an Elgin Club celebration after the designation of the Las Cienegas NCA, (*left to right*) the late rancher John Donaldson (Mac Donaldson's father); Donaldson's partner, the late John McDonald; Karen Simms; her son, Kyle Simms; and the late Jim Kolbe, who served in the U.S. House of Representatives from 1985 to 2007 and played a major role in shaping and shepherding the legislation that established the NCA. (Photo courtesy Karen Simms.)

tinue to graze on what is now our public lands, we will be suing you." So, then the next night we went down to the community of Sonoita and had a public meeting, and one of the local ranchers, who was almost three sheets to the wind, got up and said, "Thanks for all the information, but just so you know, we don't trust you. We know you're here to get rid of all the livestock so we're going to be suing you."

After the Sonoita public meeting, a community member approached Juen and suggested he talk with a local skilled facilitator, Carlos Nagel, with the goal of developing the resource management plan in collaboration with the community.[48] Nagel arranged a series of meetings that led to the formation of the Sonoita Valley Planning Partnership (SVPP), an ad hoc, broadly based community group with participants from more than a dozen communities in southeastern Arizona, along with representatives of conservation organizations, grazing interests, recreational user groups, NGOs, and federal, state, and local agencies.[49]

As Juen explains,

> What Nagel formulated for us was a community engagement plan, where we invited all the potential players in Sonoita that we thought could be involved. Recreationists, horseback riders, the environmental community, conservation groups, sporting groups, and so on. We did a mailing in every mailbox in Sonoita, and he had us set up a meeting where every interested organization had a booth, [where they could say], "Here's who we are, here's what we are passionate about, and here's what we really like about these lands." But he also set up a forum where anybody could speak about their fears, their worries. It was [arranged around a] potluck. He designed it so that everybody had to bring food to share.
>
> At the end of about two hours of people talking and sharing, we all sat down and broke bread together. What it created was an environment that wasn't about planning at all. It was about that landscape, and telling their history, how they are connected to [the land] and what they love about it, what they are worried about, why they are scared that the government is here, and what they would like to see. [At that time, it wasn't] a normal thing for BLM to do [in preparing a plan].

To develop a community-based vision for managing the Empire Ranch, the SVPP continued to meet monthly for five years, working together, sometimes harmoniously and other times less so.[50] Juen recalls, "There were times when everybody would get frustrated and throw their hands up and say, 'God, when are we going to finish this thing?' But at the end of five years, the Sonoita Valley Planning Partnership said, 'Okay, BLM, we did our work; now you go write this damn thing in whatever format you've got to put it in, and then bring it back to us and we'll make sure it has all of our things.'"

Linda Kennedy, biologist and retired director of the Appleton-Whittell Research Ranch of the National Audubon Society, captures the spirit of the meetings:

> [The] Sonoita Valley Planning Partnership brought the community into the BLM planning process. That's community writ large. That's the community of individuals living in and around Las Cienegas, that's the conservation commu-

nity at a larger scale, and it was the recreation community, it was the ranching community. . . . It brought them into the planning process in a very structured way and therefore provided a sense of ownership. I think that's the key: ownership.

Everybody that was involved in the Sonoita Valley Planning Partnership felt like it was theirs and not in a "it's mine and nobody else's" way. [More like] "They value what I have to say. They value what my concerns are." I cannot emphasize that enough. I think one of the reasons why Las Cienegas has been such a success for all of these communities is from that initial planning process that conferred a sense of ownership to large numbers of people.

Central to guiding the SVPP process to a successful conclusion was a young BLM field biologist, Karen Simms, who was assigned to live and work on the Empire Ranch in 1988. Just out of graduate school, her initial task was to inventory biological resources on the ranch. Over the course of the next seven years, she developed relationships with experts from the academic community involved in assembling baseline information that would eventually be used in the BLM RMP, ranchers John and Mac Donaldson, staff members at other federal and state agencies, and innumerable members of the Sonoita-Elgin community interested in the long-term fate of the Empire. In recognition of the breadth of her relationships and deep knowledge of the Empire, Jesse Juen asked Simms to assume responsibility for developing the RMP for the ranch in collaboration with the community.

Karen Simms played a pivotal role in collaborating with Juen and Carlos Nagel to organize a potluck event held at the Sonoita Fairgrounds, which served as a catalyst for community discussion. She recalls the effort to ensure that attendees at the potluck would span a broad range of interests:

We just kept trying to get as many different stakeholder groups [as possible]. We had bird-dog people who participated in field-dog trials on the open grasslands, people representing conservation groups, and recreationists like hikers, mountain bikers, OHV enthusiasts, and birders. We had all the different groups bring their displays to the Fairgrounds and talk about what was important to them in the watershed. There were over one hundred people that came. There's just something about that whole Cienega watershed–Sonoita Basin that's pretty amazing and people have really strong connections to it.

TEXT PORTRAIT: LINDA KENNEDY

Linda Kennedy received her PhD in botany and plant ecology from Arizona State University in 1999. For the next twenty years, she served as director of the Appleton-Whittell Research Ranch of the National Audubon Society, an eight-thousand-acre sanctuary and living laboratory in the grasslands of southeastern Arizona. During her twenty-year tenure, Kennedy played a key role in advancing the ranch's mission: to formulate, test, and demonstrate methods to rehabilitate and safeguard the bioregion and aid community members and policy makers in their efforts to protect and steward native ecosystems.

A very early memory of mine was being in a car with my mom, dad, and one of my aunts and uncles. I was probably four at the time. On that drive, we passed a hillside covered with orange flowers. It was stunning. None of these four adults, who were like gods in my eyes, had any idea what those orange flowers were. Looking back, right then, was probably the start of my interest in knowing what plants were.

But it took me a long time before I was able to indulge in an intellectual quest to understand plants, and why they are where they are. I followed a pretty nonlinear life path for forty-five years before I started to study plants in earnest. I was a bank teller in a small town in Kansas until I was in my early forties. At one point, I became furious with the vice president, quit the job, and started driving back and forth 160 miles a day to finish my bachelor's degree.

After receiving an undergraduate degree in field biology, I entered a master's program, where I studied small mammals. When I decided to go on for my PhD, I was a single mom with a small child, so I couldn't spend six months a year in the field studying mammals. But I could study plants, and I loved it.

When I first arrived at the research ranch, the Sonoita Valley Planning Partnership was meeting to discuss how to manage the area that became Las Cienegas National Conservation Area. I, along with everybody who was involved in the Sonoita Valley Planning Partnership, felt ownership of the process. So many times, somebody would come in with a bone to pick, but by the end of a meeting they saw that they were heard and saw that everybody else was heard. So that to me is one of the major reasons why SVPP was a success. Even though SVPP itself is not active anymore [it has been superseded by the Cienega Watershed Partnership], I think Las Cienegas NCA is still reaping the benefits of that initial work.

An important part of that planning process was the creation of a biological planning team, the group that I was the most involved with. Biological planning plays a big role in adaptive management of the resource. We take in ideas, try them out to see how they work. We collect data and go back and see if implementation of an idea is meeting its objectives. If it is we continue. If not, we adjust, try something else, and continue to monitor. I believe the results of the planning partnership and the bio planning efforts have contributed greatly to the health of the Cienega Creek watershed.

Other BLM offices took notice of the success of the planning process and invited representatives of the planning partnership to share their experiences. Rancher Mac Donaldson remembers, "the SVPP became a real example of the BLM's [working collaboratively with the community]. Members of the SVPP would go and talk to different BLM offices about what was done, how it was done, how conflict that was just rampant was resolved, and how we actually accomplished the goal of creating a resource management plan."

TEXT PORTRAIT: KAREN SIMMS

Karen Simms received a BS in zoology from University of California–Davis and an MS in wildlife biology from the University of Arizona. In 1988 Simms began her thirty-year career with BLM as a wildlife biologist in the Tucson Field Office, where she later served as assistant field manager as well as the manager for Las Cienegas National Conservation Area.

In 1995 Karen assumed the role of planning team leader for the Las Cienegas Resource Management Plan. The RMP planning process adopted what was at the time an innovative collaborative approach to land-use planning: stakeholders working together to achieve community-oriented solutions to issues affecting public lands in the Cienega Creek watershed. Simms now works as Natural Resources Division manager in the Pima County Natural Resources, Parks and Recreation Department.

Many people don't know this, but I was born in Cambridge, England, and emigrated to the United States. I first came to the States when my father, who was a biochemist, brought our family to the United States on a sabbatical visit. A few years afterward, we returned permanently after he accepted a position at the Oregon Health Sciences University. I was about five years old at the time.

Throughout my formative years our family did a good deal of camping and traveling. In 1976 we all became U.S. citizens. I remember being very touched by the oath you took when you became a citizen. That, combined with our travels through the West, made me want to be of service to the country by devoting myself to conservation of public lands.

I attended the University of California at Davis for undergraduate studies and found it a fantastic place. During the summers, I took internships working with the U.S. Forest Service on a spotted owl project and a mountain lion and deer project in the Sierra Nevada. My experience there led me to think seriously about a career in wildlife biology.

I returned to Oregon for a year or two between undergraduate and graduate school. During that time, I worked as a volunteer in Columbia Gorge Ranger District of the Mount Hood National Forest and later as a biological technician working primarily on wildlife mitigation projects.

Those experiences solidified my interest in wildlife management and wildlife habitat. When I finally came to the University of Arizona for graduate work, I was eager to work on a project focused on endangered species. I wound up working on the masked bobwhite quail reintroductions on the Buenos Aires National Wildlife Refuge (BANWR), and it was there that I began to get an idea of some of the conflicts that come about with managing public lands.

In establishing the refuge, the U.S. Fish and Wildlife Service (FWS) purchased several ranches, but instead of leasing the land back to the ranchers to allow grazing to continue at some level—the practice followed on BLM lands and on the ranches acquired by Pima County—the FWS removed cattle from the BANWR. As you might imagine, the ranching community became really upset.

I lived near the refuge during the whole time I was in graduate school. During that time, I listened to many different perspectives: from the refuge staff, from the ranchers in the area, and from environmentalists. I felt at the time as if the FWS could have forged a win-win solution that could have satisfied both the ranchers and the conservation goals of the BANWR.

Toward the end of my graduate career, I applied for positions with the FWS and was offered one on the bison range in Kansas. The problem was that the position was in law enforcement, in which I had zero interest. I finally asked a friend—the son of Arizona BLM State Director Dean Bibles—if the BLM had any positions available. I guess he spoke to his dad, and the next thing I knew I was being considered for one on the Empire Cienega Ranch, which the BLM had just acquired [in 1988]. It was for a wildlife biologist position, which was great—aligned with exactly what I wanted to do.

That's where my history with this landscape began. When [my husband] Jeff and I drove out here in August of 1988, it was just amazing to see this grassland valley, so close to Tucson, and so different from the Sonoran Desert. I remember seeing the houses at the Empire Ranch for the first time. It was just so incredibly beautiful with the backdrop of those cottonwoods. There were gray hawks calling. It was astonishing.

We started out living at the Empire Ranch headquarters where rancher John Donaldson was our neighbor. We lived there at the field station for about a year and a half before the BLM and John worked out an agreement that allowed us to move over to the Cienega Ranch—between three and four miles east of the ranch headquarters.

Empire Ranch was our home for close to three years. Living near John and his son, Mac, and hearing their perspectives over the years really made an impact. My early experiences at the Empire Cienega made me more open to listening to different voices, and more aware of opportunities to find common ground among them.

When the BLM acquired the Empire, we knew we needed to create a resource management plan for this area. They started out by following the traditional BLM way of doing planning: you go out, scope issues with people, go back to the BLM office, write up the issues and the agency's proposed solutions, and come back to the public and present those alternatives. Our first attempt went over like a ton of lead bricks.

At that time, Jesse Juen—who had been appointed to be the field manager at the BLM's Tucson office—had been exposed to the idea of collaborative conservation. Jesse decided to take a little detour before we really started working on the land-use plan for the Empire Ranch to see whether this approach could be used to develop an ecosystem management plan for the Muleshoe region. Muleshoe was an area between Willcox and Benson that was jointly managed by the BLM, the Forest Service, and The Nature Conservancy.

In putting together the plan, we reached out to a number of stakeholders and worked out a collaborative plan with these folks, developed the Muleshoe Ecosystem Management Plan together, and then put it out for public comment. We received some comments, but none of them really caused any major change in the draft plan. Muleshoe was my learning ground for how to carry out a collaborative planning process.

After the Muleshoe experience, Jesse asked me to take over as planning lead to develop a draft RMP for the Empire using the collaborative ecosystem approach that worked successfully for Muleshoe. And with that, we started a five-year process that culminated with the Sonoita Valley Planning Partnership's and the BLM's working together to develop the management framework for what became Las Cienegas NCA.

FIGURE 2.26 Karen Simms working at the Empire Ranch early in her career with the BLM. After spending almost thirty years with the BLM, Simms now serves as Natural Resources Division manager, Pima County Natural Resources, Parks and Recreation. (Photo courtesy Karen Simms.)

Two years after the first SVPP meeting, Karen Simms assumed the role of meeting convener and facilitator, a role she continued to fill until 2001. Naturalist and University of Arizona research scientist David Bertelson comments:

> Without Karen Simms it would have all fallen apart. I don't have any question about that. To me she's one of the most amazing people I've ever met and she was able to hold all these people together—all having a lot of different opinions—keep us happy and not shouting at each other, while not trying to control the meeting. We decided everything by consensus. There were no votes at all. That was one of the things Karen insisted on from the beginning was that everything would have to be [decided by] consensus and that was key.

Larry Fisher, research professor at the School of Natural Resources and the Environment, echoes Bertelson: "Karen Simms was able to provide the continuity of leadership and the connectivity to the stakeholder groups that was and is so critical to success."

TEXT PORTRAIT: JEFFREY SIMMS

Jeffrey Simms retired in August 2020 from the BLM, where he served for nearly thirty years as a fishery biologist. He has extensive academic training and field experience working with aquatic amphibians and reptiles. He is generally acknowledged as the most knowledgeable observer of endangered aquatic species and other aquatic fauna in the Cienega watershed. He has worked extensively with ranchers, agency managers, and biologists in the Sonoita Valley and elsewhere in southeast Arizona.

I was born in Ann Arbor, Michigan, and moved from there to Redwood City, Oklahoma City, and Phoenix before arriving in Tucson in 1971. I was an avid outdoorsman, I think because my father loved to hunt, fish, and camp. He used to take me out of school every fall and we'd spend a week in the White Mountains with nobody else there, just us.

When I was in high school, I took advanced chemistry and somebody in the class gave me a course catalog for the University of Arizona. I flipped through and said, "You've got to be joking: fisheries and wildlife science? You can't get a degree in that and get a job, can you?" Finding out that you indeed could, I applied to and was accepted to the University of Arizona and set my course straight as an arrow for one major—fisheries science.

After I received my bachelor's degree from the U of A, I applied for graduate school and was accepted. As part of my master's work, I went up to Flagstaff and worked on a lake where trout had for some reason stopped growing. I looked at lake conditions, and what I found was that the lake was getting more and more turbid over time. Trout are sight-feeders, and they can't really feed themselves in the dark of chocolate-milk-colored water. As a result, they were stunted and not very healthy.

What was causing the problem wasn't the silt and clay in the watershed as much as the livestock disturbing the ground cover, allowing it to be exposed to rain, which led to erosion and transport of the soil down to the lake. So, if you removed the cows, you'd have more ground cover. You wouldn't have as much silt and clay entering the lake. That was my master's study—looking at cause and effect for poor performance of stocked rainbow trout.

I met Karen at the University of Arizona in a graduate class we took together. We began to date and not surprisingly we enjoyed lots of outdoor activities. We eventually got engaged, and when Karen was hired by the BLM to work on the Empire Ranch, I moved with her to the ranch. As a result, I was between jobs for about a year, so I volunteered for the BLM and helped Karen carry out studies on the ranch. I enjoyed the heck out of it and applied for a job with the BLM in Safford.

Because I'd been volunteering, managers knew of me and had some confidence that I could do the job. I got the job, and because Karen and I had to commute in two different directions, we decided to move to Benson to make that possible. So she'd drive west to the Empire Ranch and I'd drive east to Safford. After a year or two, the BLM had an opening in the Tucson Field Office for a fishery biologist to work on the San Pedro River and Cienega Creek. I applied for that position and transferred to the Tucson Field Office.

During the next ten years, I worked on Cienega Creek studying the populations and habitats of the three native fish species (Gila chub, Longfin dace, and Gila topminnow) and on Aravaipa Creek, where I dealt with the native fishery, which was being invaded by green sunfish, mosquitofish, the dreaded red shiner, and bullheads. I then spent some time at the state office of the BLM and worked on the environmental impact statement for the uranium mines that were being proposed along the Grand Canyon.

One thing that has inspired me over the years and continues to motivate my commitment are the concepts behind Aldo Leopold's land ethic: the idea that human beings are a part of the animal community and ecosystem. We are not separate. The problem is most human beings see themselves as separate. So this whole idea of a land ethic is seeing yourself as part of the ecosystem, part of the community, the plant and animal community.

Extending the Community Vision to the Entire Sonoita Valley

In the course of hundreds of meetings, the SVPP expanded discussions beyond working with the BLM to develop a land-use plan for the Empire Ranch to establishing a vision for the future of the entire Sonoita Valley. The seeds for these discussions had been sown a decade earlier. Toward the end of his tenure as BLM state director in Arizona, Dean Bibles and his successor, Henri Bisson, envisioned creating an open-space corridor extending from the Mexican border to the northwest extent of the Catalina Mountains near Oracle, Arizona. Bibles had an even bolder vision in mind: an open-space and wildlife corridor extending from the Mexican to the Canadian border. When Bibles left Arizona in 1989, "we were working on an exchange to put land into public ownership so that we connected all the way [from the headwaters of Cienega Creek in the Canelo Hills], into the Coronado National Forest through the Rose Tree [Ranch], and then the Empire and Cienega ranches, and then make a connection to the Saguaro National Monument," now Saguaro National Park East.

He describes his dream:

> It didn't happen, but I thought if we could connect to the Saguaro National Monument then we could go ahead and connect [through other public lands], up and through the Kaibab and on into Utah next to public lands there. If you went on north, just east of Provo, the national forest splits. You could either have a corridor that would go over to the east and on up into Wyoming, or if you went north up the Wasatch Front you'd go up by Bear Lake, the corner of Idaho's national forest, and then hook up to the Tetons, which would then hook into Montana, and you could go all the way into Canada on the corridor.

In parallel, Julia Fonseca recalls, in 1986 "Chuck [Huckelberry] and I worked together on a proposal that would form an open-space corridor that would stretch from the Mexican border to the Oracle State Park. It was a pretty visionary thing. Chuck, I believe, had some pretty high-level discussions with Jean Hassell, who was the state land commissioner at the time and people in the BLM."

Another factor that influenced the SVPP to enlarge its focus to the full extent of the Sonoita Valley was a parallel effort initiated by the Sonoran

Institute. Founded to "connect people and communities with the natural resources that nourish and sustain them," the institute works with "rural communities around the West to help them identify the vision for their community and scope out how to realize this vision." In service of this goal, the Sonoran Institute provided funds and a facilitator to initiate discussions regarding the future of the towns of Sonoita and Elgin and the Sonoita Valley writ large.

Again, an unlikely overlap of relationships played a significant role in the institute's choosing to work in the Sonoita Valley. Luther Propst, one of the founders of the Sonoran Institute recalls,

> I'd say our coming to Sonoita was probably 50 percent serendipity and 50 percent analysis. When I first started the Sonoran Institute, I had a grant to [fund the institute to facilitate] workshops first in Jackson, Wyoming, and then later, in communities around the greater Yellowstone region. [The goal was] to help these communities address the dramatic change that was happening as they became hotbeds for tourism and for retirees.
>
> So, we put together a process, some materials, to do successful community workshops. At the time there were several people who spent time both in the greater Yellowstone region and in southern Arizona. [I think especially of] the late Jake Kittle [who moved to Sonoita in 1993], along with a few others who were familiar with my work in Wyoming, and who just by virtue of personal relationships encouraged us to come and look at Sonoita. At the time we met, Jake had a ranch in central Wyoming, but he spent a lot of time in the Jackson area and was familiar with our work that way. Jake was a larger-than-life figure in every way.

Propst continues, "Our analysis told us Sonoita was a good place to work. High conservation value coupled with a growing threat from the issues that we dealt with: growth and land-use planning and water planning. So it just made sense for us. I consider it now one of the most successful of probably two dozen or so of those workshops that we did."

Former Sonoran Institute project manager Susan Culp enlarges on Propst's comments, saying the institute believed

> that enduring conservation only really could happen if you got diverse interests— from large-scale landowners, ranchers, to the business community and entrepre-

FIGURE 2.27 A meeting of the Sonoita Crossroads Community Forum aimed at developing a vision for the future of the Sonoita Valley. (*Left to right*) Bill Branan (Appleton-Whittell Research Ranch of the National Audubon Society), Shel Clark (hydrologist), the late Annie McGreevy (community activist), the late Jake Kittle (rancher and key member of the Sonoita Crossroads Community Forum and SVPP), Bill Eifrig (president of Sonoita Crossroads Community Forum), and Sonoita residents Valerie Hing and Evelyn and Walter Karl. (Archives of the Crossroads Forum.)

neurs in the region, other advocates for conservation, just community members who cared about the place they lived—around the table and that people could [then discover] commonly shared visions. This was an opportunity for the Sonoran Institute to do something that was really in the organization's wheelhouse in a very special place [the Sonoita Valley] in Arizona.

With help from the Sonoran Institute, Sonoita Valley residents formed the Sonoita Crossroads Community Forum to grapple with growing exurban encroachment on open space—an issue of particular concern given the still vivid memory of a potential satellite city on the Empire Ranch, located between Sonoita and Tucson. There was considerable overlap between those involved in the SVPP planning process and in the Crossroads Forum, and a shared and growing sense of urgency regarding the importance of protecting the landscape and character of the Sonoita Valley and the upper Cienega Creek watershed.[51]

Advocating for Establishment of Las Cienegas NCA

As discussions in the Sonoita Valley evolved, the SVPP began work on a proposal to protect lands spanning the extent of the Sonoita Valley: from near the headwaters of Cienega Creek to the Cienega Creek Natural Preserve. Throughout these discussions Jesse Juen and SVPP members kept Congressman Jim Kolbe, his staff, and Arizona's two senators apprised of progress in shaping the RMP for the Empire Ranch and of their larger conservation goals. In late 1999 and 2000 individuals from the BLM, the Sonoran Institute, SVPP, and the Sonoita Crossroads Community Forum traveled to Washington, D.C., to discuss various options for protecting lands identified by the SVPP as conservation worthy.

The BLM's Jesse Juen recalls,

Secretary [of the Interior] Babbitt was working on the National Landscape Conservation System as part of a strategy to transform the BLM into an agency that had land conservation as well as livestock and mining on its plate. Among his strategies were declaration of national monuments that would be managed by BLM. [At the end of 1999] there were three potential national monuments [under consideration for] Arizona, and Las Cienegas was one of them.

[Babbitt] had made a trip down [to Arizona] as he was touring the country and talking to different key political folks about [potential monument] designations. As [President Clinton and Babbitt] were getting near the end of their administration, Babbitt was looking to leverage [the president's power to use the Antiquities Act to establish national monuments]. Babbitt wanted to meet with us out on the ground and talk to us about where we were in the process of planning, and to ask, "What did we think about the possibility of an NCA designation as an alternative to a monument designation?" If so, how would we frame it, who would we talk to, and all that kind of stuff.

I shared with him that I thought it would be best if he just met with the Sonoita Valley Partnership first and ask them all the same questions that he was asking me. He said, "well, why the partnership?" I explained to him the background of the partnership and the hurdles that we had overcome, and how they had evolved and done such a great job. Members of the partnership hosted a luncheon out at the Empire Ranch and Babbitt met with those folks, stayed another night at the ranch, and laid it out: "If you guys want this to be a national conservation area"—which the partnership did, they didn't want it to be a presidential proclamation of a national monument—"then you've got to get on board. You've got to get your congressional delegation lined up. You've got to get a bill put together." He just laid it out there. "I'll help in any way I can."[52]

Karen Simms remembers the unease shared by residents of the area after hearing that the Clinton administration might declare a national monument in the Sonoita Valley: "People were worried if that happened, all of their work collaborating on a management plan might not be honored, and decisions such as not allowing grazing could occur. We were already five years into meeting as a collaborative group, developing the desired conditions, and basically had all the foundations and some of the meat on the bones so to speak of a collaborative plan for that area." The SVPP quickly agreed that seeking legislation to establish an NCA was the right course.[53] Simms recalls, "I think that decision to really go for an NCA had everything to do with how much time had already been invested [in the planning process]. When they do those executive orders to create national monuments, it can take [management of those lands] out of the hands of local people, and they [the SVPP and citizens of the Sonoita Valley] wanted it to stay in local hands."

Secretary Babbitt remembers the individuals and external factors which led to the establishment of the NCA: "There was a lot of good local participation moving [a plan for land conservation] along when I showed up theorizing about asking President Clinton to use the Antiquities Act (to declare a national monument); that really gave focus to the efforts. They really started moving because they understood I only had a few more years in office, and unless we got something going legislatively, there would be the backdrop of the Antiquities Act. I must say it's worked out very nicely."

Luther Propst of the Sonoran Institute summarizes Babbitt's role: "I think it is important to recognize the important role that Babbitt played as a catalyst. He knew exactly what he was doing, in terms of showing up, not explicitly pointing his finger at somebody saying, 'if you don't do this I'm going to do that,' but he sent a very clear message that he was serious about creating a national monument if stakeholders couldn't agree to push for a national conservation area."

Armed with support from the SVPP and residents of the Sonoita Valley, Congressman Jim Kolbe took the lead in shaping and shepherding the enabling legislation for an NCA designation through Congress. Julia Fonseca recalls one important factor that motivated Kolbe's commitment establishing an NCA in the Sonoita Valley: "Jim Kolbe had the vision of a demonstration area where he could say, 'Here's an example of where livestock grazing can be shown to be compatible with conservation of biological resources.' So I think that interest of his was really important." His upbringing in the area and his childhood connection to the Empire Ranch no doubt further fueled his enthusiasm for pushing through the legislation.

Rancher Mac Donaldson recalls, "The designation of the NCA, which was done with Kolbe's leadership, was done in concert with the people that were involved with the Sonoita Valley Planning Partnership. Anybody that was going to be against it already had [had] a voice. When Kolbe proposed to make it an NCA, there was very little opposition."

On December 6, 2000, President Clinton signed a bill creating the forty-two-thousand-acre Las Cienegas National Conservation Area "to conserve, protect, and enhance . . . the unique and nationally important aquatic, wildlife, vegetative, archaeological, paleontological, scientific, cave, cultural, historical, recreational, educational, scenic, rangeland, and riparian resources and values of the public lands within the NCA, while allowing livestock grazing and recreation to continue in appropriate areas."[54]

FIGURE 2.28 Rancher Mac Donaldson in the grasslands of Las Cienegas National Conservation Area. (Photo courtesy the Sonoran Institute.)

The NCA is centered on the Empire Ranch property. However, its boundaries encompass only the central portion of the Sonoita Valley. When the legislation was passed, final decisions regarding which lands could be placed within the boundaries of the NCA had not been made. To accommodate the possibility of including additional lands within the NCA, the enabling legislation established a Sonoita Valley Acquisition Planning District encompassing one hundred thousand additional acres of public, private, county, and state trust land. The legislation further authorized the secretary of the interior "to negotiate with landowners for the acquisition of lands . . . suitable for Conservation Area expansion" and specified that any land acquired within the SVAPD be managed in accord with the BLM management protocols for Las Cienegas NCA.[55]

The largest fraction of the land within the SVAPD is state trust land. However, attempts to acquire those lands through exchanges between the BLM and the State Land Department are currently precluded by a 1990 Arizona Supreme Court decision, *Fain Land and Livestock Co. v Hassell*,[56] which con-

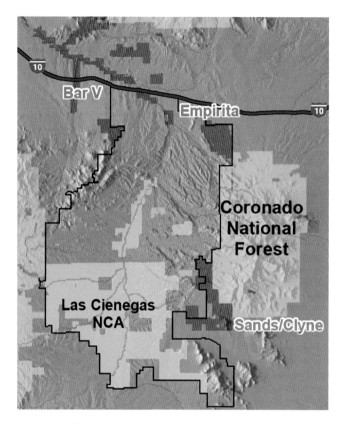

FIGURE 2.29 Sonoita Valley Acquisition Planning District (black outline with northern boundary along I-10). The parcels labeled Sands/Clyne, Empirita, and Bar V were acquired by Pima County as part of the Sonoran Desert Conservation Plan (chapter 3). (Photo courtesy of Pima County.)

cluded that exchanges of state trust land (such as those carried out in Babbitt's and Bible's time) violate the state constitution by selling or exchanging land without an auction. The theory behind the decision is that public auction offers transparency into the land sale process, ensuring that any transaction yields the maximum return to the school trust fund. Several initiative campaigns to amend the Arizona Constitution to allow for exchanges all failed at the ballot box. Thus, at present, any attempt to expand Las Cienegas into the larger Acquisition Planning District would require a combination of creative state leadership and federal legislation to provide mutually agreed-upon compensation to the State Land Department in return for transferring management of trust lands within the SVAPD to the BLM.[57]

FIGURE 2.30 Celebrating the declaration of Las Cienegas National Conservation Area. (*Left to right*) Jesse Juen (Tucson field manager, BLM), Denise Merideth (Arizona state director of the BLM), Dean Bibles (BLM), Karen Simms (ecosystem planner, BLM), and the late Henry Bisson (district manager, Phoenix District Office, BLM). (Photo courtesy of Karen Simms.)

Managing Las Cienegas NCA: A Collaborative Adaptive Management Approach

The legislation enacted in 2000 to establish the NCA mandates that the area's management align with the principles that evolved through the extensive series of meetings conducted by the Sonoita Valley Planning Partnership. Their plan, calling for "adaptive management" of the conservation area, was formally incorporated into the BLM Resource Management Plan for Las Cienegas NCA adopted in 2003.[58]

Adaptive management is a process that involves using agreed goals and measurement objectives to inform management policies, learning from the outcomes of management actions, and changing and updating management protocols in accordance with realities on the ground. To implement adaptive management successfully requires ongoing assessment and monitoring of the status of ecosystems within the NCA: understanding how livestock grazing and recreation on the NCA can be managed so that rangeland and riparian areas remain healthy; developing plans to ensure that recreation and ranching impacts on species habitat and migration are minimized; and protecting or if necessary restoring wildlife habitats.[59]

To guide the adaptive management of the NCA, the SVPP and the BLM initiated two formal processes: twice-yearly biological planning meetings involving stakeholders and experts from the nearby University of Arizona as well as knowledgeable staff from NGOs and the BLM; and an annual discussion of the ecological health of the region, Science on the Sonoita Plain. During the early phases of implementing the adaptive management plan, the BLM and the SVPP engaged The Nature Conservancy to guide identification of monitoring targets and to provide experienced-based advice on implementing adaptive management strategies.[60]

Larry Fisher of the University of Arizona provides a few specific examples: "You had it written into the RMP that we are going to hold twice-annual meetings and carry out adaptive management. There were triggers and thresholds written right into the plan that if the vegetation cover did not reach a certain level, certain grazing practices would be changed. Or if a species number went to a certain level, then management of the creek would change." The model developed by the SVPP—adaptive management guided by a collaborative dialog with the community—represented a pioneering example of what has become known among policy makers as collaborative adaptive management, or CAM.

In 2006 the Sonoita Valley Planning Partnership and a sister organization—the Cienega Corridor Conservation Council, created to develop strategies to protect land between the northern boundary of Las Cienegas NCA and Saguaro National Park—combined to form an umbrella organization: the Cienega Watershed Partnership (CWP). Since that time, the CWP has taken responsibility along with the BLM for organizing the two elements of the adaptive management process.[61]

Larry Fisher provides an overview:

The Cienega Watershed Partnership grew out of those two efforts [SVPP and Cienega Corridor Conservation Council] as an attempt to provide a formal organization, that would continue to convene still active members of the SVPP and [Cienega Corridor Conservation Council]. [CWP organized] biological planning events, the twice-yearly activities where citizens and BLM staff and scientists would go out to Las Cienegas. They would look at the monitoring data and they'd say, "What's going well, what's not going well, what do we need to change?"

FIGURE 2.31 Participants share results of scientific studies and land management activities during the Science on the Sonoita Plain symposium. The meetings are sponsored by the Cienega Watershed Partnership and National Audubon Society, with support from The Nature Conservancy and the BLM. (Photo by Tahnee Robertson.)

They'd work with Ian Tomlinson [the rancher who currently holds the grazing lease in the NCA] and talk about current management, and then make decisions about changing management practices. Ian Tomlinson is very committed to adaptive management. He's been a great partner. He put out some of his own cash to support the biological planning in times when the BLM was unable to support it.[62]

Shela McFarlin, who served as Manager of the BLM's Tucson Field Office during the time that adaptive management was first put into practice on the NCA comments that "These workshops we have, like Science on the Sonoita Plain, things that are meant for the public and for scientists and managers to get together, they are successful, they continue to be attended, and we've gotten some great products out of them which are aiding BLM managers."

Now-retired Arizona Game and Fish biologist Kurt Bahti worked on the NCA for more than two decades and participated in the seminal SVPP meetings in the late 1990s. He reflects on the success adaptive management has achieved on the Empire Ranch over the past twenty years:

> Just by driving across and being on the ranch, I would say that adaptive management is functioning well. Of course, when you have good partners like the ranchers—they had John and Mac Donaldson, and now it's Ian Tomlinson—when you have good partners that's what makes the plan work. Take the Donaldsons. They both had a very strong love for the land and wanted to see it taken care of and would always say, "If what I'm doing is hurting it, I'm going to pull my cattle out and that's it." That's a great attitude. Just looking at the ranch from passing through I'd say it's in very good shape.

When the adaptive management model was written into the enabling legislation for Las Cienegas NCA in 2000, the approach represented a radical departure from the then-typical BLM practice of developing a resource management plan: proposing the plan at public hearings, formally adopting it, and adhering to its protocols for twenty years thereafter. Owing to the success of the adaptive management approach in Las Cienegas NCA and other places where it has been tried, the BLM and the U.S. Forest Service have begun to adopt some form of the approach in managing a growing number of parcels under their purview.

In 2007 the Department of Interior issued a guide to adaptive management practices.[63] The guide cited the Sonoita Valley Planning Partnership as an example of a group that had shaped and implemented a successful collaborative adaptive management plan where "stakeholders are involved and committed to the process; progress is made toward achieving management objectives; and results from monitoring and assessment are used to adjust management decisions."

In recognition of Sonoita Valley Planning Partnership's work in developing a collaborative approach to large-landscape

FIGURE 2.32 Rancher Ian Tomlinson, who holds grazing leases on Las Cienegas NCA and continues a tradition of adopting grazing practices guided by the collaborative adaptive management plans developed by the BLM and Cienega Watershed Partnership. (Photo by Tahnee Robertson.)

conservation, the organization received the Clarence Burch Award from the Quivira Coalition in 2004. In 2005 SVPP representatives were invited to participate in the White House Conference on Cooperative Conservation, and in 2013 the successor to the SVPP, Cienega Watershed Partnership, received the U.S. Department of Interior's prestigious Partners in Conservation award.

Karen Simms's dedication to engaging stakeholders during the critical SVPP meetings that led to advocacy for establishing Las Cienegas NCA was recognized not only in the above awards but by the 2007 Faces in Conservation Healthy Landscape Award from the Sonoran Institute and the 2010 Sky Island Alliance Agency Leadership Award.

Future Challenges in the Sonoita Valley

The Cienega Watershed Partnership continues to bring together teams of experts and stakeholders to work collaboratively with the BLM in service of evaluating and updating adaptive management protocols.

However, from its founding the CWP has had a larger vision: protecting the health of the full extent of the Cienega watershed from the Canelo Hills to the Pantano Wash in the Tucson metro area. The organization is committed to "ensuring that the Cienega watershed will be a healthy ecosystem enjoyed by future generations by facilitating cooperative actions that steward its natural and cultural resources. Our first priority is the ecosystem, and we believe human uses are compatible in so far as they do not harm its sustainability."

To achieve this vision, CWP decided to supplement its annual Science on the Sonoita Plain symposium and twice-yearly biological planning meetings with a gathering aimed at assessing the state of the Cienega Creek watershed writ large.[64]

CWP Board member Larry Fisher recalls,

> We started convening this process to ask, "what's happening at the whole watershed scale? What do we need to be aware of, what do we need to be concerned about, and what do we need to be advocating for?" So, we started that process, and after about three years of general meetings, we agreed to develop a set of indicators that would give us an annual snapshot of the watershed: climate and water, ecosystem issues, species and habitat things, and then social and economic indicators. Then every year during our March meeting we could

stand up, like the president stands up in front of Congress, and says, "This is the state of our watershed."[65]

Since 2010 the CWP has held an annual State of the Watershed meeting during which a broad range of experts and stakeholders examine the current status and long-term trends in four categories: *water:* surface and ground-water flows and levels; *ecological:* grass and shrub cover, invasive species intrusion, wildlife populations, and wildfire frequency; *sociocultural:* land use, housing developments, and recreational use; and *climate:* precipitation patterns and temperature. With this information in hand, the CWP attempts to shape programs to address challenges to watershed health, to make citizens aware of these challenges, and if needed, to advocate for changes in federal, state, or local practices or policies.

Water-Related Trends and Challenges

The Pima County Regional Flood Control District monitors flows of surface water and groundwater levels within the Cienega Creek Natural Preserve. Their measurements show a significant decrease in base flows (flows measured between storm events in units of cubic feet per second) by a factor of 3 over the 23-year period between March 1994 and January 2017. Not surprisingly, the total length over which surface water is observed along Cienega Creek has decreased as well, from 9.5 miles that flowed perennially in 1985 to only 1.5 miles before the onset of summer monsoons in 2016. Since 1995 groundwater levels have decreased by 12 feet.

These trends reflect an increase in withdrawal of groundwater along with the effects of a twenty-year drought that has decreased the rate at which groundwater is recharged. University of Arizona emeritus professor of hydrology Thomas Maddock emphasizes the threat to the creek ecosystems posed by these trends:

If you start to deplete the water from the system you immediately affect the cottonwood-willow system and the [surrounding] mesquite bosque. Mesquite's not so bad [as its roots go deeper]. The cottonwoods and willows go quick. That's usually one of the first things that happens. I noticed passing over the Cienega Creek—for example on I-10—the old riparian area's pretty much mesquite now. Mesquites have a very deep taproot, so they can survive longer than large [riparian-dependent] trees. [At] one time there was a big mesquite bosque along the Santa Cruz River, but it's gone too because the groundwater pumping has depleted the aquifer below the levels of the reach of even the mesquite.[66]

Rangeland ecologist Dan Robinett is concerned about the potential threats of development, mining and agriculture on surface and groundwater in the Cienega watershed:

Groundwater use here, and a subsequent reduction in lowering of water tables and reduction in stream flows, can be caused by new exurban development, but also with mining in this region. And agriculture—and by agriculture I mean the vineyards popping up in the area—although [agriculture seems to be having] pretty low impact right now. I see the proposed [Rosemont] mine up in the Santa Rita Mountains as potentially having a really major impact on the groundwater and water tables in Cienega Creek just by intercepting that part of the Santa Rita catchment that goes into Cienega Creek and making it unavailable to the water table and stream flow down there. As far as new ex-urban development, I don't know [quantitatively what the effects on the whole watershed might be]. There are pockets here of pretty high-density housing

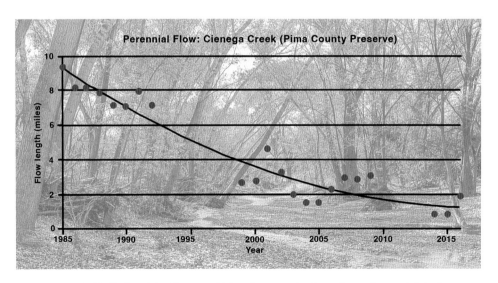

FIGURE 2.33 The length in miles over which surface water has been observed perennially in the Cienega Creek Preserve. (Courtesy of the Cienega Watershed Partnership.)

where there has already been a lowering of the water table by over one hundred feet in twenty years.

Invasive Species and Shrub Encroachment

Teams organized by the Cienega Watershed Partnership in partnership with BLM and The Nature Conservancy have monitored ground cover by native grasses; invasive species such as Lehmann lovegrass, as well as shrubs and mesquite; along with the frequency and extent of grassland fires. The results: native grasses are slowly being replaced by invasives, while the long-term trend of shrub encroachment in Las Cienegas NCA appears to have been reversed somewhat thanks to vigorous efforts to remove mesquite from the grasslands. The BLM and CWP partners continue to monitor the efficacy of various mesquite removal treatments—grubbing to dig out mesquite, chemical treatment, and prescribed burns—and to apply one or more of those techniques in their continued efforts to restore the grasslands.[67]

Dan Robinett laments,

> Every year we have a disturbance that results in a loss of perennial grasses. We are living in a time of drought, especially winter moisture deficits. Both drought and fire during drought kill perennial grasses. Drought and fire can kill nonnative grasses like the African lovegrasses and old-world bluestems just like it kills native grass species, but those [invasive] species are so well adapted to grow back after disturbance that they end up just slowly taking over. They really decrease the diversity of native grass and forbs species.
>
> If you lose diversity in native grass and forb species, you're going to lose diversity in animal species as well. I think that's probably one of the biggest changes I see up here [over the past thirty years]. It has maybe even accelerated now with recent changes in climate.

Fire Policies

The grasslands and forests in the Cienega watershed are adapted to fire. Before human occupation, grasslands burned every ten years or so, and forests every seventy years. Ignited by lightning, these naturally caused, low-intensity fires kept the grasslands free of brush and the forest floors cleared of fuels that might ignite high-temperature blazes. The challenge faced by residents of the Sonoita Valley and federal agencies is how to balance the need to restore natural fire regimes safely, with human needs in mind.

Both to protect the increasing number of homes built in the grasslands or adjacent to the Coronado National Forest and to adhere to the "no-fire" policies of the BLM and Forest Service, grassland and forest fires in the past have been extinguished as quickly as possible. Mary Nichols of the U.S. Department of Agriculture (parent agency to the Forest Service) comments, "There are a lot of folks who are interested in bringing fire back to the landscapes, but it's a really complex problem because people don't want to see smoke. It's difficult to actually come up with and implement plans to do prescribed burning on a lot of these watersheds." However, both agencies are beginning to change their policies and to reintroduce fire into grasslands and forests in some areas.

Nichols summarizes what happens when the natural cadence of fire in forests and grasslands is disrupted:

[If] fires burn really hot, soils could become hydrophobic, in which case they lose their capacity to absorb runoff [through infiltration and percolation]. . . . Basically, the surface just becomes sealed.

The problem with fires burning hotter, that's a matter basically of the fuel loads that are out there. Historically fires burned through these grasslands with small mesquites I think every 7 years or so. That was enough to keep the mesquites knocked back. Now in absence of fire, big mesquite trees are there,

FIGURE 2.34 A prescribed fire in the grasslands of Las Cienegas National Conservation Area. (Courtesy BLM.)

there's a large fuel load so when the fires come through, they burn really hot. A cool-burning fire [like those occurring naturally] will serve to recycle the nutrients. Shortly after fires grass greens up. There is seed on-site. If the fire burns really hot it can kill the seeds.[68]

The use of prescribed burns in the area has been limited, and the restorative effects of fire on grassland health have yet to be fully evaluated. The ongoing drought in the Southwest, which favors establishment of shrubs, makes it challenging to tease out the effects of fire in reducing shrub cover and the role of drought in favoring shrubs over grass.

Climate Change

The evidence for global warming caused by greenhouse gas emissions is overwhelming. The rate at which temperatures throughout the world are increasing is far greater than rates observed in preindustrial times. Moreover, temperature changes over the past one hundred years in both magnitude and rate track expectations based on measurements of atmospheric concentrations of the two most important greenhouse gases: carbon dioxide and methane. Global warming in turn effects long-term climate patterns throughout the world. Evidence of climate change in response to global warming is manifest in large-scale changes in atmospheric and oceanic circulation patterns, more frequent high-intensity storm events, and more severe drought conditions.

While global warming can be measured and linked quantitatively to greenhouse gas concentrations, predicting changes in climate depends on sophisticated modeling by atmospheric scientists. Despite quantitative differences in detail, all climate models to date agree that over the next century, the American Southwest will become increasingly hot and dry, with wintertime precipitation from Pacific storms falling dramatically.[69]

The Sonoita Valley has experienced significant warming over the past fifty years. The late University of Arizona professor Tom Meixner reflected on the current and potential effects of climate change:

The recent [twenty-year] drought probably precipitation-wise isn't that extraordinary compared to historical and pre-Columbian droughts that have occurred in the region, but it [took place when it] was significantly warmer than the best analog we have from the 1950s drought. It's about a degree

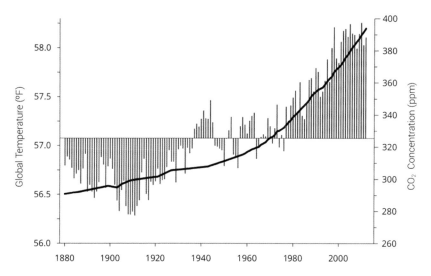

FIGURE 2.35 Global temperature (colored bars) and global carbon dioxide concentration (black line) from 1880 to 2015. (Rebecca Lindsey and Luann Dahlman, "Climate Change: Global Temperature," Climate.gov, January 18, 2023, https://www.climate.gov/news-features/understanding-climate/climate-change-global-temperature.)

centigrade to a degree centigrade and a half (two to three degrees Fahrenheit) warmer in our region and that likely has hydrologic and biological effects. If you get less rain and it's also hotter, there's more water demand by plants.

If climate trends continue,

in fifty years Sonoita will have the climate of Tucson; Tucson will have the climate of Phoenix; Phoenix will have the climate of Yuma. Yuma will have the climate of a place approximately inhospitable to live in. So that's an ever-present threat in the region and to the watershed. [If that happens] you can imagine instead of grassland, it's creosote scrubland with some interspersed grass. That would be a profound change to the watershed and would likely impact the perennial flows of [Cienega Creek] in a variety of ways. Parts of the stream might continue to flow perennially because of time lags [between the decrease in precipitation and depletion of the groundwater system]. The groundwater system is pretty large, and it might take quite a while for it to respond to that changing climate, but it would eventually respond.

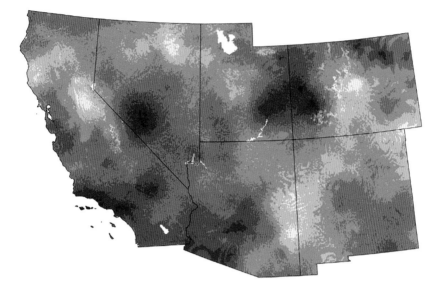

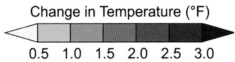

Change in Temperature (°F)

0.5 1.0 1.5 2.0 2.5 3.0

FIGURE 2.36 Observed temperature change in the American Southwest from 1901 to 2016. The figure depicts the temperature difference between the average of temperatures measured between 1901 and 1960 and the average of those measured between 1986 and 2016. Significant temperature changes have already taken place since the rapid industrialization of the United States. (Patrick Gonzalez et al., Fourth National Climate Assessment, fig. 25.1).

Plant biologist Linda Kennedy looks ahead to the future of Cienega Creek's riparian areas in light of current climate models:

As winter moisture both diminishes in amounts, and variability in winter moisture received increases, I think we're going to have impacts on stream flow and water tables in those riparian systems. I think they're a key zone in this watershed. Higher evaporation [from soils] and transpiration [from plants] due to increasing temperatures are going to have an impact as well on riparian areas. Degradation there will have impacts that are felt many hundreds of miles away from here because the riparian corridors are also huge migration corridors, especially for bird species.

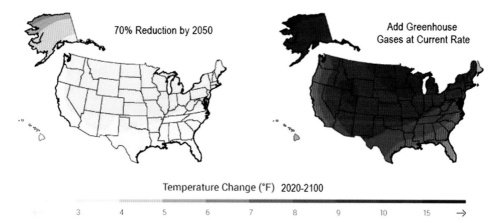

FIGURE 2.37 Average surface air temperatures predicted for 2071–2099 under two assumptions: a reduction in global greenhouse emissions by 70 percent before 2050 (*left*) and continuing to inject greenhouse gases at the same rate we are today. (John Walsh and Donald Wuebbles, "Climate Change Impacts in the United States," National Climate Assessment, 2014, https://nca2014.global change.gov/report/our-changing-climate/recent-us-temperature-trends.)

And if riparian areas degrade or disappear, other species that depend on the cover and nutrition they provide will be forced to find more suitable habitat, if indeed such habitat can be found locally.

Range ecologist Dan Robinett has already seen changes in the mix of plant species found in the Sonoita Valley. "We're seeing more cactus up here now. A species of prickly pear from the Sonoran Desert, Engelmann prickly pear, is starting to pop up here and there in the Sonoita grasslands, which is kind of unheard of. If warming continues, plains grasslands [here] may well change to more of a desert grassland, and then shrub species, including mesquite, mimosa and vachellia, and some of the lower-elevation cacti are going to become more prevalent."

Robinett references work by University of Arizona research scientist David Bertelson: "About thirty plus years ago he started hiking up Finger Rock Canyon trail in the Catalina Mountains" north of Tucson. Throughout the four thousand feet in elevation spanned by the trail, Bertelson "classified the plants he saw and reported their phenology—in other words, when were they dormant, had they greened up, were they in flower, were they in seed—as well as their abundance."

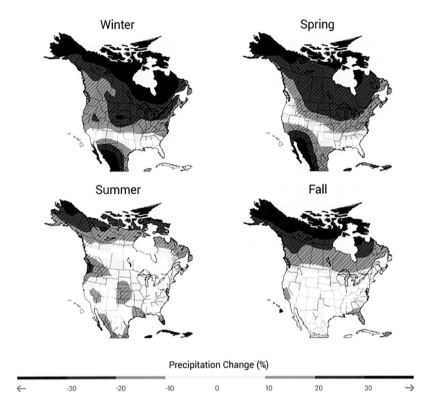

FIGURE 2.38 Seasonal changes in precipitation patterns predicted for 2071–99 compared to historical records for 1970–99 if we continue to inject greenhouse gases at the same rate that we are today. In that scenario, winter and spring precipitation in Arizona and New Mexico will drop dramatically, while summer and fall precipitation remain similar. The predicted precipitation differences will have major effects on the health of grasslands in the Sonoita Valley. (National Climate Assessment.)

In the course of his monthly hikes, Bertelson observed six hundred types of plants. More than 15 percent of the species he studied now bloom at elevations as much as one thousand feet higher than they did when he first began keeping records. His observations are consistent with the notion that temperature increases in the Southwest have driven some plants to higher, cooler elevations in order to survive.

Considering the already evident changes in and around the Sonoita Valley wrought by global warming, and the even more dramatic alterations in climate predicted for the future, the Cienega Watershed Partnership pondered how to respond to the impact of these changes. Would the indicators of watershed health selected following years of data collection and discussion still be adequate to assess watershed health over the next decades? If not, how might adaptive management protocols linked to those indicators evolve to accommodate those changes? Might there be some way to identify factors most essential to best stewarding the watershed in the face of climate change?

To examine the likely response of watershed systems to climate change and other potential stressors, the partnership initiated a scenario-planning exercise—which might be likened to the war games carried out by the Pentagon to evaluate strategic responses to potential battlefield events. Although the scenario-planning process is still ongoing, the CWP has identified two actions critical to watershed health: continuing vigorous efforts to maintain and restore the health of riparian areas (see chapter 6), and emphasizing landscape protections that will allow species to migrate to higher elevations or to more northerly latitudes. The former lies within the purview of the CWP and its BLM partners, while the latter requires a region-wide response that will entail land acquisitions to secure connected wildlife movement corridors.

The partnership is also committed to incorporating scenario planning into its collaborative adaptive management protocols by continuing its monitoring programs, evaluating the efficacy of key indicators, and altering the mix of indicators in response to changing realities on the ground. That approach requires that experts, community members, and BLM managers remain open to adopting new approaches and, if need be, modifying protocols that were often implemented following long, sometimes contentious, discussions.

The consequences of pumping groundwater are well summarized in this chapter: degradation of riparian areas and species that depend on cover and nourishment in those areas, as well as a consequent increase in susceptibility to flooding events. Some combination of citizen awareness, water conservation, public acquisition of additional lands and accompanying water rights, and groundwater recharge will be needed to preserve Cienega Creek and keep the watershed as a whole healthy.

Fragmentation

Another perhaps less immediately dramatic but equally consequential threat to ecosystems in the Sonoita Valley is fragmentation of habitat and restriction of wildlife movement. Emily Burns of the Sky Island Alliance reflects on the need for unfragmented corridors to connect viable habitat patches, particularly for wide-ranging species:

If you think about black bear, mountain lion, some of the deer species, [and ask,] "what do they need to move around and what's stopping them?" It becomes clear, it's not about watershed boundaries. It's not even about who owns the land, but it's about the big impediments to movement, like our highway system, the border wall, things like that, that we worry about. Then we think about the network of resources that are spread across these areas. Because it's not just connected land without those obstacles, it's also "is there enough water, are there food sources?"[70]

Burns suggests steps that might mitigate fragmentation:

I think we know on the landscape scale where there are potential barriers to wildlife movement [and thus where we need to avoid putting in new roads]. There has to be climate adaptation planning to ensure that we have water being absorbed in our mountains, feeding the ecosystems not only in the upland habitats but then downstream. We don't want to see severe fires eliminate the habitats that are really at risk because of climate change because that would create wastelands that animals then would be trying to move across. . . . My vision is really about having a connected network of water sources that are resilient to climate change, helping these ecosystems adapt to changing conditions, and then working to [create paths] in the network where we presently have obstacles to make it as permeable as possible. We're not going to create full connectivity, but we have to look at these really critical pinch points where we're seeing a lot of animals being killed on highways or whole populations being separated by the border wall and focus on those places where the impact of that infrastructure is disproportionately high.

Julia Fonseca comments that there may be an option to establish a wildlife corridor from the Cienega Creek Natural Preserve to Saguaro East National Park, achieving a portion the vision put forth by the Cienega Corridor Conservation Collaborative in the early 2000s:

There is an ongoing effort by the Forest Service and the Arizona Trail Association to put forward the idea that we need to set aside open-space corridors along that trail [in service of preserving its scenic character]. Since the trail passes through Saguaro National Park to Colossal Cave to Cienega Preserve down to Las Cienegas, there is a [natural wildlife movement] pathway there, but [land] would have to be acquired. One of the potential sources of funding might be the Land and Water Conservation Fund,

a fund established by Congress in 1964 to safeguard natural areas, water resources, and cultural heritage and to provide for recreational opportunities, using earnings from offshore oil and gas leasing. As of this writing, the plan is still in its formative phases.

The Status of State Trust Lands

Even a casual glance at the land-use map (fig. 2.39) for the Cienega watershed reveals a potential long-term threat: development of the seventy-thousand-acre block of state trust lands between the northern extent of Las Cienegas NCA and the Rincon Mountains.[71]

The State Land Department is at present obligated to auction trust lands in a manner that maximizes return to the school trust.[72] Significant development on private lands has already crept eastward from Tucson city limits to the Vail area, and nothing at present suggests that migration to the American Southwest will decelerate any time soon. More development on those lands would have dire consequences for the Cienega Creek watershed, the rich ecosystems it now supports, and the corridors on which a variety of species depend in order to reach viable habitat spaces.

In the words of longtime Pima County administrator Chuck Huckelberry, "the single greatest threat to the whole issue of habitat connectivity, connecting the open spaces, is really state trust lands." Given the near impossibility of effecting swaps of state trust lands and federal land, slowing or preventing development rests in the hands of Pima County. Huckelberry mentions a few options:

If you're a local government like us, Pima County, you don't facilitate [state land] transition to other uses by putting in infrastructure that facilitates urbanization or anything dealing with development. To that extent, you can basically forestall development for a long period of time [because that land] won't be marketable to develop.

The other thing we can do is to use our zoning powers, which usually infuriates the State. [So when we established] the Cienega Creek Natural Preserve

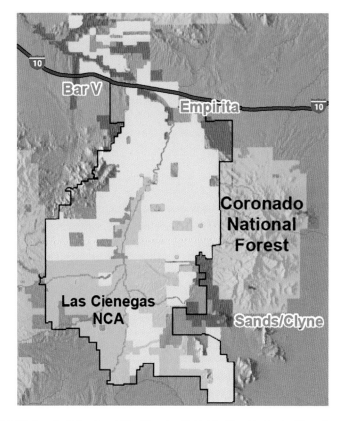

FIGURE 2.39 Sonoita Valley Acquisition Planning District (outlined in black with northern boundary coincident with I-10). State trust lands are shaded blue. Note that the Sands/Clyne, Empirita, and Bar V parcels were acquired as part of the Sonoran Desert Conservation Plan. The narrow orange corridor surrounding Cienega Creek as it crosses I-10 and courses northwestward is the Cienega Creek Natural Preserve. (Adapted from a figure courtesy of Pima County.)

> [we basically sent a] signal to anybody like a developer who thinks they're going to get [land near the preserve] released from state trust land, that they're going to have a devil of a time getting the zoning [to make a development profitable] through the county. [The area around the preserve] remains in the unincorporated area,

so the county has authority over land use. However, nothing in life or politics is certain, and the state trust lands will one day surely attract the attention of developers.

For the moment, the threat of state trust land development remains fairly low. Environmental attorney and water rights expert Peter Culp notes,

the Land Department has, in keeping with what it believes to be its fiduciary obligations, focused its efforts largely on the highest value lands with the highest, lucrative dispositions. [In practice, that] has meant that the vast majority of the Land Department's planning resources have really been focused on land in north Phoenix, Scottsdale, the Houghton Road corridor in Tucson, places like that, where they could theoretically command tens if not hundreds of thousands of dollars per acre. By contrast, [those areas south of I-10 in the Cienega watershed], while there's a lot of growth pressure there, it's not necessarily nearly so attractive a place to invest resources when you can sell land in, say, north Phoenix. For example, in Phoenix, the Land Department has a million acres of land inside the development boundary in the metro area. [Given its budget and staff, the department] can grind out only 1,000 to 1,200 acres a year in disposals.

Chuck Huckelberry is even more direct: "The only saving grace is that the State Land Department has been extraordinarily inefficient in disposing of their lands."

The Rosemont Mine

The potential development of an enormous copper deposit in the Santa Rita Mountains presents a major threat to the Cienega Creek watershed and to the Sonoita Valley.

Copper was discovered in the Santa Ritas in 1875, and by 1894 the town of Rosemont and a smelter had been established. With a decline in the copper market, the once-burgeoning mining enclave became a ghost town by 1921. Mining in the Santa Ritas remained moribund until the 1970s.[73]

The Anamax Corporation purchased the Empire Ranch along with its water rights in 1974 as part of its plan to establish a large copper mine in the Rosemont District. (Large amounts of water are needed in the process of extracting copper from ore-bearing material.) Owing to a significant decrease in copper prices during the early 1980s, building the infrastructure for the Anamax mining operation no longer made economic sense. The BLM was able to acquire the Empire Ranch and its water rights as part of a three-way purchase and exchange, and Anamax later sold its mining rights in the Santa

FIGURE 2.40 Artist conception of the HudBay mining facility looking west from the Sonoita Valley across the Santa Rita Mountains to Green Valley. The pit is 1.5 miles in diameter. (Courtesy Save the Scenic Santa Ritas, Rosemont Mine Truth, https://www.rosemontminetruth.com/three-arizona-tribes-file-federal-law-suit-against-u-s-forest-service-seeking-to-block-hudbays-rosemont-copper-mine/).

Rita Mountains to the Asarco mining company, which then sold them to three individuals.

In 2005 Augusta Resources (renamed Rosemont Copper Company in 2007), a Canadian firm, purchased the oft-transferred mining claim and initiated studies to evaluate the potential yield of the copper deposit, along with options for mining and transportation of copper ore processed on-site. In 2014 another Canadian copper company, HudBay Minerals, purchased the Rosemont Copper Company. HudBay estimates that the Rosemont deposit contains 5.9 billion pounds of copper and 194 million pounds of molybdenum, with a total estimated worth more than $7 billion in 2022. If approved, HudBay Minerals' mining operations would create a pit 1.5 miles in diameter and 3,000 feet deep. Mining would continue on the Rosemont site for 20 years.

Opposition to the mine in the Sonoita Valley has been fierce, as residents in both Pima and Santa Cruz Counties are concerned that air and water pollution from mine operations will create both short- and long-term health issues. Indigenous groups have argued that the mine and its tailings will encroach on cultural sites, while businesses in Sonoita, Elgin, and Patagonia fear negative effects on tourism. The volume of trucks carrying treated ore from the site to Tucson will require not only road building to the mine but widening of State Route 83, the main artery between the mine site and Tucson. Wildlife will suffer as habitat is fragmented and the hum of machinery intrudes on formerly silent and isolated savanna and oak scrubland.[74]

Proponents counter that the mine will bring well-paying jobs, fill state and federal coffers with tax revenues, and reduce U.S. dependence on foreign mineral sources.[75] Economic analyses by opponents suggest that jobs gained during construction and operation of the mine not only will be temporary but will be more than offset by tourism jobs lost.[76]

Less quantifiable would be the loss of a breathtaking view across the foothills of the Santa Rita Mountains—one that often finds individuals and families stopped at an overlook along State Route 83, drawn by the beauty of the landscape to point their cameras and iPhones toward the potential mine site.

Thomas Maddock, professor emeritus of hydrology and atmospheric sciences at the University of Arizona, puts it directly: "As far as the future of Cienega Creek, if the Rosemont Mine goes in, you can kiss it goodbye. That is a blunt statement but it's exactly what would happen." If you dig a deep hole, as would happen were the Rosemont Mine to go in, "instead of the water going to the creek it goes into a big hole. Cienega Creek would basically dry up."

Chris Easthoe of the University of Arizona adds, "What [the mine] will affect the most throughout the medium term is the water supply coming out of Davidson Canyon into Cienega Creek downstream of Marsh Station. In addition to the pit, [HudBay] will have ponds for mine waste removed from the pit as they expand it. That will be a pollution source in Davidson Canyon which will then eventually be a pollution source in the Tucson basin."

Gayle Hartmann of Save the Scenic Santa Ritas echoes Easthoe's concerns. A big worry, she says, is "the toxic water getting into the groundwater table and then leaking down into Barrel Canyon and McCleary Canyon and others and then into Davidson and Cienega Creek. About 10 percent of Tucson's drinking water comes from the Cienega basin, so [the effects of the

FIGURE 2.41 Looking eastward from near the proposed HudBay site. The view of the landscape in the foreground would be severely affected by the waste rock storage, dry stack tailings, and a processing plant. (Aerial photo by Stephen Strom.)

FIGURE 2.42 Davidson Creek as it flows toward its confluence with Cienega Creek. (Aerial photo by Stephen Strom.)

mine] would not be trivial for people who are drinking water, particularly on the east side of Tucson."

The Rosemont Mine project epitomizes the 150-year-old conflict in the West between short-term economic gains and benefits to one group of citizens (in this case mining corporations and the miners they employ) and long-term effects on habitat, for wildlife and for humans. The eventual need for minerals is real, and for some, mining provides a well-paying job, dignity, and a path to a comfortable life. Real as well is the loss of open space, of a healthy watershed, and of the spiritual value of the land to both Indigenous peoples and more recent arrivals alike.

At present, the fate of the HudBay's proposed mine rests with the courts. But the challenges vivified by the battle over Rosemont speak to larger cultural, economic, and environmental issues that must be addressed before they are essentially mooted by unchecked development. The Cienega Watershed Partnership, Save the Scenic Santa Ritas, Pima County, Santa Cruz County, the City of Tucson, and numerous supporting organizations are continuing efforts to stop mining in the Santa Rita Mountains permanently.

Maintaining Effective Collaborative Management of the Cienega Creek Watershed

Effective stewardship of Las Cienegas National Conservation Area relies on the productive collaboration between the Bureau of Land Management and the Cienega Watershed Partnership. This collaboration enables the BLM to access expert advice and community input essential for designing and executing adaptive management protocols. However, both CWP and the BLM face ongoing challenges that could diminish the effectiveness of the collaboration.

The partnership traces its origins to the citizen-based efforts of the Sonoita Valley Planning Partnership and the Cienega Corridor Conservation Council: both ad hoc volunteer groups.[77] While the CWP has raised modest funds from various sources, it is still a volunteer organization that depends almost entirely on contributions of time from community members, University of Arizona scientists, stakeholders, and NGO staff.

CWP board member and University of Arizona professor Larry Fisher comments:

We've never had fundraising capacity or the resources to hire the staff that we would like to have to manage our programs. Historically we've had a really close and successful relationship both with the BLM and with other agencies, BLM obviously being our closest partner. And, [while she was at the BLM Tucson Field Office,] Karen [Simms] helped us look for funds and write the contracts and work with the contracting officers to get us funded for many of the projects that we worked on together. In the last four or five years funding for these kinds of collaborative initiatives has dried up. Also, changes in BLM policy at the national level has made it more challenging for a nonprofit such as the CWP to apply for agency funds.

Bureau of Land Management

There is universal agreement that the success of the Sonoita Valley Planning Partnership was tied not only to a high level of civic engagement but to the leadership of the BLM's Jesse Juen and the long-term commitment, expertise, and commitments of BLM Tucson Field Office planner and manager Karen Simms. Simms's involvement first with the Empire Ranch, then with the SVPP and Cienega Corridor Conservation Council, and later with management of Las Cienegas NCA spanned twenty-nine years, from 1988 to her retirement from the BLM in 2017. The relationships she built and the trust she earned among a broad range of stakeholders was fundamental to the adoption and implementation of a collaborative adaptive management plan for Las Cienegas that has won national recognition. There is no person, with the possible exception of Karen's husband, biologist Jeff Simms, who has walked through, studied, and understands the area as thoroughly as she has.

However, BLM field managers rarely remain in the same positions for more than three to five years. Former BLM Tucson district manager Shela McFarlin notes that since Karen Simms retired,

You had changes in managers, people who were not tied into the original adaptive management and [collaborative] partnership approach. That has become an extreme problem. We understand where it comes from: the administration's goals and priorities, [along with] reduced resources. BLM's resources to do partnerships began to decline. Around 2017 we began noticing a decline in resources available. And that's not just handing [CWP] money or grants: their staff capacity [in Tucson] dropped. We had fewer people to deal with. They had fewer people out on the land. . . . As their capacity has dropped, their ability to engage with CWP [and their partners and experts] has been reduced.

It means that anyone who wants to work with BLM to help them out, to meet on the ground, has to really compete for their attention. So that's another change that's affected us all, whether you're talking about Las Cienegas or whether you're talking about the Ironwood Forest National Monument. There is simply not enough BLM staff. Partnerships [like CWP] are considered a kind of drawdown on that staff, and so it's difficult doing business with BLM today.

Meeting the challenges of funding successful collaborative conservation organizations such as the Cienega Watershed Partnership, reducing the cadence of staff turnover at the BLM, and providing more capacity at the agency all require policy and funding changes. If we expect to meet the challenges of large-scale conservation in an era of rapid climate change, small, community-based organizations like the Cienega Watershed Partnership will need funding for staff and contractors to provide expert advice to evaluate and monitor the health of ecosystems.

The federal agencies most responsible for stewarding our public lands need to recognize the value of managers' having the time to build relationships and trust in service of better meeting stewardship goals. And more broadly, citizens need to advocate for funding so that the BLM, U.S. Forest Service and U.S. Fish and Wildlife Service are staffed at a level consistent with their missions to steward the lands and waters of the United States both for this generation and for generations to come.

Education: Raising Public Awareness Today and Involving Tomorrow's Stewards

To build support for its conservation efforts and to connect today's young people to the Cienega watershed, the CWP has worked with partner agencies and organizations to offer three citizen participation and education opportunities. The first is a citizen science program that offers opportunities for volunteers to collect data such as local precipitation patterns and phenology (seasonal variations of plant sprouts, leaf-out, and blooms) and elevation migrations of plant species.[78] The second encourages citizen participation in a variety of programs, including one aimed at restoring washes and arroyos to prevent erosion.[79]

The third, and perhaps most important to achieving long-term conservation goals in the Cienega watershed and beyond, is the CWP's Youth Engaged Stewardship (YES!) program.[80] The program aims to connect young people to public lands in the hope of engendering lifelong appreciation and care for natural resources. Individuals with the BLM, Arizona Game and Fish, The Nature Conservancy, and the U.S. Fish and Wildlife Service, along with local ranchers, work with teenagers to carry out a variety of monitoring and restoration projects on the ground at Las Cienegas National Conservation Area. Recently, Pima County has been working with CWP to potentially bring this program to county properties, including Bar V Ranch and Cienega Creek Natural Preserve (see chapter 3).

Highlights of the program have included improving a pond for leopard frog reintroduction, restoring a sacaton plain, removing invasive species such as buffelgrass and Lehmann lovegrass, surveying and collecting data on a prairie dog restoration site, and removing invasive species from a frog habitat pond.

Without continued citizen participation in organizations such as the Cienega Watershed Partnership, impetus and support for the program will likely decline as individuals active in its formation retire or devote their energies to other efforts. More broadly, additional funding is needed to support active engagement in conservation endeavors throughout the nation and to foster a collective sense of stewardship for our living environments and the ecosystems we rely upon.

SYNOPSIS

OVERVIEW

The Sonoita Valley, located thirty miles southeast of Tucson, is a six-hundred-square-mile basin of rolling grasslands and oak-studded savannas surrounded by a ring of mountain ranges. The range of life zones in the valley supports a rich and varied population of plant and animal life. Streams in the valley feed two major rivers in southeast Arizona: the San Pedro and Santa Cruz.

Two-thirds of the land in the valley is managed by the U.S. Forest Service and the BLM, while the remainder is largely held by ranching families, individual homeowners, and the State Land Department. In the past, the valley's mineral-rich mountains supported mining and expansive grasslands supported successful ranching operations. Today, ranches play a central role in preserving large tracts of open space and species habitat.

CATALYSTS FOR ACTION

In the early 1970s, Gulf America Corporation planned a thirty-thousand-unit housing development on the forty-one-thousand-acre Empire Ranch in the heart of the valley, which would over time have fragmented wildlife movement corridors, lowered groundwater levels, and increased the threat of downstream flooding.

In 1974 Anamax mining company bought the land and proposed development of a large, open-pit copper mine. Along with the land, the company purchased the rights to pump surface and groundwater from Cienega Creek, threatening a key watershed for the Tucson metro area as well as habitat for wildlife.

Shaken by two close calls, government leaders and citizens in Pima and adjacent Santa Cruz counties pondered ways to preserve the Empire Ranch property.

MEETING CHALLENGES

In 1988 the Bureau of Land Management gained ownership of the Empire through a complex sequence of land trades.

The agency embarked on a collaborative effort to develop a resource management plan for the Empire, working with a broadly based group of stakeholders: the Sonoita Valley Planning Partnership.

In 2000 legislation embraced by the SVPP and championed by Congressman Jim Kolbe established the forty-two-thousand-acre Las Cienegas National Conservation Area and identified an additional one hundred thousand acres in the valley as a target for acquisition and incorporation in the NCA.

ELEMENTS OF SUCCESS

- Vision and leadership of BLM staff at the state and federal level; openness to collaborative development of a resource management plan

- Informal meetings with stakeholders in social settings before initiating more formal planning meetings; time taken to build trust
- Meetings publicized widely and frequently to encourage broad participation; information regarding discussions disseminated widely to the community
- An outside facilitator developed a successful method of moving forward by consensus
- Hundreds of meetings held, open to all, with participation by county, state, and federal agencies, community members, and experts from the University of Arizona, NGOs, and other community institutions

ACCOMPLISHMENTS

- Protocols developed for monitoring the environmental health of Las Cienegas National Conservation Area lands and adapting management practices to conditions on the ground; ongoing participation by local stakeholders and outside experts working with the BLM on management of the NCA
- SVPP transitioned to a formal 501(c)(3) to raise funds needed to facilitate stewardship of the natural and cultural resources of the watershed
- Annual State of the Watershed open meetings summarized ecosystem health
- Volunteers monitored watershed function, wildlife, and grassland health, engaged in watershed restoration projects, and carried out education and public outreach programs

FUNDING

- Funding from the Sonoran Institute provided support for initial meeting facilitation
- The BLM, NGO grants, individuals, and foundations fund ongoing work

ONGOING CHALLENGES AND THREATS

- Arizona State Trust land now leased to ranchers could be auctioned for development or other uses
- Cienega Watershed Partnership lacks permanent staff
- BLM Tucson Field Office and Arizona State Office staff changes frequently
- The BLM Tucson Field Office suffers from a decline in resources and manpower
- The U.S.-Mexico border wall represents a barrier to north–south wildlife movement

■ ■ ■ ■ ■ ■ ■ ■

CHAPTER 3

Creating the Sonoran Desert Conservation Plan

Great communities are no accident. They are born out of natural strength and beauty and have a deep respect for ecology, history, culture, and diversity. They are inspired by the vision of residents drawn to them. They are brought to maturity through hard work and investment. And they survive because of compromise and consensus. In a sense, they achieve balance. Such balance is at the heart of the Sonoran Desert Conservation Plan.

—PIMA COUNTY'S SONORAN DESERT CONSERVATION PLAN

We turn our attention next to Pima County, Arizona, which developed one of the most far-reaching large-landscape conservation and urban planning efforts in the United States: the Sonoran Desert Conservation Plan. The SDCP, in tandem with Pima County's Comprehensive Land Use Plan, provides a framework for both protecting the region's biological heritage and supporting economic vitality in a county whose population currently increases by 25 percent each decade. In what follows, we recount how the county's residents came to support a combination of investments, incentives, and regulations aimed at ensuring that the beauty and natural environment of the region will endure for generations to come.

The Natural Setting

Pima County encompasses more than 9,000 square miles of south central Arizona and spans two ecoregions, the Sonoran Desert and the Madrean Archipelago.[1] The eastern reaches of the county are distinguished by mountain ranges and valleys characteristic of the Basin and Range province, while the western parts are dominated by desert lands. Maximum mountain elevations range as high as 9,000 feet in the east but reach only 4,000 feet in

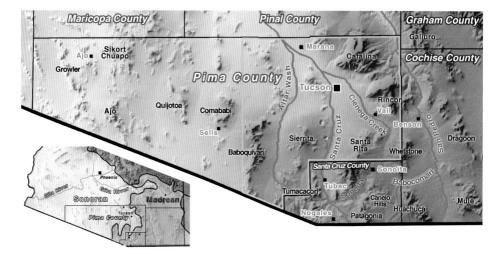

FIGURE 3.1 A map of southeast Arizona depicting (1) mountain ranges (black); (2) rivers (blue); (3) county names (white); and (4) city names (dark orange). The area covered by the Sonoran Desert Conservation Plan is outlined in turquoise. (Map by Stephen Strom.)

the west. Winter daytime temperatures average between 65 and 70 degrees Fahrenheit, while in the summer temperatures in desert regions can reach well above 100 degrees. Precipitation in desert valleys ranges from 3 inches annually in western Pima County to 20 inches in the eastern basin valleys. The wide range of temperature, precipitation, and elevation supports a rich diversity of plant, reptilian, mammalian, and avian life.[2]

Pima County's beauty is an acquired taste. Rugged and arid, the desert landscape at first appears sparse, dominated by spiny cacti and spindly palo verde and mesquite. But on a spring day following just the right amount and cadence of rain, the desert can burst into bloom, with tens of wildflower species carpeting the floor. Find a mountain perch, and in the desert's dry, clear air, you can spot ribbons of green—cottonwoods and willows—marking the path of the Santa Cruz or San Pedro River, Cienega Creek, or the Tanque Verde Wash. Look around and you'll find yourself in an oak or pine forest, perhaps near a spring trickling downward toward the desert floor. Cast your eyes outward and experience a view that is at once exhilarating and humbling: mountains and desert extending outwards for a hundred miles in all directions.

Stand in the open desert in evening, listen for coyotes, watch for javelinas, and catch a glimpse of scurrying lizards or desert rats. Or find a natural blind near a riparian area and watch the birds gather for an evening drink, then shelter for the night.

The People, from Prehistoric Times to the Present

Pima County's current population of 1.1 million reflects its history: 38 percent have Hispanic heritage, 4 percent are drawn from two Indigenous nations, the Tohono O'odham and Pascua Yaqui, and the remainder are the descendants of immigrants from throughout Europe, Asia, and Africa. The overwhelming majority of the county's populace lives in and around Tucson, a city whose climate, culture, educational resources, and natural setting have made it a magnet for growth in eastern Pima County.[3]

Lands comprising the county have been inhabited for at least twelve thousand years. Early ancestors of today's Tohono O'odham and Pascua Yaqui at first lived in small, mobile groups, hunting game and gathering plants. Between 3000 and 2000 BCE, Indigenous peoples began to develop farms along the region's rivers, some making use of floodplains, while others developed grids of sophisticated irrigation canals.[4]

Canal systems dating to 1200 BCE discovered near the Santa Cruz River may be among the oldest on the North American continent. They provided water that sustained permanent villages until 1400–1500 CE, when some combination of extended drought, religious strife, or intertribal wars triggered the collapse of Indigenous societies throughout the Southwest. When the Spanish explorers Fray Marcos de Niza and Francisco Vázquez de Coronado first arrived in the region during the mid-sixteenth century, permanent Indigenous settlements along the rivers had been abandoned and replaced by small, widely separated encampments.

Extensive Spanish engagement in the region began late in the seventeenth century, with the arrival of Jesuit Father Eusebio Kino, who committed the latter half of his life to bringing the teachings of Christ to Indigenous peoples in the Pimería Alta—northern Sonora Mexico and southern Arizona. In the course of twenty-four years, Kino organized forty expeditions to explore the Pimería Alta, established eleven missions, and introduced Native peoples to European crops and the raising of livestock.[5] Two missions in Pima County still stand as monuments to Kino's work: Mission San José del Tumacácori (originally called San Cayetano del Tumacácori) near Tubac, now a national historic park, and San Xavier del Bac, a magnificent structure sixteen miles

FIGURE 3.2 Mission San Xavier del Bac. (Philcomonforterie, Wikimedia.)

south of Tucson, still used as a center of worship by members of the Tohono O'odham and Pascua Yaqui nations.[6]

Following Kino's expeditions, Spanish settlers gradually moved into the Pimería Alta. However, their settlements were frequently attacked by Apache raiders. To protect their stake in the northern reaches of New Spain, Spanish authorities established a presidio (or fort) in Tubac in 1851.[7] Fourteen years later, Hugo O'Conor, an Irishman working for the Spanish king, founded Presidio San Agustín del Tucsón. Following the Mexican War of Independence, in 1821 the town of Tucson surrounding the presidio was incorporated into the newly established Mexican state of Sonora.[8]

In 1853 the United States entered into negotiations with Mexico to purchase the northern part of Sonora in service of providing land needed for a southern cross-continental railroad route. Following what became known as the Gadsden Purchase, land comprising the bootheel of New Mexico and today's Arizona south of the Gila River became part of the New Mexico Territory.[9]

During the Civil War, the New Mexico Territory was the site of ongoing fighting between Confederate and Union forces. When part of the territory seceded from the Union, the U.S. Senate responded by passing the Arizona Organic Act, which established the Arizona Territory in the western half of the original New Mexico Territory, with the stipulation that slavery be outlawed within its boundaries.[10]

The first Arizona Territorial Legislature created four counties: Mohave, Yavapai, Yuma, and Pima. The original Pima County was enormous—extending eastward from its boundary with Yuma County (near today's Organ Pipe National Monument) to the New Mexico border and southward from the Gila River to the Mexican border. Later, Cochise, Graham, and Santa Cruz counties were carved out from the original boundaries of Pima County.[11]

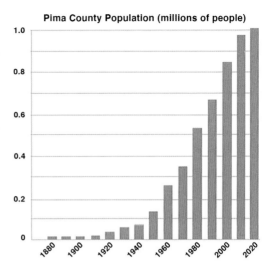

FIGURE 3.3 The population of Pima County from 1880 to 2020. (François-Michel Le Tourneau and Fabrice Dubertret, "Space and Water, Key Factors of Urban Growth in the Southwestern United States: Case Study of Tucson and Pima County [Arizona]," trans. Valentine Meunier, *L'Espace Geographique* 48, no. 1 [2019]: 39–56, https://www.cairn-int .info/article-E_EG_481_0039--space-and-water-key-factors -of-urban.htm.)

With the completion of the Southern Pacific Railroad in 1881, Pima County began to benefit from robust connection with markets throughout the United States. Shipment of minerals, livestock, and produce no longer depended on lengthy and inefficient transport by stagecoach. Growth in the area, modest prior to the arrival of the railroad, began to accelerate.[12]

With growth came grave environmental damage. Farming and ranching along Pima County's rivers consumed groundwater far more rapidly than it could be replaced. Once lush riparian areas disappeared as wood cutting, overgrazing, and groundwater depletion all took their toll. By 1920 the Santa Cruz River, once the major riverine artery in Pima County, had been reduced to a dry wash over much of its length.

From the 1890s until the early 1950s, Pima County's population grew steadily. The livelihood of its citizens waxed and waned in sympathy with the vicissitudes of climate and ever-changing demands for minerals, agricultural products, and livestock. After World War II and the advent of widely available air conditioning, migrants began to arrive in droves, drawn by the salubrious climate, the scenery, and the new opportunities created by burgeoning tourism, the growing aerospace and high-tech industries, and the University of Arizona.

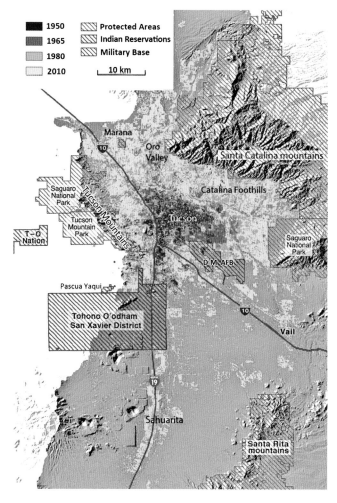

FIGURE 3.4 A map depicting the outward growth of Tucson from 1950 to 2010. (Adapted from a map in Le Tourneau and Dubertret, "Space and Water.")

Since the 1950s the county's population has grown on average by fifteen thousand new residents per year: a growth rate of nearly 3 percent per year, or three times that of the United States as a whole during the same period. Each year the developments needed to house and provide services to newcomers consume ten square miles of desert land per year. Most building takes place on the ever-expanding periphery of Tucson, where land is much less expensive than the remaining highly priced undeveloped parcels closer to the city core.

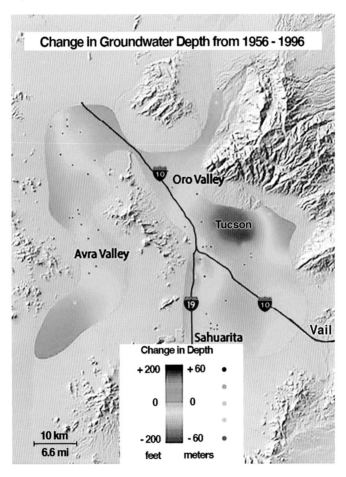

FIGURE 3.5 A map depicting the change in groundwater depth in the Tucson vicinity between 1956 and 1996. In some parts of Tucson (deep orange), groundwater depletion lowered the water table by nearly two hundred feet over a span of forty years. (Adapted from a figure in Le Tourneau and Dubertret, "Space and Water.")

During the last quarter of the twentieth century, many residents of Pima County became alarmed by the rapid outward growth of the Tucson metropolitan area, which threatened the open spaces and wild landscapes that had drawn people to the county in the first place. Their concerns were further elevated as the relentless pumping of groundwater to serve the needs of new arrivals—a critical problem as far back as the 1920s—continued to deplete underground aquifers filled slowly over thousands of years by rainwater seeping through mountains and alluvial fans. Thirty miles and more from the old Tucson Presidio, large ranch holdings were sold as the demand for land outside city limits created strong incentives for families to sell part or all of their land to developers, threatening the last remaining extensive areas of open space in the county. And as they witnessed the march of urban and suburban development, they realized that the rich diversity of plant and animal species in the region was diminishing as habitat and habitat connectivity were lost to ever-spreading grids of roads and streets.

Residents began to ponder how the community they loved might find ways to adapt more harmoniously to natural constraints lest it lose not only its rugged natural beauty and wildlife diversity but something perhaps ineffable: a culture built on the freedom offered by wide open spaces, the promise of new beginnings, and a deep connection to a landscape that is at once majestic and humbling.[13]

Attempts to Constrain Growth of Tucson: Three Decades of Environmental Churn

Beginning in the 1970s, conservation-minded Pima County residents initiated a series of efforts aimed at mitigating the environmental threats to the Tucson metro area posed by unchecked growth. By the end of the 1990s, these pioneering efforts had set the stage for developing a plan for managed growth: growth that considers the need not only to accommodate an increasing population but to live more harmoniously with the natural environment.

Restricting Access to Water

The first approach involved attempts to limit the supply of water. In 1972 the Arizona Legislature passed House Bill 333, which authorized creation of a water commission for Maricopa, Pinal, and Pima Counties, charged with overseeing water use from the Central Arizona Project (CAP).[14]

FIGURE 3.6 (a) Central
Arizona Project canal. (Aerial photo by U.S. Bureau
of Reclamation.) (b) Map
depicting the path of the
Central Arizona Project
canal, which carries water
from the Colorado River
near Lake Havasu to the
growing cities of Phoenix
and Tucson. (Map by
Central Arizona Project.)

Maricopa and Pinal counties quickly approved formation of a Central Arizona Water Conservation District. However, in Pima County, a group of concerned citizens claimed that CAP water would be unfit to drink and that the canals and aqueducts needed to transport water from the Colorado River in far-western Arizona to Pima County would harm the environment.

Their real concerns ran deeper, as they believed that importing CAP water would further fuel rapid growth of Tucson and environs, transforming the city into a Los Angeles– or Phoenix-like megaplex. They believed that Tucson should instead aspire to become a sustainable, medium-sized city, using wastewater recycling and other water-capture mechanisms to meet the needs of its population. However, the Pima County Board of Supervisors ultimately rejected the arguments of citizens opposed to using CAP water.

Environmentally minded citizens of Tucson continued to believe that water was a key to constraining growth. In 1974 they succeeded in electing three supporters to the city council, and with that election, the environmentalists held a majority on the council. In the summer of 1976, the newly constituted city council faced two pressing problems: a water-delivery system taxed by population growth and a water shortage resulting from years of drought.[15]

In response, they voted to raise water rates for all residents in the city and also included a pumping fee to account for the added cost of pumping water from lower elevations to the rapidly expanding developments along the slopes of the Catalina and Rincon Mountains. Residents of the central parts of Tucson saw their rates increase by nearly a factor of two, while those in the mountain foothills discovered that their water bills had increased by fivefold or more. City residents were furious, as were builders, whose representatives argued that "the city is using the new rate structure to slow growth on the city's outskirts by making it too expensive to live there."

Council members argued that the increases were needed to upgrade the water system as well as to charge residents for the true costs of delivering water. They also believed that the generally less affluent residents of the central city should not bear the cost of infrastructure and water delivery to the more affluent owners of homes in the mountains. And although the council members who voted for the increase insisted that their support for it was solely related to water delivery, they were nevertheless on record as believing that groundwater and recycled rainwater would be sufficient to supply the city, provided that the city grew slowly and sustainably.

Enraged Tucsonans gathered sufficient signatures on a petition to recall four members of the council. In an election held in January 1977, three of the four council members were recalled and replaced by individuals who vowed to rescind the rate increases. With the turnover in membership, the council was once again firmly supportive of builders and growth advocates. By the early 1990s, CAP water from the Colorado River began to flow into the metro Tucson area in a quantity seemingly sufficient for unlimited growth.[16]

Creating Parks at the Periphery of Tucson
Tucson Mountain Park

In the 1920s, when Tucson's population numbered fewer than fifty thousand people and the city limits extended outward only a few miles from the old presidio site, a group called the Tucson Game Protective Association became concerned that growth might one day overrun the Tucson basin. In response, they proposed to withdraw land to the west of the city from mining and homesteading and create a park and game refuge. In 1929 the Department of Interior responded to their proposal and withdrew thirty thousand acres from further development, and in 1932 the Tucson Mountain Recreation Area was opened to the public. Over the years, the northern part of the recreation area became part of Saguaro National Park, while the southern part became the core of Tucson Mountain Park. The latter continues to grow incrementally, as Pima County purchases additional parcels adjacent to the park.[17]

Colossal Cave Mountain Park

In the foothills of the Rincon Mountains on the far east side of Tucson, the nucleus of another park began to take form in 1917. After extensively exploring a cave in the Rincons over a period of several years, German businessman Frank Schmidt started to bring tourists to what became known popularly as Colossal Cave. He was able to lease state trust land surrounding the cave and over the next eight years constructed a lighting system that permitted tourists to observe its haunting calcite formations. In 1934 the New Deal Works Progress Administration invested funds and manpower to improve public access, and soon thereafter Pima County hired Schmidt to operate Colossal Cave as a park. The cave remained state property until 1992, when the county purchased it and a surrounding five-hundred-acre parcel from the state.[18]

FIGURE 3.7 Saguaro cactus forest and desert scrub in Tucson Mountain Park. (Aerial photo by Stephen Strom.)

Catalina State Park

In the beginning of the 1970s, a group of conservation-minded Tucson residents formed the Southern Arizona Environmental Council with the goal of slowing the accelerating pace of development in Pima County. In 1972 a Phoenix-area developer, John Ratliff, announced plans for a major housing development on 4,200 acres of former ranchland on the northwest periphery of Tucson adjacent to the Catalina Mountains.[19]

That galvanized action by Southern Arizona Environmental Council members, who reached out to a broad range of groups—recreationists, sportsmen, environmentalists, and some business interests—and created the Rancho Romero Coalition to oppose Ratliff's ambitious proposal to build seventeen thousand homes bordering two major washes. In order to achieve his vision, Ratliff needed the agreement of the Pima County Board of Supervisors to rezone the ranch property. The coalition galvanized community opposition to the project, and when the rezoning proposal was brought before the Pima County Planning and Zoning Commission, it was put on hold.

Tucson-area citizens then began a campaign to have the Rancho Romero property become the nucleus of a fourteen-thousand-acre park. In No-

vember of 1972, a strong supporter of conservation issues, Ron Asta, was elected to the board of supervisors. Buttressed by support from the Rancho Romero Coalition, Asta persuaded the board to vote against rezoning the property.

In 1973 Pima County residents approved a $4.5 million bond issue to acquire properties at the periphery of the Tucson metro area in order to create a greenbelt. Southern Arizona Environmental Council, the Rancho Romero Coalition, and a newly formed citizens group, the Oracle Road Green Belt Committee, lobbied to have the county purchase Rancho Romero from Ratliff for $3 million. Ratliff rejected the proposal, perhaps justifiably, as it was appraised at twice that amount.

Enter State Representative Charles King, who served the area around Rancho Romero and the proposed park. King orchestrated a land swap with the State Land Department that allowed Ratcliff to pursue his development by purchasing state trust lands to the west of Rancho Romero, while allowing ranch property to be included in what eventually became Catalina State Park. Legislation creating a park was signed into law by Arizona Governor Jack Williams in May 1974. Although significantly reduced from the fourteen thousand acres envisioned by its advocates, the 5,500-acre Catalina State Park stands as a monument to the success of a growing conservation movement in Pima County.[20]

Flood Control Funds and the Protection of Watersheds

The 1983 floods triggered by Tropical Storm Octave set in motion a series of actions that have shaped land use in the county for more than forty years. From his perch as a former member of the Pima County Board of Supervisors, David Yetman observes,

> In the aftermath of the floods, I worked very closely with Chuck Huckelberry, who at the time served as director of Pima County Transportation and the Flood Control District. One of the first things that emerged was the necessity of the county's acquiring flood-prone properties, and then adopting policy changes to keep building from encroaching into the hundred-year floodplain.
>
> Chuck and I at that time worked very closely, and we agreed that part of the long-range strategy should be the acquisition of as much as possible of lands that might one way or another contribute to flooding, to keep them from developing. That really didn't start to take shape until after the 1984 elections, when I was reelected [as a county supervisor]. First of all, we had to repair the broken infrastructure: repairing the bridges and starting to fill in along the Santa Cruz and Rillito with soil cement, to retard further erosion of the banks. That basically took two years to get all that up and running.
>
> Then a long-term strategy emerged: acquisition of lands that might contribute to flooding directly or indirectly. Everything that happened afterwards is a result of recognition of [the importance of land acquisition] by Huckelberry. I became chairman of the board of supervisors at that point, by which time that work was well under way. We worked fairly quietly [to use flood control monies to acquire those lands], but there was no opposition because nobody was in favor of flooding.

The first major acquisition using flood control district funds was land surrounding a twelve-mile stretch of lower Cienega Creek east of Vail. The goals of the purchase were to preserve riparian habitat and to reduce the potential of flooding around and downstream from the creek. With a strategically essential four-thousand-acre strip surrounding the creek now in hand, the county formally established the Cienega Creek Natural Preserve in 1986.[21]

Soon thereafter, the county envisioned increasing the tax levy that provides funds for the flood control district in order to raise the resources needed to purchase the Empire Ranch, fifteen miles upstream from (and south of) the natural preserve. If the Empire were developed, the protections afforded by the natural preserve along lower Cienega Creek would be severely undermined. Though the county's effort was ultimately unsuccessful, their main goal was achieved as the ranch was eventually transferred to the Bureau of Land Management via a land exchange with a private developer in the Phoenix area. Pima County representatives continued to be deeply involved with discussions regarding its management and eventually in the efforts to have the lands within and around the Empire included in Las Cienegas NCA (see chapter 2).

A few miles to the east of the Cienega Creek Preserve, Pima County used flood control district funds to purchase another property vital to protecting riparian areas around the creek: Empirita Ranch.[22] The county was able to leverage its investment by entering into an agreement with a local rancher who held grazing leases adjacent to the Empirita. In exchange for the rancher's continuing to have grazing access to portions of the Empirita, he agreed to manage both the ranch and his leases in accordance with environmental principles set forth by the county.[23]

A similar arrangement was made when flood control district funds were used to purchase La Posta Quemada Ranch near Colossal Cave. The ranch itself spans 470 acres and is surrounded by eight thousand acres of state trust lands that were leased from the State Land Department by the Pima County Parklands Foundation. The ranch purchase and acquisition of leasing rights on adjacent state trust land enabled protection of an important tributary of Cienega Creek.[24]

While the primary motivations for using flood control district funds for land purchase are watershed protection and flood mitigation, those purchases serve another critical purpose: preserving large areas of open space on the outskirts of the Tucson metro area, a limited but important step toward creating an open-space belt around the city.[25]

The Pima County Open Space Committee

In the mid- to late 1980s the Pima County Board of Supervisors sought to develop a more comprehensive plan for preserving open space in the rapidly growing eastern portion of the county. To guide that effort, the supervisors appointed an Open Space Committee with a mandate to "inventory and classify open space in Pima County, and to make recommendations as to the mechanisms by which the County can begin to preserve our open space resources."[26]

The core committee's thirteen members included five members drawn from Pima County staff and commissions, two from the City of Tucson, two from the public at large, and four outside experts. Representatives from surrounding towns and villages, the Tohono O'odham Nation, the Arizona Game and Fish Department, the Pima Trails Association, and members of the public also contributed to the committee's efforts.

The Open Space Committee worked for two years to establish a framework to preserve both urban and rural open spaces and recommended that the county focus on two primary goals: to create an interconnected regional open-space system and to develop mechanisms for protecting designated open space. They urged prompt action, noting that "dramatic changes in our surrounding landscape brought on by rapid growth have made it imperative that we protect those open-space values essential to the quality of life in eastern Pima County. The lush Sonoran Desert and [our] spectacular open spaces . . . are central to what makes life here unique and special."

Committee members identified six key elements of a county open-space system: preservation of desert washes; protection of mountain ranges, foothills, and scenic vistas; a community-wide system of recreation, aesthetic, and wildlife corridors; creation of natural buffers around public preserves; establishment of a desert belt around the Tucson metro area; and protection of natural landmarks.

To guide selection and acquisition of properties to create an open-space system, the committee placed highest priority on areas critical to supporting biodiversity and protecting watersheds, sites of historical or archaeological importance, regions of high aesthetic value, and parcels well-suited to expansion of county parks and recreation facilities.

The committee concluded their report with a set of suggested mechanisms for acquiring land, along with recommendations for ordinances and zoning policies to shape future development in and around high-value areas.

To implement their open-space proposal, the committee urged Pima County to establish a Parks and Open Space District with the power to generate funds to establish parks and acquire open-space parcels using monies from county-wide increases in property assessments and from taxes levied on real estate transfers and new developments.

The report's wide-ranging scope, along with its potential to affect growth patterns and tax policies, generated considerable controversy among home builders, the public, and county offices. Gayle Hartmann, an influential member of the Open Space Committee, recalls, "Ultimately because our plan was so [ambitious] it had the developers scared to death, and as a result the board of supervisors voted to 'accept' rather than 'adopt' our proposals."

Open-Space Bonds

Despite the county's unwillingness to formally adopt the land-use plan proposed by the Open Space Committee in 1988, the committee's efforts contributed to increasing public awareness and support for the idea of preserving open spaces. In 1997 Pima County voters approved a $28 million bond issue to expand mountain parks and acquire land rich in archaeological and cultural resources, as well as riparian areas and wetlands. In order to select and arrange for purchase of properties, the county established an Open Space Acquisition Review Committee. Over the next four years, the funds were used to acquire lands adjacent to Tucson Mountain Park and to purchase lands surrounding the Tortolita Mountain Reserve northwest of Tucson, Agua Caliente Wash on Tucson's east side, and lands surrounding the Empire Ranch.[27]

Perhaps most noteworthy was a purchase of a significant fraction of Canoa Ranch, which lies along a stretch of the Santa Cruz River, thirty miles south of Tucson and adjacent to the community of Green Valley. In the tenth century, Indigenous peoples dug canals to irrigate lands near today's Canoa Ranch as their agricultural settlements grew and flourished along the banks of the river. In the eighteenth century, the Spanish appropriated the land, and after the Mexican War of Independence in 1821, the newly formed Mexican government granted "San Ignacio de Canoa" to a rancher who had worked the land for more than half a century. He owned it until he sold his ranch to an Anglo man in 1876. The Canoa Ranch was later purchased by a succession of Anglos and ultimately grew from the initial seventeen-thousand-acre land grant to five hundred thousand acres—from the Santa Cruz River west to the Baboquivari Mountains—after it was acquired in 1912 by Levi Manning, a former Tucson mayor and land surveyor. Manning introduced purebred Herefords onto the property in 1917 and turned open range on the ranch into rotation pastures. Levi's son, Howell, took over ranch operations in 1921.

After the tragic death of Howell's son Howell Manning Jr. in 1951, Manning Sr. began selling parts of the ranch; by 1967 only six thousand acres remained. In 1993 the property was acquired by Fairfield Homes. In 1995 Fairfield proposed a major development to the Pima County Board of Supervisors, which approved rezoning that would allow Fairfield to build up to thirty-seven thousand homes on the ranch. In doing so, they ignored the findings of the Pima County Open Space Committee, which had identified Canoa Ranch as "an important natural landmark that is significant for its important riparian areas and its scenic and historic values."

In 1997 Supervisor John Even passed away and was replaced on the board of supervisors by Ray Carroll, a Republican with strong environmental leanings. With his appointment, the board's attitude toward growth changed.

Over the following three years, citizen activists, Fairfield Homes, and the board grappled with the decision of whether to permit Fairfield to pursue its ambitious plans or to have the county acquire the ranch for conservation purposes. Pima County Administrator Chuck Huckelberry proposed a compromise: to allow some development while preserving the majority of the 6,000-acre parcel for conservation purposes.[28] In March 2001 the supervisors voted to permit Fairfield Homes to build 2,200 homes on 1,200 acres; the remaining 4,800 acres would be purchased from Fairfield with funds drawn from the 1997 open-space bond issue. Today, the Canoa Ranch is protected permanently by Pima County as open space and wildlife habitat. Historic landscape features such as Canoa Lake have been restored, and ranch buildings have been rehabilitated. Pima County manages the area around the buildings as a national historic site. The Canoa Ranch has been renamed the Raúl M. Grijalva Canoa Ranch Conservation Park in honor of the former Pima County supervisor and current (as of 2023) Democratic congressman who was born and spent part of his childhood at Canoa Ranch.[29]

The Endangered Species Act and Large-Landscape Conservation

After twenty-five years of environmental churn beginning with the effort in 1972 to create the Catalina State Park, advocates for open-space and land conservation had achieved a great deal. But success in developing a comprehensive plan for land use in the county had thus far eluded them. On March 10, 1997, an unlikely catalyst precipitated an effort that culminated with Pima County's adoption of perhaps the most far-reaching land-use plan in the United States: a tiny, six-inch-long, 2.5-ounce raptor known as the cactus ferruginous pygmy owl. The rust-striped birds dwell in stately homes: the iconic saguaro cacti of the Sonoran Desert. As urban growth extended ever-farther into the desert, habitat for the pygmy owl had decreased to a point where fewer than thirty owls remained.

Starting in 1992, the Center for Biological Diversity, an often-controversial advocate for environmental causes, started a campaign to have the pygmy owl listed as an endangered species by the FWS.[30] In 1997 the group succeeded.

The listing of the owl had an immediate and profound effect on development in Pima County. Building projects that threatened pygmy owl habitat would be suspended or delayed until they satisfied the terms of the Endangered Species Act of 1973, which required that habitat for listed species be preserved. In 1982 the act was amended to allow developers to take habitat of endangered species, provided that suitable habitat space was set aside either on-site or elsewhere.[31] With the ESA and its 1982 amendment in hand, the U.S. Fish and Wildlife Service was empowered to negotiate agreements with developers, cities, and counties to develop habitat conservation plans.[32]

FIGURE 3.8 Cactus ferruginous pygmy owl. (Sky Jacobs, Wikimedia Commons.)

After the pygmy owl was listed, Pima County leaders began to explore how the amended Endangered Species Act might be used to forge a plan that could balance growth and environmental values.[33] They looked first to Southern California, where the act had been used successfully to catalyze two major land-use plans.

Habitat Conservation Plans in San Diego County and Orange County California

Upon assuming leadership of the Department of Interior in 1992, one of the first challenges Secretary Bruce Babbitt faced was to find a way to resolve two increasingly bitter disputes between builders poised to expand devel-

FIGURE 3.9 California gnatcatcher. (Andy Reago and Chrissy McClarren, Wikimedia Commons.)

opment along the Southern California coast and environmentalists determined to preserve remaining open space by holding developers to the strict legal requirements of the ESA.[34] The battles unfolded in two of the fastest-growing areas of the United States: Orange County and San Diego County, California.

Much of the land eyed by home builders was habitat to a small, unprepossessing bird, the California gnatcatcher, which had been listed as endangered by the FWS. Until the dispute between builders and environmentalists could be settled, building in the area would remain at a standstill. To break the impasse, Babbitt helped to facilitate development of two habitat conservation plans in which takings of gnatcatcher habitat by home builders would be compensated by preservation of large tracts of contiguous habitat elsewhere in the county.

Until Babbitt assumed leadership of Interior, the FWS lacked the support and commitment from higher-level Interior Department management needed in order to make forceful use of the ESA. As secretary of the interior, Babbitt had management authority over the U.S. Fish and Wildlife Service, the agency charged with ensuring that requirements of the Endangered Species Act were met.

Upon arriving at Interior, he observed that "the agency simply could not seem to get the hang of negotiating habitat conservation plans. Field biologists, trained for tranquil lives out researching the migratory habits of birds and the population dynamics of butterflies, found themselves confronted with rooms packed with angry landowners and hostile environmentalists, each contending that the other had no rights on the land." By injecting himself into the California land-use disputes, he aimed to show how the FWS could wield the power of the ESA to effect creative compromises.

Babbitt and his staff first met with their counterparts in Orange County, California, along with the sole shareholder of the Irvine Company, Donald Bren, who controlled the largest parcel of private land in the county. Together, they agreed to forge a land-use plan that would allow development to proceed while protecting habitat not only for the gnatcatcher but for a broad suite of other endangered species. By negotiating a multi-species conservation plan (MSCP) to cover a range of endangered and threatened species, developers and environmentalists would no longer be faced with species-by-species conservation battles. After several years of negotiation, an Orange County Habitat Conservation Plan was completed in 1996.[35] Central to the plan was the Irvine Company's establishing two preserves encompassing more than thirty thousand acres to protect habitat for the gnat catcher and thirty-two other threatened and endangered species: land that compensated for habitat loss resulting from coastal developments that were authorized to proceed following approval of the MSCP by the FWS.

The secretary was effusive in crediting the Irvine Ranch for providing the land needed to forge the Orange County MSCP: "The settlement with Irvine Ranch was a defining moment in the emergence of the Endangered Species Act as a land-use planning statute, capable of forging a balance between development and the preservation of large ecosystems. [Donald Bren from the Irvine Ranch gave] credibility to a statute that might not have survived much longer without some demonstrable evidence that it could be made to work on private property."

While negotiations with Orange County were proceeding, Babbitt met with representatives from adjacent San Diego County and the city of San Diego to urge them to resolve land-use disputes by developing a MSCP. In response to the secretary, county and city leaders and their staff initiated a yearlong process to compile species inventories, research landownership records, and to carry out economic studies. Importantly, they invited both civic leaders and citizens to participate in the process. Stitching together habitat preserves in land already heavily developed and significantly fragmented required a combination of artful zoning and land acquisition. In 1998 the city and county approved a large-scale MSCP that ultimately included two hundred thousand acres of habitat and protected more than one hundred species.[36]

Despite the success of the Endangered Species Act in catalyzing land-use planning, Babbitt lamented that the San Diego City and County MSCP emerged well after subdivisions and highways had already fragmented habitat and left little open space around developed urban and suburban lands. He hoped that other rapidly growing areas would take heed of the challenges faced by San Diego and the opportunities presented by the Endangered Species Act to engage in large-scale land-use planning before allowing unregulated growth to restrict options for supporting both sustainable expansion and a healthy environment.

A Comprehensive Land-Use Plan for Pima County

In reflecting on the origin of efforts to develop a comprehensive land-use plan for Pima County, Linda Mayro, director of sustainability and conservation, remembered that "discussions about land use were at an impasse until the cactus ferruginous pygmy owl was listed. The need to protect the habitat of the owl required by the Endangered Species Act affected all construction: schools, roads, you name it." As her words suggest, the county needed to act lest innumerable construction projects and plans grind to a halt.

Following the listing of the cactus ferruginous pygmy owl, the Pima County Board of Supervisors instructed County Administrator Chuck Huckelberry to "develop and improve strategies to deal with rapid urban growth in eastern Pima County." In a memo to his staff Huckelberry noted that in structuring a land-use plan "the challenge is how to direct growth and protect the lifestyle and quality of life that makes Pima County a unique and wonderful place to live."

In response, county staff initiated a series of meetings and study sessions to address growing community concerns related to land-use decisions that now needed to take into account requirements of the Endangered Species Act.[37] After discussions spanning nineteen months, Huckelberry's staff synthesized community and expert advice and prepared a draft report to the board of supervisors entitled the "Sonoran Desert Conservation Plan."[38]

In his cover letter to the report, Administrator Huckelberry noted, "Development of this plan has been in response to the policies and visions stated by the board in discussing urban growth issues in Pima County and the need to balance economic, environmental, and human interest. The draft plan itself is the merger of active citizen discussion regarding growth with the coalition for the Sonoran Desert Protection and others, along with integration of a number of past and present County activities that are [related to] natural resource protection."

FIGURE 3.10 Carolyn Campbell, executive director, Coalition for Sonoran Desert Protection. (Courtesy Coalition for Sonoran Desert Protection.)

Early in the process, county staff and the community decided that habitat protection mandated by the Endangered Species Act should include not only habitat important to the pygmy owl but a

range of vulnerable species. Carolyn Campbell, executive director of the Coalition for
Sonoran Desert Protection, remembers,
"When they kicked off the conservation
plan at a board of supervisors meeting, the
secretary of interior attended the meeting
and talked up multi-species habitat conservation plans."[39]

As was the case with their counterparts
in Orange and San Diego Counties, the Pima
County supervisors saw the advantage in
avoiding land-use battles each time a new
species was listed as endangered or threated.
But rather than simply following the template provided by the California multi-
species conservation plans—providing alternative habitat spaces to offset takings (of
habitat) by developers—the report proposed
a far bolder six-part plan: to not only protect
critical habitat for endangered species but establish and protect biological
corridors, restore riparian areas, conserve working ranches, create and expand mountain parks, and preserve historic and cultural sites.

FIGURE 3.11 Julia Fonseca, Pima County Office of Sustainability and Conservation. (Pima
County/U.S. Fish and Wildlife Service.)

Julia Fonseca reflects on the decision to create a plan with the ambition
and scope of the Sonoran Desert Conservation Plan. In formulating the plan,
Chuck Huckelberry and board of supervisors member Raúl Grijalva

were looking at what the community had valued in the past, what the voters
had supported. It was clear to them that people valued recreational opportunities, the multicultural heritage of the area, ranching, and the future of water
supplies. It was clear that people also cared about wildlife, not necessarily
endangered species that got in the way of particular developments, but they
sure cared about wildlife in general. These are the values that had proven to
be successful generators of action in the past [the flood control district investments; the 1986 and 1997 open-space bond issues]. There wasn't that much
speculation [about what the community supported]. What was genius was
broadening land-use discussions instead of just saying, "Ah, let's just solve one
problem. Let's just deal with the pygmy owl," because that is the train wreck

TEXT PORTRAIT: JULIA FONSECA

After receiving a graduate degree in geology at the University of Arizona, Julia Fonseca joined the Pima County Regional Flood Control District staff in 1986. Over the years, the focus of her career shifted away from hydrology and floodplain restoration to species protection efforts. Fonseca's broad range of expertise enabled her to play an instrumental role in the development and implementation of the Sonoran Desert Conservation Plan. In recognition of her many contributions to the SDCP, she was named Natural Resource Professional of the Year by the Arizona Game and Fish Commission in 2013. From 2013 to her retirement in January 2023, Fonseca served as senior planning manager for the Pima County Office of Sustainability and Conservation.

I was born in Tulsa, Oklahoma. When I was six years old, my mom, then a single mother supporting two children, moved us to Houston, Texas. At the time, I hated Houston; it had no rocks and was surrounded by oppressive vegetation. Sometime before I was ten, I developed an interest in archaeology and geology. The moment we first went to New Mexico—I think I was eleven—I immediately thought, "I want to live in the Southwest. I do not want to live in Texas!"

In 1983 I came to Tucson to study geomorphology, the science of the earth's surface and the processes that affect it. As part of our fluvial geomorphology class at the university, we studied the effects of the 1983 floods triggered by Tropical Storm Octave. I remember being out in the field with Bill Bull, an outstanding field teacher who worked with Luna Leopold and others in developing the science of geomorphology, especially for western landscapes. He was particularly interested in arroyo cutting and the response of a landscape to both changing climactic and tectonic forces. When I graduated, I was offered a position with the Pima County Regional Flood Control District, which was quite fortunate as my husband had fallen in love with the desert as well.

I was hired as a hydrologist, in part because of my studies on the 1983 flood and my understanding about the forces of erosion and flooding. I quickly got to know Chuck Huckelberry, who was then director of the Department of Transportation Flood Control District. He was clearly a man of vision, and there were actions taken by the county after the flood that were astounding examples of his leadership. It made me want to stay.

The flood control district commissioned a number of studies aimed at improving our understanding of how the watersheds in eastern Pima County function. The set of people who were there at the time were

that brought everybody to the table, but looking more broadly, that was the genius.

Huckelberry noted that "while this is the first time that we have articulated how these [six] elements combine to form one plan, past Pima County actions have pursued independently and often at different paces, implementation of all [six] plan elements." Indeed, Pima County had been building toward an effort of this scope for the better part of twenty-five years. To recall thinking about how to mitigate the effects of future floods and improve the health of the watersheds, not just building a channel to sluice the floodwaters through faster.

The rapidity of the response to the 1983 flood was also stunning. There was a $64 million dollar bond that passed the next year. It included a good deal of money not only for infrastructure repair but for monies to purchase flood-prone land as a nonstructural alternative to building and stabilization. Many of those funds went to buy out people whose homes were in the floodplain so they wouldn't get harmed again. It was a very compassionate response because there was no federal funding that could come in rapidly enough to deal with people's problems. The county purchased homes at their full value prior to the flood so that people could afford alternative housing away from the floodplain.

The funds from the bond issue were also used to purchase land around lower Cienega Creek—the area that became the Cienega Creek Natural Reserve. When I started my job in the flood control district, I was handed responsibility for the reserve. This was the first time that the flood control district was put in charge of managing land. That was a transformational act, one that created a new mission, a new purpose for the agency. Up until that point, there just hadn't been any kind of stewardship role for the flood control district. But Chuck Huckelberry's vision, our vision was to protect the Cienega Creek watershed.

During that time, I was beginning to meet with many of the individuals who now are considered the fathers of conservation biology: John Terborgh, the late Michael Soule, and Reed Noss, people like that. Co-incidentally, my husband became involved with the *Conservation Biology* journal, so I was being exposed to a lot of new ideas. Just as I was immersing myself in conservation biology, Chuck Huckelberry came up with the bold idea of creating an open-space corridor from the Mexican border through the Canelo Hills to the Rincon Mountains. Based on my growing understanding of conservation biology precepts, I was able carry out a study that demonstrated the importance of that corridor to wildlife.

What has sustained me over these past forty years, I think, is related to artistic or spiritual connections to landscapes. I think I've always responded deeply to landscapes that I've known: the vegetation, the rocks, the visual content of it. You can fall in love with a landscape as much as you can fall in love with a person. It's complex, maybe even more complex than a person.

a few examples: open-space bonds were used to purchase Rancho Romero in the 1970s and the Empirita and Canoa Ranches in the 1990s; a major effort to repair riparian areas was funded by the flood control district; biological corridors around Cienega Creek, Agua Caliente, and Colossal Cave were protected with both open space and flood control district funds; Tucson Mountain and the Tortolita Mountain Parks were extended with open-space bonds; and the initial acquisitions for Canoa Ranch National Historic Park were funded in part by open-space bonds.

In presenting the draft concept for the Sonora Desert Conservation Plan, Huckelberry suggested that a more mature version of the plan concept could serve as a central element of the County Comprehensive Land-Use Plan.[40]

Per the state-adopted Growing Smarter Acts of 1998 and 2000, municipalities and counties in Arizona are mandated to update their general or comprehensive plans once every ten years. The due date for Pima County's plan: the end of 2000. That gave the county just over two years to bring forward a Sonoran Desert Conservation Plan template that could win the support of the community and the supervisors. The county's aspirations were not only bold in scope but expansive in reach. If adopted and successfully implemented, the SDCP would "potentially include a land base that is ten times the size of the San Diego Multi-Species Conservation Program, which is considered to be the most complex permitted conservation plan in the United States." In the end, the area covered in the Sonoran Desert Conservation Plan spanned 5.9 million acres.

Following receipt of Administrator Huckelberry's draft report, the board of supervisors approved the concept proposed for the Sonoran Desert Conservation Plan on March 2, 1999, and authorized county staff to fully develop plan elements.[41] By also accepting the recommendation that a robust version of the plan be incorporated in the mandated county comprehensive plan, the board of supervisors had implicitly given Huckelberry and his staff a deadline: turning the SDCP concept into a more detailed framework in time to meet state requirements.

Creating and building support for the Sonoran Desert Conservation Plan would require outreach to and participation by citizens and experts on a scale as ambitious as the plan itself. But Huckelberry and the county saw this as an unprecedented opportunity:

[Developing] the work plan will open the door to the broad formal public process necessary to undertake regional endangered species planning and program implementation with federal natural resource agency partners. Perhaps more importantly, it will enable the local community to accept responsibility for . . . defining balanced and rational solutions. To date, community options have been defined primarily by conflict and a winner-take-all approach. Now the board can reverse this trend by establishing a process that will frame the choices available to the community in terms of consensus-building and an approach that honors multiple obligations. Through this process, we will have greater opportunity to protect the pygmy owl, achieve lasting conservation goals on an ecosystem and multi-species level, and foster acceptance of, and pride in, environmental values that can be upheld across the community.

The work ahead was daunting as the board of supervisors instructed county staff to submit an updated version of the Sonoran Desert Conservation Plan that would include three elements: a MSCP that would meet the requirements of the Endangered Species Act, gain the approval of the U.S. Fish and Wildlife Service, and provide clear guidelines to developers; a plan to provide not only comprehensive conservation of vulnerable species but preservation of contiguous habitat on a landscape scale; and land-use policies that could be integrated with the County Comprehensive Land-Use Plan.[42]

The first step taken by the county was to appoint a steering committee to develop options for the plan, along with information gathered by other teams and committees. In forming the steering committee, the county believed that success of the process depended crucially on its inclusiveness. County staff were instructed to appoint to the committee "interested government entities and each of the non-governmental organizations and individuals who have [expressed interest in becoming] members of the steering committee, contingent upon their willingness to [attend] a twice per month series of educational seminars and workshops. Everyone expressing an interest will be invited to participate."[43]

FIGURE 3.12 Congressman Raúl Grijalva, who served as chair of the Pima County Board of Supervisors from 2000 to 2002, when the Sonoran Desert Conservation Plan was incorporated into the County Comprehensive Land-Use Plan. (U.S. Fish and Wildlife Service.)

In the end, eighty-six individuals drawn from a broadly representative cross-section of the community served on the steering committee. Members included conservation-minded individuals and groups, neighborhood groups, ranchers, miners, landowners, private property advocates, developers, home builders, the real estate industry, and water interests. Representatives of the Tohono O'odham Nation were regularly consulted when the committee discussed cultural resources. The choice to open the process to all interested parties signaled a commitment to develop a report that could earn the support of Pima County residents. Over the four-year planning process, the steering committee and its advisory teams and groups held more than four hundred public meetings, along with educational sessions and workshops—all open to any interested resident of the county.

FIGURE 3.13 A public meeting of the Pima County Board of Supervisors during the period when the Sonoran Desert Conservation Plan was taking shape. (U.S. Fish and Wildlife Service.)

Next to take form were teams comprised of individuals representing each element of the plan. To ensure that individuals involved in shaping the MSCP and the broader conservation plan had access to the best scientific advice, the county appointed a science and technical advisory team (STAT) comprising biologists and federal agency scientists who had the expertise needed to define credible science-based plans. In the end, more than 150 scientists contributed to the team's efforts. To insulate the STAT from the politics of the SDCP planning process, the county created a "firewall" between the activities of the STAT and the steering committee to ensure that STAT conclusions were both based solely on the team's best scientific judgment and perceived by the public to be the case. Review of STAT studies by nationally recognized peers with no stake in the outcome of the SDCP process provided additional assurance that STAT studies and conclusions were entirely fact based.[44]

To coordinate the work of the steering committee, STAT, and other committees, the county formed a management team comprising representatives from Pima County and Department of Interior agencies. The team was led by Project Manager Maeveen Behan, who was universally acknowledged as the driving force behind the SDCP planning process. Her energy, vision, and diplomatic skill in drawing together the of elements of the planning process proved critical to forging the plan.

Congressman Raúl Grijalva, chair of the Pima County Board of Supervisors during the time the plan was developed, summarized her role: "The plan's policy concept was from Chuck [Huckelberry]. The policy direction was from the county board of supervisors. The framing of the whole effort, the mechanism, the details—those were the areas where she was head." Her passing at the relatively young age of forty-eight was mourned county-wide.[45] Her efforts in bringing the SDCP to fruition continue to be recognized as "work that changed the nature of the county's growth debate that for decades had pitted development against conservation."

FIGURE 3.14 Sonoran Desert Conservation Plan Project Manager Maeveen Behan. (U.S. Fish and Wildlife Service.)

Once the organizational framework for developing the plan was in place, steering committee members began a period of intense study aimed at familiarizing themselves with the panoply of issues they would face in the course of the planning process. Behan and Huckelberry urged the committee to begin meeting at least twice per month "to acquire knowledge in a variety of subject areas if . . . the Committee members are to make a credible recommendation on a regional conservation program that will impact land-use planning and development for decades into the future. These sessions will bring the entire group up to the same place in their knowledge of various aspects of multi-species conservation, and prepare the steering committee for their most important role: recommending a [habitat] preserve design." To ensure transparency, meetings of the steering committee and other elements in the planning process were open to the public.

Linda Mayro, director of sustainability and conservation in Pima County, remembers the intensive efforts to hammer out the SDCP as follows: "There were a scary amount of people who met monthly at the Arizona Sonoran Desert Museum. It was every stripe from the property-rights types to developers to Tohono O'odham to others, just across the board, ranching community, manufacturers, all of them. So we had these boot camps that would educate people" on all topics pertaining to the planning process.

Rancher Mac Donaldson, who had participated in the Sonoita Valley Planning Partnership and was recruited to serve on the SDCP ranching committee, noted that "Maeveen did something similar to [what Karen Simms did for] the SVPP where [she] contacted everybody and got them involved and held educational forums. The Sonoran Desert Conservation Plan really was successful I think because of that diversity of the different groups that were trying to create it and how it was created." Several other Pima County staff members also cited the SVPP process as a model for many elements adopted in shaping the SDCP planning effort.

University of Arizona professor of anthropology Tom Sheridan amplified Donaldson's observation: "I think what was happening in Cienega Creek was one of, if not the major catalyst for the Sonoran Desert Conservation Plan because I think it goes back to the fight against the development of the Empire Ranch. I think that really scared enough people in the metro Tucson area to pay attention to what was happening" outside city boundaries.

In another nod to the SVPP process, Pima County hired a facilitator to help the steering committee set ground rules for discussion and decision-making. Absent a facilitator, the planning process could easily have gone awry given the number of steering committee participants and the magnitude and complexity of the SDCP process. Funds to hire the facilitator and to support the activities of the steering committee and the science and technical advisory team were made available thanks to a $3 million earmark obtained by the Arizona congressional delegation working in concert with then secretary of the interior Bruce Babbitt.

Key Elements of the Sonoran Desert Conservation Plan
The Conservation Lands System
Developing a Multi-Species Conservation Plan

The final version of the MSCP component of the Sonoran Desert Conservation Plan provides a succinct summary of the county's intent in adopting the multi-species approach: "The overall goal of the Pima County MSCP is to balance the need to comply with the Endangered Species Act while allowing for the future growth of the built environment."[46]

The decision to develop a multi-species conservation plan required identifying a list of threatened or endangered species and mapping their habitat. That task fell naturally to the science and technical advisory team, which began intensive studies aimed at locating key habitat patches for vulnerable plant and wildlife species, along with unfragmented corridors connecting those patches. Their research initially focused on one hundred species recognized as imperiled or in decline, which was later reduced to fifty-six "priority vulnerable species" and the habitat that sustains them.[47]

To pinpoint species habitat for an area as large as eastern Pima County (2.2 million acres), STAT made use of geographic information system (GIS) tools to map known habitat for priority vulnerable species, then identified potential habitat for those species by locating areas with environments with biotic and abiotic features (e.g., vegetation, soils, and availability of water) similar to those in known habitat patches.

Biological Planning on a Regional Scale

As their studies and deliberations proceeded, STAT decided to expand its goals to "ensure the long-term survival" not only of the fifty-six priority vulnerable species comprising the core of the MSCP but "of the full spectrum of plants and animals that are indigenous to Pima County through maintaining or improving the habitat conditions and ecosystem functions necessary for their survival." To meet these goals, STAT recommended to the steering committee that Pima County design a plan to develop a county-wide system of biological reserves that would form the central element of a Conservation Lands System (CLS).[48] The basic organizing principles of the CLS included perpetuating the comprehensive conservation of vulnerable species, reserving those areas that contain large populations of vulnerable species, and connecting reserves on a landscape scale by providing functional movement corridors.[49]

The Conservation Lands System Guidelines

The Conservation Lands System defined four categories of "primary conservation areas" for protection: important riparian areas selected to have high water availability, species richness, and diversity; biological core areas identified as high-value habitat for five or more vulnerable species; and special- and multiple-use management areas chosen for their potential to provide habitat through enhancement or restoration projects. The CLS also identified areas essential to creating or sustaining connection between critical habitat, along with a set of specific conservation targets, including riparian areas, streams, grasslands, and caves. In its final form, the CLS encompassed approximately two million acres, or three thousand square miles, in eastern Pima County.[50]

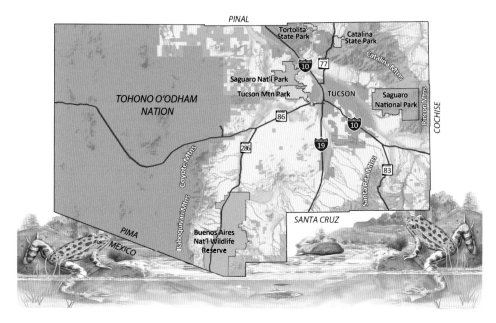

FIGURE 3.15 Priority riparian areas (blue/turquoise) identified for protection in the Sonoran Desert Conservation Plan. (Map from Pima County, modified by Stephen Strom.)

While discussions regarding other elements of the Sonoran Desert continued until 2003, the Pima County Board of Supervisors voted to include the Conservation Lands System as the environmental element of the County Comprehensive Land-Use Plan in 2001.[51] In so doing, they adopted the largest multi-species conservation plan in the United States.

But the scope of the CLS was much broader than its MSCP elements in that it proposed a county-wide system of biological reserves that not only would conserve critical species habitat but would also preserve intact and functional ecosystems and retain connections between habitat with functional corridors. Former secretary of the interior Bruce Babbitt praised the Pima County plan: "Pima County is a really important model because it is a comprehensive, general land-use, habitat protection plan. It goes a long ways beyond the specific requirements" of the Endangered Species Act.

To achieve the goals of the CLS, developers who propose rezoning or other use changes in primary conservation areas are required to set aside conservation land. The CLS assesses the value of the property for achieving conservation goals to determine how much land should be left in its natural state when a parcel is developed. For example, to develop one acre of

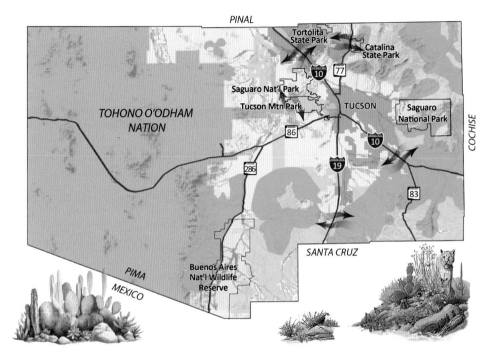

FIGURE 3.16 Map of the Maeveen Marie Behan Conservation Lands System. Priority biological areas are indicated in darker green, multiple-use areas in lighter green. Connecting corridors are illustrated using purple arrows. (Map from Pima County, modified by Stephen Strom.)

land identified as "biological core habitat," a builder would need to mitigate depletion of habitat either on-site or by purchasing land offsite. Different mitigation ratios apply to each of the four land-use categories.

The CLS guidelines place stringent requirements on development in primary conservation areas and, as a consequence, serve to funnel urban growth into areas of lesser biological importance. By identifying biologically sensitive areas, the CLS also provides the county with a prioritized set of high-value open space and conservation properties to acquire outright.[52]

Between 1986 and 2015, Pima County voters approved upward of $200 million for conservation land purchases comprising 80 properties spanning a total of nearly 60,000 acres. Along with state or federal land leased for grazing, protected lands in Pima County now exceed 230,000 acres, most of which were acquired following the adoption of the Conservation Lands System.

From 2001 to 2016 county decisions regarding land use were guided by mitigation requirements for the four primary conservation area elements of the

Conservation Lands System. After years of negotiation, Pima County and the U.S. Fish and Wildlife Service formally agreed to protection guidelines for a set of forty-four "covered species" (a subset of the fifty-six species identified in the CLS)–species for which taking of habitat by a private developer would require offsets in the form of protected mitigation habitat purchased by the county.[53]

In 2016 Pima County received a Section 10 permit from the FWS, which allows for "incidental taking" of covered species habitat for a period of thirty years. As a result of Pima County's having acquired adequate mitigation lands via open-space bond purchases, builders can now proceed with some certainty that their developments will not be subject to challenges based on their violation of the Endangered Species Act so long as they adhere to the stipulations of the Section 10 permit.[54]

Julia Fonseca looks back over her thirty-year career working in Pima County: "Habitat conservation [served as] a tool to resolve long-standing community conflicts around development. Way back before the [1983] flood, there had been conflicts about development and people not liking the idea of surrendering their open spaces that either provide them visual comfort or aesthetic values or places to recreate and enjoy them." The MSCP and the CLS played pivotal roles in ameliorating the ongoing tension between development and conservation, allowing Tucson to grow while preserving the biological integrity of surrounding lands.

In perhaps the most poignant moment during the two-decade-long effort to shape and implement the Sonoran Desert Conservation Plan, the county voted unanimously to rename the CLS as the Maeveen Marie Behan Conservation Lands System. Minutes afterward, as she watched the award ceremony on TV, Maeveen Behan took her last breath.[55]

Restoration and Protection of Riparian Areas

Riparian areas are essential to proper functioning of watersheds and provide critical habitat and shelter for aquatic and avian species as well as mammalian wildlife. Ecologists estimate that between 60 percent and 75 percent of all species in Arizona depend in some ways on riparian areas. However, as described previously, groundwater pumping, grazing, and development have drastically impacted the health of riparian areas throughout Pima County. As a result, the SDCP places high priority on protecting remaining functional riparian areas and restoring others where possible.[56]

Pima County's efforts to save and restore riparian areas began two decades before its adoption of the SDCP in 2003. Following the destruction wrought by the massive floods arising from Tropical Storm Octave in 1983, Pima County responded by not only instituting local flood-mitigation strategies along rivers and streams but investing in regional flood control efforts.

To do so required thinking on a watershed level. The county's first step was to acquire land along the course of Cienega Creek, and later to invest in restoration of functional riparian areas adjacent to the creek in what became the Cienega Creek Natural Preserve. The second step was to look thirty miles southeast of Tucson to acquire the Empire Ranch so that Cienega Creek, upstream from Tucson, was protected from development.

In Julia Fonseca's recollection, "the flood control district was saying, 'we want to buy this land.' We want the whole watershed to be part of an open-space corridor from the Mexican border all the way to Oracle. I was astonished. This was really big-picture thinking on the board's part and a huge political risk. That catalyzed the involvement of the Bureau of Land Management and the congressional delegation to create, ultimately, the Las Cienegas National Conservation Area."

"It was an idea that was way ahead of its time, to protect the floodplains upstream of Tucson so that the capacity of the [bank-protected river] channels in Tucson would not be exceeded by future development," continues Fonseca. Conceiving flood control as a regional rather than a local problem could well be seen as the genesis of the philosophy that guided the SDCP planning effort. Fonseca suggests that the 1983 flood "was a justification before the Sonoran Desert Conservation Plan, for acquiring and protecting large watersheds that are upstream of Tucson, because there is a relationship between retaining all that vegetation and topographic complexity along natural floodplains and the storage they provide."

In addition to protecting the watershed, the county embarked on efforts to restore riparian areas in and around the Cienega Creek Natural Preserve. The first step was to find a way to develop grazing strategies that would protect rather than destroy riparian areas. Looking back, Julia Fonseca remembers, "I was asked to lead a group of people who wanted to demonstrate that livestock could be compatible with grazing: a managed grazing regime." After they agreed to exclude livestock from the stream banks "in 1995, by 2003 you could see there was a whole new forest of cottonwood trees within the willow corridor. So that was an example of natural restoration" of a riparian area.

FIGURE 3.17 Riparian area surrounding Tanque Verde Creek near its confluence with Agua Caliente Wash. (Photo by Stephen Strom.)

The county also experimented with more active riparian restoration. Fonseca recollects,

> This was an area that was called the "Pantano Jungle." Up until that time, the flood control district had not done any revegetation of abandoned farmlands in floodplains. It's a sixty-acre parcel within the current boundaries of the preserve that was cleared for flood control in 1974. It was our first foray into restoring [riparian areas] in abandoned farmlands. [By addressing erosion and other problems] over the years this area has recovered quite a bit and trees here have grown quite a bit as well.
>
> It was the beginning of the flood control district's riparian restoration program which became much bigger. It grew larger because we were able to also get the Army Corps of Engineers to let us use the revegetation efforts there to satisfy the requirements of the Clean Water Act for mitigation [i.e., to replace the loss of wetland and aquatic resource functions in a watershed]. So it was the first offsite mitigation project that the flood control district had ever done. So these things just set the stage for an expansion.[57]

In the course of the discussions that led to adoption of the Conservation Lands System, STAT and the steering committee developed a map to guide efforts to restore or protect riparian areas.[58] To date, the county has invested in acquisitions of riparian areas along Tanque Verde Creek, the San Pedro River, the Agua Verde Wash, and Sabino Creek.

Ranch Conservation

Early in the twentieth century, cattle ranching, mining, and farming were the three pillars of the Arizona economy. At one time, almost two million cattle grazed in Pima County's shrub and grasslands and along rivers and streams. Over time ranching decreased in economic importance but retained its near-mythical hold on the imaginations of Arizonans. Today, virtually all of the 2.4 million acres in eastern Pima County is devoted to ranching. In essence, ranchland defines Tucson's urban boundary, helps to prevent urban sprawl, and serves as a vast reserve of undeveloped open space.[59]

Those who choose the ranching life do so in large measure because they enjoy the challenges of raising cattle and working the land. Keeping an operation going in the face of the vicissitudes of weather and the market requires a combination of optimism and endurance. For many ranchers, profit margins are slim and unpredictable.

Ian Tomlinson, who grazes cattle in the Sonoita Valley on his Vera Earl Ranch, the Empire Ranch, and surrounding state trust land in Pima and Santa Cruz Counties, captures the challenges and romance of the ranching life: "I always had a connection to it from when I was a little kid and my grandparents owned the Vera Earl. I just was always drawn to the area and the ranch, then when my grandmother passed away somebody in the family needed to come down and run it. When I arrived, I knew nothing about running a ranch, but I've always liked challenges. So I learned, made my share of mistakes and found that I really liked it."

Tomlinson continues,

> It's a hard business. We've grown way beyond what I ever envisioned. In what I'll call "the beef business," you have to be multifaceted to make money, and you have to have so many different irons in the fire. You have all the nostalgic stuff as well, getting up in the morning, being on the ranch, looking out your window, those kinds of feelings.
>
> You have to compartmentalize it some because if you get too swayed by the nostalgia and the mythical part of being a cowboy and a rancher, you're going to lose your ass. I love the challenge of growing the business and having to make money every year and the finances of it, and then the day-to-day challenges with running a cattle operation, the health of the cattle, and the landscape and the weather. It's a hell of a challenge.

Most cattle operations in Arizona require access not only to land owned by a rancher but to surrounding state trust or federal land. It is typical for a rancher to own, say, five thousand acres but to lease five to ten times that much land from the state, the U.S. Forest Service, or the Bureau of Land Management.

Today's ranching families are often descendants of homesteaders who arrived in Arizona after 1880. As ranching families age and as the demand for lands beyond the urban boundary increases, there is great temptation for owners to sell their lands unless their children or younger relatives aspire to take over the operation. Finding a way to preserve ranchland in the face of the economic and personal incentives for current landholders to sell represents a critical component of the Sonoran Desert Conservation

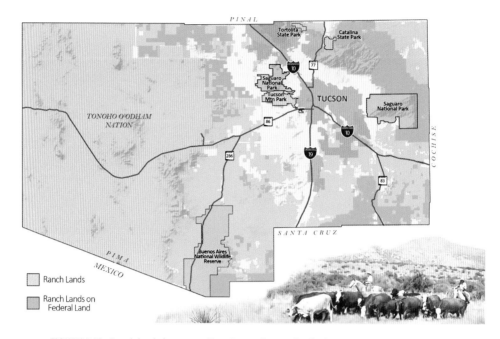

FIGURE 3.18 Ranch lands in eastern Pima County (green shading). In essence, ranchland defines Tucson's urban boundary. (Map from Pima County, modified by Stephen Strom.)

Plan. University of Arizona professor Tom Sheridan vivifies the challenge of preserving ranchlands outside the Tucson metro area: "I would say at least 80 percent of the value of these ranches lies in their speculative real estate value, not their value as actual working ranches."

Linda Mayro notes the importance of preserving ranchland to achieving the goals of the SDCP:

> There's a quote that Tom Sheridan attributes to me and it's that "ranch conservation is the key to preserving all elements of the Sonoran Desert Conservation Plan." It's really a true statement because you are preserving and conserving land at a [large] landscape level. . . . There are a variety of environments on any ranch, from mountains down to riparian areas. [Ranches provide essential links to the] cultural landscape, biological landscape, and are often roadless areas that provide connectivity for wildlife. So ranch conservation became a key part of the SDCP.

The challenge faced by the SDCP's framers was how best to conserve as much ranchland in eastern Pima County as possible. The solution proposed by the SDCP ranch conservation team was to purchase ranches using open-space bond monies but to allow the sellers—individual ranchers or ranching families—to continue their cattle operations. The county assumed responsibility for working collaboratively with each rancher to ensure that the land continued to be well managed and that the ranching operation remain sustainable. The solution proposed by the SDCP ranch conservation team had another important benefit: ensuring that adjacent state trust lands leased to the ranchers for cattle grazing would also be well managed, to the benefit of the ranchers as well as the ecological health of the land.

Julia Fonseca credits the dialogs catalyzed by Sonoita Valley Planning Partnership with serving as a model for the SDCP ranch conservation team:

> The SVPP discussions among [BLM staff members] Jesse [Juen] and Karen [Simms] and the stakeholders in the watershed was certainly a model for what became the ranch conservation element of the Sonoran Desert Conservation Plan. [Finding that] an alliance could be struck between environmentalists and ranchers and the county to conserve large areas was really important. A lot of enduring relationships came out of what happened in the Cienega watershed.

Conserving a significant fraction of the priority biological resources included as part of the Conservation Lands System—riparian areas, habitat, habitat connectivity—required acquisition of ranch land. Funds from the open-space bonds approved by voters in 1997 and 2004 were used to purchase the Bar V, Empirita, Sands, and Clyne ranches in the Cienega watershed; the Marley, Rancho Seco, Sopori, and Canoa ranches in the Upper Santa Cruz and southern Altar Valley watersheds; King and Diamond Bell Ranches and Buckelew Farm in the northern Altar Valley watershed; the Carpenter Ranch in the Tortolita Mountain Preserve; and the Six Bar and A-7 ranches in the San Pedro River Valley.

Acquisition of these ranches created an effective greenbelt surrounding the Tucson metro area, thereby encouraging home builders to concentrate developments closer to the urban core. By doing so, the county was able to preserve open space and to significantly limit the potential budgetary impacts of providing infrastructure and services to developments in remote areas.[60] Huckelberry considered ranch acquisitions a linchpin in implementing the SDCP.[61]

Purchasing the ranches key to meeting CLS goals often involved delicate negotiations. The Arizona Land and Water Trust served as an important partner with the county in approaching ranching families with offers to pur-

TEXT PORTRAIT: TOM SHERIDAN

Tom Sheridan currently holds joint appointments as a research anthropologist at the Southwest Center and professor of anthropology at the University of Arizona. Over a research career spanning more than fifty years, he has conducted ethnographic and ethnohistoric research in the Southwest and northern Mexico.

Since 1997 Sheridan has been involved in land-use politics in Arizona and the Southwest. He has played a major role in both shaping and implementing the Sonoran Desert Conservation Plan, serving as chair of the Ranch Conservation Technical Committee and on Pima County's Conservation Acquisition Commission. The latter group advises the county on which lands to purchase in order to conserve biodiversity, open space, and working ranches. Sheridan also serves on the board of the Altar Valley Conservation Alliance, an organization of ranchers committed to the conservation of open space, biodiversity, and working ranches in the Altar Valley southwest of Tucson.

I grew up in Phoenix, but growing up, I spent many summers up in the Mogollon Rim country. Beginning as a teenager I began backpacking in the Mazatzal Wilderness and other wilderness areas. During those hikes, I'd meet up with ranchers and mountain lion hunters. That didn't interfere with my love of wilderness; it added to it. I thought, "This is wild country and yet there are people back here who are making a living in it." I developed a very different view from that subset of environmentalists who can't stand the sight of cow dung on a hiking trail. I think those early experiences made me sympathetic to ranching. Then it was a small step to my viewing ranching as vital to large-landscape conservation, especially in the American West.

In 1997 I was awarded a fellowship at the Udall Center for Studies in Public Policy at the University of Arizona to look at ranching issues on both sides of the border between Arizona and Sonora, Mexico. While I was at the center, Les Corey and Andy Lorenzi of the Arizona chapter of The Nature Conservancy came to the center following the angry reaction of ranchers to the conservancy's decision to remove all the cattle following their acquisition of the fifty-five-thousand-acre Muleshoe Ranch near Willcox.

The cattlemen believed that the conservancy was aligned with the anti-cattle and anti-rancher policies advocated by many environmental groups ("cattle free by '93"). Les and Andy told us, "We think we got off on the wrong foot with the ranching community. Can you help us mend fences?" We sat down with Les and Andy, along with ranchers Jim Chilton and Clay Parsons from the Altar Valley, and met over dinner. Our discussions led to formation of the Arizona Common Ground Roundtable—an effort to bring environ-

chase ranches using open-space bond funds. Diana Freshwater of the Arizona Land and Water Trust recalls the beginning of what became a fruitful collaboration with the county:

> In 1997, following passage of the first open-space bond initiative, an opportunity arose for us to help Pima County with an acquisition of an area near

mentalists, ranchers, and state and federal land managers together to see if these different groups could find common ground.

Those who chose to take part in the roundtable asked, "What could bring us together instead of tearing us apart?" The major issue that concerned us all was real estate development and land fragmentation, where valleys in Arizona like the San Pedro Valley were being subdivided and carved up. As a result, grazing lands and habitat for both cattle and wildlife were being lost at a rapid rate, and wildlife corridors between mountain ranges were getting blocked and fragmented.

Addressing the issue of fragmentation became an issue that environmentalists, ranchers, and land managers could agree on. Other groups of ranchers were coming together at that time as well: first the Malpai Borderlands Group (see chapter 4) in the early nineties, and then the Altar Valley Conservation Alliance in 1995, and the Diablo Trust up in the Flagstaff area.

At about the same time, Pima County began to develop the Sonoran Desert Conservation Plan. Early on, they identified ranch conservation as an essential element of the plan. Because I was involved with the roundtable, they asked me to chair a technical advisory team focused on ranch-related issues. I later became a member of the committee that made recommendations about the types of land the county should buy to meet the objectives of the ranch conservation, riparian protection, and other land-use goals of the plan.

In the course of my work with the Sonoran Desert Conservation Plan and the Altar Valley Conservation Alliance, I've seen people who are willing to put the time in and to sit down with each other, respect one another, find common ground, and work to achieve common goals. It takes a lot of discipline, but basically, it's a process of developing trust and recognizing that the rancher sitting across from you at the table is not the demon that some of your colleagues in the environmental community say that he or she is. Or that a realtor is an entirely reasonable person.

I've seen it work. There are two things. One, it takes an enormous commitment of time. It happens over years. Two, you have to be really respectful, find what you agree on, concentrate on that, and then agree to disagree about things that might tear a group apart.

At times in my life, wild country is the only thing that's kept me sane. The older I get, the less faith I have in humanity and in the philosophical systems that place us at the center of the natural world. We instead need to see ourselves as part of the natural world, not above it, not separate from it. Large-landscape conservation reflects the issues that I care about most deeply: to try and save as much biodiversity and open country as we can, and to support people who know how to live and make a living from that country sustainably.

Robles Pass, close to Tucson Mountain Park. So that was the beginning of our relationship. Basically, we served as intermediaries. We would meet with the landowner and explain that the County had some funds for open-space acquisition, and they were interested in the parcel that the landowner had. We would then work with the landowner and shepherd them through the process.

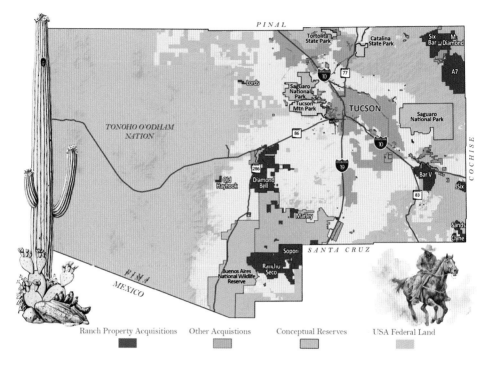

FIGURE 3.19 Properties acquired with open-space bonds approved by Pima County voters in 1997 and 2004, shown in dark blue. In combination with federal and state lands, these properties serve as a broad greenbelt surrounding the Tucson metro area. Land acquisitions from other sources are shown in light blue, while areas targeted for future reserves are shown in pink. Federal lands (national parks and wildlife reserves) are shown in dull green, while state parks are coded light salmon. (Map from Pima County, modified by Stephen Strom.)

Freshwater stresses the importance of gaining the trust of landholders:

> You're often having a discussion with somebody considering selling the thing that is most precious to them. [A successful negotiation] comes down to relationships and a respectful approach. The land trust had developed relationships with some of these ranchers for years. Even so, it took a very careful and empathetic approach, realizing how hard it would be for a landowner to sell their land that had been in their family for, in some cases, generations.

She also notes that in some cases, landholders have an aversion to working with government agencies and find it far more comfortable to work with a land trust: "Because we were representing an agency, but we weren't agency employees, we had a better time of it, I think, and were very successful in in coordinating many, many transactions for the county that protected tens of thousands of acres."

Working ranches acquired by Pima County are managed using adaptive management principles: assessing the health of rangelands, identifying any problems and defining goals, designing a management plan that incorporates these goals, implementing the plan and monitoring its impact, and changing approaches in the face of conditions on the ground.

Rangeland ecologist Dan Robinett, who served as a member of the ranch technical team when the SDCP was forged, says,

> I was really pleased to see that the county, in the development of the Sonoran Desert Conservation Plan, listened to the people on the land, the ranchers, and their concerns about what the county was proposing to do and how to develop the plan to accommodate those concerns. I really like the way that plan progressed and the way the county has used open-space funds to buy properties out there and remove private land from that potential pool of exurban development.

Mountain Parks and Natural Preserves

For the better part of a century, mountain parks have played an important role in Pima County, both conserving natural and cultural resources and providing recreation opportunities for county residents. At present, the county manages three mountain parks: Tucson Mountain to the west of Tucson, Colossal Cave to the east, and Tortolita Mountain to the north. The core of Tucson Mountain and Colossal Cave parks was acquired in the 1920s and 1930s, the former in response to concern that growth might one day overrun the Tucson basin and the latter to both protect a unique natural resource and to attract visitors.[62]

In addition, Pima County has established two natural preserves: Cienega Creek Natural Preserve, established to protect lower Cienega Creek and its riparian areas, and Bingham Cienega Natural Preserve, to protect a spring-fed marsh along the San Pedro River as it courses through the northeast corner of the county.

FIGURE 3.21 Looking northward along Altar Wash. The distinctive profile of the Baboquivari Mountains—sacred to the Tohono O'odham Nation—can be seen on the left. Ranch Seco

FIGURE 3.20 An aerial view of the A-7 Ranch on the east side of the Catalina Mountains above the San Pedro River Valley. Waters flowing through the drainage seen at the center of the image eventually make their way to the San Pedro. (Aerial photo by Stephen Strom.)

(foreground) and Marley Ranch (further north along Altar Wash) are located on the east side of the wash. (Aerial photo by Stephen Strom.)

TEXT PORTRAIT: DAN ROBINETT

Dan Robinett received his undergraduate and graduate degrees in range management from the University of Arizona and has served for thirty years as a range conservationist for the Department of Agriculture Soil Conservation Service (now the National Resources Conservation Service, NRCS). Robinett's research work has focused on the effects of drought, fire, cattle, and climate on grassland ecosystems. His expertise has proven critical to guiding vegetation management in the Cienega watershed and to formulating the ranch component of the Sonoran Desert Conservation Plan. Over the years, Robinett has worked with many ranchers and land managers as a trusted expert to develop grazing plans that are sustainable and economically viable. Since retiring in 2018, he has been running a consulting firm, Robinett Rangeland Resources.

I was born in Illinois but left for Arizona when my dad came out here in the early 1950s, after World War II. I grew up in Tucson on the edge of the city and was always outside; I loved the out-of-doors. From an early age, I thought I wanted to be a forest ranger when I grew up. My mother often referred to me as "her little forest ranger."

I started college at the University of Arizona in 1968. I first thought about majoring in forestry, but I looked around Tucson, and thought, "There's not a lot of trees here." But I loved hunting and fishing, so I started out studying wildlife biology. Near the beginning of my sophomore year, wildlife biology professor Roger Hungerford pulled me aside. He said, "Dan, I've got thirty students in wildlife biology. Each year there are only two jobs available with Arizona Game and Fish Department. I know you'll need a job when you get out. Why don't you go talk to Phil Ogden about range management?" When I went to Phil, he told me, "You've come to the right place because we have a small program. We have one or two people graduate each year, and usually three or four range management jobs available if you're willing to locate somewhere in the West." I said, "I'm willing to go anywhere in the West." So I switched into the range management program.

When I finished school, the Vietnam draft was still going on, I had a low lottery number and was drafted. I went into the army, and when I came back, I was hired quickly by Soil Conservation Service. In 1979 I was offered a job here in Tucson as the area range conservationist, a position that involved managing the range program for southern Arizona. It was a job I really wanted, and I stayed there for the rest of my career, thirty years, until I retired in 2007.

During the 1960s and 1970s, a variety of environmental laws and policies came into being. Livestock grazing came under increased scrutiny during this period, especially on public lands in the West. Federal

Tucson Mountain Park

Spanning twenty thousand acres, Tucson Mountain Park is one of the largest urban natural resource parks in the United States. Its relatively undisturbed Sonoran Desert lands serve as an important biological reserve for a wide variety of plants and animals.

However, the steady westward expansion of Tucson has threatened to render Tucson Mountain Park a biological island. In response, the county has agencies had to make some hard decisions relating to the numbers of animals on public lands and how those lands were grazed. Implementation of those decisions put many ranchers in a defensive posture.

The University of Arizona's Agricultural Extension stepped up and helped mediate disputes between ranchers and the agencies and developed monitoring techniques we could use to look at the impacts of grazing on plant communities and soils. Those of us in the Soil Conservation Service helped ranchers to develop grazing plans by conducting a basic inventory of ecological sites and conditions and providing assessments of alternatives to deal with problems.

Of course, my roots are here in the Sonoita Valley. I think the high-elevation grassland here is unique. It's very similar to the Great Plains grasslands we see in western Kansas, when Linda [Kennedy] and I go back. And then the watershed, bounded by these wonderful sky island mountain ranges: the Santa Ritas, Whetstones, Huachucas, and Rincons. So it's just an incredible place—the diversity of country and the diversity of habitats.

I think another thing special about being here was the opportunity to work with the Sonoita Valley Planning Partnership. It played a major role in framing how public lands in the area should be managed. The hundreds of discussions held by the partnership produced many positive outcomes, of which bringing the public together with the land managers and the ranchers was perhaps the most important. I was pleased to have been able to play a part in it.

There are not many places like the Sonoita Valley left in the Southwest. They're all threatened by growth, groundwater depletion, and increasing temperatures. And I think they're all worth fighting for. The big question today is, how are we going to manage development in the future? What Pima County chose to do through the Sonoran Desert Conservation Plan represented a positive approach to answering that question. I had the privilege to be involved in that effort by serving on the Ranch Conservation Committee.

The SDCP was a successful process because it was inclusive of all sides and respectful of the importance that private and state rangelands as well as federal lands played in the conservation of plants and animal resources. I was really delighted with the way it worked out in the end. As to shaping the future of lands in the West: it's up to us.

---

acquired parcels carefully selected to preserve wildlife corridors to connect the park to other conservation areas and to create a buffer around biologically critical lands within the park. Since 1997 the county has used open-space bond funds to acquire more than one thousand acres to expand park boundaries.

In the foothills of the Tucson Mountains, the county purchased lands that now comprise the Sweetwater Preserve, which both protects a major drainage from the mountains and provides habitat for a number of rare or endangered species.

At Robles Pass near the south end of the park, bond monies were used to acquire land containing an important archaeological site settled in 950 CE by

FIGURE 3.22 Looking down on the forest of saguaro cacti in Tucson Mountain Park. (Aerial photo by Stephen Strom.) ancestors of today's Tohono O'odham peoples. Known by archaeologists as the West Branch Site, it was at one time among the largest Indigenous villages in the Tucson basin.

Some of the other lands purchased recently by the county are intended to serve as buffers around areas of high ecological value. The county has invested in new pedestrian and bike trails and other amenities to channel high-impact recreational use of the park to buffer areas.

Tortolita Mountain Park

Tortolita Mountain Park lies to the north of Tucson along the county line separating Pima and Pinal County. As late as 1990 the Tortolita Mountains lay beyond the periphery of the Tucson metro area. Since then rapid expansion from Tucson northward to Oro Valley and beyond has reached the foothills of the mountains.

The park now provides a welcome relief from suburban sprawl for nearby residents and also serves as an important reserve for the unique and symbiotic ironwood tree–saguaro cactus–palo verde tree plant community. Incorporating alluvial fans and washes located along the mountain flanks in the park protects these areas from encroaching developments. This ensures that they maintain their roles as a natural source for groundwater recharge and flood mitigation.

The county has used open-space bond monies to make strategic investments in both buffer areas around Tortolita Mountain Park to serve as recreational areas for hiking and biking, and in properties that either offer scenic views or preserve important archaeological sites.

In May 2006 county residents approved a one-half-cent sales tax measure dedicated to a variety of transportation-related projects proposed by the Pima County Regional Transportation Authority.[63] During the following fifteen years, the county invested $45 million dollars of transportation au-

FIGURE 3.23 Ironwood–saguaro–palo verde plant community in Ironwood Forest National Monument, west of the Tortolita Mountain Reserve. Branches of the trees comprising the Ironwood Forest are covered with delicate pink flowers that emerge in late spring. Many of these cacti visible started their lives sheltered by ironwood and palo verde trees, which served as "nurse plants." (Aerial photo by Stephen Strom.)

thority funds to design and construct structures designed specifically to facilitate safe passage of wildlife across a landscape highly fragmented by urban growth. Carolyn Campbell of the Coalition for Sonoran Desert Protection recalls initial reactions to the proposal to use transportation authority monies for road under- and overpasses dedicated to wildlife use:

> When I started working on the committee, people looked at me like I was from Mars, asking for money for wildlife bridges. Now, it's just a thing. There is a bridge over Oracle Road. There is an underpass under Oracle Road. There are a lot in north Pima County and Oro Valley, and we have two underpasses

near Kitt Peak [west of Tucson] that we worked with the Tohono O'odham Nation on, and they are designing two bridges down by Kitt Peak for bighorn sheep.[64]

When more funds become available, the county intends to build additional structures to allow wildlife to pass above or below railroads and major roads and to restore vegetation along these manmade corridors to encourage wildlife to follow these crossing structures.[65]

Colossal Cave Mountain Park

In 1989 the county initiated efforts to establish a county park surrounding Colossal Cave by acquiring La Posta Quemada Ranch. The ranch and other parcels acquired with 1997 and 2004 open-space bonds are now part of Colossal Cave Mountain Park. These purchases have preserved important habitat for the endangered lesser long-nosed and a number of other bat spe-

FIGURE 3.24 (*top*) Wildlife crossing under Oracle Road, north of Tucson. (Elizabeth Duepree, supported by LightHawk.) (*bottom*) Artist conception of a wildlife overpass connecting the Tortolita and Catalina Mountains. (Coalition for Sonoran Desert Protection.)

cies, protected a rich riparian area along Agua Verde Creek, and expanded a wildlife corridor connecting Colossal Cave Mountain Park with the Cienega Creek Natural Preserve.

The cave itself, along with adjacent recreation areas, is leased and managed separately. A tourist destination since the 1930s, Colossal Cave and the surrounding mountain park attract more than one hundred thousand visitors annually. While many come to explore the cave and its haunting limestone formations, the park also provides extensive opportunities for hiking and horseback riding.

The Arizona Trail passes through both the Cienega Creek Natural Preserve and Colossal Cave Mountain Park. In the future, the county hopes to acquire land along the trail to establish a broad natural corridor connecting the Rincon Mountains to the northern end of Las Cienegas National Conservation Area. If Pima County succeeds, Dean Bibles's and Chuck Huckelberry's vision of a wildlife corridor between the Mexican border and the Catalina Mountains will be one step closer to being realized.

Cienega Creek Natural Preserve

Earlier we related the importance of the county's efforts to use flood control district funds in 1986 to acquire four thousand acres along a twelve-mile stretch of lower Cienega Creek. Indeed, acquisition of the lands that would later comprise the Cienega Creek Natural Preserve represented a seminal moment for the county's conservation efforts.

Since then the county has sought to expand the preserve in service of enhancing its roles in supporting natural flood control, healthy riparian habitat, recharge of a key aquifer serving the Tucson area, and wildlife migration from upper Cienega Creek to Colossal Cave Mountain Park.

Properties acquired with open-space bonds and flood control district monies now protect riparian woodland along a main tributary to Cienega Creek—Agua Verde Creek—and provide habitat for twenty-seven of the fifty-six priority vulnerable species identified in the Conservation Lands System as critically in need of protection.

In order to further protect lower Cienega Creek and ensure that the preserve continues to serve its essential role in the Conservation Lands System, the county acquired the Bar V and Empirita ranches. The former protects the area surrounding Davidson Creek and Davidson Canyon, while the latter protects Cienega Creek upstream from the preserve.

Access to the preserve is limited in order to minimize human impact on its sensitive biological resources; visitors must obtain a permit from the county in order to enter the area. But once there, hikers have access to a world apart from the desert: one of the last remaining riparian areas in southern Arizona, where dense groves of cottonwoods and desert willows shade Cienega Creek.

Bingham Cienega Natural Preserve

The San Pedro River supports a rich variety of aquatic, amphibian, and mammalian species and serves as one of the most important avian flyways in North America. In view of its extraordinary biological importance, the county has taken a number of steps to preserve the area surrounding the river and its surrounding riparian area, despite the fact that only a short segment of the San Pedro passes through Pima County.

Using open-space bond funds, the county purchased three hundred acres along the river to preserve Bingham Cienega, a spring-fed marsh along the San Pedro. The Bingham Cienega Preserve is located in far northeast corner of the county.

To further protect the San Pedro River corridor, the county purchased two large ranches. The first was the twelve-thousand-acre Six Bar Ranch

FIGURE 3.25 Davidson Creek passing through the Bar V Ranch. (Aerial photo by Stephen Strom.)

located along the east flanks of the Catalina Mountains. Drainages from the Catalinas pass through the Six Bar on their way to the San Pedro and support groves of cottonwood and sycamores, while the bajadas extending from the mountain sides to the San Pedro Valley are covered with dense saguaro forests. Owing to the broad range of habitats within its boundaries, much of the ranch was classified as a core biological area within the Conservation Lands System. The Six Bar serves as home to a number of priority vulnerable species, including the lesser long-nosed bat and desert box turtle. It is still a working ranch, managed using adaptive management protocols by a local family under a ranch management agreement with Pima County.

The second is the A-7 Ranch, which spans forty-one thousand acres and is located southeast of the Six Bar, following the east flank of the Catalina and Rincon Mountains along the San Pedro River. Oak woodlands occupy the upper elevations of the ranch, while desert grasslands populate the valleys. Riparian areas are found along the San Pedro River and in some canyon bottoms. The A-7 also occupies a biological core area of the Conservation Lands System. A local ranch family now manages the A-7 under a ranch management agreement with Pima County. Pima County also has a staff person living on the ranch who serves as a ranch liaison for the lower San

Pedro ranches, managing projects, monitoring the health of the land, and providing general oversight.

Both the A-7 and Six Bar ranches contain significant archaeological sites, including Alder Wash, Second Canyon, Davis Ranch, and Reeve Ruin. Excavations along river indicate that areas around the San Pedro near the A-7 and Bar V have been occupied for more than ten thousand years.

Together, the ranch properties provide an unfragmented wildlife corridor connecting the Rincon and Catalina Mountains with the Galiuro Mountains to the east and also serve as a link between the Chihuahuan Desert, Sonoran Desert, and Madrean Archipelago ecoregions.

Cultural and Historic Resources

Over a period spanning more than ten thousand years, first Indigenous, then Hispanic and Euro-American peoples have called Pima County home. Citizens of Pima County value their collective cultural heritage, just as they do the county's natural resources.[66]

To recognize and preserve the county's cultural heritage, the SDCP steering committee charged a cultural resource team to compile an inventory of important historic and cultural properties throughout the county.[67] They ultimately identified two hundred "priority cultural resources."

Since the adoption of the SDCP, the county has acquired, preserved, or otherwise protected a range of cultural resources: prehistoric and historic, urban and rural. Ten major sites were purchased, and some restored, using voter approved bonds.[68] Archaeological sites acquired for preservation were identified in collaboration with the Tohono O'odham Nation.

Preservation of these cultural and historic resources serve as tangible reminders of the amalgam of peoples who have contributed to the vibrant culture of Pima County.

Education and Public Outreach

Public engagement was key to shaping and adopting the Sonoran Desert Conservation Plan, and support from Pima County voters was essential to providing funds for acquisitions essential to achieving SDCP goals. However, the SDCP is now more than twenty years old, and responsibility for advancing the legacy of its founders—balancing environmental protection

FIGURE 3.26 (*a*) Students studying seeds in an Environmental Education program by the Pima County Natural Resources, Parks and Recreation Division. (*b*) A guided evening nature walk for an Environmental Education program. (Pima County Natural Resources, Parks and Recreation.)

and economic vitality—is passing into the hands of a new generation. In service of both educating that new generation and continuing to engage the energies of citizens of all ages, framers of the SDCP mandated establishment of an Environmental Education section in the Pima County Natural Resources, Parks and Recreation Department.[69] The mission of the section is to promote awareness of and foster understanding of environmental issues and to facilitate citizen participation in activities that deepen understanding of how natural and cultural resources contribute to the vitality of Pima County.

Since 2006 the Environmental Education team has engaged more than three hundred thousand people in a wide variety of programs: field studies carried out by K-12 pupils, wildlife watching activities, nature walks, a multidisciplinary art and science school program (the Living River), and a variety of community events.[70]

The Nature Conservancy's Peter Warren underlines the importance of Pima County's commitment to environmental education. "Thinking about the conservation challenges ahead, one of the biggest ones is that people can't care about something that they don't know about. [To get] people to care about something, to protect it, to conserve habitat or whatever, first they've got to learn about it, understand it, and then develop some kind of personal connection from that. So early education in the natural world is so important."

In person programs are a mainstay of Environmental Education's activities. Environmental Education staff involve preschool children, K-12 students, and adults in educational sessions held in county parks, schools, and community centers. Environmental Education also supports a robust website and a series of do-it-yourself education kits that reach approximately 1,200 people each month.

Environmental Education Program Manager Julie Strom echoes Peter Warren:

> Getting people out [in one of our parks], seeing what it is we're doing and why we're doing it and leaving with a sense that this is a place worthy of protection [is a really important element of our efforts]. [In some programs, we also give] them a hint as to how they can add to protecting the environment, whether that is coming out to remove [invasive] buffelgrass or just being a worthy spokesperson for what it is that we do or the space they visited.

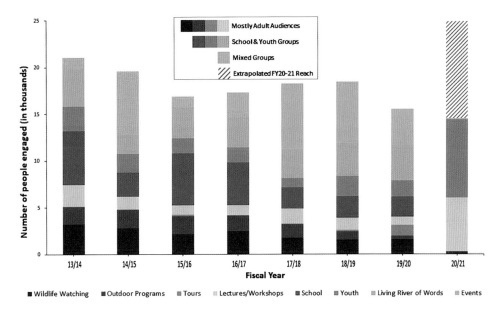

FIGURE 3.27 Participants in Pima County's Environmental Education Program for Pima County from fiscal years 2013–14 to 2020–21. Note that FY 2020–21 participation was extrapolated from that of the first seven months of the year. (Pima County Environmental Education Program.)

We have birding and nature walks and hikes. We have lizard walks. We started what we call WYSIWYG walks [what you see is what you get], where the idea is that you're not trying to get from point A to point B or talking about a specific topic. Rather, we're going to come out, and together as a group we're going to be looking around and discussing the things that we see and making connections that way.

In that same vein, Environmental Education staff member Christine Hoekenga describes "an activity we do with the kids in some of our programs where we just have them spend ten or fifteen minutes, which can feel like an eternity, observing with their senses and thinking about the things they notice, the things that they wonder about, and the things that they're reminded of being there."

Hoekenga credits the framers of the SDCP with having the vision to mandate creation of, and ongoing support for an environmental education program: "The recognition that [this program] needed to exist and needed to be funded, and needed to be staffed is one of the things about that plan that I think is unique or certainly rare."

Adoption of the Sonoran Desert Conservation Plan

In 2001 the Pima County Board of Supervisors approved an update of the County Comprehensive Land-Use Plan (CLUP)—required of all counties in Arizona by the Growing Smarter Initiative approved by state voters in 1998. The Pima County comprehensive plan adopted as its centerpiece conservation principles and land-use policies embodied in the SDCP's Conservation Lands System. Approval of the CLUP by the supervisors was accompanied by a resolution of cooperation adopted by the Tohono O'odham Nation, whose lands lie within county boundaries.

By adopting the plan, Pima County achieved something exceptional: combining a strategy for protecting natural and cultural resources with a land-use plan to guide future development. As Julia Fonseca notes, Most other conservation or land use "approaches try to deal with one thing at a time. What was remarkable about the SDCP was that it didn't set narrow parameters on the scope" of the plan.

Moreover, the plan embraced an undeniable reality—Pima County will grow. To quote Administrator Huckelberry: "The SDCP is not about *whether* Pima County will continue to grow; it is about *where* the county grows." To add to his point, the SDCP also provides an overarching vision for *how* the county grows. As a testament to the planning process's success in bridging what were once chasm-like divisions between conservation advocates and developers, Bill Arnold, a prominent local property rights advocate, was quoted in *Time Magazine* saying, "We believed it was better to be at one table rather than have a huge fight. Everyone emerged as a winner in the end."

Gayle Hartmann notes the importance of strong support from the Pima County Board of Supervisors throughout the SDCP planning process: "The board, bless their hearts, they really bought into this and got a lot of reinforcement from the public. It really comes back to [county voters] electing a good group of supervisors." Carolyn Campbell picks up from Hartmann: "Raúl Grijalva," who chaired the board during the critical period between 2000 and 2002, "was pretty much the linchpin in all this, pushing the supervisors in the right direction."

Since 2001 the Sonoran Desert Conservation Plan has guided conservation of important natural areas and informed decisions regarding expenditures of open-space bonds and other public funds used to advance the goals of the six key elements of the plan.[71]

Ten years after the plan was adopted, County Administrator Chuck Huckelberry offered these reflections on the plan, its import, and its future:

> Transformative ideas seldom emerge fully formed. Ideas that lead to lasting change typically are shaped over long and, at times, arduous discourse. And as was the case for Pima County, effective change required thoughtful collaboration among groups that may have started out as adversaries, but through fair and open dialog ended up coming together in the interest of a common good.
>
> The goals of the Sonoran Desert Conservation Plan continue to be at the forefront of county land-use and environmental planning efforts. Our land acquisition programs are an extension of the various policies that, cumulatively, were derived from the plan's development process. . . . [Neither] the Sonoran Desert Conservation Plan nor our land acquisition programs emerged fully formed from the vision of any single individual or from a specific moment in time. Instead, they emerged from intense public debate, determination, hard work, political will, patience, and an enlightened electorate. The plan is organic, not static, and its overarching vision will continue to further this community's values.

The SDCP has received numerous local, national, and international awards, including for Best Plan and Multi-Agency Coordination (Arizona Planning Association, 2001), Distinguished Leadership (Arizona Planning Association, 2001), GIS Approach to Reserve Design (ESRI User Conference, 2001), and Public Education (Arizona Planning Association, 2002).

Former secretary of the interior Bruce Babbitt was effusive in his praise of the Sonoran Desert Conservation Plan:

> I'm a big fan of the Sonoran Desert Conservation Plan. I think Chuck Huckelberry is a real hero for putting that all together and growing it across the last thirty years. It originally started off as a reaction to an endangered species issue involving the cactus ferruginous pygmy owl, and what they've done is to grow it in a remarkable way. It's a model example of habitat planning under the En-

dangered Species Act and related federal conservation programs administered by Fish and Wildlife Service.

Conservation biologist Ron Pulliam, who served in the Interior Department during the Clinton administration, echoes Babbitt: "The plan that Pima County has put together is one of the very best in the country."

The Future of the Sonoran Desert Conservation Plan

Fulfilling the goals of the Sonoran Desert Conservation Plan will require acquisition of additional conservation lands. Before 2014 Pima County citizens voted to support multiple open-space bond issues, most passing with significant majorities. In November of that year, they rejected a package of seven bond propositions that would have funded a variety of new and improved public facilities throughout the region.[72] As of this writing, the county has not put forward another proposition seeking funding to support any of the six elements of the SDCP.

Nevertheless, the SDCP has achieved extraordinary success in preserving and protecting biologically sensitive lands, riparian areas, ranches, and historic and cultural sites in eastern Pima County. That success is perhaps best illustrated by figure 3.19, which depicts areas acquired by the county over the years. Combined with federally administered national parks, national monuments, and national forests, the amount of connected, biologically important land is impressive.

However, a quick glance at a land-use map suggests a potential long-term threat to SDCP goals: auctioning of blocks of state land within and adjacent to key elements of the Conservation Lands System. In a 2021 conversation, now-retired county administrator Chuck Huckelberry was blunt: "The single greatest threat to the whole issue of connecting the open spaces—it's really state lands." Huckelberry continues by noting that Pima County has the option of "inhibiting [state land] transition to other uses by not putting in infrastructure that facilitates urbanization or anything dealing with development. To that extent, you can basically forestall development for a long period of time because the land won't be marketable."

Julia Fonseca comments, "Mr. Huckelberry is trying to guide the State Land Department toward investing in areas that make sense from multiple

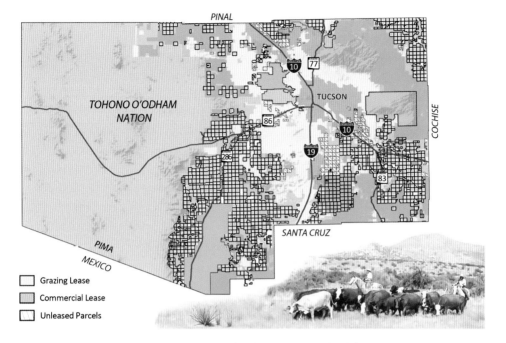

FIGURE 3.28 Arizona School Trust land sections (one-square-mile blocks) superposed on the SDCP ranch lands map (fig. 3.18). State land sections leased for grazing are shown in light blue. Those leased for commercial activities are shown in light red, while unleased parcels are illustrated with light blue cross-hatching. Note the importance of state trust lands to the future of conservation efforts in eastern Pima County. (Map of state trust lands courtesy of Arizona Land Department; underlying map from Pima County, modified by Stephen Strom.)

standpoints to develop" and to avoid biologically sensitive areas. "He can tell you a lot more about how Pima County has an economic development plan and how the State Land Department can play a role in that but it's not an easy relationship."

As discussed in chapter 2, in the judgment of the Arizona Supreme Court, the State Land Department is precluded from trading trust land parcels for federal or other lands, even in cases where such trades might provide the state with lands favorable for development.[73] Instead, all trust lands must be disposed of in public auctions.

Most of the state trust land located within the Conservation Lands System is leased by ranchers. Without continuing access to trust lands, nearly all ranching operations in Pima County would no longer be viable. As a result, ranchers and the Arizona Cattle Growers Association would hardly look kindly on any effort by the State Land Department to auction trust lands adjacent to major livestock operations.

Both conservationists and ranchers for the moment can take some solace in the fact that the State Land Department disposes of land at a rate of only a few thousand acres per year, largely in the Phoenix area, where sale of state lands yield significant returns for the school trust fund.

But as they look to the future, those most closely involved in shaping land use in Pima County share deep apprehension about the fate of state trust lands. Gayle Hartmann, who has been an active participant in conservation efforts for almost fifty years comments "I have to say, that in spite of all the accomplishments in Pima County, I'm very concerned. As Chuck [Huckelberry has] said, 'the elephant in the room is the state trust land.' If we can't keep a large portion of that out of development, we're doomed."

SYNOPSIS

OVERVIEW

Pima County spans more than nine thousand square miles of south central Arizona. Its mountains, grasslands, and deserts support a rich diversity of plant, reptilian, mammalian, and avian life. .

The overwhelming majority of the county's 1.2 million people live in and around Tucson. Since 1950 the county's population has increased by 3 percent annually: doubling every twenty-five years.

Each year, developments consume ten square miles of desert land.

CATALYSTS FOR ACTION

In the 1970s county residents became alarmed by the growth of the Tucson metro area. The Sonoran Desert landscape was disappearing at a rate of twenty acres per day. Wildlife habitat was being destroyed and movement corridors fragmented.

Water was pumped without limit, lowering the water table in some areas by more than two hundred feet. Rich riparian areas disappeared, once-broad rivers were confined to narrow channels, and developments crept ever closer to flood-plains.

In 1983 floods provided a stark reminder of the potential for significant environmental damage posed by unconstrained growth.

In 1996 the cactus ferruginous pygmy owl was listed by the U.S. Fish and Wildlife Service as an endangered species. The owl listing threatened to impact home construction in Pima County, leading county leaders to explore how the Endangered Species Act might be used to forge a plan balancing growth and environmental values.

MEETING THE CHALLENGES

After the 1983 flood, the Pima County supervisors began to purchase land for watershed protection and flood mitigation.

In response to the 1996 listing of the pygmy owl as an endangered species, the county adopted a regional land-use plan spanning 5.9 million acres: the Sonoran Desert Conservation Plan.

The plan built on the foundation of parks, open-space expansion, and watershed protection begun in the 1980s.

The SDCP was designed to establish and protect biological corridors, restore riparian areas, conserve working ranches, create and expand mountain parks, and preserve historic and cultural sites.

Central to the plan was the Conservation Lands System, a county-wide system of biological reserves that conserve intact ecosystems and retain functional habitat corridors.

Developers who propose rezoning in biologically critical land must set aside conservation land either on-site or elsewhere.

The Conservation Lands System provides a prioritized set of high-value open-space and conservation properties to acquire outright.

The plan met the requirements of the Endangered Species Act while providing clear guidelines for further development in the county.

Pima County voters approved open-space bond issues, which provided more than $200 million to acquire ranches and other properties selected to meet the goals of the SDCP.

ELEMENTS OF SUCCESS

- Leadership by Pima County who recognized the value of regional land-use planning
- Seed funding from the Department of Interior during the 1990s
- Extensive engagement of a broad group of citizens and stakeholders in shaping the SDCP
- Early involvement of a facilitator during the SDCP planning process; coordination of the planning process by a uniquely talented and charismatic individual
- Proactive and frequent communication with the public; hundreds of open meetings with discussion results disseminated broadly
- Participation by experts from the University of Arizona, NGOs, and scientists from throughout the country who provided critical background information
- Involvement of land trusts in negotiating purchases of ranches and other open-space lands

ACCOMPLISHMENTS

- Identifying areas essential to connections between critical habitats, along with specific conservation targets
- Achieving public support for open-space bond issues totaling more than $200 million
- Purchasing key conservation targets included in the Conservation Lands System
- Keeping purchased ranches as working ranches with management plans for land use
- Protecting 230,000 acres; expanding and creating new parks in the Tucson metro area
- Investing in the restoration and protection of riparian areas
- Developing and funding an environmental education program and public outreach effort
- Preserving hundreds of cultural and historic resources

FUNDING

- Seed funding from the Department of Interior for meeting organization and facilitation
- More than $200 million from open-space bond issues
- Funds from federal agencies for restoration work

ONGOING CHALLENGES AND THREATS

- Continued growth pressures
- The potential for development on state trust land
- Climate change

CHAPTER 4

■ ■ ■ ■ ■ ■ ■ ■

The Malpai
Borderlands Group

Only a community can live a way of life into being and then bequeath it to succeeding generations.

— JAMES A. CORBETT, *SANCTUARY FOR ALL LIFE*

The Natural Setting

The land the Malpai Borderlands Group is committed to stewarding is vast: an area almost 900,000 acres (about 1,400 square miles) in size, spanning southwestern New Mexico and southeastern Arizona. The landscape encompasses the rugged, forest-covered peaks of the Animas and Peloncillo Mountains, oak woodland hillsides, green riparian corridors, and grasslands stretching for miles along the Animas and San Bernardino Valleys. Its topography is characteristic of the Basin and Range province, with valley floors located between 3,000 and 5,000 feet above sea level and mountaintops reaching elevations of 7,000 to 8,500 feet.[1]

Large diurnal and seasonal temperature variations reflect the region's aridity and topography. In the valleys, summertime highs can reach 95 degrees Fahrenheit with lows in the seventies, while wintertime temperatures typically range from 65 to below 30; the temperatures atop the mountains are 15 to 20 degrees cooler than those in the valley.[2]

Precipitation patterns are typical of its location within the Madrean ecoregion. The valley floors on average receive twelve inches annually, while mountain peaks may receive up to twenty inches per year. Summer monsoon rains provide the majority of annual precipitation, with winter storms accounting for the remainder. However, precipitation in the borderlands can be fickle. Rain and snowfall from winter storms can vary greatly from year to year, and while summer rains are more predictable, they too can be ca-

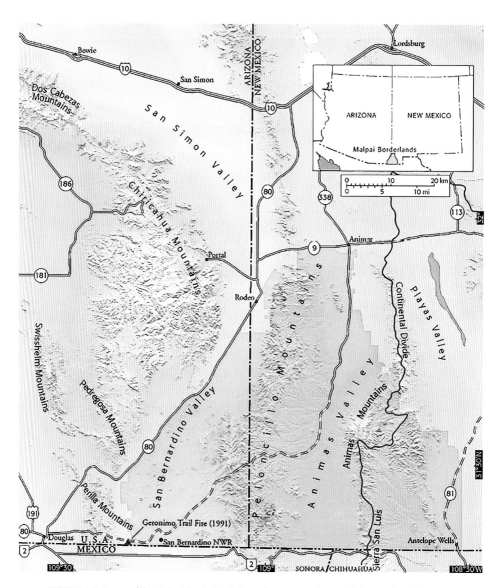

FIGURE 4.1 A map of the Malpai Borderlands (green) superposed on a relief map of southeast Arizona and southwest New Mexico. (Adapted from Nathan F. Sayre, *Working Wilderness: The Malpai Borderlands Group Story and the Future of the Western Range* [Tucson: Rio Nuevo Press, 2006].)

pricious. The name Malpai owes its origin to early Hispanic ranchers, who called these lands Mal Pais, or "badlands," perhaps in recognition of the challenges of maintaining secure livelihoods in lands where decades of drought could follow years of bounteous rains.[3]

The range of precipitation, temperature, and elevation found within the Malpai provides a wide gamut of ecological niches for a broad array of plant and animal communities drawn from the Rocky Mountains to the north and the Sierra Madre to the south, and from the Chihuahuan Desert to the east and the Sonoran Desert to the west. As a consequence, the diversity and richness of plant and animal species in the region is extraordinary, earning the borderlands designation as a biological hotspot. Surveys of the region have catalogued 400 species of vertebrates, including 264 birds, 55 reptiles and amphibians, and 80 mammals. The borderlands serve as winter homes for most North American grassland bird species and support the highest diversity of bees in the nation.

The Malpai region is home to some of the American Southwest's last remaining extensive expanses of native grasslands. The Animas Valley alone contains more than fifty species of native perennial grasses. Among the most common of the native grasses are blue grama, sideoats grama, plains lovegrass, cane beardgrass, and at lower elevations, tobosa grass.

The valleys of the borderlands as well provide exceptional habitat for a wide range of grassland specialists, and their generally unfragmented state furnishes movement corridors more than fifty miles in length for iconic wide-ranging mammals such as the northern jaguar, black bear, and mountain lion. Embedded within the grasslands are riparian areas and wetlands that support extensive amphibian populations, including threatened species such as the Chiricahua leopard frog.

The fauna and flora of the grasslands and uplands of the borderlands supported human populations for at least the ten thousand years before European arrival: from Paleo-Indian hunters (10,000–7000 BCE), through Archaic period foragers (7000 to 1500 BCE), through the first farming communities (1500 BCE to 200 CE), to more established settlements and villages (200 to 1500 CE).

Historical Background

The first Europeans to enter the area were the Spanish explorers Fray Marcos de Niza and Francisco Vázquez de Coronado, who led expeditions through

FIGURE 4.2 West side of the Peloncillo Mountains after the summer monsoons in 2022. (Photo by Stephen Strom.)

the Malpai in 1539 and 1540–42, respectively. However, it wasn't until the end of the sixteenth century that the Spanish attempted to establish permanent settlements and cattle ranches in the area. Their efforts were largely thwarted by Apache raids, which continued through the eighteenth century and late nineteenth century. Life in the borderlands remained precarious and settlements sparse despite the establishment of multiple presidios in the borderlands region, and assumption of political control of the region by Mexico after the 1821 revolution.

The acquisition by the United States of the bootheel of New Mexico and lands south of the Gila River to the present southern border of Arizona through the 1854 Gadsden Purchase presaged major changes in the Malpai Borderlands. An early arrival to the region described the newly acquired lands in southwestern New Mexico and southeastern Arizona as they appeared in the mid-1850s:

The valley bottoms were covered by a dense growth of perennial sacaton grass, oftentimes as high as the head of horseman and so thick and tall that cattle, horses, and men were easily concealed by it. The uplands were well covered with a variety of nutritious grasses, such as the perennial black grama, and the many annuals that spring into growth during the summer rainy season. The abundant vegetation, both on highlands and in valley bottoms, restrained the torrential storms of the region so that there was no erosion in valley bottoms. Instead the rainfall soaked into the soil and grew grass. Sloughs and marshy places were common along the San Simon, the San Pedro, the Santa Cruz and other streams, and even beaver were abundant in places.[4]

When news of seemingly limitless grasslands circulated, the region appeared ready to draw in a substantial wave of settlers. However, the outbreak of the Civil War (1861–65) briefly halted westward migration. Once the war concluded, a surge of fresh settlers, in search of new homes and opportu-

FIGURE 4.3 Storm over the Animas Mountains, with mixed forbs and grasses in the foreground. (Photo by Stephen Strom.)

FIGURE 4.4 Grasslands in the Animas Valley viewed from the Krentz Ranch after an unusually active summer monsoon season in 2022. The round, grass-covered hills (*left*) are volcanic cinder cones, a signpost of relatively recent volcanic activity in the region. (Photo by Stephen Strom.)

nities, set out for the Southwest. John Ross captures the spirit of the time as follows: "Most Americans embraced the West as an untapped Eden, not as the barren edge bounding the American nation, but as the very place in which it would fulfill its national destiny."[5]

An early settler of the borderlands, Joe Yarborough, noted in wonder that as he rode from El Paso, Texas, to Animas, New Mexico, in 1880 that his stirrups were never out of the grass. John Pleasant Gray, founder of the Gray Ranch (later the Diamond A) wrote that "going eastward from Tombstone [Arizona], you cross the Dragoon Mountains into the Sulphur Springs Valley, thence through the Chiricahua Mountains into the San Simon Valley of New Mexico, and right there under the shadow of Animas Peak was a big green meadow of about a thousand acres which was at the time covered with red top clover and watered by numerous springs. . . . This was the spot we had picked for a cattle ranch and it seemed just right for the purpose." And Henry Brock, an early cow boss at the Diamond A, captured the grassland bounty: "I've seen it down along the border and the southern end of the Playas valley . . . when the wind would just blow it, and it would sweep around just like an oat field. You couldn't see the ground at all."[6]

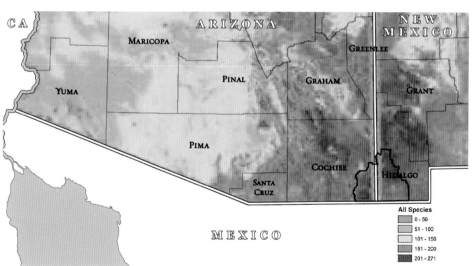

FIGURE 4.5 Species richness in southeast Arizona and southwest New Mexico. Superposed on the map are county lines in Arizona and New Mexico along with an outline (heavy black) of the Malpai Borderlands region. (Map by Stephen Strom, with data from K. G. Boykin et al. "A National Approach for Mapping and Quantifying Habitat-Based Biodiversity Metrics Across Multiple Spatial Scales," *Ecological Indicators* 33 [2013]: 139–47, https://www.epa.gov/sites/default/files/2015-09 /documents/boykin_et_al_2013_mapping_biodiversity_metrics.pdf.)

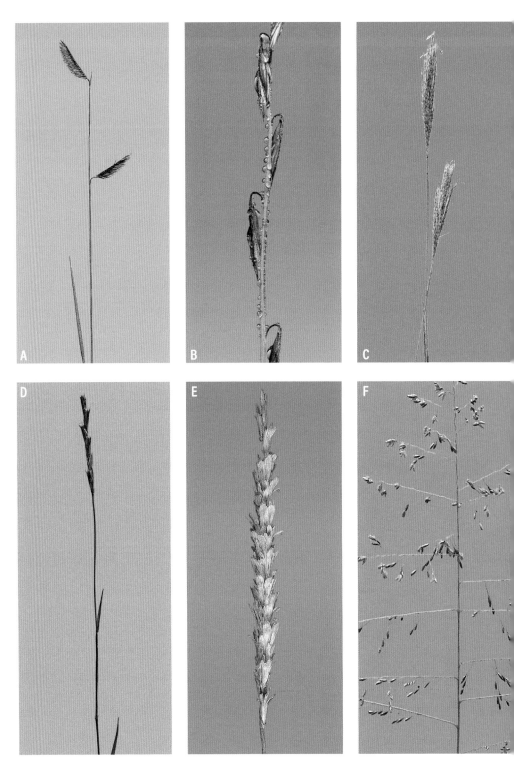

FIGURE 4.6 (*a*) Blue grama; (*b*) sideoats grama; (*c*) cane beardgrass; (*d*) curly mesquite; (*e*) tobosa; (*f*) plains lovegrass. (Photos by Stephen Strom.)

FIGURE 4.7 Chiricahua leopard frog. (Jim Rorabaugh, U.S. Fish and Wildlife Service.)

At first, ranchers and cattlemen from Texas and Colorado began to run enormous herds of cattle through the open rangelands. By the end of the 1870s, venture capitalists from the eastern United States and Europe started to use their financial power to acquire vast tracts of rangeland for industrial-scale ranching. By 1880 foreign syndicates grazed enormous herds of cattle on twenty million acres of grasslands in the American Southwest. The era of the cattle baron had begun.

Markets for cattle burgeoned as demand from local settlements, mining towns, and nearby military posts exploded. The completion of railroads linking the borderlands to a continental network toward the end of the 1870s and in the 1880s provided the means of transporting cattle from range to slaughterhouses to distant markets without the time and expense of months-long cattle drives. More and more cattle foraged on the range-lands to satisfy the demands for beef by families throughout the country. During the peak of the cattle baron era, the southern Arizona and New Mexico grasslands were home to more than ten million cattle, well more than an order of magnitude above the numbers those lands could support in the best of times.[7]

A belief in the endless bounty of these arid-land grasslands was shattered in 1891 and 1892, when a summer drought decreased available forage, leading to a precipitous decline in livestock numbers, and ultimately, the end of the cattle baron era:

> The summer of 1891 had been unusually dry in southern New Mexico and in fact all across the Southwest. In Grant County and on west into Arizona, cattle already in poor condition went into the winter on heavily overstocked ranges that were shorter of grass than cattlemen had seen them in many years. On top of that it was a mild winter that lacked the moisture needed to bring on spring feed. No rain of any consequence came; ranges lay bare and sere, and cattle began dying by the thousands.[8]

By the end of the nineteenth century, large portions of the once-rich and dense grasslands of southwestern New Mexico and southeastern Arizona had been altered dramatically.

Environmental Damage to the Borderlands Region
Overgrazing

Intensive grazing affected the extent of grass and forb coverage, the mix of vegetative species, and the physical state of grasslands. As large herds of cattle consumed available grasses, they left the land bare, providing a niche for woody species to become established. With grass coverage reduced, cattle started consuming woody plants and spread mesquite and shrub seeds as they roamed denuded grasslands. As a result, shrubs and woody plants began to take over grasslands.

As patches of grass between shrubs and woody plants decreased in size, it became more difficult for lightning to ignite grasslands fires and for blazes, once ignited, to propagate. As a result, the frequency and intensity of landscape-wide grassland fires was reduced, thereby greatly diminishing an essential natural source of shrub control. In some places, once-plentiful grasslands morphed into shrubland.[9]

With little grass available to slow surface runoff, water from summer monsoons rushed over the landscape. Waters that once infiltrated gentle grassland slopes no longer recharged the water table in the valleys below but instead carried off the fertile soil critical to regenerating grasses and incised the hillsides, creating gullies and arroyos.[10]

Peter Warren of The Nature Conservancy, who has worked in the borderlands for more than thirty years, well captures the destruction wrought between the late 1870s and the end of the 1890s:

FIGURE 4.8 Mesquite takes over a grassland following extensive grazing. (*top*) Santa Rita Experimental Range, 1903; (*bottom*) same landscape, 1941. (Santa Rita Experimental Range Photo Archive, U.S. Forest Service.)

Following the drought years, researchers from the University of Arizona interviewed some of the ranchers who had been out there during that time in the 1890s when this big drought hit. They estimated that half to a quarter of the livestock on the southern Arizona ranges starved to death in the mid-1890s. As they were starving to death, they were just ripping out any grass they could find. So there was a tremendous amount of damage done in the 1890s. That was when the big period of arroyo cutting started. That was the time all these wagon roads were going in up and down the valleys, and when it rained, water rushing through the ruts triggered a lot of down-cutting, which drained the water table in some of these sacaton grass bottoms.... I think the level of destruction in the 1890s is something that's hard to grasp. We are still suffering from the damage that was done then.[11]

While the extreme overgrazing of the 1880s and 1890s proved disastrous to much of the grassland in the Southwest, those that initially escaped major damage nevertheless continued to degrade over the ensuing century despite increasing efforts to better match herd sizes to the carrying capacity of the land. Many factors, both human- and natural-caused, continue to threaten grasslands in the borderlands.[12]

Disruption of Natural Fire Regimes

Before the arrival of settlers in the borderlands region during the latter half of the nineteenth century, studies of soil sediment carbon content and tree fire scars indicate that naturally occurring fires, ignited by lightning strikes, took place at intervals of five to ten years.

Once large herds of cattle were introduced in the region, ranchers began to extinguish grassland fires to protect their livestock. During the twentieth century, policies adopted by the Bureau of Land Management and the U.S. Forest Service required that fires on grasslands managed by these agencies also be extinguished promptly.

Absence of fire leads to an increase in shrubs and woody plants. Frequent fires prevent the establishment of shrubs by rendering their seeds unviable, as well as by killing young shrubs and woody plants before they can grow and spread new seeds. As a consequence of fire suppression over the past 140 years, mesquite, creosote, acacia, tarbush, and juniper brush have propagated widely in regions where grass once dominated.[13]

Once shrubs begin to take over more than a third of a grassland area, topsoil erosion by water and wind make it difficult to impossible to reestablish healthy grass populations, even if shrubs are removed. Rangeland ecologists who study historical grassland conditions have found that the current dominance of woody plants in the grasslands of southwest New

FIGURE 4.9 In late May and early June 2022, the Foster Fire burned through more than 7,500 acres of oak savanna grassland in the Peloncillo Mountains. By early September, the fire-charred land was covered with a rich mix of grass and forbs. By contrast, the oaks and shrubs exhibit significant fire damage (red leaves, bare limbs and stalks). (Photo by Stephen Strom.)

Mexico and southeast Arizona has no precedent in the past five thousand years.

As grasslands morph into shrublands, food, water, and shelter for avian, aquatic, and mammalian species dependent on grassland ecosystems are reduced or no longer available. As a result, both the number and diversity of those species decrease dramatically. Although we now recognize the importance of fire in maintaining grasslands, it is difficult to implement policies that allow natural fires in healthy grasslands due to their proximity to expanding exurban developments. It is also challenging to introduce controlled burns in areas where we can still limit the spread of shrubs and woody plants: ranchers need to protect their livestock, and nearby exurban residents want natural fires extinguished and are leery of controlled burns.

Soil Erosion and Formation of Gullies and Arroyos

The extensive overgrazing of the borderlands region during the cattle baron era began to degrade once-rich grasslands. As noted, during the drought of 1891 and 1892, hungry cattle consumed all available forage, leaving the ground bare and exposed in many areas. With the resumption of the more normal summer monsoon rain in the following years, water rushed over the denuded lands, stripping soil and incising the landscape with gullies and deepening channels. In dry periods, wind took over the role of water in removing topsoil crucial for supporting grasses, forbs, and the fauna that depend on a healthy mix of grassland flora.

Droughts in the 1930s and 1950s accelerated erosional processes as vegetative cover decreased, and absent plant roots, the soil became less porous and more susceptible to runoff during monsoon rains. If anything, drought conditions in the Southwest have become more dire over the past two decades, and although most grassland ranges are not overgrazed today, they are unfortunately still susceptible to erosion as well as gully and channel formation.

Climate Fluctuations and Long-Term Climate Change

Since the arrival of large numbers of U.S. settlers in the nineteenth century, temperatures in the Southwest have risen by 3 degrees Fahrenheit. Nearly all of the observed increase has taken place in the last 70 years. As temperatures rise, shrubs begin to outcompete native grasses. With increasing temperatures, water contained in surface soils evaporates more rapidly. Grasses whose roots extend downward for less than a foot are starved of water, while shrubs can access waters at depths of up to 10 feet; mesquite has been known to put roots down to 150 feet.

Climate change models for the Southwest predict both increasing temperatures along with increasing severity of droughts, and greater variability in winter precipitation. Combined, these factors will promote the spread of woody plants and shrubs even in the absence of cattle grazing.

The warming temperatures over the past 140 years have increased the length of the grass-growing season in both spring and fall. Rangeland ecologist Dan Robinett has observed that native grasses begin growth in the spring

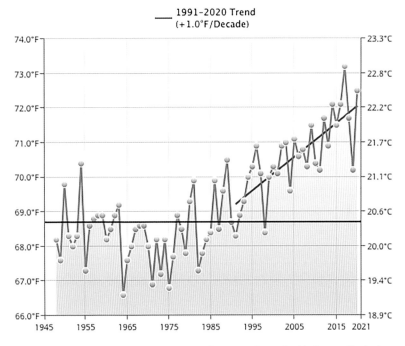

FIGURE 4.10 Year by year average temperatures (January to December) in Tucson. The horizontal line represents the average of yearly temperatures between 1948 and 2000 (68.7 degrees Fahrenheit). From 1991 to 2020, the temperature rose at a rate of 1 degree per decade. ("Climate at a Glance: City Mapping," National Center for Environmental Information, National Oceanic and Atmospheric Administration, https://www.ncei.noaa.gov/access/monitoring/climate-at-a-glance/city/mapping/2/tavg/202305/60/value.)

when average daily temperatures reach about fifty degrees Fahrenheit. As recently as the 1980s, this used to occur on or about April 1 in typical parts of the borderlands. At present, grasses begin to grow in early March, and begin to use soil moisture a month earlier. If winter rains are sparse, they run out of moisture and die before monsoon rains arrive in early July.

Grasses that start to grow following summer monsoons have in past years gone dormant in mid-October after nighttime temperatures drop below fifty degrees. In today's warming climate, grasses continue to grow through mid-November. As a result, grasses use up soil moisture that would otherwise support growth in the spring season. The reality of this grim glance into the future is manifest in the data collected by Dan Robinett, who observed high grass mortality following the dry winters of 1989, 1996, 2002, 2006, 2011, and 2017 in southeast Arizona.

As the climate warms, plants need more water to cool living tissue. As a result, they draw more water from the soil, leaving less water for production of more grass and forbs. Lower grass and forb density means that grasslands can no longer support as many cattle, and lower stocking rates reduce income for ranchers already operating on slim margins.

Climate change affects not only ranchers. Changes in the times plants begin to grow, flower and seed will affect the numerous bird species whose migration patterns and routes are finely tuned to a rhythm of plant phenology that already reflect the temperature increases of the past half century. In the near future, many avian species may not be able to find the food and cover they need when they need it during their fall and winter sojourns.[14]

Introduction of Invasive Species

During the 1930s, the Soil Conservation Service and the Soil Erosion Service introduced two African grass species to Southwest grasslands in response to ongoing severe drought conditions: Lehmann lovegrass and Boer lovegrass. In doing so, they hoped to provide forage for cattle and to stem erosion and loss of topsoil.

The two nonnative grasses spread rapidly. Where they have taken hold, they have outcompeted the mix of native grasses that once dominated the landscape. In some regions, a rich diversity of grass and forbs has been replaced by a near-monoculture of African grass.

FIGURE 4.11 (*left*) Lehmann lovegrass; (*right*) Boer lovegrass. (Photos by Stephen Strom.)

These grasses have altered fire regimes in Southwest grasslands. While both African and native grasses burn, African grasses recover more quickly after a fire. Once established, African species provide more fuel for fire than do native grasses. Consequently, they can facilitate the spread of fires across large areas of grassland. As African grasses outcompete native grasses post-fire, each fire acts to increase the fractional area covered by these nonnative species.

Species attuned to habitat comprised of native vegetation suffer when African grasses begin to take over a grassland.[15] The most significantly impacted are grassland birds, small mammals, insects, and the predators that rely on these species for their food. Although livestock can still thrive in African grass-dominated systems, the more diverse mix of grass and forbs in a native community offers a higher quality diet.[16]

Exurban Development and Landscape Fragmentation

Human population in the Southwest has increased dramatically since the 1950s. While much growth in the region has been concentrated in urban areas, grasslands have not been immune to the influx of new residents drawn by a love of open space, sweeping views, and relatively temperate climate at elevations between three thousand and five thousand feet.

The effects of subdivision and development in the grasslands has been dramatic. Roads and fences have fragmented a once open landscape. As a result, wide-ranging grassland denizens such as pronghorn and large predators such as mountain lions, jaguars, and bears can no longer roam unimpeded. As roads and residences proliferate, water flow over the landscape changes, often catalyzing erosion and gully formation. New residents need water, and unregulated pumping from a plethora of new wells can lower water tables and dramatically alter vegetation patterns and species diversity.

FIGURE 4.12 El Jefe, a male northern jaguar discovered in 2013 in Arizona's Santa Rita Mountains, has been photographed roaming as far south as central Sonora. El Jefe's wanderings (well over one hundred miles) speak to the large range of these apex predators. Until cattle rancher, hunting guide, and Malpai Borderlands Group member Warner Glenn observed a jaguar in the Peloncillo Mountains on March 7, 1996, these powerful and graceful predators were thought to be gone from the American Southwest. (U.S. Fish and Wildlife Service.)

The encroachment of houses and ranchettes (homes built on twenty-to-forty-acre parcels) in the grasslands means that any fire must be extinguished quickly lest there be extensive loss of property and lives. But as we have seen, elimination of natural fire regimes has deleterious effects on the health of the grasslands and the species that depend on them.[17]

Given the multiplicity of factors that can affect grassland health, it is difficult if not impossible to tease out the dominant cause or causes behind the radical alteration of grasslands in the Southwest. But there is no doubt that humans have played a significant, if not dominant role. Considerable degradation of grasslands surely arose from ignorance of the ability of arid lands to support large herds of cattle, and from a refusal to recognize and mitigate the effects of overgrazing on erosion and encroachment of woody species. Other choices, like suppression of fire or introduction of African grasses, seemed to make sense at the time given the state of rangeland science and the pressing need to feed cattle and mitigate erosion.

Today, it is within our power to preserve remaining healthy grasslands and to heal others. To do so requires that we reflect on past mistakes and commit to thoughtful management of rangeland: matching stocking rates to the carrying capacity of the land; introducing fire to control shrubs and woody plants in areas where shrub encroachment is still low enough that grasslands can be restored; reducing erosion by restoring the natural flow of water over the landscapes; and slowing the fragmentation of productive grasslands by exurban developments.

In the next sections, we discuss the efforts of the Malpai Borderlands Group to protect and restore more than nine hundred thousand acres of grassland in the borderlands of southeast Arizona and southwest New Mexico. Members of the group recognize the importance of healthy grasslands to both humans and other species and share a deep connection to lands whose expanse and beauty is central to their and our heritage.

An Opportunity to Protect and Restore Grasslands in the Malpai Borderlands

The maps from surveys carried out by The Nature Conservancy (figs. 4.14 and 4.15) vividly capture the landscape-scale changes wrought since settlers arrived in the area 140 years ago. Of thirteen million acres of grass-

FIGURE 4.13 An example of fragmentation of rangeland south of Rodeo, New Mexico, at the northern end of the Malpai Borderlands. (Aerial photograph by Stephen Strom.)

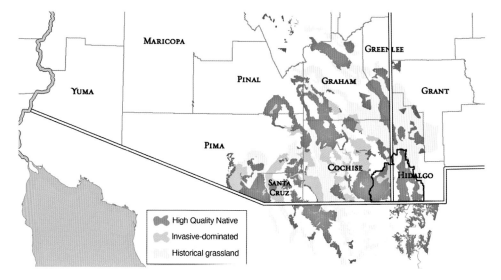

FIGURE 4.14 Changes in grassland quality in southern Arizona, southwestern New Mexico, and northern Chihuahua and Sonora, Mexico. The boundary of the Malpai Borderlands region is outlined in thick black. Today, high-quality grasslands (dark green) occupy a significantly smaller region of the borderlands than degraded grasslands (yellow) and those now dominated by non-native grasses (light green). (The Nature Conservancy.)

land in southeastern Arizona, southwestern New Mexico, and adjacent regions in northern Mexico, 36 percent are now dominated by shrubs and woody plants; 32 percent have significant shrub cover; 12 percent have a significant population of nonnative grasses; and only 17 percent of the vast tracts of native grasslands described so poetically by Joe Yarborough, John Gray, and Henry Block in the nineteenth century remain relatively intact.[18]

Superposed on these maps are the boundaries of the Malpai Borderlands area. In contrast with other parts of the Southwest, the borderlands region still contains shrub-free native grasslands, as well as grasslands where intrusion by shrubs and woody plants is small. But these relatively intact areas are nevertheless still threatened by the factors that have degraded grasslands since the 1890s—increase of woody plants and shrubs and soil erosion—as well the more recent issues that arise from exurban development.[19]

Today, nearly all of the 900,000 acres (1,410 square miles) comprising the borderlands area is devoted to ranchland. At present, there are 35 ranches in the region, whose privately owned acreage accounts for nearly 60 percent

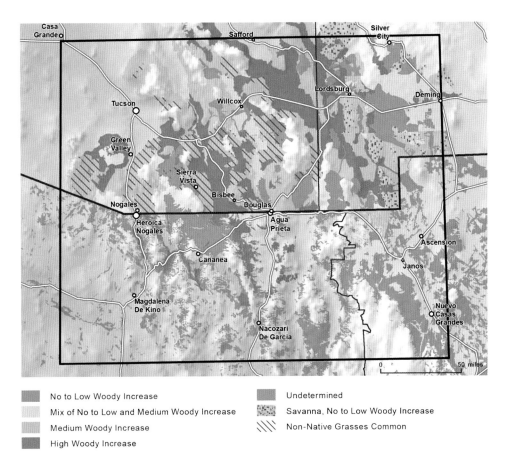

No to Low Woody Increase

Mix of No to Low and Medium Woody Increase

Medium Woody Increase

High Woody Increase

Undetermined

Savanna, No to Low Woody Increase

Non-Native Grasses Common

FIGURE 4.15 Grassland conditions and shrub encroachment in southern Arizona, southwestern New Mexico, and northern Chihuahua and Sonora, Mexico, February 2010. (The Nature Conservancy.)

of the lands in the Malpai. The remainder is managed by either the federal government or the state governments of Arizona and New Mexico.

Most ranches in the region range in size from 15,000 to 40,000 acres. In the Malpai and other rangeland in the West, a viable ranching operation depends on stock having access not only to the private lands held by an individual ranching family but to nearby, typically larger tracts of leased state (Arizona State Land Department or New Mexico State Land Office) or federal lands (BLM or U.S. Forest Service) adjacent to a ranch. Should state or federal lands be sold to home developers or mineral interests, most ranches—nearly all of which currently operate on the slimmest of margins—would fail.

Identifying Threats and Developing a Shared Vision for the Future

At the beginning of the 1990s, ranchers in the Malpai began to meet among themselves to discuss threats to the future of the region.[20] First on their list was the potential for housing developments to encroach on the grasslands, and with them, fragmentation and loss of habitat for wildlife, and continuous corridors for wildlife movement.

They looked with concern at land near Douglas, Animas, Rodeo, and Portal that had been sold to developers who divided once-rich rangeland into 20-to-40-acre parcels. Peter Warren of The Nature Conservancy recalls,

> The big club hanging over the head of the Malpai is the threat of development of this land if it's subdivided. When a ranch is subdivided these days, it goes online and it's viewed globally by people who are shopping for land. [One example I recall was a] ranch that was sold down there near Silver Creek. Five thousand acres was divided into 20- and 40-acre parcels. There are hundreds of them. More than half of the buyers were from out of state and the buyers represented 20 different U.S. states as well as Canada. They came from as far away as California, New York, and Florida. The ranch was hopelessly, irreparably subdivided.
>
> [People see a picture] with the Chiricahua Mountains in the background and they go, "oh, I want a piece of that," and they buy it sight unseen. Once that happens, a road gets put into every parcel. Fencing goes around every parcel. Suddenly there's watershed dysfunction due to all these roads creating erosion, and fencing breaking it up as wildlife habitat. So some ranchers go right to this: "If ranching is a marginal economic activity why waste your time?" The choice is between trying to find a way to keep the ranch going or letting that place get subdivided and having that piece of ground become an ecological disaster. So you've got to figure out how to keep the ranch going.

Bill McDonald, one of the founders and leaders of the MBG, emphasizes that the ranchers' concerns were not restricted to the economics of cattle grazing:

> We ranchers were concerned about what the future of this landscape would be, not just for the sake of ranching but for the sake of wildlife, the open-space

FIGURE 4.16 Rancher Bill McDonald, Malpai Borderlands Group. (Maya Springhawk Robnett and KAWC, Colorado River Public Media.)

values that are here. There's a lot of pressure to the west and the north, what they call exurban development, that is, subdivisions that aren't connected to a metropolitan area. We thought it would be a tragic thing for everyone who values what's out here, whether they be ranchers or not, if this area were to start getting cut up and developed.

The second concern was the encroachment of woody plants and shrubs on the grasslands and the resulting decline in forage for livestock and the decrease in wildlife diversity. In a presentation prepared by the Natural Resources Conservation Service, Bill McDonald noted,

Some of it undoubtedly could be traced to the fact that active fire suppression followed that period of heavy grazing when there was a big reduction of fuels, and the combination had a profound change on the landscape in that it tended to work to the detriment of the grasses and to promote woody species growth. This was a problem that we recognized from the standpoint of forage for cattle, and the environmental community recognizes from the standpoint of species diversity and diversity of habitat.[21]

Larry Allen, formerly of U.S. Forest Service and currently chairman of the MBG, echoed McDonald's comments in the NRCS presentation:

> Fire played a major role I think in controlling that in the past. We had enough grass and ground fuel to carry fires. We had virtually no suppression efforts. When the large numbers of cattle came in, they altered the fuels. Fires ceased to spread. Then by I would say in the fifties we're starting to get on top of the problem, but about then was also when the federal agencies became pretty skilled and had modern equipment and got good at putting fires out.

Both U.S. Forest Service and BLM adhered to policies that required extinguishing fires on public lands as soon as they were detected, thus preventing propagation of fires which in the past had renewed grasslands and kept them shrub free.

Peter Warren summarized:

> As we look at the needs of this landscape, one of the overwhelming needs is to burn periodically to rejuvenate the grasslands and maintain that balance of grass and woody species. We see that climate is driving this system toward a woodier, shrubbier condition. It requires periodic intervention of fire to maintain the balance. It turns out that without someone on the land to manage [fire], it really wouldn't happen very often. We've pretty much come to the conclusion that there needs to be somebody, a landowner, a land manager, who is out there taking an active interest in managing that landscape in order to take the actions that need to be done to sustain that grassland habitat.

The third threat to ranching in the Malpai came from the many environmentalists who argued that cattle grazing on public lands represented an existential threat to grasslands and associated watersheds. They believed fervently that such lands should be reserved solely for wildlife and recreation, and that the grazing fees charged by state and federal agencies were so low that they amounted to welfare for ranchers. "No Moo by '92" and "Cattle Free by '93" became rallying cries for many in the environmental movement.[22]

Ranchers' fears were amplified as failing ranches or those teetering on the brink were purchased by The Nature Conservancy, the BLM, and the U.S. Fish and Wildlife Service, following which cattle that once roamed the grasslands were removed.

If the environmental movement were successful in its campaign to eliminate grazing from public land use, most ranches in the West would fail, as access to grazing leases is essential to their viability. As a result, "at livestock association meetings, the 'enviros' were routinely called communists or agents of the UN."[23]

A Fire Catalyzes Action

Thus, as the 1990s began, relations among ranchers, environmentalists, and public agencies were fraught, and the future of ranching in the Malpai seemed uncertain, if not grim. Then, on July 2, 1991, a lightning-caused fire ignited in a remote region of the borderlands, along one of the few gravel roads that traverse the region, the Geronimo Trail. The rancher on whose private property the fire started urged that it be allowed to burn, but the Forest Service, following long-standing agency policy, refused and extinguished the blaze.

After learning of the incident, ranchers in the borderlands believed strongly that the Forest Service should have honored their neighbor's wish. Extinguishing the fire catalyzed a series of events that would culminate in the formation of the Malpai Borderlands Group and usher in an era of cooperation rather than animus among ranchers, environmentalists, and federal agencies.

Two months after the Geronimo Trail Fire, several ranchers in the area met on Warner and Wendy Glenn's Malpai Ranch to discuss their concerns about the future of the valley.[24] Joining them were environmentalists who were asked to meet at the Glenn's Ranch by Drummond Hadley.

Hadley was an heir to the Anheuser-Busch family fortune, who upon graduating from the University of Arizona worked as a vaquero in northern Mexico before purchasing the Guadalupe Canyon

FIGURE 4.17 Drummond Hadley at the University of Arizona Poetry Center, 1984. (Photo by LaVerne Harrell Clark, 1984. Courtesy of The University of Arizona Poetry Center. © Arizona Board of Regents.)

Ranch in 1973. A poet and writer, Drum, as he was known, and his then-wife Diana raised their children in the borderlands region. Over time, he developed strong relationships with his fellow ranchers. Hadley believed that grazing cattle and preserving the environment were compatible and that the ranching and environmental community could find common ground.[25]

Bill McDonald recalls,

> We started out as something of a discussion group. One of our principles here by the name of Drummond Hadley was active in the world of literature and had made friends with folks who were, in some ways, outspoken critics of the livestock industry in the Southwest. He had friends in the environmental community, [some in] the extreme environmental community, as well as his ranching neighbors. He had the perception that we all wanted the same thing and we shouldn't be at loggerheads with one another. So with this in mind, he invited some of us to get together and start talking to each other. Many of us went along simply because we didn't know how to say no to a friend, but after the first meeting we realized that there was something to this.

Peter Warren builds on McDonalds' comments:

> One common attitude that we're faced with in discussing the work we're doing out here, this collaboration of conservationists and ranchers, is disbelief that we really share enough in common so that we can successfully achieve our mutual goals. And in fact, when we look at maintaining the grassland quality of this landscape, the grassland and shrub and savanna mosaic, our goals are almost completely overlapping. We both share the goal of maintaining a vigorous, healthy native grassland.

Forging the Malpai Agenda

During the following two years, conversations among ranchers and environmentalists continued. They were joined by pioneering ecologist Ray Turner, who added a scientific perspective essential to what soon become called the Malpai Group, in recognition of their first meeting on the Glenn's Malpai Ranch.

At Drum Hadley's urging, Harvard graduate–turned–goatherder Jim Corbett was invited to participate as well: "Part ascetic, part philosopher, Corbett believed human communities are part of the natural world, not outside of it, and that striving for sustainable coexistence with nature is both a spiritual and a practical calling. Instead of being radically opposed, livestock and wilderness become mutually reinforcing, even mutually dependent."[26]

Bill McDonald recalls Corbett's seminal role in early Malpai Group meetings: "I think that certainly when we put the group together we took a lot from Jim in terms of how we structured things to bring [his philosophical views] into it. Jim expressed things beautifully. Maybe some of the rougher ranchers might not express it [Jim's] way or think that way, but everybody who's out here is out here because they love the land or they wouldn't be here."

Although discussions regarding the compatibility of cattle grazing and health of the environment continued to be fraught, the group did achieve consensus on two key principles: that the land in the borderlands should remain open and free of development, and that conversion of grassland to shrubland represented an existential threat to both ranching and the environment.

In a meeting on Drum Hadley's ranch in July 1992, the Malpai Group codified its agreements in a remarkable document, "The Malpai Agenda for Grazing in the Sonoran and Chihuahuan Bioregions."

The first element of the Malpai Agenda Program Areas was designated "Common Ground," which called for continuing dialog: "If ranchers and anti-grazing conservationists can agree on conservation principles, the resolution of many of their differences would be a matter of verifiable facts. They would then have a common ground for cooperation, study, and joint efforts."

The second, "Information and Education," committed the group to gather data essential to evaluating the health of the two bioregions. The goals of this element were to provide information to ranchers so that they could adapt range management practices to landscape conditions and to provide the public with insight into "ranching, range management and concerns about livestock impacts on native biotic communities."

The third element urged ushering in an era of collaborative decision-making among ranchers operating on private land, the state and federal agencies responsible for managing leased lands critical to the viability of ranching in the borderlands region, and environmental groups. "The ranches here aren't owned outright. They include private land as well as leased land from the state of Arizona or the state of New Mexico, the Bureau of Land Management in the Department of Interior, and the USDA, the U.S. Forest

THE MALPAI AGENDA FOR GRAZING IN THE SONORAN AND CHIHUAHUAN BIOREGIONS

On September 10, 1991, a group of ranchers met at the Malpai Ranch in southeastern Arizona to discuss the campaign in the United States against grazing on public lands. The group felt that the public's perception of ranching is based on misleading stereotypes and misinformed generalizations but with a persuasive mixture of truth about damage that has been done to arid lands by livestock. These misperceptions are often reinforced by media coverage and political organizing that polarize highly complex issues into a simple win-or-lose contest between conservationists and ranchers—a polarization often aggravated by the hardline partisans among ranchers. To reverse this polarization, which is a no-win situation for the land and everyone concerned, the Malpai Meeting proposed that a concerted effort be made to identify the conservational common ground that unites all of us who love the land, then to create programs in which we can work together to implement the values we share.

There is a love of wilderness as scenic grandeur, as an Eden unspoiled by human sins, and as a re-membrance of harmonies humanity lost when we learned to live by taming nature. And there is the love of a specific wildland as one's home. The love of land that is pristine, unscarred, and uninhabited—of virgin wilderness—has different roots from the love of a family homeland that is the best hope of a good life for unborn generations. Yet, in both cases, "love" means valuing the land in itself, and this is the foundation for establishing basic rights for native biotic communities.

In the Sonoran [and Chihuahuan] bioregion[s] and most of the arid West, ranching is now the only livelihood that is based on human adaptation to wild biotic communities. Few dispute that livestock have done serious damage and continue to do so in some places. Few dispute that yearlong, sedentary grazing will degrade plant communities in arid lands. To continue in [these bioregions], livestock grazing must discontinue practices that degrade the land. The real issue is the preservation of the last remnant of the livelihoods based on human adaptation to wildlands—pastoral adaptation that seeks to fit into the un-tamed biotic community, not to remake the land and replace its natives to fit our civilization.

All who love the land agree that it should not be cashed in or mined out and that its health takes pre-cedence over profits. They agree in their opposition to "development" that bulldozes and fractures the land, drains away its waters, and poisons it with wastes. In debates that pit preservation against development, all who know and love a wildland are on the side of its preservation. Conservationists who are ranchers are divided from many other conservationists by their belief that ranching can be stewardship that preserves the health and unreduced diversity of the native biotic community.

Much more is at stake here than the future of a few ranch families. Wildlands teach those for whom they are home an outlook and insights to which others are blind. Some of these lessons take many gen-erations to learn. Among newcomers, insight often begins with a turnaround. For example, Aldo Leopold tells of having experienced such a conversion after he joined in shooting one of the last gray wolves in the Southwest. As he watched "a fierce green fire d[ie] in her eyes," he realized that "there was something new to me in those eyes—something known only to her and to the mountain." These lessons come hard, and no society that eradicates or discards those among its members who have acquired this kind of wisdom can mature into a people that is truly at home in its land. How to fit in responsibly, as supportive members of a biotic community, is a meaningful question only for those who live by fitting in somehow.

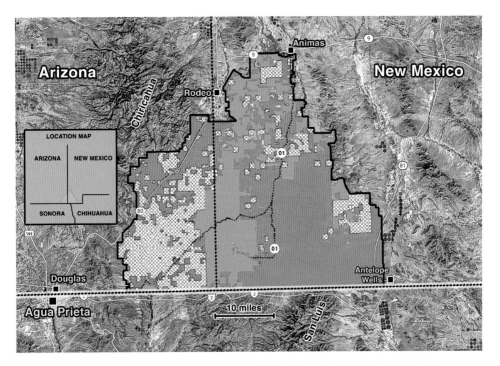

FIGURE 4.18 Landownership in the Malpai Borderlands region. Privately held land is shown in red; Arizona and New Mexico State Trust Land is cross-hatched; federally held lands are shown in green. Ranchers in the borderlands depend on having access to leased state trust lands. The Diamond A (formerly the Gray Ranch) occupies much of the large red block on the eastern side of the borderlands. (Prepared by the Malpai Borderlands Group and adapted by Stephen Strom.)

Service. We consider them partners because they are partners," Bill McDonald says.

The importance of collaboration in defining the future of ranchlands is well captured in the MBG founding document:

Livestock have been most destructive in the Sonoran and Chihuahuan biore-gions when the common use of land hasn't been matched by community decision-making. Where community decision-making is undeveloped, every-one may see what needs to be done to save our common heritage of life-supporting soils, waters, native plants, and wildlife, but no one can do anything about it. Where a community agrees about its conservation principles and how to implement them, it can enact its land ethic as the law of its land, formulated in conservation covenants.

Developing a Consensus Fire Management Policy

Discussions within the group continued after July 1992, and on March 28, 1993, thirty individuals from nineteen ranches reached consensus on a proposal to develop a fire management plan for the region and to collaborate with federal agencies in developing and implementing the plan: "We, the undersigned, are committed to the development of a fire management plan for the area encompassed by the ranches we represent. We request that the agencies involved coordinate with us in the development of this plan."

Four weeks later, representatives from the Arizona State Land Department, the New Mexico State Land Office, the Soil Conservation Service (now the Natural Resources Conservation Service), the Coronado National Forest, and the New Mexico State Forester's Office met at the Gray Ranch to consider the group's proposal. At the end of two days of intensive discussion, participants reached consensus: fire control policies of state and federal agencies would be "informed and guided by the management goals of the ranchers." Starting with a memo of understanding with the Malpai Group in 1993, collaborative meetings between ranchers and agency representatives would eventually lead to adoption of a comprehensive fire management plan for the borderlands, including a commitment to landscape-scale controlled burns.[27]

In a presentation prepared for Stewardship with Vision, Science Coordinator for the Malpai Borderlands Group Ben Brown recalled, "We agreed that we needed to do a prescribed burn. Our experience with the agencies and how they came on board with fire convinced the ranchers that if they were willing to get out front on some of these issues that they could set the agenda as leaders and not just as followers."[28]

A New Paradigm for Protecting Ranchland from Fragmentation

After discussions among the Malpai Group and other stakeholders in the region, two of the challenges facing the borderlands were on a path toward resolution: environmentalists and ranchers agreed to keep talking with one another in service of developing approaches to ranching based on scientific assessment of the grassland ecosystem, and federal and state agencies committed to collaborative efforts to develop fire management policies aimed at mitigating encroachment of woody plants and shrubs on rangeland. One major threat had yet to be resolved: the potential for development and fragmentation in the borderlands region. A breakthrough came with the purchase of the largest ranch in the region—the Gray Ranch—by The Nature Conservancy.

Near the end of the 1980s, the ranch came close to failing. During the eighties, conservation groups throughout the country had become aware of the incredible richness and diversity of flora and fauna on the ranch and looked to the ranch as a prime conservation target. Among them was The Nature Conservancy, which identified the Gray Ranch as one of earth's "Last Great Places" and eagerly sought to acquire and protect it. After a year of difficult negotiations, the conservancy purchased the 321,000-acre ranch in January 1990 and soon began to remove cattle from its new acquisition. The initial reaction of local ranchers was far from enthusiastic. Historian of the Gray Ranch George Hilliard captured local sentiment as follows: "Some local ranch people foresaw an invasion of crystal-worshippers and tree huggers; and a short future was predicted for the first Nike-shod, camera-wielding tourist who strayed onto private ranch land. Others anticipated the introduction on the ranch of gray wolves that, they were sure, would devour their livestock, and very likely their children and house pets as well."[29]

Enter John Cook, a staff member from The Nature Conservancy assigned to locate an organization or individual to assume responsibility for stewarding the ranch.[30] The Nature Conservancy's Peter Warren recalls Cook's willingness to try something that was at the time radical: "There was a lot of pressure at that time to make the Gray Ranch into a big wildlife refuge managed by the U.S. Fish and Wildlife Service. John instead decided and really pushed on the idea of making it a demonstration for private land conservation. John really kind of broke new ground, coming up with private ranching as a significant conservation solution."

Cook found a partner in Drummond Hadley. He recognized Drum as a knowledgeable rancher who had committed his life to preservation of land and wildlife, and one who had the financial means to purchase and operate the Gray in accordance with environmentally sound principles. In 1994 The Nature Conservancy sold the Gray to the Animas Foundation, a nonprofit founded and funded by Drum Hadley and his family.[31]

A critical stipulation of the deed transferring the ranch to the Animas Foundation was a *conservation easement*, a legal agreement between the foundation and The Nature Conservancy requiring that the Gray Ranch (renamed the Diamond A) remain intact and serve as habitat for wildlife for all time. To ensure adherence to the easement terms, The Nature Conservancy reserved the right to monitor the health of the ranch.[32]

Before forging the agreement with Drum Hadley, Cook had moved to the borderlands from his base in Florida and, according to Peter Warren,

> started talking to all the neighbors. John's having had experience running a nonprofit organization in Florida [shared with the ranchers his belief in the importance of] having a board of leaders who can keep an organization going. The ranchers decided they needed a formal organization based on the premises that wildlife and livestock could coexist; that economically viable ranching was the best way to preserve open space; and that ranchers, environmentalists and government agencies could learn to get along.

To capture the motivating spirit of the new organization, Bill McDonald coined a phrase: *the radical center*, a place where previously warring parties could meet to find common cause.

FIGURE 4.19 Animas Creek coursing through the Diamond A Ranch. (Aerial photo by Stephen Strom.)

In 1994 the Malpai Borderlands Group was formally established as a non-profit 501(c)(3) corporation. Its mission statement reflects the aspirations and philosophy of the MBG:

> The goal of the Malpai Borderlands Group is to restore and maintain the natural processes that create and protect a healthy, unfragmented landscape to support a diverse, flourishing community of human, plant, and animal life in our borderlands region. Together, we will accomplish this by working to encourage profitable ranching and other traditional livelihoods, which will sustain the open-space nature of our land for generations to come.

MBG is governed by a broadly based board of directors, which as of October 2022 included a number of local ranchers, a scientist, a vice president of The Nature Conservancy, a retired member of the Arizona State Land Department's Natural Resources section, a range conservationist, and a retired member of the U.S. Forest Service; it is funded through grants from private foundations, tax-deductible contributions, and grants from state and federal

TEXT PORTRAIT: PETER WARREN

After receiving his doctorate from the University of Arizona, Peter Warren served as a biologist and field representative at The Nature Conservancy for more than thirty years. During his career, Warren worked with landholders and ranchers in southeast Arizona and southwest New Mexico to protect grasslands, riparian areas, and watersheds. He continues to be involved with both the Malpai Borderlands Group and the Cienega Watershed Partnership.

I was raised in Southern California, near Whittier. I trace my interest in biology to my grandfather. Agriculture was the love of his life, but my grandmother told me that at one point he realized he couldn't make a living in agriculture. So they packed up and moved to California and he became an architect. When I heard that story, I thought early on that "I'm going to try to pursue what I really care about."

My grandparents owned about one hundred acres that included an avocado and citrus orchard in Southern California, which we called "the ranch." It was inland from Camp Pendleton in Fallbrook, near the Santa Margarita River—a little stream that flows through the camp into the ocean at Oceanside. My vision of a great life was being in a place like this where you could go down to a creek and catch crawdads and find horned toads in the sand flats.

While at the "ranch," I helped to take care of the orchards. But when I was done with my daily chores, I went hiking back up through the chaparral to the ridge top behind the ranch, looking for rattlesnakes and other creatures. My vision of a truly great landscape was one that included both natural and agricultural components. Agriculture, love of the natural world, and fascination with living things were all components of the ideal world I've imagined since I was a kid.

Probably one of the reasons that drew me specifically to the Southwest was the relatively brief time I spent in the Four Corners area while growing up. Both my parents were Quakers, and during World War II

agencies.[33] Its legal status allows the corporation to both accept tax-free donations and, importantly, to hold and manage conservation easements on lands within the borderlands.

Following formal establishment of the corporation, the Animas Foundation, represented by Drum Hadley, and the MBG began to discuss a highly innovative way to achieve two of the group's objectives: protecting the region from further fragmentation and development, and maintaining or improving grassland conditions. Their idea was to make part of the enormous reserve of native grasses on the 321,000-acre Diamond A Ranch available to ranchers who wished to rest and restore their grazing lands in exchange for placing a conservation easement on their land. The terms of the easement would preclude subdivision of the ranch in perpetuity, while use of the Diamond A grass bank would allow a rancher to keep his cattle operation viable while his own pastures recovered.[34]

my dad was a conscientious objector. Conscientious objectors were required to do some kind of alternative service. One of the things he did was to work on a survey crew with the Coast and Geodetic Survey in the Four Corners area along the San Juan River. I loved it. It's interesting how your early experiences shape your worldview. I think it's just inescapable as humans that we're often drawn to landscapes that we experienced as kids.

Not surprisingly, I chose to pursue an undergraduate degree in biology. Following college, I enrolled in graduate school at the University of Arizona to study ecology. In graduate school I realized I just wasn't cut out for the academic world. I'm more of a practical, problem-solving kind of guy. After receiving my master's degree, I took a job with The Nature Conservancy. It was an ideal position for me: working with agricultural producers and ranchers in order to find ways to preserve big intact landscapes as part of a core strategy for protecting ecologically important landscapes.

One of the conservancy's key goals is to see land protected as natural habitat for wildlife. The traditional path followed by The Nature Conservancy in the 1970s and 1980s was to buy parcels of land and then transfer them to the federal government to manage. However, the federal government alone can't protect large landscapes and watersheds. As a result, the conservancy now focuses on collaborative approaches involving private landowners and land managers from the BLM and Forest Service. In the early 1990s, the conservancy decided we were going to make the Malpai Borderlands an example of private land conservation and set the mark for how you stimulate these collaborations for big landscape conservation among diverse land ownerships: private and public.

When ranchers in the Malpai saw ranches being divided and sold off, they felt that their family, heritages, and traditions were being lost, and with them, an intimate link with the land that they're making a living on. And in everything we're doing around the world, the conservancy is now working with groups like the Malpai ranchers and with local communities to find sustainable ways of using the land that are compatible with the biological diversity goals that we have for these natural landscapes.

Peter Warren describes what happened following Hadley's proposal to the MBG:

Four ranchers who were willing to try something different stepped forward. The four people were Billy Darnell, who had been the sheriff of Hidalgo County for three terms, so everybody knew him. At that time conservation easements were a very suspicious thing in the ranching community. Many people thought—and [many still] do think—it's just a trick for these conservation groups to find a way to take over your land. So when Billy Darnell who everybody knew and who was a sheriff decided to do a conservation easement [it made it easier for others to embrace the concept].

Edward Elbrock, another guy, Billy's neighbor, runs a well-drilling service. [He owns] the store there in Animas. So everybody who needed a well drilled or a well fixed, they called Edward, so Edward knew everybody. [He's also a] somewhat creative, innovative guy. So Edward decided to do a conservation easement and [take part in the grass bank exchange].

A third guy was Wart Walters. Wart was just a salt of the earth, ordinary rancher. His idea of a good time is to go out there with a can of beans and work on fixing the fence. Everybody knew Wart. He was from one of the longtime families there. He was just a regular guy. He was neighbors to Edward and Bill so he decided to do it too. So if a guy like Wart would do it, it kind of opened the door to others.

Finally, the fourth person was Mary Winkler. Mary ran the ranch because her husband, Rich, was a lawyer and was a judge for a while. Because he was a judge in the county, everyone knew Rich Winkler also. So there was a confluence of four well-known, trusted people willing to take a leap of faith because they trusted Drum, because Drum had been around for thirty or forty years, to do a conservation easement. It was at that time like jumping off the deep end of a pool when you can't swim. Again, just that example of having a critical mass of local leadership to try something different.

Today, the MBG also funds and administers another conservation easement program. Ranchers in the borderlands who wish to keep their land intact and free from development can sell a conservation easement to the MBG corporation. The price of the easement is set by an independent appraisal of the value of potential development rights. Once an easement transaction is completed, the MBG assumes responsibility for monitoring and enforcing the terms of the easement. Funds to purchase conservation easements in the region come from donations to, and in some cases from grants to the MBG. Bill McDonald emphasizes the importance of conservation easements in achieving one of the major goals of the MBG: "Conservation easements are the major tool that we've used to avoid land fragmentation. We're very serious about keeping this land in open space."

Not all ranchers are open to placing conservation easements on their land. They view the restrictions on land use for all time by easement agreements to be a violation of property rights. Their opposition increases even more when funds from the federal government or from an NGO they view with suspicion are involved in the transactions. But a significant number of ranchers in the borderlands region share the sentiments expressed by the late rancher Wart Walters and captured by Peter Warren before Walters passed away:

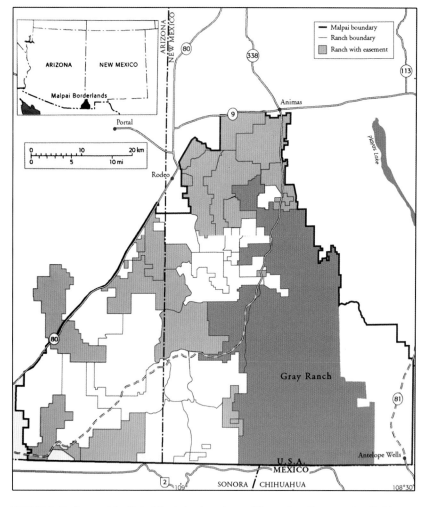

FIGURE 4.20 A map of the Malpai Borderlands region and its ranches. Those ranches that have been placed under conservation easement are shaded in light gray-green. The Diamond A (formerly the Gray) Ranch, also under conservation easement, is shaded in darker gray-green. (Malpai Borderlands Group.)

I ran into Wart Walters, just a seat-of-the-pants old guy, one time at the little coffee shop in Animas; it's now closed.

I stopped in there to get a cup of coffee on the way home. I was sitting there and Wart came in, so I started talking to him. I asked him, "Hey, Wart, you don't seem like the kind of guy who would have done a conservation easement. Why did you decide to do this conservation easement?" He said, "You know, I spent my entire life out there. I love that place and I just couldn't stand the thought of my kids splitting it up." So Wart, he was looking to the future, looking at his family, and he did it because he just didn't want his kids to be able to split the place up.

As of October 2022, ranchers from the borderlands have sold or exchanged conservation easements under the grass bank program that together have protected approximately 87,000 acres. Together with the easements already in place on the Diamond A Ranch, almost 340,000 acres, or nearly 75 percent of the private lands in the Malpai region, are under conservation easement.

The Effects of the U.S.-Mexico Border Wall on MBG Goals

An essential motivation for pursuing ambitious efforts to place lands in the borderlands region under conservation easement was to maintain open spaces and linkages among wildlife habitats. In the words of recently retired MBG executive director Rich Winkler, "The connection of the mountains and grasslands of the Malpai Borderlands to the Sierra Madre Occidental Mountains in Mexico provides crucial wildlife movement corridors that connect and enhance the abundance and diversity of wildlife throughout the region."[35]

Until the late 1990s, cross-border movement by both wildlife and humans was relatively unimpeded. Bill McDonald remembers, "We used to just walk across the line there at Guadalupe, you could just walk right across there and we'd go back and forth. We traded cattle back and forth, just going through the [border] fence."

The relative ease of rancher-to-rancher exchanges was significantly curtailed as drug smugglers from Mexico began to make use of the Malpai region to carry drugs into the United States. In the same spirit that informed collaborative relationships with other government agencies established during the 1990s, the MBG hoped to engage representatives of the U.S. Customs and Border Patrol Agency (CBP) to develop cooperative efforts to mitigate both drug smuggling and illegal border crossings.

Initial efforts to engage with CBP proceeded slowly until 2010, when MBG rancher Rob Krentz was murdered, apparently by a drug smuggler on his way back to Mexico from the United States.[36] After the slaying, the CBP became far more open to listening to suggestions from and partnering with ranchers in the borderlands region. More agents were assigned to the area, and patrols became more frequent. The government installed vehicle barriers comprised of old railroad tracks, making it far more challenging to cross the border by auto, while ranchers worked with CBP to place surveillance towers on their land.

Thanks to the increased level of collaboration between MBG and the CBP, border crossings dropped significantly. Toward the end of the ensuing decade, the number of illegal border crossings had decreased by more than a factor of ten, and smuggling in the area had decreased dramatically.

In 2019 MBG learned of plans by the Trump administration to build a thirty-foot-high wall along the U.S.-Mexico border east of Douglas, with segments extending into the New Mexico bootheel. If those plans came to fruition, one of the two major goals of the MBG coalition would be undermined: maintaining unfragmented open space.

In May 2019, Rich Winkler summarized the views of a large majority of MBG members:

> Every member of our group recognizes the need for security along the border in the Malpai Borderlands, but we also understand that a border wall is not the best means to achieve security in remote areas.
>
> The Malpai Borderlands Group has worked hard for a quarter century to maintain an unfragmented landscape free of excessive infrastructure, housing developments and roads.
>
> The proposed border wall in the San Bernardino Valley shows a glaring lack of respect for our efforts. The construction of this border wall will fundamentally interfere with the core mission of the Malpai Borderlands Group, and the open-space nature of the land will be significantly altered for generations to come.[37]

Throughout 2019 representatives of CBP assured the MBG that the borderlands area was not a priority for constructing a border wall. But in early 2020, CBP announced a decision by the Trump administration to install a wall along the border east of Douglas near the San Bernardino National Wildlife Reserve and adjacent to the properties of three MBG ranchers. By time the agency informed the group of the construction plans, it was too late to challenge the government.

FIGURE 4.21 The U.S.-Mexico border wall near the San Bernardino National Wildlife Reserve. The wall is a barrier to movement by mammals, especially megafauna such as the iconic northern jaguar. Floodlights along the wall disrupt the normal daily rhythms of many species, mammalian and avian, that depend on darkness to hunt and travel. (Photo by Stephen Strom.)

FIGURE 4.22 A view into Mexico from the U.S. side of the border south of the San Bernardino National Wildlife Reserve. (Photo by Stephen Strom.)

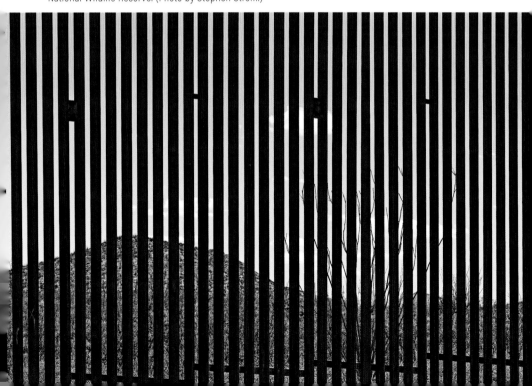

At the time, Roy Villareal of the CBP argued that while illegal activity in the Douglas sector had been down, "it would be a mistake to assume that it will remain that way. What I do not want to have happen is a resurgence, and once again have us become the epicenter of the Southwest border." But MBG members believed that election-year politics was the real reason behind the sudden decision to proceed with the wall: a desire for the administration to show significant progress on the wall before the November 2020 elections.[38]

When Bill McDonald learned of the decision, he said, "I personally felt like I kind of failed. I thought we had something there that we didn't have," a collaborative relationship with CBP. He lamented, "I should have spoken up earlier. Maybe if we had fought them politically, we could have made a difference. I feel like I've let down the generations to come, because we're going to have that ugly scar out here. It just makes me sick."

By mid-2020, two segments of a thirty-foot high wall spanning twenty-five miles were erected along the southern boundary of the Malpai Borderlands region. In a matter of a few months, wildlife was cut off from water supplies and habitat severed. No longer could jaguars, mountain lions, and other mega-fauna move freely along biological corridors established millennia in the past.

In March 2020 the *Washington Post* reported that as the wall neared completion near the San Bernardino National Wildlife Reserve, "remote video cameras on the refuge have captured pumas, bobcats, wild turkeys and other species streaming through the last remaining gaps in the barrier before construction crews finish the job."[39]

Maintaining and Improving the Health of Grasslands in the Borderlands

The MBG's conservation easement programs have gone a long way toward accomplishing one of the goals articulated in the group's mission statement: protecting an unfragmented landscape. The second—supporting a diverse, flourishing community of human, plant, and animal life—requires that management of lands in the Malpai region be guided by careful assessment of the current state of the land and by sound scientific advice.

Using Science to Guide Land Management

Early on in its history, the Malpai Borderlands Group embraced the need for good science to guide land management decisions in the region. The group established a scientific advisory committee whose members include academic researchers, knowledgeable representatives from NGOs, and representatives from state and federal agencies. Currently serving on the advisory committee are academic researchers from the University of Arizona, University of California–Berkeley, Colorado State University, and University of South Florida; scientists from The Nature Conservancy, the American Museum of Natural History, Jornada Experimental Range, Santa Lucia Conservancy, and Savannah River Ecology Lab; and experts from the U.S. Forest Service, Natural Resources Conservation Service, U.S. Department of Agriculture, and the U.S. Fish and Wildlife Service.[40]

The committee meets yearly with ranchers in the Malpai region to discuss management of grassland ecology, share results of monitoring programs aimed at assessing current conditions in the region with the community, and discuss how best to enhance rangeland conditions and ecosystem health. Over the past two decades, ranchers and scientists have worked together on programs to inventory species, monitor vegetation in the area, and carry out research aimed at better understanding the distribution and habitat of endangered species in the area.

The MBG also serves as a nexus for catalyzing and holding discussions with state and federal agency representatives and scientists from NGOs throughout the year. Though the group tries to provide ranchers with advice informed by the best available scientific thinking, MBG doesn't control or try to influence management by local ranchers. "The management is all done by the local ranchers. The Borderlands Group provides assistance on projects when there are landowners that want to do it. Like repairing a fence or putting in a new fence, some grass restoration work like brush removal. Malpai group will also help do cost-share managing for specific range improvement projects," says Peter Warren, who serves on the group's board of directors.

Active Management of Erosion and Fire

As part of their commitment to "restore and maintain the natural processes that create and protect a healthy, unfragmented landscape," the MBG has initiated a number of efforts aimed at controlling erosion. Some areas have been reseeded, with the result that rainwater no longer creates gullies or arroyos as it rushes unimpeded across the landscape. In other parts of the region, ranchers have placed gabions (rock-filled wire containers) in arroyos

FIGURE 4.23 View toward the Peloncillo Mountains from Bill McDonald's Sycamore Ranch. (Aerial photo by Stephen Strom.)

and stream channels or constructed dikes to slow the flow of water and thereby prevent or mitigate erosion.

Bringing back fire to the landscape remains one of the primary goals of the Malpai Borderlands Group. Natural Resources Conservation Service Range Management Specialist Ron Bemis, who has helped to guide the effort, noted in a presentation to the NRCS that "part of the mission of the Malpai Group is to bring fire back in and turn around the brush encroachment trend, not to remove anything, but to look at the subtleties and manage the resources that are in front of us to improve ecologic function and in turn have diverse and healthy wildlife populations while we have a sustainable livestock production on the resources."

The development of a memorandum of understanding among MBG and nine federal, state, and county agencies in 1993 led to the adoption of fire management policies that allowed fire to be used to enhance grassland con-

ditions. In 2003 collaborative discussions among MBG ranchers and agencies culminated in approval of the Bootheel Fire Management Plan, which codifies fire policy guidelines for the New Mexico portion of the MBG. A year later, MBG and the U.S. Forest Service developed a fire management plan for the Peloncillo Mountains, memorialized in the Peloncillo Programmatic Fire Management Plan. And most encouraging in light of past bitter disagreements between ranchers and the Forest Service, MBG members and the U.S. Forest Service plan and carry out controlled burns collaboratively.[41]

Efforts to restore or improve MBG rangelands have been funded from a variety of sources: successful proposals to the Natural Resources Conservation Service's Environmental Quality Incentives Program, or funding from the U.S. Forest Service or Fish and Wildlife Service. Individual ranchers, rather than the MBG organization, apply for funds and work with the agencies. However, MBG frequently provides scientific guidance and assistance in navigating often complex bureaucratic hurdles.

Finding a Path from Conflict to the Radical Center

In the nearly three decades since its founding, the Malpai Borderlands Group has continued to meet the challenge of establishing civil and productive relationships among individuals, agencies, and environmental groups whose interests and ideologies don't always mesh. MBG and its partners have worked diligently to understand the landscape and to find paths toward ranching sustainably and living harmoniously with the ecological communities on which they depend.[42]

The animating philosophy that lies behind the successes of the Malpai Borderlands Group in "finding the radical center" is perhaps best captured by Drummond Hadley in the founding document for the Animas Foundation:

> Working ranches . . . are the result of intricate relationships between humans, cattle and their direct dependence on rain, sunlight and grass. Here, in spite of intense grazing for over one hundred years, cattle ranching has protected from development a last remaining intact natural system of southwestern grasslands and mountainous uplands. The Animas Foundation respects and engages the traditional skills of the ranchers, brush country vaqueros, cowboys and homesteaders of our region. These skills include tracking, the herding of cattle through vast open spaces, the roping and sorting of cattle, the gentling of colts and the training of working horses.
>
> We believe that to sustain these grazing livelihoods is key to solve two issues facing the West: how to maintain productive and healthy lands in the face of ever-increasing human encroachment, and how to manage native grasslands which are rapidly being converted to desert and shrubland.
>
> In this time of world-wide habitat loss for both human beings and wildlife, The Animas Foundation believes that these commitments to carefully managed open lands can support stable rural economies and healthy natural communities of grasslands, mountains and deserts. We believe that vast lands such as these can bring to our society understandings crucial to this time in how to live in communion with the land and with each other.

SYNOPSIS

OVERVIEW

The Malpai Borderlands spans a nine-hundred-thousand-acre area in southwestern New Mexico and southeastern Arizona characterized by forest-covered mountain ranges, oak woodlands, and broad grasslands.

Ecologists have designated the borderlands as a biological hotspot, owing to the richness and diversity of plant and animal species in the region.

The borderlands comprises a mix of privately owned lands, state trust land, and federally administered public lands. At present there are thirty-five ranches whose total privately held acreage amounts to nearly 60 percent of the lands in the Malpai region.

CATALYSTS FOR ACTION

Ranchland on the periphery of the region was being divided into smaller parcels.

Ranchers in the region were concerned that the economic benefits of selling land for development would lead to sale of ranchland for subdivision, with a resultant loss of healthy grasslands, habitat, and corridors for wildlife movement, and the ranching culture.

A steady encroachment of woody plants and shrubs on the grasslands resulted in both a decline in forage for livestock and a decrease in species diversity. The natural fire regime was disrupted by federal policy which required extinguishing grassland fires.

Many environmentalists urged that cattle be removed from public lands. Absent the option to lease public lands for cattle grazing, most ranches would no longer be economically viable.

MEETING THE CHALLENGES

Ranchers began to meet informally to discuss the triple threats of ranch sales and fragmentation, encroachment of shrubs, and environmental activism aimed at removing cattle from public land.

In 1991 a lightning-caused fire ignited on a ranch in a remote region of the borderlands. The rancher urged the U.S. Forest Service personnel to let it burn. Bound by extant policy, the Forest Service refused, and in response, several ranchers gathered at the Malpai Ranch to discuss their concerns about agency response to fire as well as the long-term future of the borderlands. They were joined by a group of environmentalists along with the largest landholder in the region, Drummond Hadley.

The meetings later included representatives from federal and state agencies, knowledgeable rangeland ecologists, and other experts, and after two years the group codified their agreements in "The Malpai Agenda for Grazing in the Sonoran and Chihuahuan Bioregions."

The first element of the agenda called for continuing dialog. The second committed the group to gathering data needed to evaluate the ecological rangeland health so that ranchers could adapt management practices to extant conditions. The third urged adoption of collaborative decision-making among ranchers, state and federal agencies, and environmental groups.

Collaborative decision-making led to adoption of a comprehensive fire management plan for the borderlands, including a commitment to landscape-scale controlled burns.

A portion of the grasslands on the 321,000-acre Gray Ranch was made available to ranchers who wished to rest and restore their grazing lands in exchange for granting a conservation easement on their land precluding subdivision of the ranch.

ELEMENTS OF SUCCESS

- Purchase of the 321,000-acre Gray Ranch (now the Diamond A) by The Nature Conservancy in January 1990
- Placing the Diamond A under conservation easement
- Using the rangeland on the Diamond A as a grass bank in exchange for granting conservation easements
- Taking the time to build trust, first through meetings held among ranchers, then with federal and state agency staff, then extending to environmentalists, scientists, and NGO staff
- Commitment to finding "the radical center": a place that embraces civil and productive relationships among individuals, agencies, and environmental groups whose interests and ideologies don't always mesh

ACCOMPLISHMENTS

- Developing and implementing a fire management plan with federal and state agencies
- Carrying out six prescribed burns, including the largest successful prescribed fire in U.S. history
- Organizing the MBG as a 501(c)(3) corporation, able to hold conservation easements and to raise funds needed to support restoration and land stewardship efforts
- Monitoring the health of the grasslands and other ecosystems in the region
- Placing 75 percent of the ranchland in the borderlands region under conservation easement
- Forming a science advisory committee to inform rangeland management

- Holding discussions with state and federal agencies and scientists from NGOs
- Protecting endangered species by maintaining habitat and movement corridors
- Demonstrating that ranching can contribute to large-landscape conservation efforts

FUNDING

- Private donations
- Cash and in-kind support from NGOs
- Federal grants from U.S. Department of Agriculture and the U.S. Fish and Wildlife Service

ONGOING CHALLENGES AND THREATS

- Possible sale or development of state trust lands; curtailing or removing access to federal lands currently used for grazing
- The U.S.-Mexico border wall: wildlife cut off from water supplies and habitat severed
- Future of state lands and the clause in all extant easements in the borderlands that enables ranchers to opt out should grazing leases no longer be available on public or state trust lands
- Resistance to conservation easements by some ranchers in the borderlands region who view the restrictions on land use in perpetuity by easement agreements to be a violation of property rights
- Development of state trust lands: leasing on trust lands is essential to maintaining the economic viability of ranches in the borderlands region

CHAPTER 5

■ ■ ■ ■ ■ ■ ■ ■

Cienega Ranch

What's the value of a Chiricahua leopard frog? Of a Yaqui topminnow, a fairy shrimp, or
a Triops? Of native pollinators? What's the value of dark space so you can actually see
the sky? Keeping land like this in ranching is one of the best options to keep those open
spaces and to protect wildlife that rely on this country. It is really important to me that
Cienega stay wild and undeveloped in the future.

— JOSIAH AUSTIN

The Natural Setting

The Sulphur Springs Valley lies just to the west of the Malpai Borderlands
region. Bounded by the Chiricahua and Dos Cabezas Mountains on the east
and the Dragoon and Mule Mountains on the west (see fig. 1.11), the valley contains one of twelve priority grasslands in the Southwest borderlands
identified as prime targets for conservation and potential restoration by The
Nature Conservancy and the National Fish and Wildlife Foundation.[1]

Cienega Ranch lies in the southern part of the Sulphur Springs Valley
along the eastern flank of the Chiricahua Mountains, adjacent to the Coronado National Forest and the Fort Bowie National Historic Site, and just to
the north of the Chiricahua National Monument.

The mapping tool HabiMap, developed by the Arizona Game and Fish
Department, shows that Cienega Ranch contains habitat that supports more
than sixty species identified by the department as having the greatest conservation need.[2] Moreover, the ranch's strategic location relative to nearby protected areas provides wildlife with long, unfragmented movement corridors
between the Dos Cabezas Wilderness Area; Fort Bowie National Monument;
the Bowie Mountains, a BLM scenic area of critical environmental concern;
and the Coronado National Forest.[3]

FIGURE 5.1 Entrance to the Cienega Ranch in the Sulphur Springs Valley. (Photo by Stephen Strom.)

But just twenty miles to the west of Cienega Ranch, an ever-increasing area of once grass-rich bottomlands have been converted to vineyards, nut trees, and irrigated cropland. Agriculture in the western Sulphur Springs Valley has proven far more lucrative than ranching, which at the best of times operates on the slimmest of margins.[4]

Moreover, the valley and environs provide winter homes and stopovers for an enormous number of bird species. As such, it is a veritable mecca for bird enthusiasts, and over the years, many birders as well as other visitors to the valley have retired or built second homes in the area. Sales of 5-acre lots, along with 20- and 40-acre ranchettes, have grown steadily as rangeland is sold off piece by piece.[5]

Michael Patrick of the Trust for Public Land emphasizes the importance of keeping the Sulphur Springs Valley grasslands healthy and intact: "The grasslands in this valley, where Cienega Ranch is located, contain critical habitat for endangered wildlife, support large working cattle ranches for America's food supply, and provide substantial amounts of carbon storage to help mitigate climate change."

Protecting and Preserving Grasslands in the Sulphur Springs Valley of Arizona

Enter Josiah Austin. Raised on a farm in Maryland, Austin began his career as a financial analyst. He soon grew tired of city work and yearned to return to open spaces and to working the land. On a vacation trip to Arizona in the early 1980s with his then-wife, Valer, Austin became enamored with

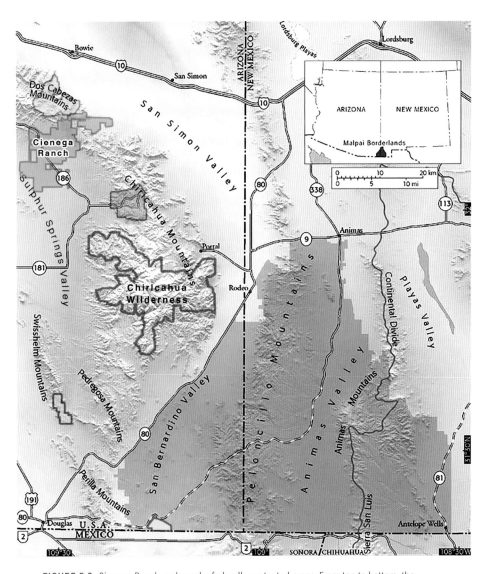

FIGURE 5.2 Cienega Ranch and nearby federally protected areas. From top to bottom, the enclosed polygons mark Dos Cabezas Wilderness (light green); Cienega Ranch (red); Chiricahua National Monument (gray); Chiricahua Wilderness (white with green outline); Leslie Canyon National Wildlife Area (light purple polygon); and San Bernardino National Wildlife Reserve (yellow polygon). The Malpai Borderlands region is shaded olive green. (Map adapted from Nathan F. Sayre, *Working Wilderness: The Malpai Borderlands Group Story and the Future of the Western Range* [Tucson: Rio Nuevo Press, 2006].)

FIGURE 5.3 Aerial view of Cienega Ranch. (Photo by Stephen Strom.)

the open rangelands in the Sulphur Springs Valley. Starting in 1982, he and Valer began to purchase ranches—the HYL, Bar Boot, and El Coronado—along the western slope of the Chiricahua Mountains with the goals of preserving healthy grasslands and improving ranches that had fallen victim to the effects of overgrazing. Over the years, the combined acreage of the ranches in the valley purchased by both Josiah and Valer Clark Austin grew to more than one hundred thousand acres. The Austins' vision was to demonstrate that properly managed working ranches could be both economically viable and provide habitat favorable not only for cattle grazing but for wildlife.[6]

"Josiah and Valer Austin are more than simply neighbors of the Malpai Borderlands Group," writes chronicler of the Malpai Borderlands Group Nathan Sayre. "Although they . . . fall outside the primary planning area [of the MBG], they have been supporters, partners, and exemplars for the group from its inception."[7]

Acquiring Conservation Easements

In 1989 Austin purchased Cienega Ranch, and over the years he has collaborated with the Trust for Public Land and the New Mexico Land Conservancy to put conservation easements on the property. "I just would hate to see the area I'm in now developed," says Austin. "That's one of my motivating factors in putting easements on the ranch. I pretty much have all the ranch under easement, and as a result, [Cienega Ranch] will never get developed."[8]

Most of the funds to purchase the initial easements on the ranch came from the Department of Agriculture's Natural Resources Conservation Service's ACEP (Agricultural Conservation Easement Program). ACEP is designed "to help private and tribal landowners, land trusts, and other entities such as state and local governments protect croplands and grasslands on working farms and ranches by limiting non-agricultural uses of the land through conservation easements." However, the ACEP provides only a portion of the funds needed to purchase an easement. The remainder must come from private sources.[9]

Michael Patrick notes that "normally the NRCS will provide up to 50 percent of the land's assessed value. However, if you can qualify for a category called 'grasslands of special environmental significance,' NRCS will provide up to 75 percent of the purchase price for the easement. The Nature Conservancy maps depicting the status of grasslands in the southwest made it fairly easy to convince the NRCS Arizona state office that Cienega Ranch qualified for that category," as the Cienega Ranch is centered on one of the conservancy's priority grasslands. "So then the trick was, how do we get the matching money?"

Over several years, Michael Patrick and Josiah Austin raised private contributions to match ACEP funds for the first two easement purchases from the Nina Mason Pulliam Charitable Trust and the National Fish and Wildlife Foundation's Acres for America program, supported by Walmart. "We're always struggling to find matching non-federal funds," says Patrick. "On our most recent easement purchase on Cienega Ranch, we received some money from a friend of Josiah's who really loved what he was doing. Then we got money from the Malpai Borderlands Group, and the final piece we needed from The Nature Conservancy of Arizona."

Cattle rancher and MBG board member Rich Winkler explains why the MBG enthusiastically supported Austin's efforts to protect Cienega Ranch and environs: "The Malpai Borderlands Group decided to get involved in this project because it supports all the same values that the Malpai Group stands for: sustaining wild, working landscapes by helping ranchers protect their private lands."[10]

Austin uses some of the proceeds from his sale of conservation easements on the Cienega Ranch to purchase nearby ranches as they come on the market and to add their lands to those already protected on the Cienega property. The ranch has grown in size from the nine thousand acres originally acquired in 1989 to around sixty thousand acres in 2022.

The additions have enhanced habitat connectivity for endemic and migrating species. "This whole valley contains some spectacular grassland that is home for birds, bats, jaguar, deer, and, of course, cattle," says Austin. "I hope people understand that keeping land like this in ranching is one of the best options for our society to keep those open spaces and protect the wildlife that rely on this country. It is really important to me that Cienega stay wild and undeveloped in the future. I want to protect the lands *for* future generations and *against* future generations."

Restoring Rangeland

Protecting grasslands is only one of the goals Austin hopes to achieve. The proceeds from each easement sale have also been reinvested in programs to restore ranchland damaged by overgrazing and drought, and to provide habitat for threatened and endangered species. Water and its interactions with the grassland ecosystem has been a primary focus of Austin's work over the years. He says, "One of the things I've been concerned with since I came into this part of the country forty years ago was the water cycle: slowing down runoff and trying to get the runoff into the ground versus taking topsoil when it flows over the ground. So that's one of the major restoration tools that I've been doing for the past forty years."

Austin continues,

> I've done a lot of it with earthen dams I call gully plugs. I've put in thousands of loose rock structures, probably thousands of gully plugs over the years, quite a few rock and cement structures, and gabions [wire baskets filled with rocks]. When I walk the land, I'm always looking at ways to improve the water cycle. I'm always looking at canyons with rocky steep sides that could be used for either loose rock structures or gabions or cement-and-rocks. When I look at washes, I always look at areas that I could slow the water down with a gully plug. The intention is not to impound water but rather to slow the water down, repair erosion, to get the water into the ground.

FIGURE 5.4 Josiah Austin. (Courtesy Josiah Austin.)

FIGURE 5.5 (*a*) Josiah Austin inspects one of the cattle and wildlife drinkers on Cienega Ranch. (*b*) Josiah Austin inspects cement-rock structures (leaky weirs) fitted into channels to slow surface water flows. (Courtesy Josiah Austin.)

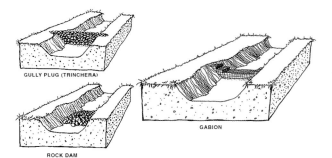

FIGURE 5.6 Three rock detention structures installed to slow the flow of water over the landscape and to prevent erosion. (Courtesy of U.S. Geological Survey, drawing by Chloe Fantel.)

By slowing down the water, it no longer incises the land. Instead, silt washing downhill accumulates behind the gabions or plugs and over time serves to support and nourish new vegetation. The newly vegetated areas in turn further slow rushing waters, allowing them instead to infiltrate into the ground rather than erode the land.

Gita Bodner of The Nature Conservancy explains that by installing these structures, "the net result is that you prolong the availability of a big rainfall on the landscape. You end up with the plants having access to the water longer, the animals having access to the water longer, either in pools or in moist soil or in the plants themselves."

She continues: "The biggest and broadest benefits are to soil moisture and everything that depends on [it]—the whole world of plants and animals that depend on soil moisture. With erosion control, there are places where rivers [like the San Bernardino River] are flowing on the surface for miles longer than they used to. Erosion control, watershed enhancement . . . that's the kind of intervention I feel very positive about."

Gully plug by gully plug, gabion by gabion, Austin has restored eroded washes, slowed runoff to allow water to seep into the ground, and created pools, re-created wetlands, and reestablished creek flows. As aquatic conditions are restored, aquatic, amphibian and avian wildlife will return and flourish.

As we wandered across the Cienega Ranch on a mid-November afternoon, Austin pointed to an area behind one of the gully plugs he installed:

> There's no water in there now, but after a rain it will contain Triops and fairy shrimp. It's just fascinating coming over and just looking down in there and seeing this little Triops in there. It's just so neat. You look at people that just think of landscapes, and they think of cows, and something that's productive,

FIGURE 5.7 Grass filling in the area behind a small earthen structure (outlined by the black ellipse) created to slow the flow of water over the landscape and create conditions where vegetation can flourish and thus further slow stormwater and prevent soil erosion and incision by gullies. (Photo by Stephen Strom.)

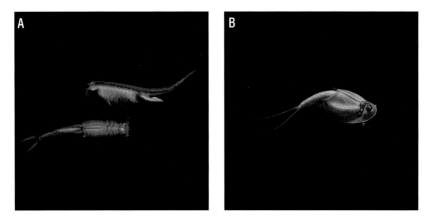

FIGURE 5.8 (a) Fairy shrimp; (b) Triops. (Photos by Bruce Taubert.)

and they don't look at these fairy shrimp and these Triops. I personally think they're as important as everything else. They've [survived on earth] for two hundred million years and haven't changed.

I remember talking to somebody about what excites me about the land and I was about ready to say "fairy shrimp." It's just such a unique creature. They said, "How can you be excited about a fairy shrimp?" I'm thinking, how can you *not* be excited about a fairy shrimp or a Triops, which has been around hundreds of millions of years and hasn't changed?

Using Science to Guide Restoration Work

Before beginning any major work on the ranch, Austin consults with experts or staff members from various agencies, NGOs, and universities:

> For example, I'll be talking to a native bee guy, Bob Minckley, from the University of Rochester. I'll say, "Bob, I'm thinking about moving a lot of this mesquite. Is it going to affect the solitary bees?" Or I'll ask Randy Babb [Arizona Game and Fish biologist], "When I'm grubbing out [mesquite], is there anything I need to be careful about?" And Randy said, "Yes, leave the rat dens. Don't disturb the rat dens." So when I grub out a field I try not to grub out the mesquite that are growing through a kangaroo rat den, because you'll disturb turtles and snakes and vertebrates and everything like that in there. I do ask people, "If I do this, what are the consequences?"

During the time Austin has owned the ranch, he has worked with biologists to reintroduce threatened or endangered species, including the Chiricahua leopard frog and the Gila and Yaqui topminnows. In collaboration with the National Wild Turkey Federation, Austin has introduced flocks of Gould's turkey on the western slopes of the Chiricahua Mountains. He has also planted large numbers of agave, whose springtime blooms provide nectar for rare species of bats. As of this writing, prairie dogs have been reintroduced on the ranch, and Austin is discussing the prospect of reintroducing pronghorn with Arizona Game and Fish biologists.[11]

Funding Restoration Projects

While a significant fraction of the funds used for restoration on Cienega Ranch come from proceeds from the sale of conservation easements, the

FIGURE 5.9 (a) Gould's wild turkey. (Tuvas, Wikimedia Commons.) (b) Black-tailed prairie dog. (Joe Ravi, Wikimedia Commons.)

Natural Resources Conservation Service has also provided funds through its Environmental Quality Incentives Program.[12] Through the program, "NRCS works one-on-one with producers to develop a conservation plan that outlines conservation practices and activities to help solve on-farm resource issues. Producers implement practices and activities in their conservation plan that can lead to cleaner water and air, healthier soil and better wildlife habitat, all while improving their agricultural operations."

Austin uses funds from the Environmental Quality Incentives Program along with monies from the sale of conservation easements to remove fences, reintroduce native plants, disperse water drinkers throughout the ranch for both cattle and wildlife, and adopt grazing patterns that provide for long rest periods for pastures. To ensure that his range management practices on Cienega Ranch take account of the best available science, Austin speaks regularly with individuals from the NRCS, The Nature Conservancy, Arizona Game and Fish, U.S. Fish and Wildlife Service, and the Forest Ser-

vice. He also makes a point to keep in close touch with the Malpai Borderlands Group, attending their annual science meeting as well as the regularly
scheduled meetings of the MBG Board.

The Environmental Significance of Protecting and Restoring Grasslands

Overgrazing, drought, altered fire regimes, shrub and woody plant encroachment, conversion to farmland, and introduction of invasive species over the
past 140 years have dramatically altered grasslands in the Southwest. Of
the 13 million acres of native grasslands that filled the valleys of southeast
Arizona and southwest New Mexico before American settlers arrived in the
1870s and 1880s, only 2.6 million acres remain intact.[13]

Today, increases in temperature and changes in precipitation patterns
along with encroaching developments threaten remaining grasslands in the
borderlands region. Loss and degradation of grasslands is hardly restricted
to the borderlands: it is a worldwide problem that has raised alarm among
ecologists who identify grasslands as one of the planet's most endangered
ecosystems.

FIGURE 5.10 One of the drinkers on the Cienega Ranch constructed from discarded mining truck tires. According to rancher Josiah Austin, "Cattle now don't have to walk more than a half mile to water because of the pipelines I've put in to fill those drinkers. Every tire tank goes in with a wildlife ramp. Wildlife booms around these tire tanks." (Photo by Stephen Strom.)

In thinking about value to humans, grasslands' role in providing forage for livestock comes first to mind. However, grasslands provide a number of critical practical benefits, among them sustaining healthy watersheds, controlling erosion, sequestering carbon, hosting pollinators essential to the survival of a wide variety of plants, and supporting a large and diverse population of flora and fauna.[14]

Watershed Function and Erosion Control

In grasslands degraded by overgrazing or covered by woody plants and shrubs, when rains come, water rushes across the land, carries away topsoil, and pours through gullies, leaving little water to seep into the ground.[15]

In healthy grasslands, both grass above ground and its root system below intercept storm water as it courses across the land and slow its flow. Instead of removing topsoil and eroding the land, rainwater infiltrates the soil and over time recharges the aquifer. Moreover, as water slowly makes its way to the aquifer, it passes through layers of soil and loose rock that act as filters to remove any pollutants. Well-functioning grasslands serve as nature's water purification facilities.

Grassland Carbon Sequestration: Carbon Storage in Plants and Soil Organic Carbon

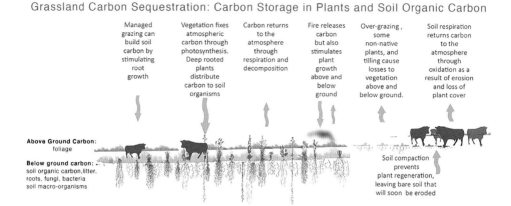

FIGURE 5.11 Illustration of how grasslands sequester carbon. Vegetation fixes atmospheric carbon through photosynthesis and stores the carbon in the soil. Some carbon returns to the atmosphere via soil decomposition, plant respiration, and fire. The green arrows indicate the flow of carbon to soil and plants, while the yellow arrows indicate flow of carbon back into the atmosphere. The size of the arrows is proportional to the magnitude of sequestration and loss for each process. Note the negative effects of overgrazing and the positive effects of carefully managed grazing. (Illustration adapted from "Carbon Sequestration in Grasslands," Minnesota Board of Water and Soil Resources, https://bwsr.state.mn.us/carbon-sequestration-grasslands.)

Carbon Sequestration

Healthy grasslands trap carbon and can thereby contribute to mitigating rising atmospheric carbon dioxide levels, a primary contributor to global warming and climate change. Figure 5.11 is worthy of careful examination: it details the positive carbon sequestration provided by carefully managed grazing in contrast to the negative effects of overgrazing on carbon storage.[16]

Healthy grasslands thus serve as an important carbon sink, and their importance may grow as the earth warms. At present, grasslands store about 30 percent of the world's carbon stock, with forests accounting for much of the remainder. However, forests sequester most of their carbon above ground in leaves and wood, while grasslands primarily store carbon underground. Both forests and grasslands are subject to fire. But when forests burn, most of their stored carbon is released back into the atmosphere. By contrast, while grassland fires release some carbon when shoots above ground burn, most carbon remains stored in root systems and in the soil. Moreover, grasses recover quickly after a fire and soon begin to remove carbon dioxide from the air and again start to store carbon in the soil. By contrast, regrowth of forests and restart of carbon sequestration by new growth takes place on a much longer timescale.[17]

As forest wildfires are anticipated to become more frequent with rising temperatures and aridity in the West, it would be unwise to overlook the significance of preserving expansive, healthy grasslands as a dependable carbon sink. Moreover, partially degraded grasslands offer the possibility of providing additional carbon storage if steps are taken to restore them to a fully healthy state. Based on its study of priority grassland landscapes in the borderlands region, The Nature Conservancy estimates that perhaps a third of the grasslands there could be restored through shrub and woody plant removal, reintroduction of fire, and managing water flow over the landscape. Combining such restoration efforts with modern rangeland grazing practices would provide a nature-based solution to the challenge of storing carbon and reducing atmospheric carbon dioxide.[18]

Gita Bodner of The Nature Conservancy suggests that efforts to preserve open grasslands should start with those areas least affected by encroachment of shrubs and woody plants and by takeover by nonnative African grasses:

> In terms of restoration that's designed to sustain open grasslands and all the species that depend on them, the best results tend to come in places that have not already been heavily impacted. So focusing first on maintaining those as open grasslands will tend to be more beneficial, and certainly provide higher return [on investment, rather] than focusing on areas that have already been really, really changed, where there's been a lot of shrub encroachment, and where it's already shifted to exotic grasses like Lehmann's lovegrass.

Healthy Pollinator Populations

Native open grasslands, with their rich mix of grass and forb species and expansive range, provide critical habitat for thousands of pollinators: bees, butterflies, beetles, bats, birds, and moths, to name a few. Pollen transferred between flowering plants produces fruit and seeds that serve to nourish a wide variety of species, while pollinators themselves serve as an essential food source for birds and other vertebrates.

Loss and degradation of native grasslands has reduced both foraging and nesting habitat for pollinators and as a result has had a devastating effect on pollinator populations.[19] Moreover, the numbers of pollinators and the species that depend on them have been drastically reduced in areas where

FIGURE 5.12 (*a*) Flowering agave. (Stephen Strom.) (*b*) Mexican long-tongued bat. (Bruce Taubert.)

native grass and forb mixes have been replaced by monocultures of invasive grasses.[20]

Sustaining existing native grasslands is critical to maintaining pollinator habitat. Restoring grasslands by reducing shrub and woody plant populations offers the possibility of mitigating the alarming decline in the number of bees and other pollinators.

Species Diversity

The eastern Sulphur Springs Valley is located at the heart of the Madrean Archipelago ecoregion: a biological hotspot noted for its impressively large variety and richness of floral and faunal species.[21]

A number of rare or sensitive species depend on the region's grasslands — the black-tailed prairie dog, white-sided jackrabbit, lesser long-nosed bat, yellow-nosed cotton rat, and white-sided jackrabbit — as do a suite of grassland birds, including Botteri's, Baird's, and Cassin's sparrows, the northern Aplomado falcon, and the western burrowing owl.

Moreover, grasslands in the eastern part of the valley have for the most part not yet been significantly fragmented. As a result, habitat patches are relatively intact and connected by long movement corridors. Here, bears, mountain lions, and wildcats find the space they need to hunt and to find mates drawn from diverse gene pools.

Elsewhere in the Southwest, mammals that depend on large habitat patches and unfragmented landscapes are disappearing, and many grassland birds are declining as grasslands are degraded or heavily severed by encroaching development.

Aesthetic and Spiritual Value

Grasslands offer deep satisfaction to the senses and the soul: silence, serenity, solitude, and communion with earth and sky. On some days, the only sounds are those of birds, the occasional insect, and grass rustling and swaying in response to a gentle breeze. Grasslands are a place whose near-infinite horizons invite introspection and humility and a renewed recognition of connection to things much larger than oneself. Perhaps the aesthetic and spiritual power of grasslands lies not only in their vastness but in their evocation of deep memories of the African savanna from which we emerged as a species eons ago. Could the sounds of a grasslands be a call to return home?

The Challenges of Protecting Grasslands

In the southwest, preserving grasslands depends on keeping large, contiguous rangeland intact and healthy. Most of the grasslands in southeastern Arizona and southwestern New Mexico are owned by ranching families. But sustaining a living by raising cattle is not only incredibly hard work; it is also economically challenging.

Josiah Austin captures the difficulties inherent in running a profitable cattle operation:

> Ranching is a terrible business. The average ranch in the United States makes minus 1½ percent on its assets. That's the average ranch. So there are many more ranches that lose even more and there are ranches that make a little better. I'm trying to figure out how to make it, I won't say profitable, I'll say sustainable. What I've done has resulted in my ranching losing quite a bit more than 1½ percent on current assets. The main reason is because of the restoration efforts I'm doing and the infrastructure that I'm putting in, the pipelines, the wells, the solar pumps, the earthen gully plugs.

Bill McDonald, Malpai-area rancher and former president of Malpai Borderlands Group, reinforces Austin's point: "If an average guy wants to go out and buy a ranch, you just can't do it. There's just no way you can buy a real ranch and pay for it with cattle."

FIGURE 5.13 Cienega Ranch grasslands at sunset. (Photo by Stephen Strom.)

FIGURE 5.14 Malpai Borderlands grasslands viewed from the Krentz Ranch. (Photo by Stephen Strom.)

Austin then summarizes the difficulty in keeping ranchland intact: "It's a tough way to make a living and pretty much anybody who owns a ranch free and clear could take that ranch, sell it, and put the money into something that pays 3 percent and you'll make 3 percent consistently forever. It would be a lot more than you will make ranching."

What keeps him going is a deep love for and connection to the land and a commitment to conserving and improving his ranch:

> Every day I drive down Arizona State Route 186 or drive through my ranch, it puts a smile on my face. It just makes me feel good to see this open space. When I sit where I'm sitting right now, I'm looking all the way over to the Chiricahuas. I'm looking all the way down to the Swisshelm Mountains. I can see all the way to the Huachucas. To me that is a tremendous dividend. Can it be converted? I mean, I can't eat that dividend. I can't take that dividend out and buy groceries or buy hay but it certainly is one of the dividends that this ranch pays me.

Bill McDonald, Josiah Austin, and others in the Malpai Borderlands Group who share their commitment to preserving grasslands have ensured that their ranches will remain intact forever by placing their land under conservation easement.[22] But Austin and the ranchers involved with the Malpai Borderlands Group have also demonstrated a path forward for others aspiring to preserve large, intact landscapes. Well-written conservation easements can be an effective tool for both helping ranchers sustain their way of life and also ensuring that land practices that support a healthy ecosystem are carried out over expansive areas now and into the future.[23]

As we gaze over the grass-covered rolling hills of his ranch, Austin reflects on the mindset required to undertake efforts to restore grasslands to full health: "It takes a long time. A lot of what I'm doing now, people won't start feeling the benefits until I'm long dead and gone. Sometimes you see immediate results and sometimes it might take 30 or 40 years before you really see it. It's like planting a tree. It's not really going to look good for 100 years." As the sun sets, Austin smiles, and says, "Look at that native grass coming up. The sun shining on it. This is one of the things that makes it worthwhile. Just looking out here, just seeing the beauty of these grasses."

SYNOPSIS

OVERVIEW

Cienega Ranch is located in Sulphur Springs Valley of Arizona, an area containing one of twelve grasslands in the Southwest identified by The Nature Conservancy as prime targets for conservation and restoration. Along with nearby protected federal lands, the eighty-thousand-acre ranch provides habitat for more than sixty threatened or endangered species, and long, unfragmented wildlife movement corridors.

Owner Josiah Austin has raised cattle on the Cienega for almost forty years. During that time, Austin has worked with the Trust for Public Land and the New Mexico Land Conservancy to place conservation easements on much of his range-land, and with federal agencies and NGOs to carry out extensive restoration projects to improve grassland health and watershed function.

CATALYSTS FOR ACTION

Over the past fifty years, much of the grass-rich bottomlands in the Sulphur Springs Valley have been converted to vineyards and irrigated cropland or been populated by houses for retirees and part-time residents. Wildlife habitat in those regions has been fragmented.

MEETING THE CHALLENGE

In 1982 Josiah Austin and his then-wife, Valer, began to purchase ranchland in the Sulphur Springs Valley with the twin goals of preserving remaining healthy grass-lands and improving ranches that suffered from overgrazing.

Over the years, the couple worked with NGOs and land trusts to place ranch-land under conservation easement, and to then use the funds received from the easement transactions to restore lands damaged by soil erosion and improve habitat for wildlife.

The North Star guiding the Austins' efforts is the belief that economically viable working ranches represent one of the best options for protecting open spaces and wildlife habitat.

ELEMENTS OF SUCCESS

- Access to personal funds and willingness to invest in land restoration and protection
- Successful collaboration with NGOs in raising funds for conservation easements
- Funds reinvested from purchase of conservation easements in further land acquisitions and in restoration efforts

- Collaboration with the Malpai Borderlands Group in advancing conservation goals and experimenting with rangeland management practices recommended by the MBG science advisory team

ACCOMPLISHMENTS

- Arresting soil erosion and incision of grasslands by gullies and arroyos
- Installing forty thousand rock structures and dams designed to slow runoff from rainstorms
- Enhancing habitat connectivity for endemic and migrating species
- Installing drinkers for both cattle and wildlife
- Reintroducing threatened or endangered species
- Planting large numbers of agave to provide nectar for rare species of bats
- Reintroducing the black-tailed prairie dog, once an apex species in Southwest grasslands

FUNDING

- Land trusts: Trust for Public Land; New Mexico Land Conservancy
- NRCS funding for conservation easements through the Agricultural Conservation Easement Program
- NRCS funding for land restoration through the Environmental Quality Improvement Program
- Foundation funding from the Nina Mason Pulliam Charitable Trust and the National Fish and Wildlife Foundation's Acres for America program, supported by Walmart
- Donations from the Malpai Borderlands Group
- Donations from private individuals

ONGOING CHALLENGES AND THREATS

- Sale of Arizona State Trust land: Cienega Ranch operations depend on leasing rangeland from the State Land Department
- Finding matching funds for the Agricultural Conservation Easement Program

■ ■ ■ ■ ■ ■ ■ ■

CHAPTER 6

Restoring and Stewarding Lands

Humanity is a biological species, living in a biological environment, because like all species, we are exquisitely adapted in everything: from our behavior to our genetics, to our physiology, to that particular environment in which we live. The earth is our home. Unless we preserve the rest of life, as a sacred duty, we will be endangering ourselves by destroying the home in which we evolved, and on which we completely depend.

—E. O. WILSON

Overview
Achieving Large-Landscape Goals Collaboratively

In the past, conservation goals have frequently been achieved in the wake of pitched battles between environmentalists and other interest groups; from top-down, agency-driven planning processes; or by executive action. The previous chapters provide examples of how a different approach—collaborative conservation—can successfully integrate human and environmental needs on ecosystem and regional scales while creating a positive social context for long-term cooperation among stakeholders.

- **Establishing a federally designated conservation area:** A broadly based collaborative, the Sonoita Valley Planning Partnership, worked for more than five years with the Bureau of Land Management to develop a plan to manage the Empire Ranch at the heart of the Cienega Creek watershed. The partnership's efforts culminated in establishment of the forty-two-thousand-acre Las Cienegas National Conservation Area. Once designated, the NCA protected large tracts of native grasslands, riparian areas and cienegas, watershed function, and an unfragmented wildlife movement corridor spanning more than fifty miles in the Sonoita Valley. The citizen-based Cienega Watershed Partnership, a 501(c)3 nonprofit, that emerged from the SVPP continues to monitor watershed function and ecological health in the valley, to restore degraded riparian areas and grasslands where needed, and to work with the BLM to inform stewardship of the NCA.

- **Developing and implementing a regional land-use plan:** Following five years of community discussions, citizens and stakeholder groups worked with Pima County to establish a regional land-use plan—the Sonoran Desert Conservation Plan. The plan provides a framework for establishing and protecting wildlife corridors; restoring riparian areas; conserving and stewarding working ranches; and creating and expanding mountain parks; preserving historic and cultural resources over an area of 5.9 million acres (9,200 square miles) in the eastern part of the county, while maintaining a healthy economy. Public support for the SDCP has enabled the county to raise more than $200 million to purchase open space or other areas critical to meeting the plan's objectives.

- **Forming a rancher collaborative to protect and restore grasslands:** Faced with the triple threats of fragmentation of grassland by sales of large ranches, encroachment of shrubs and woody plants, and environmental activism focused on removing cattle from nearby state and public lands, ranchers in the Malpai Borderlands region met in the early 1990s to consider their response. After two years of discussion, they agreed to form the Malpai Borderlands Group, with a mission "to restore and maintain the natural processes that create and protect a healthy, unfragmented landscape to support a diverse, flourishing community of human, plant and animal life in our Borderlands region." Over the past twenty-five years, more than 75 percent of the ranches in the nine-hundred-thousand-acre region have been placed under conservation easements that preclude development and consequent land fragmentation. Working in collaboration with representatives from state and federal agencies, NGO staff members, and environmentalists, the MBG has developed and implemented a fire management plan, formed a broadly based science advisory committee to inform rangeland stewardship practices, and worked collaboratively to restore grassland function and wildlife habitat.

- **Purchasing and operating working ranches to protect open space and wildlife:** Starting in 1982 Josiah Austin and his then-wife, Valer Clark, began to purchase ranchland in the Sulphur Springs Valley with the twin goals of preserving healthy grasslands in a region that has witnessed rapid conversion of land to irrigated cropland, nut trees, and vineyards, and restoring grasslands degraded by overgrazing. Over the years, Austin and Clark have worked with NGOs and land trusts to place ranchland under conservation easement and used funds received from easement arrangements to restore grasslands damaged by soil erosion and to improve habitat for wildlife. Their efforts are based on the belief—shared with the Malpai Borderlands Group—that economically viable working ranches represent one of the best options for protecting open spaces and wildlife in the West.

The Need for Landscape-Scale Conservation Efforts

These examples provide compelling evidence that groups of citizens and committed individuals can find common ground and develop creative solutions to achieving essential conservation goals. The need to incentivize and support such collaborative conservation efforts on a national and indeed global scale has never been more urgent. Urban and suburban development are continuing to encroach on natural habitat, and water use by a rapidly growing populace is depleting surface and groundwater and threatening the viability of streams, rivers, and riparian areas.

As a result, we are rapidly losing our natural heritage. Ecologists estimate that several thousand species are becoming extinct every year: about one thousand times the nominal natural rate that obtained in preindustrial times.[1] Over the past forty years, the abundance of mammalian, avian, reptilian, and aquatic life has decreased by 60 percent.[2] Continuing on this trajectory would lead to extinction of perhaps as many as 50 percent of extant species by midcentury. In the United States alone, about 12,000 wildlife species are currently threatened by extinction. Bees and other pollinators are disappearing at a rapid rate, putting crop yields at risk.[3] And over the past fifty years, the total bird population in North America has lost three billion birds, nearly 30 percent of the total avian population.

Loss of habitat is a major cause of wildlife population decline and species extinction.[4] Nearly half of the riparian areas and wetlands in the contiguous forty-eight states have been damaged or lost, while eight thousand square miles (more than five million acres) of ranch- and farmland is lost to development every decade. These trends are disturbing. Ecologists are unambiguous in their conclusions that rich and diverse plant and animal species are fundamental to the functioning of healthy ecosystems and loss of habitat means loss of species. Protecting and restoring habitat and connections between functioning habitat patches will require landscape-scale efforts.[5]

Watersheds provide another example where large-landscape conservation and planning is urgently needed. Healthy watersheds support groundwater sources, help to build fertile soil, provide nutrients for many species, and store, filter, and purify the water we drink.[6]

However, the health of our watersheds is at serious risk. Between 1950 and 2015, withdrawals of both surface and groundwater for agricultural, industrial, and human consumption across the United States increased by nearly 50 percent.[7] Groundwater withdrawals alone tripled during that period.[8] In the arid American Southwest, the combination of human impacts and drought has reached a critical point, with many river levels at historical lows and key reservoirs seriously depleted. The effects of climate change are predicted to exacerbate these trends.

Moreover, a national survey of rivers and streams in the United States shows that only 28 percent of these fluvial arteries are in sound biological condition. As a result nearly 40 percent of native fish in inland streams and waterways are endangered, threatened, or vulnerable.[9]

Developing regional conservation strategies aimed at reducing usage and protecting the biological integrity of well-functioning fluvial ecosystems on a regional scale represents an essential and compelling challenge.

Preparing to Meet Conservation Challenges

Addressing the challenges of preserving and restoring healthy ecosystems and watersheds will require an all-lands approach involving conservation efforts on public, private, and tribal lands. While our national parks, monuments and other federally managed lands contain somewhere between half and two-thirds of listed endangered species, the remainder depend on habitat found only on privately held lands.

Moreover, some recent studies have suggested that for most species to survive in the wild requires that 30 percent of their habitat and habitat range be protected. Federal lands alone do not provide sufficient habitat. A viable conservation strategy for protecting at-risk species, or more broadly for maintaining robust biodiversity must necessarily involve private as well as federal lands to provide adequate habitat and to facilitate wildlife movement.[10]

As another example, ensuring the healthy functioning of a watershed re-quires coordinating conservation and stewardship efforts across a mosaic of public and private land: national forests, privately held forests, ranches, state trust land, and privately held parcels. For example, runoff from fire-scarred forests or pollution from mines in unprotected areas miles away from creeks can affect the quality of water that both humans and wildlife depend on. Multiple housing developments on private land within a watershed might require extensive withdrawal of groundwater, which in turn could degrade riparian areas along a creek, increase the likelihood of downstream flooding during storm events, decrease species habitat, and sever wildlife movement paths essential to maintaining healthy species populations.

Protecting ecosystem and watershed functions throughout the United States will require not only an integrated all-lands approach, including both public and private lands, but an all-hands approach, involving broad public participation in shaping how to protect and steward large landscapes.

To succeed, we need to think of landscape as people plus nature, not as lands isolated from people. Furthermore, "protecting a landscape" should be taken to mean "finding ways to use land in such a way that it serves the needs of people and supports healthy ecosystems comprising a rich mix of plant and animal life." To succeed, an all-hands approach requires that the interests of all stakeholders be heard, and that all stakeholders collaborate in shaping the outcome.

In the following sections we summarize lessons learned from the four large-landscape conservation efforts discussed in chapters 2 through 5 and review all-lands options for protecting, restoring, and stewarding lands. We next outline elements that underlie successful all-hands collaborative conservation efforts and discuss options for incentivizing and supporting individuals, groups, and communities to embrace the challenge of meeting environmental, social, and economic needs.

Selecting and Prioritizing Areas to Be Conserved

Preserving healthy ecosystems or restoring ecosystem functions will require significant commitments of both financial and human resources. Because these resources are finite, individual communities and citizens nationwide will need to prioritize how time and money should be invested in order to optimize conservation outcomes. The approach taken by Pima County in forging the Sonoran Desert Conservation Plan offers one template for large-landscape conservation: the county's Conservation Lands System.

The two key elements informing the CLS are location of habitat needed to sustain populations of endangered, threatened, or vulnerable species and of corridors linking habitat areas. Over a three-year period, a team of scientists drawn from around the country compiled a list of vulnerable plants and wildlife and carried out detailed studies of habitat and habitat conditions for forty-four endangered or declining species. Using those data, along with surveys of vegetation, soil conditions, and terrain in eastern Pima County, the scientists created a biological reserve map depicting the locations of critical habitat patches and connecting corridors. Of special importance to ensuring the long-term survival of plants and wildlife are aquatic and riparian areas which house the majority of vulnerable species, along with grassland, desert scrub, and cave ecosystems.[11]

The CLS map plays an essential role in guiding county land-use policies. Over the past twenty years, the CLS and associated building regulations and incentives have served to focus growth toward existing urban areas rather than in biologically sensitive areas. The CLS has also been used to identify targets for land purchases and conservation easements as well for investments in restoring the ecological health of riparian systems and grasslands.

Selecting Habitat Patches Critical to Protecting Biodiversity

The Nature Conservancy has suggested a similar strategy for guiding nationwide large-landscape conservation efforts. The conservancy proposes as an overall goal that "the United States seek to sustain the full range of terrestrial, freshwater and marine ecosystems and their native species even as they change in composition and structure in response to development and climate change." Its approach envisions identifying conservation priorities within an ecoregion (for example, the Sonoran Desert ecoregion): an approach somewhat analogous to that taken in preparing the Conservation Lands System for the SDCP.[12]

Paul Beier of the Center for Large Landscape Conservations explains:

> [The Nature Conservancy] uses what they call fine filter and coarse filter strategies. So their *fine filter* identifies habitat species by species. For example, condor habitat is well mapped. Some really endangered species, we know where

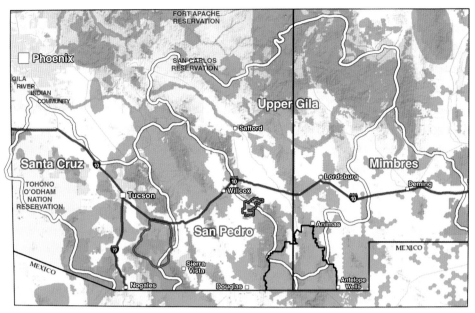

FIGURE 6.1 Regions of high biodiversity (green) in the Malpai Borderlands region, (outlined in black), Cienega Ranch (outlined in red), Sonoita Valley (outlined in light purple), and environs. Selecting lands for protection based solely on biodiversity may not provide sufficient protection for healthy watershed function. (Map adapted from The Nature Conservancy Resilient Land Mapping Tool, https://maps.tnc.org/resilientland/, with watershed boundaries obtained from the U.S. Geological Survey's Watershed Map of North America and of Major Watersheds of New Mexico and from the Arizona Department of Environmental Quality.)

they are. So we can identify critical habitat patches [for these species] using a fine filter approach. The idea behind their *coarse filter* approach is to identify habitat for species for which [habitat] studies are incomplete or lacking. For example, if I have a lot of riparian forest, it's probably going to contain habitat not only for threatened or endangered species known to depend on riparian forests but for a wide range of plants and animals that aren't well mapped.

Identify Habitat to Enable Species to Survive in the face of Climate Change

The Nature Conservancy further proposes that the highest conservation priority be given to land containing a "high diversity of species, abundant habitat, topographic and elevation diversity that provides a range of habitat types. . . . and minimal barriers that restrict adaptive movement of species or ecosystems" in response to climate change. They refer to such areas as "resilient lands," chosen in service of "ensuring that wildlife will have suitable habitat both now and in the future."

The conservancy has developed a resilience mapping tool to guide selection of key targets for conservation efforts.[13] The input data for the tool includes both (a) natural stronghold areas known to support "exemplary habitats, or rare species and [which have characteristics that suggest that they] may provide refuge . . . as climate changes" as well as (b) land having physical properties and natural communities similar to those found in natural strongholds.

Paul Beier describes this latter approach to identifying resilient land: "It's called an *abiotic coarse filter*—a combination of soil and topographic setting, elevation; things that are going to be constant even as climate changes." Land areas having high species diversity and access to refuge habitat in the face of climate change is given a high resilience score.

The Nature Conservancy's tool also provides a local connectedness metric that quantifies the barriers to wildlife movement within a landscape. A landscape rated "highly connected" promotes resilience to climate change by allowing species to move freely into areas having more suitable climate. As an example, Paul Beier suggests "we look at connectivity of abiotic settings. The most obvious one we always want is riparian connectivity. Even as climate changes, the wet areas are still going to be the wet areas. The streams are going to be at the bottoms of drainages. So let's use some of these abiotic, these geophysical settings and try and have some [unfragmented] continuity of those."

In combination with the resilience tool's local connectedness metric, The Nature Conservancy's resilience score can serve to guide the efforts of individuals, groups, communities, and political leaders with data to inform land-use and conservation investment strategies.

Lori Faeth of the Land Trust Alliance notes the importance of The Nature Conservancy's efforts "to comprehensively map resilient lands and significant climate corridors." She also mentions the Gap Analysis Project, a complementary effort by the U.S. Geological Survey to produce maps of areal range and predicted distributions for more than two thousand species; detailed vegetation and land cover patterns; and an inventory of terrestrial and marine protected areas. "Both layers of information help guide our members' conservation target selection," Faeth says.

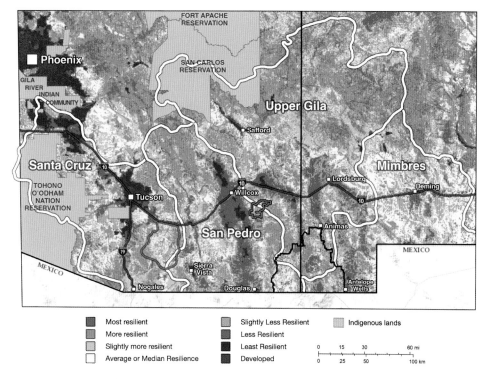

FIGURE 6.2 Landscape resilience in the Malpai Borderlands region (outlined in black), Cienega Ranch (outlined in red), and the Sonoita Valley (outlined in light purple). The most resilient areas exhibit a significant diversity of local climate conditions and low levels of human modification, thus providing species with the connected, diverse climatic conditions they will need to persist and adapt to changing regional climates. Note that selecting lands for protection solely by using a resilience index may not provide sufficient protection for healthy watershed function. (Map adapted from The Nature Conservancy Resilient Land Mapping Tool.)

Ecologist Ron Pulliam, former director of the National Biological Service, points to NatureServe as another entity that has assembled data on the location of species and ecosystems and their spatial distribution, along with models to assess extinction risks and identify priority conservation areas: "Each state has a group of biologists that are part of NatureServe. As one example of how NatureServe is used, there is an organized effort [in some states] to create a template for how you would connect habitats. Some states have taken it much further than others. Florida, for example, has developed a very widely supported plan that gets a lot of in-state funding."[14]

Including Watershed Protection in Developing Land-Use Strategies

Brian O'Donnell, director of the Campaign for Nature, suggests that landscape-scale conservation efforts be based not only on biodiversity and resilience, but on protection of watershed function: "I think watershed protection in general, and fresh water specifically, can sometimes become an afterthought. It is easy to imagine that water is automatically conserved by protecting land but that won't be true if you're not prioritizing the right places." Examination of figure 6.1, in which watershed boundaries are superposed on a map showing regions of high biodiversity, illustrates O'Donnell's concern.

Gita Bodner also emphasizes the importance of ensuring healthy watershed function when prioritizing lands for enhanced protection or stewardship:

> In the early days of conservation work on the San Pedro River, The Nature Conservancy purchased conservation easements on any place that came up near the San Pedro River. Our recent work has been much more focused on keeping water in the river, recognizing that you can protect all of the land you want but if the water isn't high enough in the ground that cottonwood roots can reach it, then you're not going to have a riparian forest. You're not going to have a live river. You're going to have a dry riverbed.
>
> So much more work on the San Pedro in recent years has focused on ways of keeping water in the river. For example, we've ended up buying or buying easements on small properties that don't have a ton of biodiversity—they've been used and abused—but they've got a shallow water table and if they had wells drilled on them, those wells would have a disproportionately large impact on the river. So it's more targeted on protecting watershed function, rather than on individual places [for example, those exhibiting high biodiversity].

O'Donnell's and Bodner's remarks emphasize that meeting the joint challenges of sustaining the richness and diversity of species along with the healthy functioning of watersheds and connected ecosystems requires conservation planning at large-landscape scale. The tools for identifying and prioritizing critical conservation lands are relatively well developed and in place. What is needed are strategies, policies, and funding to incentivize individuals, groups, and communities to undertake large-scale conservation.

Tools for Implementing Large-Landscape Conservation

Meeting the conservation challenges of the twenty-first century will require adopting new land-use policies to achieve the linked goals of protecting the integrity of ecosystems, watersheds, and wildlife habitat in the face of climate change while enhancing and sustaining the economies of both rural and urban communities.

Protecting sufficient habitat to ensure robust biodiversity or safeguarding lands essential to proper functioning of watersheds will require a combination of approaches across a variety of landownerships: protected public lands such as national parks, monuments, and conservation areas; working farms, ranches, and forests; tribal lands; and private land.

Chris Horyza, who retired in 2013 as state planning and environmental coordinator of the Arizona State BLM office, captures the magnitude of the challenges:

> When I started working on a concept for ecosystem-level planning, I realized how disjoint management and responsibility is, especially given that ecosystems are so big. For one, the missions and interests of the federal agencies are different.
>
> You have the Park Service, who has a preservationist approach to management. Then you have the Forest Service and the BLM, who have a multiple-use, sustained-yield mandate in the laws that guide their management, all while maintaining the integrity of the landscape as you do that. Next you have the Fish and Wildlife Service, who are managing [to preserve] habitat. Then you have state agencies whose goal is to generate as much revenue from those lands as they possibly can. Finally, you have private lands.
>
> If you begin to look at ecosystems, there is such a mosaic of lands, along with institutional and private goals. How do you protect something? In answering that question, you have to ask about every component in that ecosystem. And you need to figure out how all those components fit together and interact in that ecosystem.

The Nature Conservancy's Peter Warren emphasizes:

> To be successful at a large-landscape conservation effort or watershed conservation, there are two tracks. You've got to pursue both and you have to be suc-

cessful at both in order to be successful in the long run. One is protecting land from subdivision and development. Two, you've got to keep the land healthy. They are two separate things. On the protection side, there are multiple mechanisms available to prevent land from being subdivided and developed. Health involves restoration and ecological management. Large-scale conservation success in the long run depends on pursuing both of those avenues.

In what follows, we discuss a suite of options for protecting and restoring lands that together offer the promise of effective large-landscape conservation.

Strategies for Land Protection
Acquisition through Direct Purchase
Purchase by Counties

A key part of the Sonoran Desert Conservation Plan, described in chapter 3, involved acquisition of lands deemed essential to achieving ecosystem and watershed protection goals. Open-space bonds totaling more than $200 million dollars enabled Pima County to purchase both large ranches and strategic parcels critical to maintaining or restoring the health of riparian areas.[15]

The ranches acquired by the county continue to be operated as working ranches. The responsibility of proper stewardship of each ranch is shared with a representative of the county, who works with the rancher to adapt management practices to changing conditions on the ground. As a result, open-space and wildlife corridors are maintained, while an important cultural element of the rural Southwest is preserved.

Dean Bibles discusses the success of another county-based land acquisition program initiated by San Antonio, Texas, and aimed at protecting the watershed surrounding San Antonio: "I was involved in a small group, way back in 2000, who advocated for passage of Proposition 3 which required that a portion of sales tax (1/8 percent) would go to protect our watershed, the Edwards Aquifer." Between 2000 and 2005, the tax raised $45 million dollars to purchase nearly 6,500 acres located in the vicinity of the recharge zone of the aquifer. The citizens of San Antonio reapproved the tax in 2005, 2010, and 2015 with the goal of ensuring that the quality and quantity of water in Bexar County and the City of San Antonio would be maintained. Acquisitions in the recharge zone have now exceeded 150,000 acres.[16]

Purchase Through Funds Acquired by a Federal Agency

Lands identified as critical to meeting environmental goals can also be acquired by federal agencies. The late Michael Taylor, former Arizona assistant state director of the BLM, describes several options available to the agency: "There are a number of ways the BLM can acquire funding to do these acquisitions, [including] direct funding from Congress. The decisions to make those acquisitions would be included in a resource management plan. If we know there are certain specific properties we would really like to acquire, you would see those specifically identified in the RMP." He continues, "There are a number of other tools [like] the Land and Water Conservation Fund. The Federal Land Transaction Facilitation Act provides monies to the BLM from sales of BLM lands and allows those monies to be used to acquire other properties that were important from a land management standpoint, be it biological or cultural." The U.S. Fish and Wildlife Service is also able to acquire land from willing sellers through use of Migratory Bird Conservation and Land and Water Conservation Fund dollars.[17]

Purchase of Conservation Lands by Groups

Jack Williams of Trout Unlimited describes another route to acquiring critical conservation lands—purchasing from funds raised by a group of conservation-minded citizens:

> I used to sit on the board of a group called the Western Rivers Conservancy, formed to buy land along western rivers and streams to protect habitat for fish and wildlife. They acquire lands and try to put them together with existing conservation parcels. One of the early big projects was on the Hoh River in Washington State, which springs out of public lands in the Olympic Peninsula. Over many years, they've managed to purchase a lot of critical private lands right along the river, and then established the Hoh River Land Trust to oversee and manage them. Their primary approach is filling in critical in-holdings around federal lands.
>
> They've done a lot of work in Oregon too. For example, they've bought a number of big ranches along the John Day and BLM has used Land and Water Conservation money to buy them from the Western Rivers Conservancy and then turn them into publicly held lands.[18]

Purchase of Conservation Lands by Committed Individuals of Means

In chapters 4 and 5, we recounted the roles of Drummond Hadley and Josiah Austin in using their personal resources to purchase large tracts of grasslands in the Madrean ecoregion. Hadley's acquisition of the Gray Ranch played a major role in catalyzing the success of the Malpai Borderlands Group in placing conservation easements on more than six hundred thousand acres of prime grassland. Josiah and Valer Clark Austin's purchase of more than 200,000 acres of grasslands in the Sulphur Springs Valley and adjacent areas in Mexico has enabled restoration of previously degraded grassland to health and protected significant acreages of open rangeland. In both cases, the lands are stewarded using management practices informed by the best rangeland science.

Paul Beier of the Center for Large Landscape Conservation describes a similar effort:

> In Southern California [Dave Myers] committed part of his fortune to start the Wildlands Conservancy, which has purchased around two hundred thousand acres of land in Southern California for protection. I recall one campaign called Save the Saints: San Bernadino, the San Gabriel, the Santa Anas, they're "the saints." But a lot of them had a lot of private in-holdings. They made it a point to buy wherever possible, all of the private in-holdings and deed [them] to the Forest Service.
>
> [They also worked to consolidate the] the Mohave National Preserve in the Mohave Desert. When the Mohave National Preserve was created, there was BLM land in a checkerboard pattern together with other land, most of which was still owned by a few private landowners. Wildlands Conservancy went and bought all of it and told the federal government, "We'll give this to you if you make it a national preserve and don't charge people to come onto it." The negotiated for several years but they did it. I mean, that's fantastic. They just get out their checkbook and negotiated with the landowner.[19]

The Wildlands Conservancy has broadened its reach by acquiring large donations from wealthy benefactors and using their contributions to acquire important parcels of conservation lands.

Acquisition of Conservation Lands via Land Exchanges

Upon entering the Union, each state was granted state trust lands designated primarily to support public schools.[20] These lands are then sold or leased to generate funds for schools (and in some cases other public institutions) in accordance with policies adopted by state trust boards, commissions, or agencies.[21] The federal government retained possession of public lands, now managed primarily by the National Park Service, the U.S. Forest Service, the Bureau of Land Management, the Department of Defense, and the U.S. Fish and Wildlife Service.

Among the Four Corners states of the American Southwest, the fraction of remaining state trust, the fraction of remaining federal lands, and the area of each state are, as of the end of 2022, as follows: Utah, 6 percent trust, 65 percent federal, 54 million acres; New Mexico, 12 percent trust, 35 percent federal, 78 million acres; Colorado, 4 percent trust, 36 percent federal, 66 million acres; and Arizona, 13 percent trust, 39 percent federal, 73 million acres.[22]

In all states, state land departments are legally bound to manage lands in a manner that serves the best interest of the trust beneficiaries—primarily public schools—to the exclusion of other public interests.[23] In Utah, New Mexico, and Colorado, revenues generated for the trust derive predominantly from oil, gas, and mining leases and secondarily from grazing leases, timber, and land sales. In Arizona the bulk of trust land revenues come from commercial leases, rights-of-way, and agricultural and grazing leases.

In the Southwest, federal and state trust lands comprise a significant fraction of the matrix of lands that need to be managed, restored, or protected in order to meet conservation goals. Unfortunately, but hardly surprisingly, these lands are not distributed in a manner that matches conservation priorities for protecting watersheds, ecosystems, or wildlife movement corridors. In Utah, New Mexico, and Colorado, trust lands are distributed in a checkerboard pattern across the state. In Arizona the trust lands are more consolidated as a result of land exchanges from the late 1930s to the early 1960s allowed by the Taylor Grazing Act and from 1984–88 by land exchanges authorized by the Federal Land Policy and Management Act.

Incorporating state trust lands into a large-landscape conservation strategy involves two challenges: the requirement that disposal or exchange of state trust lands meet the legal obligation to maximize returns to the trust fund; and the difficulty of effecting exchanges with federal agencies that satisfy both conservation and revenue raising requirements.[24]

The challenge is even greater in Arizona, where a decision by the state supreme court in *Fain Land and Cattle vs. Hassell* (1990) concluded that exchanges of trust land violate the state constitutional requirement to sell land at public auction.[25] Before 1990 land exchanges in the state resulted in the protection of millions of conservation acres while providing the State Land Department with federal lands located in areas that enabled high-return real estate sales.

John Leshy recalls, "Dean Bibles and Bruce Babbitt really remade the map of the state of Arizona in the 1980s by primarily exchanging rural isolated scattered parcels of state land for developable BLM land. At that time, they were able to do it all administratively." Bibles comments on the care that went into the land exchanges during that time, saying they worked to make sure "that when we did an agreement, we'd have a team of state people and BLM people that would look at tracts of land and determine 'does this land have the kind of values that suggest it should stay in public ownership, or should it be in state trust, where they can use it to make the money required for the school trust?'"

Retired New Mexico State BLM director Jesse Juen encapsulates the potential value of, and impediments to, federal-state land exchanges:

> I think that there's tremendous opportunity for land exchanges that put the state trust land offices in a position of generating significant revenue from exchanged federal land. [In return,] the public could [obtain] return in terms of conservation values on the State lands. But today, the exchange process is so complicated, so difficult. It is ultimately up to the state land office to say, "Yeah, I like your appraisal," or "No, I don't." You could go through years of work and all kinds of consternations and get the appraisal and they say, "Nah, we don't like it."

Incentivizing Stewardship of State Trust Lands to Meet Conservation Objectives

Recently, a few states in the West have begun experimenting with special stewardship classifications for trust lands selected to be managed in a manner that improves or sustains the health of the land. Colorado has taken an even bolder step by creating a stewardship trust, which currently holds three hundred thousand acres of state trust lands deemed to have high conservation values. The arrangement is not permanent but will ensure that those lands will not be sold or developed for a long time.

Colorado has also initiated a conservation incentive for state trust land leased for grazing. In return for granting longer-term leases, ranchers commit to adhere to higher standards of range management on leased lands.

Similar policies could in principle be implemented on federally held lands. The adaptive management plan adopted for Las Cienegas National Conservation Area represents an exemplary illustration of how federal lands can serve both working ranching operations and long-term environmental goals.

Using Conservation Easements to Protect Important Conservation Lands

The success of the Malpai Borderlands Group and rancher Josiah Austin in protecting land from subdivision and development resulted from their placing lands under conservation easement. Easements are voluntary agreements that limit land uses in service of conservation goals.[26] They can be either sold or donated to a legally qualified conservation organization, typically a land trust or a government agency. For sold easements, the purchaser pays the current landowner an amount calculated by subtracting the estimated sale price of the property with the easement in place from the current market value of the property with development rights intact.

In the case of a donated easement, the landowner is eligible for a tax deduction of value determined by the assessed valuation of the property and the income status of the donor.

Although the use of property under conservation easement is subject to the conditions of the easement agreement, landholders retain rights, including the right to sell the land or to pass ownership to their heirs. The organization that holds the easement is responsible for ensuring that the donated or purchased land is properly stewarded.[27] In the case of Cienega Ranch, that organization is the Trust for Public Land. For the Gray/Diamond A Ranch, the Animas Foundation has that responsibility.

Advantages of Conservation Easements

One advantage of purchasing a conservation easement is that the cost of placing land under easement is usually significantly less than it would be were the land to be acquired outright. They can also provide economic benefit to landholders who are land rich but cash poor, and allow them to continue farming or ranching.

Conserved property can continue to provide economic benefit to both current and future landholders and their communities, as land under easement remains on county and state tax rolls.

Ecologist Ron Pulliam, former director of the National Biological Service, comments: "I would argue that you can do an awful lot more for conservation than [outright acquiring] big pieces of land by working with existing landowners and providing them incentives to steward their land responsibly or to place conservation easements on the land. I would focus acquisition dollars on critical habitat and the threatened connections between habitat patches."

The late Michael Taylor (formerly of the BLM) echoes Pulliam's remarks: "In looking at the relative merits of easements and acquisitions, I think it depends on the conservation importance of the property and the level of control you need to have on it. If it's super critical, maybe it's better to just purchase it. I personally think your money goes a lot further [with conservation easements] and you [still] can negotiate to get what you need" by stipulating how the landholder is obliged to steward the land.

Acquiring Conservation Easements

There are a number of avenues for acquiring the funds needed to purchase conservation easements.

COUNTY FUNDS

When the City of San Antonio passed Proposition 3, it was able to accrue funds to purchase conservation easements critical to protecting the Edwards Aquifer.[28] Gaining agreement from initially skeptical farmers and ranchers who owned land essential to meeting the goals of the aquifer protection project required artful discussions.

Dean Bibles describes the process of gaining trust and then agreement from landholders: "I was very heavily involved in visiting directly with the ranchers. I would explain to them, 'You're selling the development rights. You're not giving up any ownership. You're just saying, this land is now committed to watershed protection.' That accomplishes two things for the rancher."

He continues:

One, we do an appraisal to see what that development right is worth, which is a pretty good chunk of change. They get a pretty good piece of money for the easement. If they're in danger of losing their ranch, that usually would help. Two, it forever locks it in as an agricultural base, which in Texas means that the county cannot tax you for development purposes. That's important, because as soon as the state says, 'This could be developed,' they can tax land as development property. If that happens, most ranchers can't afford to own it anymore. So I would say to a rancher, 'If you sell this conservation easement to the City of San Antonio, you can pass your land down and keep this in ranching from now on [because it is being taxed as agricultural rather than development property].' Boy I'll tell you, they would line up. We didn't have enough money to buy all of the conservation easements people were willing to sell. So we renewed the program in 2005, 2010, 2015. It's been a very popular thing. People lined up to sell the conservation easements.

FEDERAL FUNDS

The U.S. Department of Agriculture administers the Agricultural Conservation Easement Program through the Natural Resources Conservation Service.[29] The ACEP program provides funds to "help private and Tribal landowners, land trusts, and other entities such as state and local governments protect farms from development and ensure farm viability for future generations by preventing land (including rangeland, pasture, and shrubland) from being converted to other uses." The funds are awarded to land trusts and other nonprofit organizations, as well as state and local agencies and Indian tribes. As is the case with purchased or donated easements, the entity awarded ACEP funds to acquire a conservation easement, is then responsible for enforcing its terms.

Decisions regarding where to invest these funds are made at both the federal and state level. The BLM's Jesse Juen describes the process: "There are national programs, which are being handled out of the Beltway and they'll have the parameters of what you qualify for and under what circumstances. Then there are state-level programs. Most of your state NRCS directors. . . . can decide program parameters within their specific states. They could be species-driven, they could be habitat-driven. They create committees in the state to help them understand where [they should invest]."

One advantage of funding easements through the NRCS is that ranchers and agricultural producers trust the agency "because they have a history of working with them. They're a natural partner" for doing conservation-related work, says Peter Warren. However, to receive ACEP grants, organizations must provide matching funds. Warren notes that "on the ag land easement program, NRCS will typically pay 50 percent and then partner organization(s) [provide the remainder of the funding]. If your land lies within areas designated 'grasslands of special significance,' then NRCS can pay 75 percent instead of just 50 percent. So [in doing an easement] there are three partners. There's NRCS, there's the private landowner, and then there's a local land trust or organization holding the easement."

LAND TRUST FUNDS

Land Trusts such as the Arizona Land and Water Trust and the Trust for Public Lands can purchase easements either from their own funds, or in collaboration with ACEP, private donors or other funding sources.[30]

Says Trout Unlimited's Jack Williams,

> It's been interesting to watch that easements, rather than straight out land acquisitions or water acquisitions are being favored a lot right now. It's been stimulated by the proliferation and success of a lot of local land trusts that function at a smaller geography but really get in there and work with local landowners to protect agricultural lands or scenic lands or whatever it might be. Those easement dollars go a lot farther than acquisition dollars. They're working with the local community and those dollars can go a lot farther both politically and economically in meeting conservation objectives.

Les Corey of the Arizona Land and Water Trust summarizes how the trust has been able to purchase conservation easements in the Sonoita Valley in order to protect the valley's grasslands from fragmentation and development: "We've been able to secure funding from the Natural Resource Conservation Service because of the quality of the grasslands down there. The [Arizona Land and Water Trust] has been in a strong position to raise [NRCS/ACEP] monies for easements on key ranches in that area, and then combine those monies where possible with funding from the Department of Defense through the Sentinel Landscape program."[31]

The trust's Cameron Becker describes how Arizona Land and Water Trust worked with a landholder to place a conservation easement on a key property in the Sonoita Valley:

> Let me tell you about the Rose Tree Ranch. It's a little over eleven thousand acres. It's been in one of our priority areas for acquisition for years. We fostered a relationship with the landowner, and it took probably four years or so to actually get it done. We had a lot of conversations with the landowner to first say, 'Here's the sort of work that the trust does. Tell us more about your family, your plans, what you want to see on the ranch, and what you don't want to see.' For example, this landowner said, 'I want to keep it as it is. I don't want to see a bunch of new houses or billboards. I need to be able to move my water for cattle.' So then we go out and say okay, how can acquire the funds for the rancher to be compensated for those development rights that they're giving up. Here we were able to partner with the both the USDA Natural Resources Conservation Service as well as the Department of Defense in acquiring the funds needed to purchase the easement.

The Importance of Investing Strategically in Conservation Easements

In an ideal world, limited federal, state, county, and private resources would be invested in acquiring lands or placing conservation easements on lands of highest value for protecting watersheds, ecosystems, or wildlife. However, in practice, it proves challenging to direct conservation funding in a targeted, strategic manner.

Larry Fisher notes that "a lot of conservation easements are opportunistic: they support ranchers or farmers but they don't necessarily protect ecosystems. I had a master's student, Damian Rawoot, who is now at The Nature Conservancy, [whose research focused] on the allocation of conservation easements: whether they were in fact strategically selected or whether they were opportunistic. He found that many of them were really more opportunistic than strategic."[32]

Gita Bodner of The Nature Conservancy observes,

> You could do the most thorough prioritization and the most thorough analysis of what critters exist where, and you could come up with an idealized conservation plan for a region and have it not work because the opportunities [for acqui-

sition or easements] don't line up with that idealized map. The opposite end of that approach is just sort of the willy-nilly, we'll work with anybody who wants to work with us, haphazard, scatter shot approach, totally opportunity driven.

What seems to me to in general be most effective and produce the best results for the amount of effort put into it is an approach somewhere in the middle where you have a vision of where a conservation investment will capture the most species, or the rarest habitats, or protect the most vital watershed components. You have a vision for what the ideal could look like, but you're able to be opportunistic about whom you partner with for what pieces of land and then put together the best practical solution like a jigsaw puzzle.

Challenges Posed by Conservation Easements
PROPERTY UNDER EASEMENT NEEDS GOOD MANAGEMENT

Land trusts or other organizations that hold conservation easements are responsible for sound stewardship of lands placed under easement. That requires monitoring the health of the land and working with the landholder to ensure that the terms of the easement are upheld.

"It's really important what we write into these deals," says Cameron Becker of the Arizona Land and Water Trust. "It's really a contract between our nonprofit and the landowner saying, 'These are the conservation values of the property. Here is what we've agreed together to protect.' Then it's our responsibility whether they pass it on to their kids or sell the ranch, that the land is maintained to agreed-upon standards. So, for example, if the land provides important agave and yucca habitat as well as the native grasslands, we want to make sure that we have terms in the agreement saying you can't rip that all up and put in a vineyard."

Gita Bodner cautions that "many easements don't directly affect land management, the stewardship side of it, at all." She continues,

> Managing land well is an art as much as it is a science. It takes a lot of attention. It takes a lot of resources. Restoration work takes a lot of resources. Historically people have tried to use easements both to protect land from conversion to other uses and to mandate outcomes of the more subtle management actions. They're probably not the best tool for mandating outcomes or ensuring good stewardship.
>
> Easements can work great in combination with other investments that encourage good management and facilitate good management. For example, if you have a conservation easement or some other protective mechanism in

place on a property then it would weigh in your favor when you competed for management or restoration grants. That would be a good policy. And vice versa. If you're doing a bunch of restoration work or proactive good stewardship, it would raise your likelihood of getting funded for a conservation easement.

Managing lands under easements to fully achieve conservation goals requires that nonprofits or agencies have the requisite human and monetary resources to determine whether those goals are met.

VALUE OF THE EASEMENT DEPENDS ON CONTINUED ACCESS TO LEASED LANDS

Working ranches placed under conservation easement often face an ongoing threat: canceling of grazing leases on adjacent state or federal land. State land could be sold or leased for purposes other than cattle grazing. In other cases, the resource management plan for BLM holdings or the land and resource management plan for U.S. Forest Service land might be revised either to eliminate grazing or place stricter use requirements on the land. The end result could be disastrous for a rancher whose operations depend on access to public lands.

Bill McDonald emphasizes the importance of continued access to state and federal land to the viability of ranches in the Malpai Borderlands region:

> Many of us, my ranch is a good example, depend heavily on state and public lands to graze as well as the private land. We couldn't make it on private land as a ranching enterprise, no way in the world, if it was just the private land. In recognition of that, members of the Malpai Borderlands Group have agreed that if for any reason that has nothing to do with the performance of the ranch you lose access to your public and/or state land, then the easement can be retired. We feel it is very important that ranching on those lands continue to be viable and it wouldn't be if the public or state lands are taken away from the rancher.

CONSERVATION EASEMENTS CAN SOMETIMES BE MISUSED

Although conservation easements hold great promise for conserving working lands to serve larger environmental goals, the easement process is unfortunately subject to abuse.

Tom Cors, director of lands for U.S. Government Relations, describes a particularly pernicious scheme:

A syndicator will buy 100 acres for 4 investors, for say, $100,000. Then they'll draw up plans to have this land [platted] for development. [Next], an appraiser will come in and say that $100,000 dollar piece of land is now worth a million dollars. So, the people who put in their quarter of the $100,000 price tag get to claim that the land is now worth $1 million. They'll then 'donate' a conservation easement appraised at $1 million and thereby receive a tax deduction. So each of the four individuals who invested $25,000 to purchase the 100-acre piece could receive a $250,000 deduction. The syndicators are doing things like this at about six times the pace of the conservation community's easement purchases. It's a real concern that these practices are going to jeopardize one of the big tools that we've got in the conservation community, which are easements and donated easements.

In the waning days of the 117th Congress, the House and Senate included language aimed at halting this practice.[33] Lori Faeth of the Land Trust Alliance expressed hope that the legislation will "drive a stake through the heart of this abuse. It will save the taxpayers literally billions of dollars and it will ensure that the thousands of transactions and conservation donations that happen each year in the name of true charity and true philanthropy will continue to go on."

John Leshy of the Hastings College of Law is concerned that the concept of "perpetuity" embodied in easement agreements may be under threat:

There have been a few recent court decisions that seem to make it quite easy to amend conservation easements. The whole idea behind them from the beginning was they need to be perpetual in order to qualify for a federal tax deduction. As you might imagine, clever lawyers get involved and they write in easement terms that make it possible to amend easements that essentially rob the easement of any protection. To the extent that happens, they're not perpetual anymore. But once you get the tax deduction, the federal government doesn't go back and revisit those.[34]

Use of Habitat or Multi-Species Conservation Plans

The success of the Sonoran Desert Conservation Plan and others based on multi-species habitat plans is linked inextricably to the regulatory power embodied in the Endangered Species Act.

The enabling legislation passed in 1973

> provides a program for the conservation of threatened and endangered plants and animals and the habitats in which they are found. The lead federal agencies for implementing ESA are the U.S. Fish and Wildlife Service [the FWS maintains a worldwide list of endangered species including birds, insects, fish, reptiles, mammals, crustaceans, flowers, grasses, and trees] and the National Oceanic and Atmospheric Administration Fisheries Service. The law requires federal agencies, in consultation with the U.S. Fish and Wildlife Service and/ or the NOAA Fisheries Service, to ensure that actions they authorize, fund, or carry out are not likely to jeopardize the continued existence of any listed species or result in the destruction or adverse modification of designated critical habitat of such species. The law also prohibits any action that causes a "taking" of any listed species of endangered fish or wildlife.

The ESA requirement that takings of habitat for endangered species be compensated by provision of habitat elsewhere makes it a powerful conservation tool. Bruce Babbitt suggests that "the Endangered Species Act could be considered a land-use planning statute, capable of forging a balance between development and the preservation of large ecosystems."
In *Cities of the Wilderness*,[35] Babbitt noted that

> the sponsors of the legislation acknowledged that to protect endangered species it would be necessary to preserve their habitat, in the words of the act itself, "to provide a means whereby the ecosystems upon which endangered species and threatened species depend may be conserved." This would require land-use planning. The ESA [as currently written] authorizes the U.S. Fish and Wildlife Service to negotiate plans that would give landowners permission to develop land, even though it would mean some incidental destruction of species, provided that enough space were set aside and preserved to give the affected species a fair chance of survival. By authorizing "habitat conservation plans" Congress invited the agency, and gave it the necessary discretion and latitude, to apply its expertise to work out solutions.

Babbitt cites Pima County as an example of how the ESA can be used creatively to forge a plan that achieves large-landscape conservation goals while establishing a context for growth and a vigorous economy:

Pima County . . . accomplished a first—using the listing moratorium as a springboard from which to develop, not just the legally required habitat conservation plan, but an entirely new open-space plan. They made a momentous decision: to take the process to the next level by preparing a comprehensive land-use and open-space plan for the county, encompassing not just the habitat of the owl and other threatened species, but drawn with the objective of protecting riparian areas, outlying rangeland, and other important ecosystems throughout the county. What finally emerged was a general land use plan, dedicating extensive areas of undeveloped land to open space through an adroit combination of public acquisition and regulation.

Thanks to the Endangered Species Act, "smarter [developers] tend to get together and say, 'let's get together and do a regional land-use plan to head off the prospect of draconian federal regulation.' That's happened in various places," says John Leshy. "A classic example is the Northwest Forest Plan which involved a big regional effort to protect old-growth forest species. Although it took ten years to negotiate, it resulted in a quite dramatic reduction in old-growth timber harvesting. But successful use of the ESA depends very much on leadership at the local level and leadership in key areas like the land developers or the timber industry or whoever has to participate and help make it work."[36]

A visionary Congress and administration could in the future amend the ESA to achieve even broader conservation goals, according to Bruce Babbitt:

The act should be amended to build upon the success stories, not just in identifying and listing species, but in transforming habitat requirements into effective land use plans. It should contain a broad mandate to identify and protect landscapes and watersheds and critical ecosystems, *whether or not an endangered species happens to be in the neighborhood* at a particular time. It should be expanded to include not just endangered species, but to promote the protection of open space and important watersheds, forests, and other threatened ecosystems—before the downward spiral to extinction begins. We should begin to think of the Endangered Species Act, not in bits and pieces, but as an effective mandate to conserve the ecosystems upon which all of life, including human life, depends.

Use of Conservation Leasing and Stewardship Grants, Habitat Leasing and Mitigation Banks

Conservation easements in principle provide permanent protections for lands placed under easement. Recently, several other options for long-term, albeit not permanent, conservation have been advanced.

Conservation Leasing

One such program is the Conservation Reserve Program (CRP) administered by the USDA Farm Service Agency: "In exchange for a yearly rental payment, farmers enrolled in the program agree to remove environmentally sensitive land from agricultural production and plant species that will improve environmental health and quality. Contracts for land enrolled in CRP are 10–15 years in length. The long-term goal of the program is to re-establish valuable land cover to help improve water quality, prevent soil erosion, and reduce loss of wildlife habitat."[37]

Conservation Stewardship Program

A similar program administered by the USDA Natural Resources Conservation Service is the Conservation Stewardship Program (CSP): "Through CSP, NRCS provides financial and technical assistance to eligible producers to conserve and enhance soil, water, air, and related natural resources on their land. CSP encourages land stewards to improve their conservation performance by installing and adopting additional conservation activities and improving, maintaining, and managing existing conservation activities on eligible land."[38] Such activities include practices that reduce soil erosion, improve soil fertility, conserve energy, enhance wildlife and pollinator habitat, and improve water quality. Funding is through contracts. The program is noteworthy for supporting not only new conservation initiatives but rewarding past land stewardship.

Habitat Leasing

Habitat leasing represents another path to supporting conservation on private lands. One example of the concept is an arrangement between the Department of Agriculture and the State of Wyoming that provides funding for landholders willing to rent out their property to the government to support big game wildlife migration.[39] For the duration of the lease, the landholder cannot subdivide or build on the land. Other habitat leasing programs involve renting private lands to the government in order to protect habitat or support ranching operations.

Lesli Allison of the Western Landowners Alliance regards habitat leasing as providing compensation to landholders for an environmental service they have provided for years. "They can't do that endlessly for free. Part of the reason we're losing these lands to development is because they're not able to compete economically with other land uses," Allison said in an interview with Wyoming Public Radio. "And that's because the value they're providing to public wildlife has never really been recognized."

In an interview for this book, Allison notes, "working lands folks [understand] habitat leasing but a lot of the conservation groups are still uncomfortable with it because it's not the permanent, legal protection that they're after. So we're having a conversation about permanent legal protection versus long-term stewardship because we want to see long-term stewardship part of the conversation about conservation."

Mitigation Banking

In places where it proves impossible or impractical to protect habitat or ecosystem function, mitigation banking represents a mechanism for compensating for environmental losses resulting from development.

In this system, a mitigation banker purchases ecologically valuable land and preserves or restores it.[40] In doing so, the banker accumulates credits that are sold to a developer whose project has inflicted ecological damage elsewhere. The proceeds from the transaction can be used to support management of land set aside to serve as a conservation bank or purchase of additional conservation lands.

"It works well with private developers because it's probably cheaper for them to acquire a remote private property that's near one of our county preserves and put it in that preserve than it is to set aside an equivalent amount of land that they just paid a lot of money for because they want to urbanize it. It's worked well with private developers," says former Pima County administrator Chuck Huckelberry. "We're working on an in lieu fee program where developers who can't find land suitable as offset [pay a fee that] goes into a fund. We then accumulate money and try to buy a ranch or try to buy other open space as it's available," adds Linda Mayro, Pima County director of sustainability and conservation.

As part of its land-use plan, San Diego County has identified areas of high biological value where endangered or threatened species and their habitat are most likely to be found. These are designated preapproved mitigation areas (PAMAs). The county land-use plan strongly encourages development outside PAMAs. As is the case for Pima County's lands of biological significance, home developers building in PAMAs are required to compensate habitat loss through on- or off-site mitigation. In the case of offsite mitigation, a developer has the option of purchasing mitigation credits from a mitigation bank.[41]

Payment for Ecosystem Services

Healthy natural systems—grasslands, forests, riparian areas—provide critical environmental services: maintaining water supplies; controlling flooding; sustaining productive soil; and furnishing habitat for a rich, diverse range of plant and wildlife species. Michael Dombeck, former chief of the Forest Service and former director of the Bureau of Land Management, stresses the importance of ecosystem services: "We're talking about fundamental things: natural processes producing clean air and clean water, rebuilding topsoils, stabilizing topsoils, and recharging aquifers."

Dombeck continues:

> When I became chief of the Forest Service, I asked myself, "How do we maintain support for public lands and public land management and doing what at least we, with the state-of-the-art knowledge that we have, believe is the right thing for the land?" Yes, some people care about trees. Some people want to log. Some people don't want to log. The old sort of one-liner that "everybody loves trees: some like them horizontal and some like them vertical," applies to this. How do we build support from the public?
>
> . . . I commissioned a team of scientists to take a look at the values of water flowing off national forest lands. The timber people knew the value of the wood. The miners knew the value of the ore. We knew the value of a barrel of oil, a ton of coal, but where were we with water?
>
> So we went ahead and carried out a study, and did it very conservatively, and found out that approximately sixty thousand communities depend on their drinking water directly from national forest watersheds. And most of them don't need water filtration plants because the water is clean and pure; a prop

erly functioning watershed saves them money. That was one way that I tried to emphasize the importance of public land and the value of the ecosystem services they provide.

[If we] quantify the water that comes off the national forest . . . we came with the value of $3.6 billion a year of water coming off the national forests, valuing it at $4 an acre-foot in the West and $2 an acre-foot in the East, where it rains more. An acre-foot is a lot of water. So we tried to put that on a footing with other commodity values.

To ensure that these systems continue to provide such services, a number of countries throughout the world have instituted programs to incentivize private landholders to follow sound ecological principles in stewarding their lands. Although they may have different acronyms, they fall under the general category payments for ecosystem services (PES), and involve either direct payments or other benefits for delivering a specific service: for example, providing habitat, protecting watersheds, or sequestering carbon.[42]

More precisely, a payment for ecosystem services is a voluntary transaction in which a well-defined environmental service or form of land use is bought by an ecosystem buyer (for example, a government agency) from an ecosystem provider (for example, a rancher) under the condition that the provider continues to supply the service. The concept of PES provides a carrot of incentives for good stewardship as opposed to a stick of environmental regulation.[43]

Says Peter Culp,

There's a lot of congruity of interests between maintaining the integrity of the watershed and the investments that need to occur in the landscape. [Maintaining the watershed's integrity] by keeping a ranch functioning may not actually require you to stop grazing, but instead be focused on what it takes to actually make ranching sustainable. But you would be hard pressed to find a single ranch anywhere in the Colorado River Basin that's making money. They're all losing money hand over fist because even pre-COVID they were maybe eking out 1 or 2 percent returns. And that was in areas with a lot of grass.

I think you could figure out a way ranching and cattle grazing economically work out. There are a lot of ranchers, not all of them, that would be more than happy to be involved in a watershed restoration economy as opposed to depending on solely on ranching where they can barely eke out a living doing it.

The USDA Farm Service Agency's Grasslands Conservation Reserve Program (CRP) is an example of a PES program designed to help landholders protect grasslands while supporting ongoing grazing operations.[44] In return for preserving wildlife habitat, reducing soil erosion, or protecting watershed function, for example, the Farm Service Agency will provide CRP funding for ongoing stewardship in the form of an annual rental payment or an annual payment to limit future development on grasslands.

A program like the Grasslands CRP provides supplemental income to ranchers that contributes not only to their livelihood but more broadly to the health of rural economies.[45] If sufficient, PES payments can make the differences between maintaining a ranch or selling it. Sale of working ranches often result in the conversion of a healthy grassland into a land-fragmenting exurban development or a water-intensive agricultural operation.

Conservation Reserve Program funding is also available for PES on privately held forest land through the Forest Management Initiative (FMI).[46] The goals of CRP-FMI funded activities are to improve the condition of the forest resource, promote sound management practices—including prescribed burning and brush management—and enhance wildlife habitat. The challenge is to fund programs like the CRP and CRP-FMI at levels commensurate with large-landscape conservation needs.

Payments for ecosystem services can also involve transactions between private ecosystem buyers and private ecosystem sellers. The Willamette Partnership in Oregon has devised a system whereby landholders can sell credits for projects that improve salmon habitat and regulate water temperature.[47] Potential buyers are utilities or corporations who discharge warm water into streams, thereby negatively impacting salmon habitat. Because regulations require that the buyers mitigate the damage to salmon habitat, the buyers need to purchase offsetting credits. The funds received by sellers from the sale credits are then invested in projects that improve salmon habitat on their lands. The PES approach adopted by the partnership is similar in some regards to the mitigation banks discussed earlier.

The concept of payments for ecosystem services is relatively new, as is the use of markets to establish fair-exchange practices. A challenge common to all PES efforts is placing a value on the multiplicity of services provided by properly functioning ecosystems. Resolution of these issues is very much in flux, as economists and ecologists debate how best to quantify and justify valuations, and policy makers struggle with resolving how to fund programs whose returns may not be visible or readily measurable on short timescales.[48]

There is some concern that using a market-based, PES system will lead to "commodification" of nature. That concern is well captured by Aldo Leopold: "At the beginning of the [twentieth] century, songbirds were supposed to be disappearing. Ornithologists jumped to the rescue with some distinctly shaky evidence to the effect that insects would eat us up if birds failed to control them. The evidence had to be economic in order to be valid. It is painful to read these circumlocutions today. We have no land ethic yet, but we have at least drawn nearer the point of admitting that birds should continue as a matter of biotic right, regardless of the presence or absence of economic advantage to us."[49]

How should we value the role of forest and farmland in sustaining the health of a watershed and purifying water? How much should we invest in keeping grassland systems intact and pollinators abundant? And how do we put a dollar amount on the aesthetic or spiritual value of open space or a riparian area filled with the songs of hundreds of migrating birds?

Absent a mechanism for quantifying the sometimes-ineffable values of particular landscapes, it may as a practical matter be necessary to refine, broaden, or develop new PES tools to incentivize preservation and restoration of environmentally critical lands.

Concluding Comments Regarding Land Protection Strategies

Former deputy secretary of the Department of Interior Lynn Scarlett suggests that achieving conservation goals will require an imaginative mix of land protection strategies: "There is certainly a place for land acquisition. Certainly, use of conservation easements has a significant role to play. [But] broadening the toolkit to envision these collaborative endeavors that take advantage of tools like easements, like mitigation banks and multiyear conservation grants to achieve certain purposes, that all needs to be part of the picture."

Michael Dombeck speaks to the importance of creating, or perhaps recreating, a deeper connection with our natural environment: "I often think about how most Indigenous peoples—not just Native American but Indigenous peoples on every continent—have a spiritual connection with nature while in our Euro-American cultures we don't have that spiritual connection as part of our value system. I wish we could figure out how to connect people to nature more successfully than we have."

We have numerous tools and policies designed to protect lands critical to sustaining the healthy functioning of grasslands, forests, and watersheds, and to preserve habitat needed to support the richness and diversity of the plants and animals with whom we share this earth. And as ecological understanding advances and biological surveys expand in scope, science can serve as an ever better guide to focusing conservation investments. The pressing question today is whether we can find the will to use our tools and knowledge to steward our ecological endowment to our benefit and the benefit of our children and generations to come.

Landscape Restoration

Meeting the conservation challenges of the twenty-first century will require a three-pronged strategy: protection of lands critical to biodiversity and ecosystem function; restoration of lands still able to provide habitat, connectivity, and healthy ecosystem function; and policies that support and encourage sound stewardship on public and private lands. The previous section summarized a range of options for land *protection*. Here, we provide examples of the role played by *restoration and stewardship* in meeting the conservation goals of Las Cienegas National Conservation Area, the Sonoran Desert Conservation Plan, and the Malpai Borderlands Group. We end with a summary of two additional examples of multi-stakeholder, multi-agency conservation plans that aim to address conservation challenges on a regional scale.

Las Cienegas NCA

The enabling legislation for Las Cienegas National Conservation Area establishes the NCA to "conserve, protect, and *enhance* for the benefit and enjoyment of present and future generations the unique and nationally important aquatic, wildlife, vegetative, archaeological, paleontological, scientific, cave, cultural, historical, recreational, educational, scenic, rangeland, and riparian resources and values of the public lands, while allowing livestock grazing and recreation to continue in appropriate areas."[50]

After the establishment of the NCA, the BLM was charged with implementing a comprehensive management plan for the NCA using the precepts developed by the Sonoita Valley Planning Partnership: to "perpetuate naturally functioning ecosystems while preserving the rural, grassland character of the Sonoita Valley for future generations." Achieving this vision required the BLM to develop a resource management plan that would "maintain and improve watershed health; maintain and improve native wildlife habitats and populations; maintain and restore native plant diversity and abundance; protect water quality; protect water quantity."[51]

The BLM's Tucson Field Office adopted this vision as the foundation for the Las Cienegas RMP and undertook to implement it through ongoing collaborations with a broad range of stakeholders, other agencies, and outside scientific experts.[52] To measure progress against the objectives of the RMP, the BLM adopted an adaptive management approach (see chapter 2): as the BLM obtains new information, it evaluates ecosystem monitoring data, consults with experts and stakeholders, and refines or alters implementation strategies.[53]

A key part of the RMP requires that the BLM manage the NCA with the objectives of restoring and maintaining the native diversity, natural distribution, and abundance of fish and wildlife species; minimizing habitat fragmentation; reestablishing, extending the habitat range of, or supplementing wildlife populations; and implementing species recovery plans.

Full-scale restoration efforts within the NCA began in 2002, after three years of monitoring a wide range of environmental indicators: aquatic habitat, water quantity, threatened and endangered species, native fish, and wildlife.

Restoration of Water Resources and Riparian Function

Prior to the rapid influx of settlers to Arizona in the 1870s and 1880s, the Sonoita Valley was reported to be a land of many springs and rich grasslands, with the valley bottom described as "quite boggy in the middle" and surrounded by "meadows of Sacaton and Salt Grass": a classic cienega. Today, little of that once-rich, extensive cienega persists: a result of draining surface and groundwater for agricultural uses, removal of beavers from streams, harvesting of trees, and intensive grazing within riparian areas and wetlands that led to erosion and down-cutting.[54] Sacaton grasslands, cottonwood-willow riparian areas, and mesquite bosques are now found only along short

FIGURE 6.3 Volunteers carrying out restoration work on Cienega Creek, organized by the Cienega Watershed Partnership. (Courtesy Cienega Watershed Partnership.)

stretches of Cienega Creek. As a result, soil erosion is accelerating and threatens existing stretches of riparian forests.

Restoration efforts in Las Cienegas NCA aim to reestablish riparian vegetation and reduce erosion with the ultimate goals of increasing the capacity of riparian areas and floodplains to slow storm runoff and capture sediment, and to increase aquatic and wildlife habitat.[55] In 2016 the Cienega Watershed Partnership and the BLM contracted the Watershed Management Group to survey the NCA and develop a list of priority areas for erosion control and riparian restoration.[56]

Later, CWP was awarded a WaterSMART grant from the Bureau of Reclamation to implement erosion control projects at six locations. Additional funding from the Arizona Department of Environmental Quality enabled the installation of various erosion control structures including rock and earth works (see chapter 5) at four more sites.[57] These installations slow water flow, allowing upstream areas to capture sediment and provide fertile soil to support growth of native plants.

Restoration of Grassland Function

Grassland ecologists estimate that one-third of historical grassland in the Las Cienegas region has been completely overtaken by shrubs and woody plants, indicative of a history of overgrazing, drought, and fire suppression. Of the remaining two-thirds, half shows signs of shrub encroachment.

The goals of the BLM RMP are to protect unfragmented grasslands, to keep them healthy, and to restore grasslands degraded by past practices. Achieving these goals will enhance habitat necessary to support wildlife species reliant on grasslands.[58]

Since 2007 the BLM has been working collaboratively with experts and stakeholders to implement a suite of treatments aimed at reducing mesquite cover: prescribed fires, mechanical treatments, and chemical treatments. The agency has treated approximately sixteen thousand acres to reduce mesquite, bulrush, and cattail coverage. Follow-up monitoring revealed that in the NCA region, grubbing (removing mesquite by the roots), hand cutting, and chemical spraying proved most effective. Where mesquite has been removed, grass and forbs have taken over. As a consequence, soil erosion has decreased as water now flows more slowly over the landscape.

Reintroduction of Endangered and Extirpated Species

Gita Bodner from The Nature Conservancy stresses the importance of enhancing endangered wildlife populations and reintroducing previously common species, highlighting their significance to a comprehensive conservation strategy:

> Funding to do restoration is a big [component of a successful conservation strategy]. I'll give you an example that's relevant to Cienega watershed. National Fish and Wildlife Foundation supported a Sky Islands Grasslands program that funded proposals from several different groups within Cienega watershed and outside of those boundaries across the neighboring valleys. . . . Funds from the foundation enabled a number of projects to restore habitats and species, and to carry out more detailed analyses of conservation priorities in the region.
>
> For example, the funds allowed the Chiricahua leopard frog restoration work in Cienega Creek program to grow and become much more active. Grant programs like that represent some of the most effective ways of encouraging and enabling good outcome-based conservation stewardship. The pronghorn project in the Cienega watershed and beyond also received funding from NFWF as did the program to reintroduce the prairie dog in the region.[59]

The FROG Project

The goals of the FROG Project are to recover populations of native fish and the threatened Chiricahua leopard frog. Aquatic species and those dependent on wetland habitat are under threat by invasive species such as bullfrogs, mosquitofish, and crayfish. The FROG program aims to rid the NCA and environs of these invasive species and to restore populations of native species.

By using funds from the NFWF and engaging the community, populations of nonnative aquatic species have been reduced, breeding populations of leopard frogs have been introduced at a number of sites, new frog refugia have been created, and native aquatic plants have been sowed.[60] The Cienega Watershed Partnership continues to engage the community in monitoring Chiricahua leopard frog populations as well as those of other rare and threatened aquatic species including Gila topminnow, Gila chub, Huachuca water umbel, and Mexican garter snake.

Native Fish Populations

Starting in 2011 the Arizona Department of Game and Fish, in collaboration with the U.S. Fish and Wildlife Service and the BLM, has reintroduced federally endangered native fish in seventeen locations within the conservation area. In 2016 the BLM continued the recovery efforts by

FIGURE 6.4 The threatened Chiricahua leopard frog. (Jim Rorabaugh, U.S. Fish and Wildlife Service.)

FIGURE 6.5 The endangered Northern Mexican garter snake. (U.S. Fish and Wildlife Service.)

FIGURE 6.6 The endangered desert pupfish. (Bruce Taubert.)

stocking four areas with the endangered Gila chub, desert pupfish, and Gila topminnow.[61]

Black-Tailed Prairie Dog

Black-tailed prairie dogs are considered a keystone species—a species that many plants and animals depend upon—in grassland ecosystems. They serve various essential roles: their burrowing helps sustain grasslands by preventing the proliferation of woody shrubs and fostering the growth of young grasses preferred by livestock. Additionally, their burrows offer habitat and refuge to other animals, while prairie dogs themselves act as prey for birds and other wildlife. Eliminating them can lead to a decline in the health of grassland ecosystems.

By the early 1930s, black-tailed prairie dogs in the region had been extirpated by ranchers who considered them pests. Starting in 2008, the Arizona Game and Fish Department reintroduced the black-tailed prairie dog at three sites in the NCA. The department monitors the population twice per year. Thus far, the reintroduction has been judged a success.

Pronghorn Antelope

In 2009 the Tucson office of the Arizona Game and Fish Department established a working group to develop a plan for grassland conservation and restoration in southeast Arizona. Following a series of planning meetings, the group—which called itself the Southeast Arizona Collaborative Grassland Working Group (SEAGRASS)—decided to use pronghorn as a focal species for its conservation efforts. Their primary goals were to increase pronghorn population and distribution across the region and to ensure connection among pronghorn habitats. Achieving those goals involved maintaining year-round water sources; protecting and improving habitat and forage; maintaining movement corridors; treating grasslands impacted by shrub encroachment; monitoring pronghorn numbers and distribution; and encouraging collaborations among interested conservation groups.

In parallel, a strategic planning group at the Arizona Antelope Foundation developed the framework for a Southeastern Arizona Grasslands Program Initiative, with goals that overlapped those of Arizona Game and Fish. Game and Fish and the Arizona Antelope Foundation succeeded in raising funds from National Fish and Wildlife Foundation, which, along with additional funds from the BLM, private landowners, and other nongovernmental organizations, enabled the initiative to invest $1.74 million in a program aimed at increasing pronghorn population, distribution, and connecting corridors.

Between 2012 and 2020, the initiative worked in 6 herd zones spanning more than 190,000 acres.[62] Fence modification programs facilitated pronghorn movement within each of the zones, and 13 water projects provided year-round water in four of the herd zones. Almost 8,000 acres of pronghorn grassland habitat was improved by mesquite grubbing, chemical treatments, and prescribed fire. Ninety-five pronghorn were introduced to supplement populations in the 6 herd zones, and the number of antelope in those zones increased by 548 animals.

One of the six herd zones was located in the heart of the Sonoita Valley. Establishing safe connectivity within the zone presented a major problem. To address this issue in the northern part of the zone, mesquite was removed, and pronghorn-friendly fences were installed along SR82 and SR83 highway rights-of-way. Multiple fence modifications near the southern extent of the valley enabled unimpeded movement of pronghorn between the Rose Tree Ranch and the Babocomari Ranch where pronghorn had been introduced in earlier decades.

A Proposal to Reintroduce the North American Beaver

Beavers provide essential services to streams and watershed. Their temporary, semipermeable dams slow down onrushing waters from rainstorms. In the process, groundwater is replenished, and as a result, surface water flows well into the summer months: a benefit to both fish and wildlife.

Beavers have long been absent from the Sonoita Valley: a consequence of extensive hunting which decimated beaver populations throughout the West. As of 2022 the BLM is considering reintroduction of the North American beaver in Las Cienegas NCA.[63] The expectation is that beavers will improve the health of streams and wetlands and serve to mitigate the ongoing effects of groundwater pumping and climate-change-induced drought and increasing temperatures.

Malpai Borderlands

From its founding the MBG committed "to restore and maintain the natural processes that create and protect a healthy, unfragmented landscape to support a diverse, flourishing community of human, plant, and animal life in our borderlands region." Key components of their twenty-year commitment to these principles are

- Reintroducing fire as a natural component of the grassland ecosystem in the borderlands
- Maintaining and enhancing watershed function by controlling erosion and repairing gullies and arroyos
- Halting encroachment of shrubs and woody plants by using mechanical and chemical treatments in addition to fire
- Restoring grassland productivity and habitat
- Working to conserve wildlife and native plants and protecting endangered species

In carrying out these objectives, the Malpai Borderlands Group provides assistance to area ranchers in the form of technical help in designing projects, cost-sharing, collaboration in implementing projects, and coordinating fire management.[64]

A key player in monitoring and improving grassland health is the U.S. Department of Agriculture's Natural Resources Conservation Service. The NRCS provides both funding and on-the-ground assistance to both the MBG and individual ranchers in the borderlands area. Collaborations with and funding from the U.S. Fish and Wildlife Service, the U.S. Forest Service, the BLM, Arizona Game and Fish Department, New Mexico Department of Game and Fish, the Arizona State Land Department, and the New Mexico State Land Office have also been essential to meeting MBG's goals.[65]

Bill McDonald notes the importance of collaboration with federal and state agencies in meeting MBG's conservation goals: "I think the agencies have been very supportive, especially the Forest Service. State Land is helpful, depending on the situation. BLM is certainly cooperative, but they don't do it on as regular or as intensive basis at the Forest Service does. Fish and Wildlife Service became a really good partner and hopefully will continue to be. NRCS was from the beginning a great partner and continues to be in Arizona, and now is a good partner in New Mexico as well."

The MBG's ability to establish effective working relationships with these agencies, as well as with private landholders, is indicative of the vision and effectiveness of its leadership and the commitment of its members to sound stewardship of land spanning almost nine hundred thousand acres.

Riparian Restoration

While there are relatively few riparian areas in the borderlands region, the MBG has been actively involved in maintaining and improving their function as well as enhancing habitat for aquatic species.

From its inception, the group has worked collaboratively with the San Bernardino National Wildlife Reserve.[66] The wildlife refuge contains scattered riparian, marshland, and aquatic habitats fed by artesian wells and seeps. It supports populations of federally listed fish that occur nowhere else in the Malpai Borderlands and in few locations elsewhere (chapter 4). Protecting these habitats and fish represents the primary mission of the wildlife refuge and was the principal reason for its establishment in 1982.[67]

In an interview with The Nature Conservancy, former U.S. Fish and Wildlife Service Wildlife Refuge Manager Bill Radke remarked that MBG "landowners in many cases share an agenda that is my job: restoring habitat and rare species."[68] As one example of what he calls "collaboration for the common good," Radke cites the willingness of rancher Warner Glenn to work with the San Bernardino National Wildlife Reserve to provide temporary refuge for the endangered Chiricahua leopard frog in one of his stock tanks. Radke comments, "The only reason these frogs are here in the San Bernardino Valley is because of this rancher."[69]

The MBG and the Sky Island Alliance are currently working to restore a cienega and creek in the southern part of the borderlands area: Cloverdale Valley. Over the past century, installation of levees along with erosion caused by past overgrazing has resulted in decreased water flow from Cloverdale Creek to the two cienegas. Restoration efforts are focused on slowing flood flows behind regulating structures and building up sediment deposits. Over time, native vegetation will take root and provide habitat for wildlife. Recent changes in grazing practices in the Cloverdale Valley have already led to establishment of a young cottonwood-willow forest—signaling a return to health of a once-rich riparian cienega system.[70]

Grassland Restoration
Reintroduction of Fire

One of the catalysts for forming the Malpai Borderlands Group was area ranchers' belief that periodic fire was critical to the health of their range-

FIGURE 6.7 Igniting the Baker II prescribed burn on June 9, 2003. Credited as the largest controlled burn in the United States, the fire ultimately burned 47,645 acres of open grassland and mountain terrain across Arizona and New Mexico. The land burned was composed of 23 percent private land, 21 percent state trust land, and 56 percent federal land. (Malpai Borderlands Group.)

lands. The group worked for years to develop partnerships with state and federal agencies, starting with the U.S. Forest Service, and later with the NRCS, the FWS, the BLM, and the New Mexico and Arizona state land and natural resources agencies. Together, they developed the Peloncillo Programmatic Plan to guide management of prescribed burning and of fires ignited naturally by lightning.[71] Consultations with scientists and conservationists at The Nature Conservancy and elsewhere were essential to evaluating the effects of fire on wildlife and informing the framers of the plan.

Over the nearly 30-year lifetime of the Malpai Borderlands Group, almost 650,000 acres has burned. Approximately 120,000 acres were ignited in prescribed burns, while the remainder were started naturally and allowed to burn subject to the precepts for extinguishing fires established by the group. Areas that have burned more than once have shown marked decrease in brush and woody plant density. In other areas, the fire policy has shown mixed results, depending on climatic conditions both preceding and following the fires.[72]

Erosion Control Measures

MBG and Malpai-area ranchers have undertaken a variety of efforts to control erosion over the years. Grassland has been restored in some areas, which helps to slow erosion. Elsewhere, ranchers have deployed gabions and constructed dikes and earthen reservoirs in order to restore gullies and fill in eroded stream channels.[73]

Reintroduction of Species

In collaboration with the New Mexico Game and Fish Department, the owners of the Post Office Canyon Ranch in the Peloncillo Mountains have reintroduced desert bighorn sheep.[74]

As part of the Southeastern Arizona Grasslands Pronghorn Initiative, a herd of pronghorn was reintroduced in the San Bernardino Valley, in the Malpai Borderlands region northeast of Douglas, Arizona.[75]

Although movement corridors are relatively unfragmented in the valley, two modest fencing projects have been carried out to increase connectivity. In addition, four water projects were instituted to ensure access to water for the pronghorn—a significant challenge, since pronghorn occupy a reserve zone spanning 140,000 acres. Land under conservation easement held by the MBG comprises much of the acreage in the herd zone. In 2019 an aerial survey recorded 203 pronghorn in the San Bernardino Valley zone, a number that ecologists believe can be securely sustained.

In 1999 the U.S. Forest Service introduced 102 black-tailed prairie dogs onto the Gray/Diamond A Ranch, and a Forest Service study suggests that following reintroduction, prairie dogs increased the mass and nutrient content of forbs and grasses significantly.[76] Cattle appear to favor foraging the grass near prairie dog towns. In turn, the prairie dogs benefit from the cattle's mowing of grass to heights of just a few inches, which enables the dogs to better detect predators from a safe distance. The study also suggests that prairie dogs contribute positively not only to vegetation biomass but to over-all diversity and density of some avian species and lizards.

Sonoran Desert Conservation Plan

The Sonoran Desert Conservation Plan stands out as an example of community-based, regional land-use planning that combines protection of both natural and cultural resources. The plan's primary conservation goal is "to ensure the long-term survival of the full spectrum of plants and animals that are indigenous to Pima County through maintaining or improving the ecosystem structures and functions necessary for their survival."

Achieving that goal has two components: preserving, restoring and en-hancing wildlife habitat, particularly for endangered and threatened species, and protecting large parcels of unfragmented open space and providing cor-ridors connecting them.

After almost two decades of acquiring or otherwise protecting high-priority lands using open-space bond monies, most of the county's efforts are now focused on restoration and stewardship of critical conservation targets: riparian areas, ranches, and wildlife habitat and corridors.

Riparian Restoration

Healthy riparian areas are critical to watershed function and wildlife. Over the past century, southern Arizona has lost approximately 90 percent of its riparian habitat as groundwater pumping, wood harvesting, and erosion has reduced or eliminated perennial stream flow and decimated riparian forests.[77] The loss of riparian habitat negatively affects the state's wildlife population, a large majority of which depends on access to healthy riparian areas. The Sonoran Desert Conservation Plan prioritizes the restoration of these areas to safeguard endangered or threatened species reliant on these habitats.

Cienega Creek Natural Preserve

One of the first investments in watershed protection after the 1983 flood was the acquisition of nearly four thousand acres adjacent to Cienega Creek to create the Cienega Creek Natural Preserve. In establishing the preserve, Pima County hoped to preserve one of the last remaining perennial streams in the eastern county and to protect and restore the riparian area surrounding the creek.

Julia Fonseca recalls the challenges the county faced following acquisition of the creekside lands: "The cows were eating all the vegetation. Young cottonwoods couldn't get any higher than a few inches because they would be eaten down by the livestock. There were native grasses there, but they were only several inches high." Fencing off the creek in order to eliminate grazing as well as the intrusion of off-road vehicles was a critical first step. Over time, the density of riparian vegetation—cottonwoods, willows, grasses, and shrubs—increased, and erosion of the creek channel decreased as onrushing water from storms was slowed by plants.

Fonseca further notes,

> When the grasses and cottonwoods were allowed to grow higher, vegetation that's along the creek channel presents roughness to flowing water. That slows the flow of water and induces the sediment to fall out, providing fertile soil for more plants to take root. After we fenced off the creek, we started to see pools forming. I asked some of the cowboys out there, "Did you see ever see pools before?" They said, "No, we never saw pools. We've been here since 1974. We've never seen pools. We've never seen cattails." So immediately this stream started to change just with the reduction of livestock grazing.

Since the Cienega Creek Natural Preserve was established, the county has continued to monitor stream flow and water quality in the area and to carry out restoration projects aimed at recharging groundwater and further stemming erosion.[78] Cottonwoods and willows have been planted along creek tributaries to stabilize arroyo banks and to shade the creeks. These projects contribute to the county's efforts to improve habitat for endangered species such as the yellow-billed cuckoo, Mexican garter snake, and the Chiricahua leopard frog.

Pantano Jungle Restoration

As part of the management plan developed for the Cienega Creek Natural Preserve, Pima County initiated a project to reestablish a mesquite bosque and sacaton grassland and increase the diversity of native vegetation in an area within the preserve that had been cleared for agricultural crop production during the 1970s. "It was the first restoration project at Cienega Creek

FIGURE 6.8 Cienega Creek passing through the Cienega Creek Natural Preserve near the Gabe Zimmerman Trail. (Photo by Stephen Strom.)

Preserve," Julia Fonseca remembers. "We were looking at one of these fields going like 'wow.' They ripped out the mesquite bosque that was once an essential component of the riparian area. They planted Bermuda grass and they grazed the hell out of it, and now it's abandoned pasture. . . . It was the beginning of the flood control district's riparian restoration program, which became much bigger."

Since the inception of what became known as the Pantano Jungle Restoration Project, native trees and grasses have been planted and check dams and other erosion mitigation structures have been deployed.[79] Over the years, the diversity of plant species has increased, and sacaton, saltbush, and mesquite have been successfully reestablished.

Bingham Cienega Natural Preserve

In 1989 Pima County acquired an area along the San Pedro River with the goal of preserving a rare, spring-fed marsh: Bingham Cienega. Early in the twentieth century, the area around the cienega was developed for agricultural purposes, in part by digging ditches and constructing berms to redirect waterflow to fields cleared of native riparian vegetation.

Over succeeding years, the county has initiated a series of projects to restore the cienega, beginning with installation of check dams to halt erosion and promote revegetation behind the dams. In 1998 The Nature Conservancy collaborated with the county on a project aimed at restoring sacaton grasslands, willow forests, and mesquite woodland.[80]

Santa Cruz River

At the beginning of the twentieth century, the Santa Cruz River was surrounded by healthy riparian areas along its path from Mexico through Nogales to Tucson and north toward the Gila River. Most of these areas are long gone: the result of groundwater pumping, overgrazing, and removal of riparian vegetation.[81]

Plans developed by Pima County call for maintaining the remaining natural riparian systems and restoring and increasing riparian habitat where possible. Because the water table now lies well below the Santa Cruz streambed in most places, restoring riparian areas and surface stream flows requires use of reclaimed water and effluent.

The City of Tucson and Pima County have constructed water treatment plants at two locations along the Santa Cruz as part of a $600 million project to reuse reclaimed water and agreed to devote part of the treated effluent to riparian restoration and enhancement projects. The water from the Conservation Effluent Pool has been used to create segments of a "living river—a thriving habitat for flora and fauna"—extending northwest from the city of South Tucson to the town of Marana.[82]

Monitoring conducted from 2013 to 2020 reveals the remarkable resurgence of a once lifeless river.[83] Wetland plants established themselves soon after effluent was introduced. Wildlife followed, along with fish and aquatic-dependent invertebrates (insects, crustaceans, and worms). Conditions improved significantly, allowing for the successful reintroduction of the endangered Gila topminnow, which has since flourished in the region.

Grasslands and Ranches

The ranch conservation element of the Sonoran Desert Conservation Plan plays an essential role in preserving unfragmented open space and connected wildlife habitat. Since 1997 Pima County has purchased more than fifty thousand acres of ranchland. Combined with leased state trust and federal lands adjacent to these parcels, the county now manages working ranches spanning nearly two hundred thousand acres.[84] The ranch conservation element serves as a model for coordinated stewardship of a mosaic of county, state, and federal lands: a critical prerequisite for most large-landscape conservation efforts.

To meet the conservation goals of the SDCP, the county partners not only with ranchers but with a variety of nongovernmental groups and individuals. Over the years, these collaborations have enabled the county to institute a variety of projects: to reintroduce fire, restore eroded landscapes, reintroduce wildlife, protect threatened and endangered species, and control or mitigate intrusion of invasive species.

To ensure effective management of the multiplicity of collaborative restoration and land stewardship efforts on a sprawling landscape, the Pima County Natural Resources, Parks and Recreation Department recently created a position to oversee both restoration efforts and invasive species mitigation.

Invasive Species Control

Pima County staff, in collaboration with state and federal agencies, monitor, inventory, and manage invasive species on all county lands. The highest

FIGURE 6.9 Sweetwater Wetlands: a lush riparian habitat created by treated effluent from the Agua Nueva Water Reclamation Facility. (Photo by Stephen Strom.)

priority is eradication of buffelgrass (see chapter 3), a major threat to the Sonoran Desert ecosystem. Other invasive plants (e.g., giant reed grass, fountaingrass, and tamarisk) are removed or chemically treated as feasible.

Restoring Grasslands in the Altar Valley

The Altar Valley, located about fifty miles southwest of Tucson, extends from the Mexican border through the Buenos Aires National Wildlife Preserve, and past the Baboquivari Mountains to the town of Three Points. Pima County manages five ranches in the area—Marley, King 98, and Diamond Bell Ranches, along with Rancho Seco and Buckelew Farm—all acquired between 2000 and 2010 using open-space bond monies.

Among the county's neighbors in the valley are a group of ranchers who formed the Altar Valley Conservation Alliance (AVCA) in 1995, following

in the footsteps of the Malpai Borderlands Group.[85] The group is committed to "work through a strongly collaborative, science-based, community
driven and integrated approach to conserve, promote and sustain healthy
and productive working landscapes, including soil and water conservation,
wildfire management, habitat conservation and protection of native species,
and other environmental initiatives."

The overlap in goals between the county and AVCA made for natural
partnerships on conservation projects of mutual interest. In an interview
with the Center for Collaborative Conservation, AVCA Executive Director
Sarah King remarked, "the folks of Pima County and their Natural Resources
Department really recognize the value that these ranches play and what it
takes to make them successful. That means being part of the neighborhood
and the alliance has helped to welcome them into the community and coordinate projects that we can do together." She continues, "the alliance's partnership with Pima County has evolved through a lot of years of time together,

FIGURE 6.10 Grasslands in the Altar Valley near the Diamond Bell Ranch. (Aerial photo by Stephen Strom.)

trust, projects, and successes. It's one that may not have been an obvious fit on paper, but it really has been such a success. They are an important part of the stuff that we do out here."

In order to halt and then reverse the invasion of woody plants and shrubs, AVCA, Pima County, and other partners developed a fire management plan in 2008.[86] The plan identified areas where fire could benefit grassland health, developed a plan for prescribed burns, and located resources needed to support fire management. With the advent in 2012 of the Altar Valley Fire Management Group, prescribed fires have been ignited on selected sites.

Thus far, the results have been encouraging. Trees and shrubs have decreased sixfold; bare ground has decreased by a factor of two; and grass cover and overall grass production (in pounds per acre) have increased by almost a factor of two.

However, there are still not yet enough fine fuels to carry fire in many areas, and in others, the risk to people and infrastructure is deemed too high to justify prescribed burns. As a result, while there has been some progress in restoring grasslands, they are still far from returning to a natural state.

Enhancing Watershed Function in the Altar Valley

The Altar Valley Conservation Alliance and Pima County also worked together to develop a plan to enhance watershed function in the Altar Valley.[87] The planning process was supported by the Pima County Regional Flood Control District and the Bureau of Reclamation WaterSmart program and completed in spring 2022. The plan focuses on two areas: mitigation of channel incision of the Altar Wash and its main tributaries and reducing shrub and brush encroachment in service of increasing ground cover by grasses and forbs.

The Watershed Plan lists, prioritizes, and provides conceptual plans for restoration projects. In addition, it provides guidelines for landholder stewardship, including shrub and woody plant removal, prescribed fire, and water harvesting.

Currently, several projects are already underway, including

- The La Osa Wells Riparian Project, which will create a perennial water supply for the Chiricahua leopard frog
- Altar Valley Brush Treatment Corridor, which aims to remove shrubs and woody plants on the Buenos Aires National Wildlife Refuge and adjacent ranches
- A water project to provide drinkers for wildlife on the BANWR

The partnership between AVCA and Pima County is another example of the kinds of collaborations—in this case between a group comprised of individual ranchers committed to environmentally sound stewardship and the county—that will be essential to achieving large-landscape conservation efforts.

Creating Wildlife Movement Corridors

In establishing the Conservation Lands System, the framers of the Sonoran Desert Conservation Plan identified "protection of existing wildlife habitat, removing obstacles to wildlife movement, and restoring fragmented landscapes as one of its six primary objectives."

The Coalition for Sonoran Desert Protection is currently working with Pima County to monitor wildlife attempting to cross Interstate 10, which is a major impediment to wildlife movement between the Santa Rita Mountains to the south of the interstate and the Rincon Mountains to the north. The coalition is also working to develop plans to facilitate wildlife movement between the Tortolita and Tucson Mountains.[88]

Says Carolyn Campbell of the Coalition for Sonoran Desert Protection, a key participant in developing the Sonoran Desert Conservation Plan,

> We have a big focus on wildlife connectivity, on mitigating fragmentation by roads, and creating wildlife underpasses and overpasses. We have a grant from the [Arizona] Game and Fish Department to place cameras on highways that impede wildlife movement, and to look at places, roadkill surveys, where animals are getting killed. We're looking at fixes. Do we need to fence some of

FIGURE 6.11 Completed wildlife underpass on State Route 86 west of Tucson. (Coalition for Sonoran Desert Protection.)

it? Do we need to clear out vegetation or perhaps make culverts bigger? We're now involved in land use and acquisition, using funds from the regional transportation plan for funding wildlife crossing infrastructure. We'll probably also be working with some of the ranchers in the area to get support for looking at wildlife connectivity north and south of I-10.

I was on the Regional Transportation Authority Citizens Committee when we managed to get $45 million for wildlife infrastructure. We've made fantastic progress in pushing the county to protect areas around two major arteries in the area. It's fantastic progress. We need a lot more money, because most of the $45 million is already spent.

One notable success was the construction of a wildlife overpass on Oracle Road, described in chapter 3. The coalition is currently working with Pima County and a number of stakeholders to construct a wildlife crossing point at the intersection of Avra Valley Road and I-10 that would connect the Tucson and Tortolita Mountains.

Enhancing Wildlife Safety and Habitat

As part of continuing efforts to steward ranches managed by Pima County, a number of steps have been taken to enhance wildlife safety and habitat. Drinkers with wildlife escape ramps have been installed on several ranches.[89] On Rancho Seco, a specially designed thirteen-foot-long drinker was installed to improve water access for bat colonies in the nearby Las Guijas Mountains, including two bat species covered by the county's multi-species habitat plan—Townsend's big-eared bats and California leaf-nosed bats, as well as a sizable cave colony of mouse-eared bats.

Reintroducing Species

ANTELOPE

The Arizona Antelope Foundation identified the Altar Valley as one of its six priority zones for reintroduction of pronghorn antelope. Antelope survival in the valley has proven challenging owing to loss of grass forage to mesquite encroachment, the availability of reliable water sources, and the continuing effects of a twenty-year drought in the Southwest. Habitat improvement projects both on the Buenos Aires National Wildlife Refuge and on nearby ranches have provided new permanent water sources and increased forage available to antelope following clearing of mesquite. More work needs to be done to sustain a viable population of pronghorn; at present, the number of antelope is estimated to be twenty-five or fewer.

LONGFIN DACE

The Pima County Office of Sustainability, the Pima County Regional Flood Control District, the Arizona Game and Fish Department, the FWS, and the University of Arizona worked together to reintroduce the longfin dace in two stretches of the Santa Cruz River sustained by effluent: near downtown Tucson and north of the Agua Nueva Water Reclamation Facility.[90] The tiny fish, listed in the SDCP Multi-Species Conservation Plan, was once an abundant denizen of the river.

GILA TOPMINNOW

The endangered topminnow was reintroduced into the Santa Cruz River, Agua Caliente Park (renamed Agua Nueva Park), Roger Road Nodal Park, the M Diamond Ranch, and the Clyne Ranch in the southeastern corner of Pima County.[91]

FIGURE 6.12 Gila topminnow. (Bruce Taubert.)

GILA CHUB

Large numbers of the endangered fish were salvaged from Sabino Canyon following the Bighorn Fire in the Catalina Mountains and transferred to a pond in Agua Caliente Park, which serves as a refugia for the chub and other endangered or threatened fish.[92]

The county plans further efforts to stock created aquatic features such as the Agua Caliente Park ponds with native species.

FIGURE 6.13 Gila chub. (Courtesy of U.S. Geological Survey.)

Collaborative Forest Landscape and the Wyoming Landscape Conservation Initiatives

Overview

It is thus that the people of the valleys are interested in the forests of the mountains. [Their] mountain passes are the portals through which the clouds of heaven come down to bless their gardens and their fields, and to fill the fountains from which their children quaff the water of life. . . . Before the white man came, the natives systematically burned over the forest lands with each recurrent year. By this process little destruction of timber was accomplished; but [now], forests are rapidly disappearing. The needles, cones, and brush, together with the leaves of grass and shrubs below, accumulate when not burned annually. New deposits are made from year to year, until the ground is covered with a thick mantle of flammable material. Then a spark is dropped, a fire is accidentally or purposely kindled, and the flames have abundant food. . . . But these same people are interested in the forests that crown the heights of [watershed]. If they permit the forests to be destroyed, the source of their water supply is injured and the timber values are wiped out. . . . [The] rapid destruction [of areas of good timber] is a calamity that cannot well be overestimated. These living forests are always a delight, for in beauty and grandeur they are unexcelled; but dead forests present scenes of desolation that fill the soul with sadness. The vast destruction of values, together with the enormous ravishment of beauty, have for years enlisted the sympathy of intelligent men.[93]

These quotes from explorer and scientist John Wesley Powell during his tenure as director of the U.S. Geological Survey (1881–1894) are eerily prescient in their vivid description of the economic and spiritual value of robust forestlands and the challenges of stewarding them: engaging in sustainable silviculture, managing ground cover and tree density in service of preventing catastrophic fires, and protecting the essential role of forestlands in contributing to healthy watersheds. They are as much a call to action today as they were more than 130 years ago.

The Collaborative Forest Landscape Restoration Program

In recognition of the importance of mitigating the risk of severe wildfires, protecting old-growth forests and wildlife habitat, and improving watershed health, Congress passed the Forest Landscape Restoration Act in 2009, which provided funding for a bold program: the Collaborative Forest Landscape Restoration Program (CFLRP).[94] The goals of CFLRP are "to encourage the collaborative, science-based ecosystem restoration of priority forest landscapes" and to encourage "ecological, economic, and social sustainability."

The CFLRP invited proposals with the requirement that they be developed and implemented collaboratively by a broad range of stakeholders and

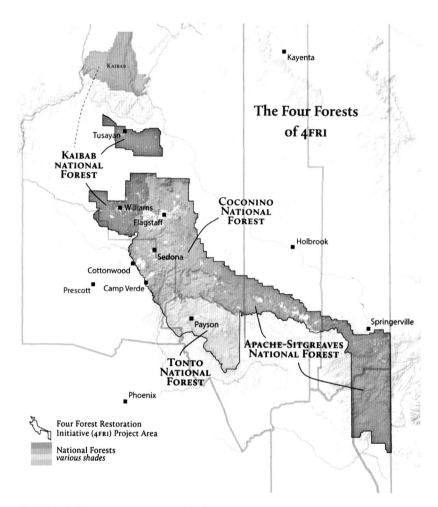

The Four Forests
of 4FRI

KAIBAB
NATIONAL
FOREST

COCONINO
NATIONAL
FOREST

APACHE-SITGREAVES
NATIONAL FOREST

TONTO
NATIONAL
FOREST

Kayenta
Tusayan
Williams
Flagstaff
Holbrook
Sedona
Cottonwood
Prescott Camp Verde
Payson
Springerville
Phoenix

Four Forest Restoration
Initiative (4FRI) Project Area

National Forests
various shades

FIGURE 6.14 Forest areas encompassed by the Four Forest Landscape Initiative. (Underlying map prepared by Stephanie Smith for the Grand Canyon Trust.)

based on a restoration plan for landscapes at least as large as fifty thousand acres.[95] Though focused primarily on Forest Service lands, the program is designed to catalyze projects spanning a mosaic of land ownership.

Requests for CFLRP funding are required to indicate how a proposed program will "reduce the risk of uncharacteristic wildfire," "improve fish and wildlife habitat," "maintain or improve water quality and watershed function," and address invasion of exotic species.[96] Each of the competitively selected programs receives up to $4 million annually for a period of ten years, renewable for an additional decade. Proposal partners are required to leverage local and private resources to match awarded federal dollars.

The program also encourages proposers to adopt adaptive management protocols and to evaluate how restoration activities can both achieve their environmental objectives and benefit local economies. Says Larry Fisher of the University of Arizona's School of Natural Resources and the Environment,

> I think that the CFLRP is one of the better examples of how the federal government can support collaboratives within an agency framework. What they did is [to] call on all the Forest Service units to develop collaborative plans with state, local government, nonprofits and landowners. [They would] then submit them in a competitive way. [Consequently, you] had this really nice federal, regional, local nexus, and you had all of the right incentives: that these programs had to be developed through a multi-stakeholder process. They had to have a landscape-scale perspective. They had to have both a restoration and an economic element, and they had to have a strong multi-party monitoring plan.
>
> [There] are projects all across the West, where they have looked at landscape-scale work, some of it watershed focused, some of it wildlife and forest conservation-focused, building the timber sector of the economy, and so on. The CFLRP has been highly successful [in building] collaborative working relationships between the Forest Service, local jurisdictions, counties, municipalities, tribes, businesses When I was working with it—I've been out of that group for a while—it was the best thing going in the Forest Service for sure. The largest of the CFLRP programs is right here in Arizona: the Four Forest Restoration Initiative—4FRI.

The Four Forest Restoration Initiative

The Four Forest Restoration Initiative (4FRI) is a restoration initiative for 2.4 million acres of ponderosa pine forestland along the Mogollon Rim encompassing four national forests: Apache, Coconino, Tonto, and Kaibab.[97] The principal goals of the program are to restore forest ecosystems so that they are more resilient to naturally and human-caused fires; increase the diversity of plants; protect springs and streams; and promote industries that depend on wood products to the benefit of local economies.

The collaboration of local, county, and state governments, representatives from industrial and environmental communities, as well as other stakeholders are committed to an ambitious program that among many objectives plans to thin one million acres over the twenty-year lifetime of the 4FRI program. The expected result: a significant decrease in destructive wildfires that both threaten homes and contaminate streams and rivers with ash that can affect both water quality and threaten aquatic species. The combined efforts of 4FRI represent the largest collaborative restoration project in the history of the Forest Service.

In addition to thinning and restoring fire to the forest ecosystem, 4FRI is involved in a number of other significant projects, including restoration of grasslands, stream channels, and wildlife habitat.

The Wyoming Landscape Conservation Initiative

The Wyoming Landscape Conservation Initiative (WLCI) was established in 2007 by a partnership between individuals and federal, state, and county agencies.[98] The WLCI's twin goals are to conserve and enhance fish and wild-

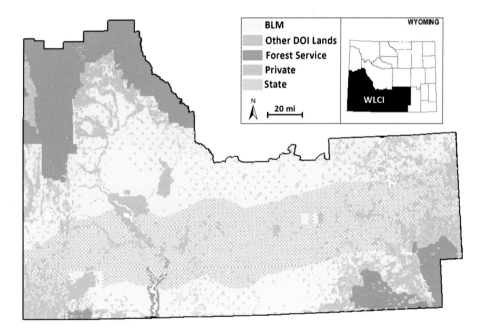

FIGURE 6.15 The mosaic of landownership in the 2.4-million-acre region that is the focus of restoration and conservation efforts by the Wyoming Landscape Conservation Initiative. (Courtesy Bureau of Land Management.)

FIGURE 6.16 Installing a steel jack fence to exclude ungulates from an aspen stand. (Courtesy Bureau of Land Management.)

life habitat at landscape scale using science-based programs, and to support responsible energy, mineral, and other development. This approach is similar to the combined conservation and economic goals of the CFLRP. The WLCI partnership comprises representatives from the BLM, U.S. Geological Survey, U.S. Fish and Wildlife Service, U.S. Forest Service, National Park Service, Natural Resources Conservation Service, Wyoming Department of Agriculture, Wyoming Game and Fish Department, six county commissions, eleven conservation districts, and industry and landholders.

In the 2018 annual report of the WLCI, former Wyoming Game and Fish deputy director John Emmerich recalled formative discussions with then–BLM state director Robert Bennett as the WLCI concept was taking form: "Our focus was a comprehensive coordinated effort to engage all agencies to work on the same goals—basically improving wildlife habitat."[99]

The scope of the initiative is vast: nineteen million acres in southwest Wyoming (an area that would encompass Massachusetts, New Hampshire, and Vermont), a mosaic of private, federal, and state trust lands spanning five counties. The landscape is diverse, comprising desert, sagebrush, and aspen forests, as well as riparian and aquatic components. More than 100,000 deer, 100,000 antelope, 40,000 elk, and 8,000 moose roam the landscape, sharing it with 151 threatened or endangered species.[100]

The area is rich in oil, coal, and natural gas. Preserving the integrity of sagebrush, aspen, and riparian areas in the face of ongoing extraction represents a significant challenge. To meet that challenge, WLCI has formed four local project development teams consisting of "land managers and resource specialists from federal, state, and local government agencies, special interest groups, agriculture and other private landowners, and industry, all having a desire to participate in cooperative conservation" and working collaboratively on the ground to design and implement projects.[101] Their landscape-wide conservation efforts are coordinated from headquarters located in Rock Springs, Wyoming.

Among the key goals of the initiative are maintaining and reconnecting corridors, improving wildlife and aquatic habitat, maintaining and restoring sagebrush ecosystems, controlling invasive species, reestablishing riparian communities, and restoring and maintaining wetlands.[102]

To achieve these goals, WCLI has undertaken a suite of restoration and enhancement projects with the aims of

FIGURE 6.17 Evidence of extreme head-cutting (*left*) and the work done to restore more natural stream flow (*right*). (Courtesy Bureau of Land Management.)

- Mitigating fragmentation by negotiating easements and by removing barriers to wildlife migration
- Reducing foraging by ungulates and removing juniper from the sagebrush ecosystem
- Removing coniferous plants, opening forested areas to increase regeneration of aspen
- Removing barriers to fish movement, protecting native fish from encroachment by invasive nonnative species, and improving stream flows to create more favorable habitat for native species
- Identifying the most efficacious treatments for removing invasive plants such as salt cedar, cheatgrass, and Russian olive which are rapidly replacing native species
- Monitoring and evaluating invasive species treatments
- Identifying priority riparian zones for restoration aimed at fulfilling their natural functions—controlling flooding, reducing erosion, recharging groundwater, and increasing stream flows—to achieve watershed-scale conservation objectives[103]

In the first decade since its inception in 2007, the initiative invested $69 million (in 2018 dollars) in restoration and environmental enhancement projects. In an essay celebrating the tenth anniversary of the WLCI, Jim Wassen, Wyoming Game and Fish WLCI coordinator, commented that "the initiative is a unique, comprehensive approach to conservation. We feel like we've accomplished quite a bit in ten years."[104]

Jill Randall, Wyoming Game and Fish Department statewide migration coordinator, echoed Wassen's remarks:

> WLCI is a very important partner in southwest Wyoming because their interests, like those of the Wyoming Game and Fish Department, include working across land ownership boundaries toward solutions that meet multiple objectives. Projects such as aspen treatments, cheatgrass management, highway crossings and fence modifications have all been completed to improve the function of our ecosystem for multiple users on our landscape including wildlife, livestock, sportsmen, and landowners.

In an interview with the BLM, Larry Hicks of the Little Snake River Conservation District remarked on the importance of collaborative partnerships

FIGURE 6.18 Pronghorn using a wildlife overpass over State Highway 191, Trappers Point, Wyoming. (Wyoming Department of Transportation.)

in enabling WLCI's efforts: "The true success of WLCI is the people partnership component. You know good things happen when we can sit down at the same table and have a discussion. We can look at the success on the landscape, but I think that [the reason why] 10 years later WLCI is still in existence is the people that care deeply about those landscapes. So, it's really a people story as much as it is a natural resource landscape conservation initiative story."[105]

Renee Dana, formerly the Bureau of Land Management's WLCI coordinator, reinforces Hicks's comments: "Successful partnerships are implemented and led from the grassroots. Local and active participation is critical. We depend on those partnerships and those folks on the ground to help us out."[106]

Investments in WLCI not only have addressed conservation objectives but have had a significant positive effect on local economies. In addition to purchasing easements, 98 percent of the funds for restoration and enhancement projects were awarded to Wyoming businesses, resulting in more than $30 million in labor income and $68 million in economic output in the Wyoming economy between 2007 and 2017, a vivid demonstration that a commitment to conservation can yield positive economic benefits.[107]

Land Stewardship

Overview

Successful strategies for large-landscape conservation will require not only instituting a variety of land protection and restoration efforts on a mosaic of public and private lands but also developing shared commitments to sound stewardship practices.

The previous sections summarize key elements of a diverse range of conservation efforts: on a privately held ranch and adjacent state land (Cienega Ranch); a single landscape comprising federal and state lands (Las Cienegas NCA); among multiple working ranches, each comprising a mix of private and state lands (Malpai Borderlands Group); in a large county that developed a regional land-use plan (Sonoran Desert Conservation Plan); and two regional plans aimed at integrating conservation and economic goals on landscapes spanning millions of acres (Four Forest Restoration Initiative and the Wyoming Conservation Lands Initiative).

While their approaches differ, they have all adopted adaptive management principles aimed at ensuring that their land stewardship practices achieved desired conservation goals.

In each case, individuals, agencies, or collaborating groups of stakeholders

- assessed current conditions and threats
- developed a shared vision for conservation goals and objectives
- consulted with a range of stakeholders and outside experts
- developed and implemented an initial plan comprising protection and restoration efforts after discussing a number of alternatives
- monitored conditions as parts of the plan were put into action
- evaluated the outcomes and adjusted the plan

A lesson common to all the conservation efforts discussed here is that effective stewardship requires that land managers, scientists, stakeholders, and communities work and learn together to create and maintain sustainable landscapes using adaptive management tools.[108]

Cienega Ranch

When Josiah Austin purchased Cienega Ranch, he had a vision: "I believe that Cienega Ranch should be a working landscape, a commercial cow-calf operation. However, I believe that any working landscape should also benefit the other native species."

But when he bought the ranch, "it was really degraded, overgrazed, just a mess," recalls Michael Patrick of the Trust for Public Lands. To achieve his vision, Austin embarked on a massive restoration program. "He started putting in tens of thousands of rock walls with the idea that they would slow down the water coming down these washes and build back the soil." To evaluate the efficacy of his efforts, "he's worked with Laura Norman at USGS as a science partner in quantifying the benefits of this work to slow down the water and let it permeate into the watershed," says Patrick. Austin attends the MBG's annual science conference and consults with representatives of the NRCS and U.S. Fish and Wildlife Service to update rangeland practices and inform his efforts to restore habitat for wildlife and reintroduce endangered species.

Vision, assessment, action, evaluation, and revision: hallmarks of sound adaptive management practices.

Las Cienegas NCA

The BLM completed the Las Cienegas Resource Management Plan in 2003 after numerous meetings with the Sonoita Valley Planning Partnership and other stakeholders. The plan outlines specific conservation objectives and commits the BLM to use adaptive management protocols in collaborative consultation with stakeholders to meet or revise these objectives.

In carrying out its mission to steward the NCA, the BLM works closely with the successor to the SVPP, the Cienega Watershed Partnership, which "values an ecosystem approach to science-based management of natural resources for the long term through collaborative efforts."

The partnership holds twice-yearly biological planning meetings on the NCA resource as well as an annual State of the Watershed gathering in the Sonoita Valley. Together, they provide forums for reporting results of monitoring key resource indicators and evaluating the results of past projects and management actions in meeting conservation objectives.

Monitoring resource indicators is central to adaptive management. The CWP, in collaboration with the BLM, other agencies, and volunteers, tracks twenty key indicators of the health of the Cienega watershed.[109]

"Monitoring is a critical part of the whole adaptive management plan," says Larry Fisher, who served for nine years on the CWP Board. Fisher reflects on the challenges faced in gathering the yearly indicator data. "To pull together the data to inform the adaptive management plan with the twenty indicators, we have to call scientists in the agencies and get their data: their annual fish monitoring data or pronghorn data or wet-dry mapping data from the county and so on."

He continues,

> It takes us weeks and weeks and weeks and weeks to pull together the information. When we do our annual State of the Watershed presentation, we get somewhere between thirty-five and fifty people from all the agencies and a lot of researchers and citizens and advocates of all kinds come to listen. Then we try to use the information we've gathered and ask, "Okay, given these trends, and given the latest data that we're seeing, what does that tell us about management?"

The BLM, SVPP, and CWP have successfully implemented textbook models for collaborative adaptive management: from developing shared goals and measurable objectives, to monitoring the resource and gathering reliable data, to using those data and the best available science to inform decision-making, and to revising processes and actions in light of new learning. Their efforts over more than twenty-five years serve as outstanding examples of cooperative stewardship of public lands for the benefit of a broad range of stakeholders and communities.

Malpai Borderlands Group

The Malpai Borderlands Group is working to restore and maintain flourishing communities of plant and animal life and the natural processes that support them on nearly a million acres of ranch land in southwestern New Mexico and southeastern Arizona.

Areas of particular conservation interest to the group include enhancement of biodiversity, preservation of pollinator habitat, control of erosion and shrub encroachment, and improvement in soil health and forage production. MBG members understood from the group's inception that following the best scientific advice for managing large ecosystems would be essential.

As part of the Malpai Borderlands Habitat Conservation Plan, the group developed a plan for adaptive management which incorporated two major goals: maintaining and enhancing soil stability, biotic integrity, and watershed function and ensuring that grassland improvements and ranching activities follow protocols that protect the habitat of endangered species.

Their adaptive management plan lays out a set of specific objectives, along with metrics devised to assess whether land stewardship actions are achieving those objectives, and a set of triggers to alert MBG and individual ranchers if remedial action is needed. Management is carried out by individual ranchers who steward their lands according to the goals and objectives set by the MBG and government agencies, as well as by collaborations among ranchers, MBG, federal agencies, and conservation NGOs. Monitoring efforts in the borderlands region focus on vegetation and species monitoring and measuring the effects of fire, livestock grazing, and the consumption of plants by native species under different climatic conditions.

Discussion of ongoing programs, landscape and habitat conditions, and possible new conservation and stewardship strategies takes place annually at the Malpai Borderlands Science Conference. To inform land management choices and to evaluate environmental health, the group has formed a science advisory committee composed of scientists whose specialties cover a wide range of disciplines relevant to rangeland, wildlife, soil, hydrological, and botanical management.

The MBG has been working in the borderlands for almost thirty years, enough time to take a first look at how well the group's conservation goals are being met. Peter Warren summarizes the conclusion of a recent retrospective study:

> Basically the Jornada Experimental Range used a large data set approach, either satellite imagery or other kinds of large-landscape data sets to compare outcomes in the Malpai area with adjacent comparable landscapes. [Its goal was] to see if there had been any measurable improvement in the ecological condition of the MBG lands, the productivity of the land, compared with adjacent areas. The upshot is that there actually was. It looks like the productivities have been higher in some areas. In some cases [productivity in adjacent areas] has declined whereas Malpai's has remained stable.

A seminal academic paper by Brandon Bestelmeyer and collaborators reaches the following encouraging conclusions regarding the efficacy of stewardship on the borderlands landscape:

In summary, our findings indicate that MBG is meeting most sustainability goals it established in 1994. Although ranch-based livelihoods have become more challenging, the MBG remains a working landscape and ranching continues as properties change. Fires have occurred over a relatively large fraction of MBG, enabled by an effective system of conservation easements that has prevented development [NB: Significant development would have made setting prescribed burns covering wide areas difficult]. Mean vegetation and bare ground cover estimates suggest a comparatively healthy landscape. While we cannot evaluate biodiversity directly, fractional cover proxies suggest comparatively favorable habitat for desert grassland species [in the MBG] properties.[110]

Sonoran Desert Conservation Plan

The Sonoran Desert Conservation Plan represents the embodiment of a community-developed vision: to balance conservation of natural and cultural resources in Pima County and maintenance of a vibrant and economically sound community. In implementing the plan, the county has acquired and managed lands critical to protecting healthy ecosystems and developed regulations and planning protocols essential to achieving regional conservation goals.

Stewardship of lands acquired through open-space bond purchases and lands falling within biologically critical areas is guided by adaptive management principles: resource assessment, adoption of indicators of resource health, monitoring, evaluation of monitoring results, and changes in implementation objectives or strategies.

The county has developed an extensive monitoring program that assesses changes in the abundance and presence of species covered by the multi-species conservation plan;[111] changes in habitat for covered species; changes in land-use patterns, such as fragmentation, that would threaten covered species; potential threats to habitat and species health such as off-road vehicle use and pollution; and changes in climate, a critical driver of ecosystem function and species richness and diversity.

Responsibility for overseeing monitoring efforts lies with a science and technical advisory team comprising representatives from federal, state, and county agencies, along with conservation NGOs.

The county is committed to monitoring and managing five plan elements—critical habitats and biological corridors, riparian areas, mountain parks,

FIGURE 6.19 Monitoring fish populations along a stretch of the Santa Cruz River revived by using treated effluent (Pima County).

historical and cultural areas, and ranches—on lands spanning 5.9 million acres. Meeting that commitment requires an all-hands approach involving a number of Pima County government departments along with state and federal agencies.

Stewardship of county owned ranches provides a sense of how the county addresses its monitoring and assessment responsibilities. According to Vanessa Prileson, Pima County Range Program manager,

> [We] have very specific standards and guidelines developed for Pima County. [Those] were developed collaboratively between University of Arizona, local range ecology consultant experts and other agencies such as the U.S. Forest Service, BLM and several scientists and rangeland ecologists in the area. Adaptive management [is] built in, and you can try creative ways to manage or restore land within those standards and guidelines.
>
> Those guidelines inform how to write coordinated resource management plans for each of our ranches and describe how goals and objectives should be based on what's actually on the ground at specific sites. We can't just use the same parameters across the board because each ranch and each pasture on each ranch is pretty unique.

I'm constantly meeting with ranchers on the ground. We conduct an annual meeting [at which we] discuss grazing planning. We discuss projects each rancher wants to do. We communicate about monitoring that the county is doing for activities other than grazing—for example, for wildlife habitat and other ecological monitoring. We have very frequent communication and field visiting . . . with each of our ranchers that we work with. We've been able to establish a good connection and relationship with each one so that we're able to better implement these standards and guidelines that then feed up to the SDCP.

Collaborative Forest Landscape Restoration Program: 4FRI

In the legislation establishing the Collaborative Forest Landscape Restoration Program, Congress set out the following goals for the program:

encourage the collaborative, science-based ecosystem restoration of priority forest landscapes through a process that: 1) encourages ecological, economic and social sustainability; 2) leverages local resources with national and private resources; 3) facilitates the reduction of wildfire management costs, including through reestablishing natural fire regimes and reducing the risk of uncharacteristic wildfire; and 4) demonstrates the degree to which various ecological restoration techniques achieve ecological and watershed health objectives and affect wildfire activity and management cost; and where the use of forest restoration byproducts can offset treatment costs while benefiting local rural economies and improving forest health.

In 2010 the Four Forest Restoration Initiative was awarded funding during the first round of project selections under the Collaborative Forest Landscape Restoration Program.[112] The environmental goals of the initiative are to restore the health of ponderosa pine ecosystems, reduce the fuels for and risks of severe wildfires, and establish and maintain conditions for rich and diverse populations of plants and wildlife. The initiative's social goals are to create and develop sustainable businesses to harvest, process, and sell wood products.

Working toward and achieving these goals is anticipated to take more than twenty years, given both the magnitude of both social and environmen-

FIGURE 6.20 The 4FRI Stakeholders Group meeting at The Nature Conservancy's Hart Prairie Preserve. The group gathered at the preserve five years after the award of CFLRP funding to assess progress, challenges, and what practices and policies might need revision. (Courtesy Tahnee Robertson.)

tal challenges and the scale of the 4FRI area (2.4 million acres). Managing progress and adapting plans and protocols along the way requires an extensive monitoring program. Fortunately, the CFLRP allocates 10 percent of the awarded funds for each project to monitor the initial state of the forest, evaluate the effectiveness of subsequent treatments, closely track the number and distribution of threatened and endangered species, and monitor social conditions.[113]

Environmental monitoring focuses on measuring biological diversity in ponderosa pine ecosystems, resilience of those ecosystems, and maintenance of soil and water resources.[114] Social monitoring is directed at gathering economic data and evaluating the efficacy of collaborative programs aimed at advancing the economic needs of nearby communities. In order to determine how well 4FRI projects are meeting desired environmental and social goals, the 4FRI collaboration has created a multi-party monitoring board. Input from the board provides guidance to enable initiative leaders to adjust plans and funding.

Wyoming Landscape Conservation Initiative

The primary goals of the Wyoming Landscape Conservation Initiative are to *conserve* and *enhance* fish and wildlife habitat across nineteen million acres in southwestern Wyoming, while supporting responsible industrial use in the area.

The WLCI partners with twelve federal and state agencies, local resource agencies, and NGOs to assess, monitor, and improve the status of natural resources in southwest Wyoming and to evaluate and mitigate the effects of energy development on wildlife habitat. Along with its partners, WLCI monitors vegetation, soil conditions, wildlife species, habitat conditions, and wildlife connectivity.

Using these monitoring data, the initiative evaluates the effectiveness of projects in meeting its conservation objectives.[115] A few examples of projects and monitoring activities follow:

- Excluding ungulates from aspen stands. Ungulate browsing limits vertical growth of aspens and prevents younger aspens from reaching maturity. WLCI partners installed temporary fences on selected aspen stands in the region to exclude browsing by livestock, mule deer, pronghorn, and other ungulates. Growth of aspen in these fenced areas is monitored until they reach a height where ungulate browsing is no longer a danger. Fencing is then moved to other aspen stands needing protection.
- Improving vegetation health on ranges crucial to mule deer during winter and the birthing season. Project participants removed and treated cheatgrass and excluded livestock from the treated area. Vegetation was monitored before treatment, and monitoring continues in order to assess the efficacy of employed methods.
- Mapping the distribution of and removing invasive species. Along the Green River, its tributaries, and wetlands, WLCI removed invasive species such as Russian olive, saltcedar, and cheatgrass in an effort to enhance habitat for sage-grouse, mule deer, pronghorn, and birds. WLCI partners and participating ranchers monitor the effectiveness of the removal treatments by returning every three to five years.

Scientists involved in WLCI projects are developing tools to incorporate remote-sensing assessment and monitoring—an essential complement to ground-based efforts on a landscape as vast as that encompassed by the WLCI. Remote-sensing assessments of vegetation cover and composition and soil characteristics are calibrated using in situ measurement of vegetation and soil characteristics.

The WLCI partnership draws on the scientific expertise of staff at the U.S. Geological Survey and the National Park Service, as well as on universities and NGOs, to inform management of the area.[116] Formal monitoring and data management teams oversee data gathering in the field and analysis of those data. Monitoring results are then used to assess project progress against WLCI objectives and to revise plans accordingly.

The adaptive process works iteratively, as lessons learned in the field and by scientists allow managers to evaluate project outcomes and management techniques, pose questions to technical experts, and work together to re-shape actions on extant programs and inform planning of new projects.

Organizing Successful Large-Landscape Conservation Efforts

"Never doubt that a small group of thoughtful, committed citizens can change the world; indeed, it's the only thing that ever has."

—MARGARET MEAD, ANTHROPOLOGIST, RECIPIENT OF
THE PLANETARY CITIZEN OF THE YEAR AWARD IN 1978[117]

Overview

Conserving and stewarding healthy watersheds, grasslands, and forests and other ecosystems requires bringing people together to develop sustainable relationships with the land.

The Nature Conservancy's Peter Warren reflects on his experiences in working with groups committed to large-landscape conservation efforts:

To achieve [success] requires continuing attention and effort to develop conservation strategies across a large area having multiple land ownerships. In order to achieve that you've got to have some kind of ongoing collaborative effort in which people share a common vision for the future: where value is placed on having large, open, ecologically healthy land, which is full of wildlife, recreation opportunities, and agricultural production in the form of sustainable ranching.

To come up with a cohesive conservation approach to something on the scale of one hundred thousand acres, or five hundred thousand acres, or a million acres for how to manage that landscape requires collaboration among different landowners and land managers. I've come to view successful collaborations as team problem-solving, troubleshooting, brain-storming efforts based on shared experience.

Motivating Action Often Requires a Threat

Motivating citizens or communities to begin the conversations needed to forge a vision for the future often requires the perception of an imminent threat. Jesse Juen of the BLM observes that

there has to be some compelling, identified need that is affecting people on a landscape. Drought, endangered species, fire, whatever the potential for impacting people's lives and economies is probably the common denominator. Sometimes [things that initiate conversation] are issue-driven: an endangered species listing; water quality that is affecting not only the ecology [of the region] but people who are using or have access to that water. It could be an economic tie, perhaps affecting an individual who sees that their livelihood might be affected by a policy change or some other action.

In the case of the Sonoita Valley, the threat of a satellite city and its potential to undermine the ecological integrity of the Cienega watershed as well as the rural character of the region precipitated acquisition of the Empire Ranch and citizen discussions regarding how it would be managed.

For the Sonoran Desert Conservation Plan, the 1983 flood, concerns about the effects of urban growth and preserving open space, water use, and the listing of the endangered cactus ferruginous pygmy owl combined to initiate community-wide discussions that ultimately led to a collaborative effort to develop a county-wide land-use plan.

The Malpai Borderlands Group was formed in reaction to the threats posed by fragmentation of ranches by encroaching subdivisions, environmental activists demanding removal of cattle from public land, and rapid intrusion of shrubs and woody plants on rangeland.

And for Josiah Austin's Cienega Ranch, concerns about fragmentation of surrounding grasslands and fear that absent a vigorous restoration effort, grassland health would continue to deteriorate motivated Austin's efforts.

Engage Citizens, Community Leaders, NGOs, and Government Agencies

Think Globally, Act Locally

Success in catalyzing discussions, developing plans, and implementing long-term stewardship programs depends on citizens having strong connection to place.[118] Larry Fisher of the University of Arizona's School of Natural Resources and the Environment notes,

> Science tells us all these reasons for linking the landscape into some kind of coherent whole, but what motivates an organic movement is the connection that people feel to their place, to "their" landscape.
>
> This is one of the things that we have to contend with, the sense of place issue. So, if you're living in the Sonoran Desert you're connected to the Sonoran Desert. You have a feeling and an empathy, kind of an emotion toward it. But the Chihuahuan or Mojave deserts, maybe not so much.
>
> [Here's] the challenge that we face: You have these natural coalitions of people trying to solve a problem over a given landscape. Then you've got these landscape designations—watersheds or ecoregions—they are large and have common composition and function characteristics. In approaching large-landscape conservation, you're trying to find a balance between the problems that people want to encounter and deal with in "their" landscape and the problems that need to be addressed on a larger scale. Somehow, we have to get people to see themselves within a larger landscape in a functioning ecosystem.

Les Corey of the Arizona Land and Water Trust emphasizes that although large-landscape conservation is essential, addressing land protection and stewardship issues on a local scale is a necessary first step:

> I think that more localized efforts, particularly in today's political climate where there is so much distrust and antagonism, have a higher probability for constructive dialog and success. It's easier if you're working together, listening to one another, trying to problem-solve together, you can overcome some of the more intractable ideological issues, or political issues that tend to color so much of

what our society has to deal with on a regular basis. I guess it's more human-scale when you're talking at a community level. When you get beyond the counties and out to the state or multi-state level, it becomes much more [challenging].

Faced with the need to confront environmental challenges, how do successful citizen groups and communities come together to meet them?

Initiate a Dialog and Commit to a Collaborative Conservation Process

Once a sufficient number of citizens agree on the need to address land-use challenges, more structured conversations can start in multiple ways.

An agency led, facilitated discussion: After informal conversations at casual dinners and breakfast meetings in the Sonoita Valley, the BLM hired a facilitator to help citizens organize what became the Sonoita Valley Planning Partnership and later to develop a consensus regarding a management plan for the Las Cienegas NCA.

A county led effort: In Pima County, the county administrator's office took the lead in organizing a land-use planning exercise in response to the designation of the cactus ferruginous pygmy owl as an endangered species. The broadly based community effort that led ultimately to adoption and support of the Sonoran Desert Conservation Plan built on more than two decades of grassroots organizing for open-space protections, water conservation, riparian area restoration, and mountain park expansion.

A self-organized group: The Malpai Borderlands Group emerged from two years of conversation among ranchers who realized that achieving their shared conservation goals would require engaging federal and state agencies, NGOs, scientists, and environmentalists in a collaborative effort.

Involve a Broad Group of Citizens and Stakeholder Groups

Successful and enduring collaborative conservation efforts depend on building consensus among diverse groups of citizens and stakeholder groups, some of whom may initially have very different opinions regarding conservation and land-use issues.

Former Arizona assistant state director of the BLM, the late Michael Taylor, summarizes how the agency initiates successful dialog: "We like to go out and engage the public in the beginning of the process. Go out and say here's where we're at now, and how do you guys want to see this land managed?" Sometimes the process of engaging the public from the get-go can be "painful, but I really, really liked that part of it because you could engage with people, you could understand what it is that they see as important."

In reflecting on his experience with the Sonoita Valley Planning Partnership, Larry Fisher recalls, "It was very collaborative and the participation was very balanced and diverse. You'd see mountain bikers show up, and wildlife advocates, and citizens and ranchers, in addition to the county and the state and federal folks."

Susan Culp of the Sonoran Institute (which played a role in both the Sonoita Valley and Pima County planning efforts) noted that "enduring conservation only really can happen if you get diverse interests—from large-scale landowners, ranchers, to the business community and entrepreneurs in the region, other advocates for conservation, community members who care about the place they lived—around the table and [discover] commonly shared visions."

Engage a Facilitator If Needed

Individuals involved in both the Sonoita Valley Planning Partnership and the Sonoran Desert Conservation Plan believed that having a facilitator involved, especially in early discussions, was critical to establishing a framework for reaching consensus. Chris Horyza, retired from the BLM, observed that from an agency perspective, "having that facilitation is critical, because neither the public nor the federal agency understands very well how to work with one another. So having a facilitator to do that, and not just a facilitator at meetings but somebody who can go out and sit down with interested public, stakeholders, and the government, and educate them on how to interact, how to work together is important. If you don't do that it's going to be a very difficult and probably an unsuccessful effort."

Agree on Goals and Take the Time to Develop a Widely Shared Consensus

Once more structured conversations begin, successful outcomes for collaborative conservation efforts depend on taking the time to build trust, agree on broad goals, and develop a consensus plan for organizing and taking action. Says Michael Dombeck, former chief of the U.S. Forest Service and former acting director of the BLM,

In order to develop a consensus on a conservation plan, three common features to success are: agreeing upon common goals, building trust and then moving forward and working successfully on low-hanging fruit first, which [in turn, begins to] cement trust.

Oftentimes, we start at too high a level and skip the common goals, like the fact that you need clean water, you need a diversity of plants, you need a functioning watershed, you need to be recharging aquifers. You need to be doing all of these things for healthy land and, for lack of a better word, something that is beautiful to look at. Often times that is skipped and we go right to the "whose ox does it gore?" "Are we going to have to reduce grazing?" "Who's going to pay for conservation efforts?"

Larry Fisher builds on Dombeck's remarks:

Thinking about the Sonoita Valley—people shared concerns about the ranching culture and the historical value of the landscape. They were concerned about the community cohesiveness, about water, about wildlife and about recreation. It's not just conservation for conservation's sake. It's looking at the landscape and saying, "How do we manage this landscape for these multiple benefits?" All those things coalesced into a plan that people could get behind. If we had tried to engineer a top-down plan from the outside [it would have been difficult to impossible].

Recognize and Embrace Cultural Differences

Building trust starts with recognizing and embracing cultural differences. Western Landowners Alliance Executive Director Lesli Allison vividly captures the polarity in viewpoints that often color conservation discussions in the rural West:

There's a rural worldview, [and] there's an urban worldview. Urban people tend to look at natural areas and say, "Nature has done all that it needs to do. It doesn't need human management. All it needs is human beings to get out of the way. We need to get people off the land. We want to make sure those areas are open for recreation so let's make more trails or let's make recreation the economic engine that supports all of that." . . .

The rural perspective says, "we're part of the landscape. We have to produce food. We need to know how, as Aldo Leopold said, [to] live on a piece of land without spoiling it. In fact, nature needs us. We need forest management. There's this whole idea of being embedded in the landscape in a meaningful way that's not just riding your mountain bike on the weekends." It's a very big worldview gap.

Gita Bodner of The Nature Conservancy believes that environmentalists and those working the land are starting to understand one another's perspectives:

I think a lot of ranchers would tell you that they are the original conservationists, and if they don't manage their lands well, they won't have grass [in] the future. I think a lot of what has changed over time is the degree to which people recognize overlap in their own long-standing cultural values: from the conservation, nonprofit side and from the rancher side. I'm not implying that there's complete overlap in values, but just that there is enough overlap that big shifts can happen when people start to see those overlaps and find affinity in them.

The late Michael Taylor reflects on his experience with efforts by the BLM to initiate land-use discussions in rural areas.

A lot of times objections to BLM conservation efforts are cultural based. You know, "My family has been here since the earth formed, and we feel this or we feel that, and we don't want to see this or that happen." You might not ever know that if you're a specialist who, say, came from Montana and you're here in Arizona, and you say, "We need to do this on this land because that's what my training, my science background says it would be best to do," not appreciating that you might be really stepping on the toes of some cultural values that people have.

Pima County range manager Vanessa Prileson suggests that

everybody [involved in rangeland conservation] should do a ranch apprenticeship at least in college or even when they're older, just so they learn this is what it's like to fix a pipeline when it's 110 degrees out and trying to get water

TEXT PORTRAIT: MICHAEL DOMBECK

Michael Dombeck spent his childhood in the northern Wisconsin Lake Country during the 1950s. He earned degrees in biology and education at the University of Wisconsin–Stevens Point and the University of Minnesota, and his doctorate at Iowa State University. During the early years of his working life, he taught biology, chemistry, zoology, and fisheries management in both universities and public schools. In 1978 he joined the Forest Service as a fisheries biologist, spending twelve years with the agency, primarily in the Midwest and West.

Beginning in 1989 Dombeck served as science adviser and special assistant to the director of the Bureau of Land Management. In 1994 he was appointed acting director of the BLM and served in that position until 1997, when he was named the fourteenth chief of the U.S. Forest Service.

Throughout his tenure as Forest Service chief, Dombeck strongly advocated for a collaborative approach to land management and stewardship. Upon his retirement in 2001 President George W. Bush presented Dombeck with the Distinguished Executive Award, one of many honors he has received in recognition of his contributions to conservation efforts throughout the nation.

I grew up twenty-five miles from a town of 1,500 people in northern Wisconsin Lake Country in the Chequamegon National Forest. My early years were spent fishing, hunting, and hiking, with eleven summers spent as a fishing guide. Two of my favorite things to do to this day are walking in the woods and being on the water.

My undergraduate training was in in general sciences and zoology. I have graduate degrees in aquatic ecology and fisheries, but I also went through an education program in college. So I have teacher training, along with biology and general science. In retrospect, I believe that generalist training might be even better than a specialist training because I think it pushes you to look at things more broadly. Once I got more involved with administration and agency leadership, that combined background in aquatic ecology, general science, and education proved really valuable.

During the Clinton administration (1993–2001), there was a good deal of exuberance about ecosystem management and greater recognition of the role of science in guiding stewardship of public lands. [Secretary of Interior] Bruce Babbitt, who became a close friend and mentor to me, and I both spent a good

to your cows, or this is what it's like to try to sell enough meat at the farmers' market to make it, or here's what it's like to try to sell enough calves at the sale barn to try to get your paycheck for the year. Looking at it from that standpoint for a little while.

She continues, perhaps wryly, "But also it would be nice to [if] some folks from more rural environments—the rancher, the farmer—if they understood kind of where some of the conservationists and biologists are coming from too. Maybe they need a city internship!"

deal of time emphasizing the importance of the health and restoration of ecosystems. We were trying to build support for integrating sound ecological science and management principles geared to the long-term health of whole ecosystems: looking at historical patterns in ecosystems or watersheds and how best to restore and sustain them over the long haul. One of my jobs was to go up to Capitol Hill to explain ecosystem management to skeptics, some of the most conservative members of Congress.

I quickly learned through painful experience that talking strictly in terms of scientific concepts was not getting us anywhere. But if you talked about place-based things and concepts, or put them in a place-based language, suddenly the whole tenor of the conversation would change. I stopped using the word *ecosystem* and I started using the word *watershed*. The concept of a watershed is not new to anyone: everyone lives in a watershed. Everybody lives in a place. People care about where they live. They can relate to the land where they live, but they can't as easily relate to more abstract concepts like biodiversity or ecosystems.

But if you say, "I live in a Blackfoot watershed, or the Chippewa watershed," that means something. I remember having a conversation with a conservative senator from the Mountain West. As soon as I started talking about watersheds, riparian areas, and soil-holding capabilities, he started to perk up and say, "Yeah, this is what happened on my neighbor's ranch in the creek when he did this," and it all began to make sense to him. Making practical, place-based arguments is maybe the best way to present things to build political support.

My hope is that we will continue to build public support for recognizing the importance of ecosystem services, continuing to tie arguments to watershed function but also to the role of forests and grasslands in storing carbon.

As chief of the Forest Service, I set forth a vision for the agency that I think still applies today:

> I envision a time when our differences no longer divide us in managing the land. I envision a time when America's lands, like the ecosystems on them, are interwoven in a seamless tapestry, a tapestry of collective and collaborative management to protect the land while meeting the needs of people, within the limits of the land. As Aldo Leopold wrote in *A Sand County Almanac*, "Conservation, viewed in its entirety, is the slow and laborious unfolding of a new relationship between people and land." I would add, "and a new relationship among the people who live and play on the land." I believe that practicing our land ethic—treating the land with respect—depends on first treating each other with respect.

Build Relationships and Trust

Harmonizing the diverse, sometimes orthogonal views of individuals and stakeholders takes time. The Sonoita Valley Planning Partnership spent five years developing a consensus plan for managing what became Las Cienegas NCA. The Sonoran Desert Conservation Plan, while forged over a similar time period, emerged from relationships built over two decades of conservation efforts. Though the core of the Malpai Borderlands Group comprised only a few dozen ranchers, it still took three years to formalize the group.

"You have to have relationships with people who don't think like you. Through those relationships, trust builds, and that's when you get things done. That's what makes it so hard because so much of it is relationships and trust, and the only way those things get built is over time and with effort from both sides," says rancher Ian Tomlinson, who runs cattle on Las Cienegas NCA and works closely with the Cienega Watershed Partnership.

He continues:

> [Over time] I learned the importance of relationships and saw the value and the trust that's produced by taking the time to talk with the agencies, talk with stakeholders. Now it's vitally important to my business operation and my business plan because I don't have nearly the number of the impediments that I would have if both sides hadn't taken the time to get to know one another and develop relationships.
>
> Ten years ago I wouldn't have been able to articulate that to you worth beans. It has evolved over time. I guess being older, I see the importance of it more so now than I probably ever have, and would put it up as probably the number one priority for anybody starting any business, but especially ranching. When I get the opportunity to talk to groups, this is one of the topics that I talk about—the importance of relationships and trust and spending the time to get there.

Research anthropologist Tom Sheridan was closely involved with efforts to create the Sonoran Desert Conservation Plan and works closely with the Altar Valley Conservation Alliance. He very much agrees with Tomlinson's analysis:

> What I've learned in these various collaborative conservation efforts [is that] the only way to end the demonization on both sides is to sit down at the table and spend enough time to establish trust. There are ranchers in the Altar Valley Conservation Alliance on [some issues] I would disagree with strongly. But I trust them, and I've seen federal, county, and state land managers come to trust them as well because we're doing conservation projects on the ground that are tangible and we're a reliable partner.

Recognize and Understand People's Fears About Future Change

Developing a long-term land-use plan almost inevitably involves change of some sort. Accepting change is difficult, and doing so in the context of seemingly unbridgeable cultural differences is perhaps doubly so. Former New Mexico BLM state director Jesse Juen captures the challenge of confronting fears this way:

> People have fears. The stronger that fear is, the easier it is to accept fiction in terms of what may or may not happen on the landscape. So as an example, I think the Cattle Growers in Arizona or New Mexico have this thought process that if public land becomes nationally designated with a conservation priority, that somehow that means it's a Park Service–driven process that says the next step is "thou shalt not enter, no cattle, no people, don't get off the road, don't pick up a rock," that kind of thing. It is that fear-based or culturally based opposition to conservation that is difficult to break until folks who are opposed initially become involved in a process that allows them to not operate on a fear-based premise but operate on "What are the possibilities? How do we sustain grazing as part of that conservation equation? How do we improve economics for rural counties? How do we enhance the experience for the public on the public lands?"

Take the Time to Ensure That All Views Are Heard

The late Michael Taylor noted the Bureau of Land Management's increasing use of collaborative efforts aimed at engaging citizens in the development of resource management plans:

> Engaging people early has become a more common practice in the BLM. [Some collaborative efforts to develop RMPs] became very successful: the Las Cienegas planning process, the Bradshaw Hassayampa process that included the management plan for the Agua Fria National Monument. That one took a long time but it included public involvement from the get-go. It was very collaborative.
>
> . . . It can take you a lot longer to develop a collaborative resource management plan than the old normal: plan; bam, bam, bam get it done; sign the plan. But that way, you're often still not done because it's in court for another three or four years. If you spend the time up front resolving issues, building

good mitigating measures for things that might have been an issue, working with the people that are out there who are really the ones who are going to care the most [it works far better in the long run]. So making sure you're hearing from all of those people is what is so important. I've found that if the views of people on the ground are considered, and if you work with them, [the] level of angst goes down.

Harmonize Economic, Cultural, and Conservation Goals

An essential feature of successful conservation efforts is gaining broad support. Lynn Scarlett, former acting director of the Department of Interior, provides an example of how conservation and economic goals can be harmonized:

> One of the great programs at Fish and Wildlife Service is the Partners for Fish and Wildlife program. It [provides funds to farmers that] helps them to invest in streambank fencing and the planting of native warm spring grasses and the restoration of shrubs along streambanks and [things like that].
>
> The interesting thing is that that funding is [not only] very good for nature but [has also] proven to be advantageous from the productivity of the cattle or dairy farmer, because it results in less waterborne hoof disease and various and sundry other things. It allows them to manage their pastures better.
>
> So my point is, it's important not to think that this is an inevitable trade-off, that is, *either* the farmer does conservation efforts *or* they have productive livelihoods. There are ways to think about how to combine them and thinking in an integrated way is important. [For example, in the case of] the Malpai Borderlands Group, a lot of the work it does [is] fire management: periodic, monitored burns both to enhance forage but also reduce invasive species. It's good for the land and species, [and] it's good for the ranchers.[119]

Recent investment work in restoration work in the Colorado River watershed provides another example. Says Walton Foundation Colorado River Lead Tom Kowalski,

> We at the Walton Foundation undertook a five-year program to initiate projects in the Colorado River Basin that address the challenge of accelerating

water use in the face of population growth and watershed sustainability. Restoration and river health was also an important part of the program. We worked [in selected areas where we hoped to demonstrate] that the health of the river was not an anathema to the local economy, [but] rather [that] you could have a healthy economy and a healthy river in the same space.

We also worked in the Escalante River basin. We worked in the San Pedro and the Verde, working on protecting flows and [improving] flows as well as working on riparian restoration: trying to bring back native plants and take out all sorts of invasive species—salt cedar, tamarisk, and the like. We also did that in the context of the delta in Mexico.[120]

Lesli Allison of the Western Landowners Alliance emphasizes the importance of working lands in achieving conservation goals:

Western Landowners Alliance is trying to catalyze [a] movement to find pathways to conservation that will support working lands. The traditional approaches of "take it out of private ownership and put it into public ownership"—that acquisition approach—is really not popular with most folks in the West who have land. By contrast, groups like Audubon, The Nature Conservancy, Trout Unlimited, Ducks Unlimited are working on the ground trying to find win-win solutions with farmers and ranchers. They don't have an 'anti agenda.' They're not anti-grazing or anti-ranching.

Find and Embrace Champions for a Community-Based Effort and Commit to a Long-Term Effort

Successful collaborative conservation or land-use planning efforts require a combination of good leadership and long-term, often multi-year commitment. "No matter how well intended, or how big, or how well developed the projects are, their success often depends on a champion or two or three, or a group that really wants to work to make them happen. You need effective leadership regardless of whether it's a national-led effort, or a state-led or a community-led effort," says Jack Williams of Trout Unlimited.

Peter Warren, who has observed the workings of the Malpai Borderlands Group for more than two decades, echoes Williams: "It takes a certain critical mass of people who are willing to put that effort in to make it work. It takes at least half a dozen people. It's better if it's eight or ten or more. It's really difficult and uncommon to find that many [committed] people. It's not the financial wherewithal, it's the visionary, personal wherewithal, to invest in that kind of an effort."

Encouraging Coordination with and Planning Among Conservation Groups

In order to achieve conservation goals on the scale of watersheds or large ecosystems, strategic planning and coordination among local collaborative groups is essential.

Says Lynn Scarlett:

> I like to think of these collaborative conservation efforts as operating on different scales, and then sometimes coalescing and combining at larger scales, and yet again larger still scales. There are limits to what can be accomplished when one is bounded at a smaller-scale level. There are emerging examples of what I call network-governed collaborative conservation efforts, where individual conservation efforts coalesce for broader common purposes.
>
> . . . You can have many individual collaborative conservation efforts that then, in common purpose, come together over a set of specific goals and projects, but still retain their individualized purposes. [They] may [later] reformulate with [other] organizations, for another set of projects and purposes.
>
> I would suggest [that] it's worthwhile thinking of large-landscape conservation and collaborative watershed conservation that pulls together multiple groups as not necessarily being defined as only those which end up with a formalized structure that embraces that larger scale. [It often proves difficult] to sustain a multi-entity large endeavor, especially if it involves combining existing organizations under the single umbrella of a more formalized effort.

As one example illustrating the successful integration of multiple conservation efforts, Scarlett cites the Crown of the Continent Roundtable:

> an endeavor that was launched with the recognition that there were literally dozens of local collaborative conservation groups in a 10-million-acre region spanning northern Montana, western Alberta and eastern British Columbia. They realized that their purposes intersected, and they could accomplish more if they could combine their efforts; for example, interconnecting watersheds or interconnecting wildlife corridors.

The Crown of the Continent Roundtable is a loose confederation. It regularly meets and there's knowledge sharing [among them]. But then, within the Crown of the Continent Roundtable some of the groups combine and jointly pursue fundraising for some larger-scale common purpose. It's not formal in the sense of having a tightly knit board of directors–governed single enterprise, but rather a kind of set of nested efforts that come together for common purpose and then re-cluster in other common purposes.

An example of federal efforts to support landscape-scale public-private collaborative efforts is the Regional Conservation Partnership Program, which promotes coordination of U.S. Department of Agriculture Natural Resources Conservation Service activities with partners to address on-farm, watershed, and regional-scale natural resource concerns.[121]

Emily Burns of the Sky Island Alliance is optimistic about the future of large-landscape conservation if local efforts can be coordinated to achieve regional or ecosystem goals: "The accumulation of really small acts on the landscape can be really incredible. People or groups working separately on several individual water sources could in combination help sustain species on the landscape over a much wider area. I just think sometimes work on local projects is very tangible for people. Our large-scale conservation work is a cumulative effort of many of those smaller projects."

Burns says that the Sky Island Alliance is in the process of bringing together individuals and groups working in the Madrean Archipelago ecoregion to carry out

large-landscape conservation planning to help manage the Sky Island landscape across jurisdictional boundaries. We support and participate in many groups, and also look for opportunities where we can talk about the region at a much larger scale: across the U.S.-Mexico boundary in addition to public land boundaries here in Arizona. There is definitely an effort to move beyond just specific projects or groups to be thinking on an ecoregional scale. There's definitely an interest in shared wildlife monitoring across the region—where species are found across the landscape and how their populations are changing over time. That is something that many groups have mobilized and come together to share monitoring data.

In order to advance large-landscape scale conservation goals, Tahnee Robertson of Southwest Decisions Resources suggests it's important to work with "local, place-based collaboratives to coordinate and to share costs. I don't think it's about one person being manager at a regional scale, [but rather to have someone in a coordinator/facilitator role] to bring them all together, [with] . . . agency support. That's what the U.S. Fish and Wildlife and the Bureau of Reclamation were funding with the Desert Landscape Conservation Cooperative: pilot [projects] for doing 'climate-smart' landscape conservation design."[122]

Robertson says of the Desert Landscape Conservation Cooperative (LCC), "The goals . . . were very ambitious and it was well funded. Then the LCCs all fizzled away when they started losing all their funding." She points out that although the Desert LCC is now "moribund, coordinator and science coordinator of the Desert LCC [Genevieve Johnson and Matt Grabau, respectively] are building on their experience with Desert LCC and developing CCAST, which is Conservation and Adaptation Resources Toolbox."[123]

CCAST enhances collaborative conservation efforts at watershed and landscape scales by facilitating issue-based, peer-to-peer knowledge sharing. By connecting hundreds of individuals from dozens of organizations across North America, CCAST helps bridge the gaps between work at project, landscape, and operational scales. CCAST answers "Who is doing what, and where? What is working and what isn't? Where can we find resources to help us improve our work on a similar issue?" The multi-organization CCAST partnership is supported by the U.S. Fish and Wildlife Service and the Bureau of Reclamation. At present "Their three priority areas are grasslands, aquatic and phenology for pollinators. They're putting together case studies and creating communities of practice around these topics," says Robertson.

Funding and Support Needed for Collaborative Conservation Efforts

Support for Essential Organizational Functions

Groups and organizations involved in large-landscape conservation need funding for monitoring ecosystem functions, hiring consultants to provide expert advice, communicating with other groups and the public, organizing meetings, and supporting travel. While there are a number of funding sources available to support specific conservation projects, obtaining support for these ongoing organizational infrastructure needs can be challenging.

"When I talk about funding for large-landscape conservation and the need for operating funding, it is actually for the people and governance that allow those ongoing adaptive efforts to continue to evolve and be sustained," says Lynn Scarlett.

> There's no question that many of the large-landscape successful efforts underway—the Malpai Borderlands Group, the Blackfoot Challenge, the Applegate Partnership—all or most of them would benefit from enduring funding. They all have to scramble year by year. Alas, [most] public funding grants in the conservation arena come in increments of one year. It's a stretch to try and get a three-year funding commitment. It's just the way that the funding cycles for conservation work. So you have a challenge in that the need [for what might be termed "infrastructure" support] is a forever need, an iterative and ongoing need, but the realities of public sector funding mean that one has to be thinking about shorter-term time horizons.[124]

Bill McDonald of the Malpai Borderlands Group captures the problem well: "Our executive director spends a lot of his time raising money. I spent an enormous amount of time grant writing when I was executive director. It was probably half of my job."

The BLM's Jesse Juen says,

> There are foundations and grant programs that provide [infrastructure support] and in addition many of the agencies, whether they be local, county or whether they be state or the federal entities, have that ability to secure a facilitator or contract out a facilitator, to help a group work through these dynamics. Federal agencies have the ability to do it at a very reasonable cost—they can make sure that folks are invited and folks are encouraged to come to meetings. They can put out the results of meetings. They can put notes together. They can do social media. There's a whole lot of that stuff that agencies are very well positioned to do or assist with or to nurture.

Federal and State Support for Collaborative Planning with Other Locally Based Groups

"In the past, most Farm Bill funding has been distributed formulaically in sort of 'random acts of conservation kindness' . . . with no real strategic focus," says Lynn Scarlett. But since 2014, a critical component of the Farm Bill has been the Regional Conservation Partnership Program.

"The RCPP program . . . took a chunk of Farm Bill funding and said, 'These are the strategic areas where we want to drive the funding.' So that funding [was] targeted at these specific high-priority areas, in order to get more clustered and more strategically focused conservation efforts by farmers within a defined region," says Scarlett, who served as acting director of the Department of Interior. "If you look at the Department of Interior and all its multitude of grant programs, in theory you could similarly allocate some of those in [a manner analogous to RCPP] rather than catch as catch can. You could strategically focus them."

She notes that "there are some state models for supporting collaborative conservation efforts that are kind of interesting. New Mexico has something called the New Mexico Collaborative Zone grants." The Zone Grant pilot project, launched in 2018, solicited proposals for one-year planning grants to support conservation collaboratives working in selected conservation zones. In the following year, eight of the fourteen collaboratives selected to receive planning grants were each awarded $135,000 to implement the plans they developed during the planning process.[125]

Scarlett believes

> the New Mexico program represents a model that is potentially replicable in other states. In theory, it could be a model at the federal level. A move to zone grants, would allow funding to be more concentrated to strategic focus areas. You could have a multitude of ranchers in some zone apply [individually] but [tied to] specific, overarching performance purposes. [The] effect would be you'd have a higher concentration of conservation efforts within that zone. [Depending] on how you develop those zones, you could even [provide incentives] to proposals where five or more ranch holders work together. You put criteria in there along those lines.

Concluding Thoughts

The options for individuals and communities to develop large-landscape conservation plans are manifold. The Nature Conservancy's Peter Warren succinctly captures the most crucial element: "The prognosis for success in trying to preserve a large landscape depends on having enough people who love that place and care enough about it to do something to protect it."

SYNOPSIS

OVERVIEW

Meeting the conservation challenges of the twenty-first century will require a three-pronged strategy: *protection* of lands critical to biodiversity and ecosystem function; *restoration* of lands still able to provide connected species habitat and healthy ecosystem function; and policies that support and encourage *sound stewardship* of public and private lands.

Protecting isolated sites as national parks or monuments for their aesthetic, scientific, or cultural value represents only one element of an overall strategy for sustaining healthy ecological functions. A landscape-scale perspective is needed.

All elements of a landscape mosaic should be considered in forging an integrated plan for conservation and land stewardship. Addressing the challenge of preserving and restoring healthy ecosystems will require an *all-lands* approach: public, private, and tribal.

Achieving large-landscape conservation goals will also require an *all-hands* approach, involving broad public participation in shaping how to protect and steward the landscapes in which citizens live.

Collaborative large-landscape conservation offers the promise of better integrating human needs and environmental needs and creating the context for long-term cooperation among stakeholders.

SELECTING AND PRIORITIZING CONSERVATION AREAS

Selection criteria for identifying the highest priority conservation lands should include

- diversity and richness of species (biodiversity)
- potential for maintaining or restoring ecosystem function
- potential for providing wildlife with suitable habitat now and in the future (resilience)
- unfragmented connection between viable species habitat areas
- protection of watersheds and other ecosystem functions

STRATEGIES FOR LAND PROTECTION

Land acquisition

- Through direct purchase by counties, federal agencies, individuals of means, groups of conservation-minded citizens, and land exchanges involving state, federal, and private entities

Purchase or donation of conservation easements

- Land trusts or other entities are responsible for monitoring easements and ensuring that the landholder adheres to the term of the easement.
- Easements provide protection against development or subdivision but are typically quite limited in their ability to mandate sound stewardship.

Single-species or multi-species habitat conservation plans
- Require adherence to the terms of the Endangered Species Act
- Preclude takings of habitat for endangered species or provision of alternative habitat

Conservation leasing, habitat leasing, and mitigation banks
- Yearly payment for removing environmentally sensitive land from production
- Payment and technical assistant to carry out conservation activities on eligible land
- Payment to rent out lands to support habitat and wildlife migration
- Purchase of ecologically valuable land by a county to serve as a bank. Developers who inflict environmental damage in turn purchase credits from the bank. The proceeds are used by the county to purchase more mitigation lands to add to the bank

Payment for ecosystem services
- Funding opportunities aimed at incentivizing private landholders to follow the sound stewardship needed to deliver one or more ecological services
- Example: the government pays a rancher to carry out or continue to carry out practices that maintain or enhance watershed function, wildlife habitat, or habitat connectivity

LANDSCAPE RESTORATION

Restoring damaged grasslands, forests, and riparian areas

- Mitigate or eliminate soil erosion, arroyo creation, channel incision
- Reduce encroachment by shrubs and invasive species
- Restore fire to forest and grassland areas
- Modify grazing practices to minimize effects on environmentally sensitive lands
- Where needed and possible, use treated water to restore riparian areas
- Create paths for wildlife movement by protecting land and creating overpasses and tunnels where roads have fragmented land
- Reintroduce endangered and extirpated species such as beavers and prairie dogs

LAND STEWARDSHIP

Effective stewardship requires that land managers, stakeholders, scientific experts, and communities work and learn together to develop goals for maintaining sustainable landscapes by

- Assessing current environmental conditions along with extant and possible future threats

- Developing a shared vision for conservation goals and objectives
- Developing and implementing a plan including both land protection and restoration efforts
- Monitoring landscape conditions following implementation of the plan
- Reassessing environmental conditions and adjusting management plans accordingly

Vision, assessment, action, monitoring, evaluation and revision are hallmarks of sound stewardship.

MOTIVATING AND CATALYZING LARGE-LANDSCAPE CONSERVATION

To develop successful conservation strategies across a large area with multiple landowners requires ongoing collaborative efforts in which people share a common vision for the future.

- Threats are often the most powerful catalysts for action.
- Most successful conservation efforts start out locally, where individuals motivated by attachment to and passion for a place initiate conversation about the effects of land use on their future.
- Conversations that endure are those that include individuals with diverse interests—from large-scale landowners and ranchers to the business community and entrepreneurs in the region, other advocates for conservation, and community members who care about the place.
- A facilitator can help groups set a framework for successful discussions and provide them with experienced-based suggestions regarding how best to interact and work together.

The collaborative conservation efforts described in this book share the following characteristics with each other and groups across the United States:

- Recognizing and respecting cultural differences
- Recognizing and understanding with compassion fears of some individuals about the future
- Taking the time to build relationships and trust
- Holding meetings in informal settings to build understanding and trust
- Harmonizing economic, cultural, and conservation goals
- Operating transparently and communicating the results of discussions promptly and widely
- Finding and supporting a good leader or leadership team
- Developing a transition plan to enable a smooth handover to next generation group leaders
- Seeking and finding agreement on a common vision and goals

RECOMMENDATIONS

- Investments in land protection and land restoration need to be strategic. Federal, state, county, and individual funds need to be directed primarily to protection of critical lands.
- Conservation easements need stronger legal protections to ensure protection in perpetuity.
- Land trusts managing conservation easements need resources to monitor lands under easement to ensure that the lands' contributions to ecosystem functions are maximized.
- The value of ranch properties to ecosystem function should be considered when making decisions about selling state trust land. Access to state and federal lands is critical to the economic viability of ranches; most ranches would no longer be sustainable without them.
- Lands under easement should be given higher priority for federal restoration funds than those that lack the development restrictions inherent in the easement.
- Similarly, landholders who invest consistently in restoration and other land stewardship efforts should be given high priority if they seek federal funds to place conservation easements on their lands.
- Non-market values (e.g., wildlife habitat, watershed function, open space) should be used in appraising the value of a conservation easement. The potential to receive a higher return for placing land under easement may motivate more landholders to place their lands under easement.
- Tax deductions for land under easement and inheritance taxes should be structured to further incentivize protection of biologically critical lands.
- The Endangered Species Act should be amended to promote the protection of important watersheds, forests, and other threatened ecosystems, whether or not they provide habitat for endangered species.
- Federal, state, and county support for collaborative planning efforts should be increased, with the goal of providing ongoing support for groups attempting to meet the challenge of protecting the most biologically sensitive lands.
- Funds for supporting the management functions of established collaborative conservation groups should be increased in order that often small, local groups have access to resources to support monitoring, hiring of consultants and scientific experts, grant writing expertise, travel, and hiring of facilitators.
- Funds for land restoration and monitoring of environmental conditions should be increased in service of incentivizing restoration of important conservation lands.
- The length of federal grants to support collaborative conservation efforts should be increased to better match the timescales needed to form and develop effective collaborative conservation groups and to carry out monitoring and restoration efforts.

Ending Thoughts

A human being is a part of the whole called by us universe, a part limited in time and space. He experiences himself, his thoughts and feeling as something separated from the rest, a kind of optical delusion of his consciousness. This delusion is a kind of prison for us, restricting us to our personal desires and to affection for a few persons nearest to us. Our task must be to free ourselves from this prison by widening our circle of compassion to embrace all living creatures and the whole of nature in its beauty.

—ALBERT EINSTEIN

The rapid growth of the West over the past century has brought with it not only transformative progress but significant environmental damage. Once wide open spaces have been fragmented by roads and homes. Grasslands, forests, and watersheds have been damaged, to the detriment of wildlife, species diversity, and water supply. Healthy ecosystems that otherwise would have stored carbon have been lost or degraded, greenhouse gases have accumulated more rapidly, and global warming has accelerated. The result: higher temperatures and historic droughts, along with more frequent and disruptive wildfires and the loss of the ineffable values of scenic beauty and solitude.

Why is it, biologist E. O. Wilson wondered, that "the delusion has arisen that people can flourish apart from the rest of the living world?"[1] In 1833 William Foster Lloyd, a political economist at Oxford University, asked himself a similar question as he reflected on the devastation of community grazing pastures in England: "Why is the common itself so bare-worn and cropped so differently from the adjoining" privately owned lands?[2] His answer: absent any external regulation, each farmer in the community acts in his own self-interest and places as many of his cattle on the commons as he can in service of maximizing profit.

"Therein is the tragedy. Each man is locked into a system that compels him to increase his herd without limit—in a world that is limited. Ruin is the destination toward which all men rush, each pursuing his own best interest in a society that believes in the freedom of the commons," wrote ecologist Garrett Hardin in a widely read, influential paper published in the December 1968 issue of *Science Magazine*.[3] "An unmanaged commons in a world of limited material wealth and unlimited desires inevitably ends in ruin." Hardin speculated that what he dubbed the "Tragedy of the Commons" could only be avoided through strict government regulation or private ownership of land by individuals motivated by self-interest to steward it well.[4]

Economist Elinor Ostrom contested Hardin's arguments. In her 2009 Nobel Prize lecture, she noted that "the National Research Council established a committee in the mid-1980s to assess diverse institutional arrangements for effective conservation and utilization of jointly managed resources." In contradistinction to Hardin's grim assessment, the committee "found multiple cases where resource users were successful in organizing themselves [which] challenged the presumption that it was impossible for resource users to solve their own problems of overuse."[5]

Much of Ostrom's research career was devoted to studies and analyses of collaborative systems developed organically in a variety of cultural and economic contexts.[6] She documented how different communities had self-organized to develop protocols for both preserving natural resources and supporting local economic needs.

The large-landscape conservation efforts described in *Forging a Sustainable Southwest*, along with the burgeoning numbers of such efforts around the country, lend support to Ostrom's optimistic, empirically based conclusion: faced with the challenge of managing common resources, communities can find a way to collaboratively develop beneficent solutions.

In many ways, the potential of community-based groups to steward resources essential to their well-being was anticipated by scientist and pioneering explorer of the West, John Wesley Powell. Powell's multiple expeditions to uncharted western lands, along with surveys he organized as director of the U.S. Geological Survey, led him to warn his country that water in the arid lands was scarce west of the one-hundredth meridian. He urged that water be managed as a common resource lest a "tragedy of the commons" result from an individual's use of water without regard to the needs of fellow settlers. "People of the West are entering upon an era of unparalleled speculation, which will result in the aggregation of the lands and waters in the hands of a comparatively few persons. Let us hope that there is wisdom enough in the statesmen of America to avert the impending evil," Powell wrote.[7]

He imagined that citizens would be motivated to form what we would today call a collaborative conservation partnership so that "the waters . . . be divided among the people so that each man may have the amount necessary to fertilize his farm, each hamlet, town, and city the amount necessary for domestic purposes, and that every thirsty garden may quaff from the crystal waters that come from the mountains."

Powell noted that such collaborative groups had taken form centuries before European settlement of the West in the nineteenth century: "The people of the Southwest came originally, by the way of Mexico, from Spain, where irrigation and the institutions necessary for its control had been developing from high antiquity, and these people well understood that their institutions must be adapted to their industries, and so they organized their settlements as pueblos, or 'irrigating municipalities,' by which the lands were held in severalty while the tenure of waters and works was communal or municipal." Elinor Ostrom might well have smiled had she read this passage.

Powell is rightly celebrated as a great explorer, an insightful scientist, and a skilled administrator. But he was also a prescient ecologist. In his writings about water, he spoke not only of the streams and rivers of the West, but the health of the watersheds within which they flowed:

> In a group of mountains, a small river has its source. A dozen or a score of creeks unite to form the trunk. The creeks higher up divide into brooks. All these streams combined form the drainage system of a hydrographic basin, a unit of country well defined in nature, for it is bounded above and on each side by heights of land that rise as crests to part the waters. In such a basin of the arid region the irrigable lands lie below; not chiefly by the river's side, but on the mesas and low plains that stretch back on each side. Above these lands the pasturage hills and mountains stand, and there the forests and sources of water supply are found.

He urged that communities that benefit from a watershed take responsibility for stewarding the lands comprising what he called a "hydrographic basin":

> Every man is interested in the conservation and management of the water supply, for all the waters are needed within the district. The men who control the farming below must also control the upper regions where the waters are gathered from the heavens and stored in the reservoirs. Every farm and garden in the valley below is dependent upon each fountain above.
>
> All of the lands that lie within the basin above the farming districts are the catchment areas for all the waters poured upon the fields below. Not a spring or a creek can be touched without affecting the interests of every man who cultivates the soil in the region. *All the waters are common property . . .* to be distributed among the people. How these waters are to be caught and the common source of wealth utilized by the individual settlers interested therein is a *problem for the men of the district to solve*, and for them alone.
>
> Let such a people organize, under national and State laws, and let them make their own laws for the division of the waters, for the protection and use of the forests, and for the protection of the pasturage on the hills. The people in such a district have common interests, common rights, and common duties, and must necessarily work together for common purposes.

Powell emphasized the interdependence of all components of the watershed and stressed the importance of the roles played by healthy forests and grasslands in the proper functioning of hydrographic basins:

> The great forests that clothe the hills, plateaus, and mountains with verdure must be saved from devastation by fire and preserved for the use of man, that the sources of water may be protected.
>
> Though the grasses of the pasturage lands of the West are nutritious, they are not abundant, as in the humid valleys of the East. Yet they have an important value. These grasses are easily destroyed by improvident pasturage, and they are then replaced by noxious weeds. To be utilized they must be carefully protected and grazed only in proper seasons and within prescribed limits. But they cannot be enclosed by fences in small fields. Ten, twenty, fifty acres are necessary for the pasturage of a steer; so the grasses can be utilized only

in large bodies, and be fenced only by townships or tens of townships. To be utilized they must be carefully protected and grazed only in proper seasons and within prescribed limits.[8]

Powell anticipated how the environmental challenges he outlined might be met: "Thus, it is that there is a body of interdependent and unified interests and values, all collected in one hydrographic basin. The people in such a district have common interests, common rights, and common duties and necessarily work together for common purpose."

There is hardly a more eloquent call for collaborative, large-landscape conservation groups to take form, and networks of such groups to join together in service of protecting, restoring, and stewarding lands.

Powell had deep faith in the ability of humans to develop locally rooted democratic institutions to address environmental challenges. As he foresaw, successfully building such institutions would start locally, with small gatherings of individuals engaging their neighbors and communities to find common ground: from citizen groups who care passionately about a nearby forest, grassland, or riparian area, to a web of groups working to ensure the proper function of a watershed or an ecoregion.

The case studies presented here affirm Powell's belief in citizens' ability to create shared land-use visions that take into consideration ecological, economic, and cultural needs. To address today's environmental challenges, we should draw inspiration from the endeavors of Josiah Austin, the Malpai Borderlands Group, the Sonoita Valley Planning Partnership, and the architects of the Sonoran Desert Conservation Plan.

Matthew McKinney, Lynn Scarlett, and Daniel Kemmis in a report for the Lincoln Institute of Land Policy suggest that forming such collaborative efforts to address large-landscape conservation challenges

might well result in a healing of not only ecosystems, but also related human systems. As traditionally adversarial conservation, community, and economic interests search for common ground, one arena of shared interest is a growing recognition that unscarred landscapes, clean water, fresh air, and a rich biodiversity based on healthy ecosystems, are becoming the best economic engine available to many local communities. *Perhaps even more appealing is the prospect that, in the course of working hard to discover and claim that common ground, the people who inhabit those ecosystems will have contributed to the strengthening of their civic culture, and to expanding their capacity to address the next set of challenges.*[9]

Nature has presented us with gifts of incalculable value: earth with its astounding diversity of plant and animal life—systems of unbound complexity and beauty, masterpieces of evolution. Can our society rediscover shared purpose in protecting and cherishing these masterpieces, stewarding our endowment, and in the process, restoring the commons? To once again quote E. O. Wilson, "There can be no purpose more enspiriting than to begin the age of restoration, reweaving the wondrous diversity of life that still surrounds us."

ACKNOWLEDGMENTS

In memory of Henri Bisson, Jim Kolbe, Tom Meixner, and Michael Taylor.

I would like to express my thanks to all the individuals interviewed for this book who took the time to educate me, and to share their insights, experiences, and in many cases personal stories and anecdotes.

I am particularly grateful to Josiah Austin, Bruce Babbitt, Dean Bibles, Diana Freshwater, Gayle Hartmann, Jesse Juen, Bill McDonald, Dan Robinett, Karen Simms, and Jeffrey Simms for providing constructive feedback and thoughtful comments on earlier drafts of the text.

Josiah Austin, Mac Donaldson, and Karen and Jeffrey Simms were kind enough to spend time with me on the ground at Cienega Ranch, Open Cross Ranch, and Las Cienegas National Conservation Areas, respectively. In the course of the hours we spent on the open range and in lush riparian areas, I was able to gain a far deeper understanding of their connection to and love for the land, as well as their commitment to caring stewardship.

Thanks as well to Alan Fitzgerald, director of Art Intersection Gallery in Gilbert, who served both as pilot of a productive Cessna flight over the Sonoita Valley and as a supporter of my photographic endeavors.

Wildlife photographer Bruce D. Taubert contributed many of his striking images of threatened and endangered species. To fully appreciate the elegance of his work, I encourage readers to visit his website (https://bruce taubert.smugmug.com/Galleries).

Finally, I am profoundly grateful to my daughter, Kathy Huntington, and granddaughter, Rebecca Robinson, for reading various versions of the manuscript with a critical eye. Their gentle but firm criticisms and ongoing encouragement helped to bring this work to fruition.

INDIVIDUALS INTERVIEWED

denotes individuals deceased since their interviews.

Lesli Allison: CEO, Western Landowners Alliance

Josiah Austin: Cienega Ranch

Bruce Babbitt: Former secretary of the interior; former governor of Arizona

Kurt Bahti: Former field supervisor, Arizona Game and Fish Department

Ron Barber: Former U.S. congressman from Arizona

Cameron Becker: Director of land programs, Arizona Land and Water Trust

Paul Beier: Professor of conservation biology, Northern Arizona University

David Bertelsen: Adjunct associate research scientist, University of Arizona

Dean Bibles: Public Lands Foundation, Bureau of Land Management (retired)

Henri Bisson*: former president, Public Lands Foundation, Bureau of Land Management (retired)

Kenneth Branch: Natural Resources Conservation Service, New Mexico

Ben Brophy: Vice president, Arizona Land and Water Trust

Gita Bodner: Conservation ecologist, The Nature Conservancy

Em Brott: Former project manager, Sonoran Desert Program, Sonoran Institute

Alison Bunting: Historian, Empire Ranch Foundation

Emily Burns: Program director, Sky Island Alliance

Carolyn Campbell: Executive director, Coalition for Sonoran Desert Protection

Shel Clark: Senior environmental scientist, TerraGraphics Environmental Engineering

Les Corey: Executive director, Arizona Wilderness Coalition; former vice president, The Nature Conservancy

Tom Cors: Director of lands for U.S. Government Relations at The Nature Conservancy

Peter Culp: Specialist in natural resource law and policy, Culp and Kelly, LLP, Phoenix

Susan Culp: Project manager, Western Lands and Communities, Lincoln Institute of Land Policy

Bill Doelle: President and CEO, Archaeology Southwest

Michael Dombeck: Fourteenth chief of the U.S. Forest Service; former acting director, Bureau of Land Management

Mac Donaldson: Retired rancher

Chris Easthoe: Adjunct researcher, University of Arizona College of Science (Geosciences)

Lori Faeth: Senior government relations director, Land Trust Alliance

Larry Fisher: Research professor, natural resources and the environment, University of Arizona (retired)

Julia Fonseca: Office of Sustainability and Conservation, Pima County (retired)

Diana Freshwater: President, Arizona Land and Water Trust

Bill Gillespie: Forest archaeologist, Coronado National Forest, U.S. Forest Service

Diana Hadley: Founding president, Northern Jaguar Project

Gayle Hartmann: Former president, Save the Scenic Santa Ritas

Christine Hoekenga: Environmental Education, Natural Resources, Parks and Recreation, Pima County

Chris Horyza: State planning and environmental coordinator, Bureau of Land Management (retired)

Chuck Huckelberry: Pima County administrator (retired)

Katharine Jacobs: Professor of hydrology and atmospheric sciences, University of Arizona

Jesse Juen: Former director, New Mexico State Bureau of Land Management (retired)

Linda Kennedy: Director, Appleton-Whittell Research Ranch, National Audubon Society (retired)

Jim Kolbe*: former U.S. congressman from Arizona

Tom Kowalski: Senior program officer, Walton Family Foundation

John Leshy: Emeritus professor, University of California Hastings College of Law

Thomas Maddock: Professor of hydrology and water resources, University of Arizona

Linda Mayro: Director, Office of Sustainability and Conservation, Pima County

Frank McChesney: Partner in the operation of Babocomari Ranch, Sonoita, Arizona

Bill McDonald: Rancher and conservationist; founding member, Malpai Borderlands Group

Shela McFarlin: Manager, Bureau of Land Management Tucson Field Office (retired)

Jen McIntosh: Professor of hydrology and atmospheric sciences, University of Arizona

Tom Meixner*: Professor of hydrology and atmospheric sciences, University of Arizona

Gary Nabhan: Research social scientist emeritus, Southwest Center, University of Arizona

Mary Nichols: Research hydraulic engineer, U.S. Department of Agriculture

Ed Norton: Founding chair, Conservation Lands Foundation

Brian O'Donnell: Director, Campaign for Nature

Michael Patrick: Senior project manager, Trust for Public Land

Ron Pulliam: Regents Professor Emeritus, Odum School of Ecology, University of Georgia

Liz Petterson: Former executive director, Arizona Land and Water Trust

Vanessa Prileson: Rangeland program manager, Pima County

Luther Propst: Former executive director, Sonoran Institute; Teton County, Wyoming, commissioner

Tahnee Robertson: Director, Southwest Decision Resources

Dan Robinett: Range conservationist, USDA Natural Resources Conservation Services (retired)

Jennifer Ruyle: Deputy director for planning and watersheds, Southwest Region, U.S. Forest Service

Lynn Scarlett: Managing director, public policy, The Nature Conservancy (retired)

Russ Scott: Research hydrologist/adjunct research professor, University of Arizona

Tom Sheridan: Research anthropologist, Southwest Center, University of Arizona

Jeff Simms: Fishery biologist, Bureau of Land Management

Karen Simms: Natural Resources Division manager, Pima County; Bureau of Land Management Tucson Field Office (retired)

Julie Strom: Environmental Education program manager, Pima County

Michael Taylor*: Deputy director, Bureau of Land Management Arizona State Office

Ian Tomlinson: Cattle rancher and vice president of Vera Earl Ranch

Peter Warren: Field representative, The Nature Conservancy (retired)

Dick White: Former mayor, Durango, Colorado

Jack Williams: Emeritus scientist, Trout Unlimited

Stephen Williams: Arizona State Land Department (retired)

Jeff Williamson: Former CEO and president, Phoenix Zoo

David Yetman: Research social scientist, University of Arizona; former Pima County commissioner

Elaine Zielinski: Arizona State director, Bureau of Land Management (retired)

Adriana Zuniga-Teran: Assistant professor, School of Geography, University of Arizona

NOTES

Introduction

1. H. Wesley Peirce and Peter L. Kresan, "The 'Floods' of October 1983," *Fieldnotes from the Arizona Bureau of Geology and Mineral Technology* 14, no. 2 (Summer 1984), https://azgeology.azgs.arizona.edu/sites/default/files/archived-articles-125th/Floods-of -Oct-1983-Summer-84.pdf; Thomas F. Saarinen, Victor R. Baker, Robert Durrenberger, and Thomas Maddock, "The Tucson, Arizona, Flood of October 1983," Committee on Natural Disasters Commission on Engineering and Technical Systems, National Research Council, January 1, 1984.

2. Pima County, "History of the Pima County Regional Flood Control District," pamphlet, August 7, 2020, https://content.civicplus.com/api/assets/d24de96a-e844-46ca-a466 -1b3cba4e4a62?cache=1800.

3. Pima County, "History of the Pima County Regional Flood Control District."

4. David Smutzer and Julia Fonseca, "Analysis of Purchasing Floodprone Portions of the Empire and Cienega Ranches," Pima County Department of Transportation and Flood Control District Long Range Planning Section, September 14, 1987.

5. "History Overview," Empire Ranch Foundation, https://www.empireranch foundation.org/empire-ranch/history/; Bureau of Land Management, "Historic Empire Ranch," https://www.blm.gov/visit/historic-empire-ranch; Public Law 106-538, 106th Congress: An Act to Establish the Las Cienegas National Conservation Area in the State of Arizona, *Congressional Record* 146 (2000), https://www.govinfo.gov/content/pkg/PLAW -106publ538/pdf/PLAW-106publ538.pdf; Em Martin Brott, "Celebrating Collaborative Conservation and Twenty Years of Las Cienegas NCA," Sonoran Institute, 2023, https:// sonoraninstitute.org/card/las-cienegas-nca/.

6. Pima County Administrator's Office, *Protecting Our Land, Water, and Heritage: Pima County's Voter-Supported Conservation Efforts, Sonoran Desert Conservation Plan,* February 2011, https://prism.lib.asu.edu/items/42546.

7. "Ecosystem," National Geographic Education, https://education.nationalgeographic
.org/resource/ecosystem/; "Ecosystem," Biology Dictionary, https://biologydictionary.net
/ecosystem/; "Ecosystem," Biology Online, https://www.biologyonline.com/dictionary
/ecosystem; "Ecoregions," U.S. Environmental Protection Agency, https://www.epa.gov
/eco-research/ecoregions.

8. "The Disappearing West," Center for American Progress, https://disappearingwest
.org/land.html.

9. "Global Warming in the Western United States," Union of Concerned Scientists,
September 15, 2015, updated June 25, 2018, https://www.ucsusa.org/resources/global
-warming-western-united-states; "As the Climate Dries the American West Faces Power
and Water Shortages, Experts Warn," United Nations Environment Program, August 2,
2022, https://www.unep.org/news-and-stories/story/climate-dries-american-west-faces
-power-and-water-shortages-experts-warn; Deborah M. Finch, *Climate Change in Grasslands, Shrublands, and Deserts of the Interior American West: A Review and Needs Assessment*, U.S. Forest Service Rocky Mountain Research Station General Technical Report
RMRS-GTR-285, 2012, https://www.fs.usda.gov/research/treesearch/41171.

10. "Conservation Timeline, 1901–2000," National Park Service, https://www.nps
.gov/mabi/learn/historyculture/conservation-timeline-1901-2000.htm; "Quick History
of the National Park Service," National Park Service, https://www.nps.gov/articles/quick
-nps-history.htm; "What Are the Differences Between National Parks and National Forests?," National Forest Foundation, https://www.nationalforests.org/blog/what-are-the
-differences-between-national-parks-and-national-forests?gad=1&gclid=CjwKCAjw44
mlBhAQEiwAqP3eVsmb0V0IFQ4XWit_xoiBiENEiJJOMGLlichpAeZQ76eevflTkbU80xo
CXagQAvD_BwE; "Federal Land Designations: A Brief Guide," Congressional Research
Service, May 19, 2023. https://crsreports.congress.gov/product/pdf/R/R45340; "Federal
Land Ownership: Overview and Data," Congressional Research Service, February 21,
2020, https://sgp.fas.org/crs/misc/R42346.pdf; "America's Public Lands Explained," U.S.
Department of Interior, https://www.doi.gov/blog/americas-public-lands-explained; "National History," Department of Interior, Bureau of Land Management, https://www.blm
.gov/about/history/timeline.

11. "The Wilderness Act," Wilderness Society, https://www.wilderness.org/articles
/article/wilderness-act; "National Parks, National Forests, and U.S. Wildernesses," Public Broadcasting System, April 18, 2012, https://www.pbs.org/wnet/nature/river-of-no
-return-national-parks-national-forests-and-u-s-wildernesses/7667/.

12. "The Origins of EPA," U.S. Environmental Protection Agency, https://www.epa.gov
/history/origins-epa; "Summary of the Clean Water Act," U.S. Environmental Protection
Agency, https://www.epa.gov/laws-regulations/summary-clean-water-act; "Evolution of
the Clean Air Act," U.S. Environmental Protection Agency, https://www.epa.gov/clean-air
-act-overview/evolution-clean-air-act.

13. Matthew McKinney, Lynn Scarlett, and Daniel Kemmis, "Large Landscape Conservation: A Strategic Framework for Policy and Action," Lincoln Institute of Land Policy,
2010, https://landconservationnetwork.org/wp-content/uploads/legacy-files/Large%20
Landscape%20Conservation-%20A%20Strategic%20Framework%20for%20Policy%20and
%20Action.pdf.

14. Aldo Leopold, *A Sand County Almanac* (Oxford: Oxford University Press, 1949), 192.

Chapter 1

1. E. D. Wilson and R. T. Moore, "Structure of Basin and Range Province in Arizona," *Southern Arizona Guidebook II: Arizona Geological Society* (1959), 89–97.

2. "Geologic Provinces of the United States: Colorado Plateau Province," U.S. Geological Survey, https://web.archive.org/web/20170709182145/https:/geomaps.wr.usgs.gov/parks/province/basinrange.html.

3. J. D. Hendricks and J. B. Plescia, "A Review of the Regional Geophysics of the Arizona Transition Zone," *Journal of Geophysical Research* 96 (1991): 12341–73, https://agupubs.onlinelibrary.wiley.com/doi/abs/10.1029/90JB01781.

4. "Weathering," Understanding Global Change, https://ugc.berkeley.edu/background-content/weathering/; "Weathering and Erosion," National Park Service, https://www.nps.gov/articles/000/weathering-erosion.htm; "Weathering and Soil," University of Houston, https://uh.edu/~geos6g/1330/weath.html; "Types of Weathering—Biological," Plant & Soil Sciences eLibrary, University of Nebraska–Lincoln, https://passel2.unl.edu/view/lesson/edd25385ca3d/4.

5. "Water: Science and Society—The Orographic Effect," InTeGrate at Penn State University, https://www.e-education.psu.edu/earth111/node/751; "Snowsports: Winter Mountain Weather," ATSC 113: Weather for Sailing, Flying & Snow Sports, University of British Columbia, https://www.eoas.ubc.ca/courses/atsc113/snow/met_concepts/06-met_concepts/06e-orographic-uplift-lee-shadowing/.

6. "Sonoran Desert Network Ecosystems," National Park Service, https://www.nps.gov/im/sodn/ecosystems.htm; Mark A. Dimmitt, "Biomes and Communities of the Sonoran Desert," Arizona-Sonora Desert Museum, https://www.desertmuseum.org/books/nhsd_biomes.php.

7. "What Is a Watershed?," National Ocean Service, https://oceanservice.noaa.gov/facts/watershed.html; "Watersheds and Drainage Basins," U.S. Geological Survey, https://www.usgs.gov/special-topics/water-science-school/science/watersheds-and-drainage-basins.

8. "Water Cycle," National Oceanic and Atmospheric Administration, https://www.noaa.gov/education/resource-collections/freshwater/water-cycle.

9. "Groundwater Connection with Streams," Groundwater Project, https://books.gw-project.org/groundwater-in-our-water-cycle/chapter/groundwater-connection-with-streams/.

10. "An Overview of Riparian Systems and Potential Problems," Oregon State University Extension Service, https://extension.oregonstate.edu/water/riparian-areas/overview-riparian-systems-potential-problems; George Zaimes, "Chapter 1: Defining Arizona's Riparian Areas and Their Importance to the Landscape," in *Understanding Arizona's Riparian Areas*, ed. George Zaimes (University of Arizona Cooperative Extension, 2007), https://cals.arizona.edu/extension/riparian/pub/UARA_07-17-07_chapter1.pdf.

11. "Ecoregions," U.S. Environmental Protection Agency; Benjamin M. Sleeter, Tamara S. Wilson, and William Acevedo, eds., "Status and Trends of Land Change in the

Western United States, 1973 to 2000," U.S. Geological Survey, 2012, https://pubs.usgs.gov/pp/1794/a/.

12. Glenn E. Griffith, James M. Omernik, Colleen Burch Johnson, and Dale S. Turner, "Ecoregions of Arizona," U.S. Geological Survey, 2014, https://pubs.usgs.gov/of/2014/1141/pdf/ofr2014-1141_front.pdf.

13. R. Brusca and W. Moore, "An Archipelago in a Cordilleran Gap—The Sky Islands of Arizona and Sonora," The Sky Islands, 2013, https://www.rickbrusca.com/http___www.rickbrusca.com_index.html/The_Sky_Islands.html; "Madrean Sky Islands," Wild Sonora, http://wildsonora.com/sky-islands.

14. "Madrean Archipelago Rapid Ecoregional Assessment: Executive Summary," Bureau of Land Management, 2014, https://landscape.blm.gov/REA_General_Docs/MAR_REA_Final_Report_Exec_Sum_Main_Report.pdf.

15. "The Sky Islands," Sky Island Alliance, https://skyislandalliance.org/the-sky-islands/.

16. "The Northern Sky Islands: Largest High-Biodiversity Habitat Block in Arizona?," Cascabel Conservation Association and Lower San Pedro Watershed Alliance, https://newsite.cascabelconservation.org/wp-content/uploads/2021/01/Fragmentation-LSPRV4b.pdf.

17. J. R. Strittholt, S. A. Bryce, B. C. Ward, and D. M. Bachelet, *Sonoran Desert Rapid Ecoregional Assessment Report*, Bureau of Land Management, May 2012, https://landscape.blm.gov/REA_General_Docs/SOD_Final_Report_Body.pdf.

18. R. M. Marshall et al., "An Ecological Analysis of Conservation Priorities in the Sonoran Desert Ecoregion," The Nature Conservancy Arizona Chapter, Sonoran Institute, and Instituto del Medio Ambiente y el Desarrollo Sustentable del Estado de Sonora, 2000, https://www.conservationgateway.org/ConservationPlanning/SettingPriorities/EcoregionalReports/Documents/SonoranPlan.pdf; "Sonoran Desert Inventory and Monitoring Network," U.S. National Park Service, https://www.nps.gov/im/sodn/ecosystems.htm.

19. "Chihuahuan Desert Rapid Ecoregional Assessment," Bureau of Land Management, October 2017, https://landscape.blm.gov/REA_General_Docs/CHD_Report.pdf; "Chihuahuan Desert Ecoregion," Chihuahuan Desert Inventory and Monitoring Network, U.S. National Park Service, https://www.nps.gov/im/chdn/ecoregion.htm.

20. Jerry R. Cox, Howard L. Morton, Jimmy T. LaBaume, and Kenneth G. Renard, "Reviving Arizona's Rangelands," *Journal of Soil and Water Conservation* 38 (1983): 342–45, https://www.tucson.ars.ag.gov/unit/publications/PDFfiles/401.pdf.

21. "Timber Management," in *Timeless Heritage: A History of the Forest Service in the Southwest*, by Robert D. Baker, Robert S. Maxwell, Victor H. Treat, and Henry C. Dethloff (U.S. Forest Service, 1988), http://npshistory.com/publications/usfs/region/3/history/chap10.htm; "US Forest Service Fire Suppression," Forest History Society, https://foresthistory.org/research-explore/us-forest-service-history/policy-and-law/fire-u-s-forest-service/u-s-forest-service-fire-suppression/; Diane M. Smith, "Sustainability and Wildland Fire: The Origins of Forest Service Wildland Fire Research," U.S. Forest Service, May 2017, https://www.fs.usda.gov/sites/default/files/fs_media/fs_document/sustainability-wildlandfire-508.pdf.

22. Benjamin F. Gilbert, *Mining Frontier*, ed. William C. Everett (U.S. Department of the Interior, National Park Service, 1959), http://npshistory.com/publications/nhl/theme-studies/mining-frontier.pdf; "Mining in Arizona," Arizona Geological Survey, https://azgs.arizona.edu/minerals/mining-arizona.

23. Conrad Joseph Bahre, *A Legacy of Change: Historic Human Impact on Vegetation in the Arizona Borderlands* (Tucson: University of Arizona Press, 1991); Nathan Freeman Sayre, *Ranching, Endangered Species, and Urbanization in the Southwest: Species of Capital* (Tucson: University of Arizona Press, 2002); Gerald R. Noonan, "The Overgrazing of Arizona Rangelands," San Pedro River Valley Human & Environmental History & Science Facts, 2011, https://scihistory.info/overgrazing.html; Arizona Game and Fish Department, "Grassland Systems Overview," Arizona Wildlife Conservation Strategy, https://awcs.azgfd.com/chapter-7-habitat-profiles/grasslands-ecosystem-group; Arizona Game and Fish Department, "Semidesert Grasslands," Arizona Wildlife Conservation Strategy, https://awcs.azgfd.com/habitats/semidesert-grasslands; Arizona Game and Fish Department, "Invasive and Problematic Species," Arizona Wildlife Conservation Strategy, https://awcs.azgfd.com/conservation-challenges/invasive-and-problematic-species; Thomas R. Van Devender and Mark A. Dimmitt, "Desert Grasses," Arizona-Sonora Desert Museum, https://www.desertmuseum.org/books/nhsd_grasses.php.

24. "Celebrating Arizona's Rivers: The Colorado River," University of Arizona Water Resources Research Center, 2012, http://wildsonora.com/sites/default/files/reports/celebrating-arizonas-rivers-colorado-river.pdf; "Celebrating Arizona's Rivers: The Little Colorado River," University of Arizona Water Resources Research Center, 2012, https://westernresourceadvocates.org/wp-content/uploads/dlm_uploads/2015/07/Celebrating-Arizona-Rivers_-The-Little-Colorado-River.pdf; "Celebrating Arizona's Rivers: The Verde River," University of Arizona Water Resources Research Center, 2012, http://www.edf.org/sites/default/files/Verde-FINAL-092612.pdf; "Celebrating Arizona's Rivers: The Gila River," University of Arizona Water Resources Research Center, 2012, https://www.edf.org/sites/default/files/GilaRiverFactSheet.pdf; Gregory McNamee, *Gila: The Life and Death of an American River* (Albuquerque: University of New Mexico Press, 1998); "Celebrating Arizona's Rivers: The Salt River," University of Arizona Water Resources Research Center, 2012, https://westernresourceadvocates.org/wp-content/uploads/dlm_uploads/2015/07/Celebrating-Arizona-Rivers_The-Salt-River.pdf; "Celebrating Arizona's Rivers: The San Pedro River," University of Arizona Water Resources Research Center, 2012, https://www.edf.org/sites/default/files/San_Pedro-FINAL.pdf; "Celebrating Arizona's Rivers: The Santa Cruz River," University of Arizona Water Resources Research Center, 2012, https://www.edf.org/sites/default/files/celebrating-arizonas-rivers-santa-cruz-062512_1.pdf; Odd S. Halseth, "Arizona's 1500 Years of Irrigation History," U.S. Department of the Interior, Bureau of Reclamation, https://www.usbr.gov/lc/phoenix/AZ100/1940/AZ_irrigation_history.html.

25. Robert H. Webb, Stanley A. Leake, and Raymond M. Turner, *The Ribbon of Green: Change in Riparian Vegetation in the Southwestern United States* (Tucson: University of Arizona Press, 2007); Barbara Tellman, Richard Yarde, and Mary G. Wallace, "Arizona's Changing Rivers: How People Have Affected the Rivers," University of Arizona Water

Resources Research Center, 1997, https://repository.arizona.edu/bitstream/handle/10150 /326060/Arizona's_Changing_Rivers_March%201997.pdf.

26. "Arizona vs. United States Comparative Trends Analysis: Population Growth and Change, 1958–2022," United States Regional Economic Analysis Project, https://united -states.reaproject.org/analysis/comparative-trends-analysis/population/tools/40000/0/.

27. Tucker Larson, "Where the Water Goes: Water in Arizonan Agriculture," Arizona State University Swette Center for Sustainable Food Systems, July 25, 2022, https:// sustainability-innovation.asu.edu/food/news/archive/where-the-water-goes-water-in -arizonan-agriculture/; Arizona Department of Water Resources, "Arizona's Water Supplies," Arizona Water Facts, https://www.arizonawaterfacts.com/water-your-facts.

28. Michael Hanemann, "The Central Arizona Project," University of California– Berkeley Department of Agricultural and Resource Economics, paper 937, 2002, http:// large.stanford.edu/courses/2020/ph240/bhatt1/docs/hanemann.pdf.

29. "Arizona Wildlife Linkages Assessment Section I—Introduction," Arizona Department of Transportation, https://azdot.gov/sites/default/files/2019/06/awlw-section -i-introduction.pdf.

30. Strittholt et al., "Sonoran Desert Rapid Ecoregional Assessment Report."

31. "Understanding and Managing the Effects of Groundwater Pumping on Streamflow," U.S. Geological Survey, January 2013, https://pubs.usgs.gov/fs/2013/3001/fs2013 -3001.pdf.

32. Russell Cohen, "Function of Riparian Areas for Wildlife Habitat," Massachusetts Department of Fish and Game, Division of Ecological Restoration, 2014, https://www .mass.gov/doc/fact-sheet-3-functions-of-riparian-areas-for-wildlife-habitat/download; "Riparian and Aquatic Ecosystem Strategy, Southwestern Region of the Forest Service," U.S. Forest Service, September 2019, https://www.fs.usda.gov/Internet/FSE_DOCUMENTS /fseprd762374.pdf.

33. "Water Quality after Wildfire," U.S. Geological Survey, April 11, 2023, https://www .usgs.gov/mission-areas/water-resources/science/water-quality-after-wildfire.

34. Aregai Tecle, "Downstream Effects of Damming the Colorado River," *International Journal of Lakes and Rivers* 10, no. 1 (2017): 7–33, https://www.ripublication.com/ijlr17 /ijlrv10n1_02.pdf; *Riparian Areas: Functions and Strategies for Management* (Washington, D.C.: National Academies Press, 2002), https://nap.nationalacademies.org/read /10327/chapter/5.

35. Randy Brooks, "After the Fires: Hydrophobic Soils," University of Idaho Forestry Information Series No. 5, https://www.uidaho.edu/-/media/UIdaho-Responsive/Files /Extension/topic/forestry/F5-After-the-Fires-Hydrophobic-Soils.pdf; "Fire Effect on Soil," Northern Arizona University, https://www2.nau.edu/~gaud/bio300w/frsl.htm.

36. Brian Segee and Martin Taylor, "Prelude to Catastrophe: Recent and Historic Land Management within the Rodeo-Chediski Fire Area," Center for Biological Diversity, July 2002, https://www.biologicaldiversity.org/publications/papers/r-c_report.pdf.

37. Van Devender and Dimmitt, "Desert Grasses"; Perry Grissom, "Lehmann Lovegrass (*Eragrostis lehmanniana*)," Sonoran Desert Cooperative Weed Management Area, https:// www.sdcwma.org/species/lehmannlovegrass.php.

38. Perry Grissom, "Protecting and Restoring the Sonoran Desert Ecosystem in Saguaro National Park," U.S. Department of the Interior, October 5, 2022, https://www.doi.gov/wildlandfire/news/protecting-and-restoring-sonoran-desert-ecosystem-saguaro-national-park.

39. Matthew Allcock and Luke Hecht, "Potential Effects of Habitat Fragmentation on Wild Animal Welfare," preprint, 2020, https://doi.org/10.32942/osf.io/hb7nm; U.S. Forest Service, "Reduce Landscape Fragmentation," Climate Change Resource Center, https://www.fs.usda.gov/ccrc/approach/reduce-landscape-fragmentation.

40. "Impact of Habitat Fragmentation on Migrant Birds," Science Daily, September 6, 2018, https://www.sciencedaily.com/releases/2018/09/180906123338.htm; "Habitat Fragmentation," NatureScot, January 18, 2023, https://www.nature.scot/professional-advice/land-and-sea-management/managing-land/habitat-networks/habitat-fragmentation; Nick M. Haddad et al., "Habitat Fragmentation and Its Lasting Impact on Earth's Ecosystems," *Science Advances* 1, no. 2 (2015), https://www.science.org/doi/10.1126/sciadv.1500052.

41. William Ripple, "Loss of Large Predators Disrupting Plant, Animal and Human Ecosystems," Oregon State University Newsroom, July 14, 2011, https://today.oregonstate.edu/archives/2011/jul/loss-large-predators-disrupting-multiple-plant-animal-and-human-ecosystems.

42. Robert Bescta, "Scientists: Wolves Helping Rebalance Yellowstone Ecosystem," Oregon State University Newsroom, July 10, 2009, https://today.oregonstate.edu/archives/2003/oct/scientists-wolves-helping-rebalance-yellowstone-ecosystem.

43. R. L. Beschta and W. J. Ripple, "Large Carnivore Extirpation Linked to Loss of Overstory Aspen in Yellowstone," *Food Webs* 20 (2020): e00140, https://trophiccascades.forestry.oregonstate.edu/sites/trophic/files/Beschta2020_FoodWebs.pdf; L. E. Painter and M. T. Tercek, "Tall Willow Thickets Return to Northern Yellowstone," *Ecosphere* 11, no. 5 (2020): e03115, https://trophiccascades.forestry.oregonstate.edu/sites/trophic/files/Painter_ESA2020.pdf.

44. "Climate Impacts in the Southwest," Environmental Protection Agency, https://climatechange.chicago.gov/climate-impacts/climate-impacts-southwest; Gregg Garfin, Angela Jardine, Robert Merideth, Mary Black, and Sarah LeRoy, eds., *Assessment of Climate Change in the Southwest United States: A Report Prepared for the National Climate Assessment* (Washington, D.C.: Island Press, 2013) https://www.resolutionmineeis.us/sites/default/files/references/garfin-jardine-merideth-black-leroy-2013.pdf.

45. "Climate Change Impacts to Grasslands," Land Trust Alliance, 2021, https://climatechange.lta.org/impacts-to-grasslands/. Prairie grasses grow in Arizona at elevations between 5,000 and 7,000 feet.

46. Alan D. Yanahan and Wendy Moore, "Impacts of 21st-Century Climate Change on Montane Habitat in the Madrean Sky Island Archipelago," *Diversity and Distributions: A Journal of Conservation Biogeography* 25, no. 10 (2019): 1625–38, https://onlinelibrary.wiley.com/doi/10.1111/ddi.12965; Teresa M. Crimmins, Michael A. Crimmins, and C. David Bertelsen, "Temporal Patterns in Species Flowering in Sky Islands of the Sonoran Desert Ecoregion," U.S. Forest Service Proceedings RMRS-P-67, 2013, https://www.fs.usda.gov/rm/pubs/rmrs_p067/rmrs_p067_033_039.pdf; Louise W. Misztal, Gregg Gar-

fin, and Lara Hansen, "Responding to Climate Change Impacts in the Sky Island Region: From Planning to Action," U.S. Forest Service Proceedings RMRS-P-67, 2013, https://www.fs.usda.gov/research/treesearch/44413.

47. Barbara J. Bentz, Jacques Régnière, Christopher J. Fettig, E. Matthew Hansen, Jane L. Hayes, Jeffrey A. Hicke, Rick G. Kelsey, Jose F. Negrón, and Steven J. Seybold, "Climate Change and Bark Beetles of the Western United States and Canada: Direct and Indirect Effects," *BioScience* 60, no. 8 (September 2010), https://academic.oup.com/bioscience/article/60/8/602/305152; Jeffry B. Mitton and Scott M. Ferrenberg, "Mountain Pine Beetle Develops an Unprecedented Summer Generation in Response to Climate Warming," *American Naturalist* 179, no. 5 (2012), https://www.journals.uchicago.edu/doi/full/10.1086/665007.

48. "National Fish, Wildlife and Plants Climate Adaptation Strategy," Association of Fish and Wildlife Agencies, 2021, https://www.fishwildlife.org/application/files/4216/1161/3356/Advancing_Strategy_Report_FINAL.pdf; "Ecosystems," U.S. Climate Resilience Toolkit, https://toolkit.climate.gov/topics/ccosystems.

49. Robin S. Reid, V. Lee Scharf, Ch'aska Huayhuaca, Stacy Lynn, Kara Loyd, and Connor Jandreau, "Collaborative Conservation in Practice: Current State and Future Directions," Center for Collaborative Conservation, https://collaborativeconservation.org/media/sites/142/2018/02/LEEcollaborative_conservation_in_practice.pdf; McKinney, Scarlett, and Kemmis, "Large Landscape Conservation."

Chapter 2

1. "Las Cienegas National Conservation Area," Bureau of Land Management, https://www.blm.gov/national-conservation-lands/arizona/las-cienegas; Jonathan Adams, "Las Cienegas National Conservation Area," LandScope America, http://www.landscope.org/article/AZ/las_cienagas/1/.

2. "The Cienega Watershed and Sonoita Valley," Cienega Watershed Partnership, http://www.cienega.org/about/our-story/.

3. "Sonoita and Elgin," Santa Cruz County, Arizona, https://www.santacruzcountyaz.gov/252/Sonoita-Elgin.

4. "Area History," Visit the Sky Islands of Arizona, https://www.visitskyislands.com/about-the-area/.

5. "Meet the Sky Islands," Sky Island Alliance, https://skyislandalliance.org/the-sky-islands/; Peter Warshall, "The Madrean Sky Island Archipelago: A Planetary Overview," U.S. Forest Service, 1995, https://www.fs.usda.gov/rm/pubs_rm/rm_gtr264/rm_gtr264_006_018.pdf.

6. "Sky Island Biotic Influences Map," Wild Sonora, http://wildsonora.com/content/sky-island-biotic-influences-map.

7. "US–Mexico Border Wall," Sky Island Alliance, https://skyislandalliance.org/our-work/us-mexico-border-wall/.

8. "Living in the Watershed," Cienega Watershed Partnership, http://www.cienega.org/explore/living-in-the-watershed/.

9. David Gori, Gitanjali S. Bodner, Karla Sartor, Peter Warren, and Steven Bassett, "Sky Island Grassland Assessment: Identifying and Evaluating Priority Grassland Landscapes for Conservation and Restoration in the Borderlands," The Nature Conservancy, 2012, https://static1.squarespace.com/static/5a7b81c690bcce74cb6144bb/t/5a8c75c2ec212d 652959a3e8/1519154724496/Sky+Islands+Grasslands+Assessment+TNC; Matt Skrotch, "Sky Islands of North America," Terrain.org, January 21, 2008, https://www.terrain.org /2008/nonfiction/sky-islands-of-north-america/; "Desert Islands," National Geographic Education, https://education.nationalgeographic.org/resource/desert-islands/.

10. Jonathan Mabry, ed., *Feasibility Study for the Santa Cruz Valley National Heritage Area*, Center for Desert Archaeology, 2005, https://www.archaeologysouthwest.org/pdf /Santa_Cruz_Valley_NHA_Feasibility_Study_web.pdf.

11. "What Is the Watershed?," Cienega Watershed Partnership, http://www.cienega.org /explore/what-is-the-watershed/.

12. Neva Connolly and Jeri Ledbetter, "Ciénega Creek Natural Preserve," Northern Arizona University Arizona Heritage Waters, http://www.azheritagewaters.nau.edu/loc _cienega.html.

13. "Wildlife," Sky Island Alliance, https://sia2023.wpengine.com/our-region/species -gallery/.

14. "Native American Lifeways (11,000 BC to the Present)," in Mabry, *Feasibility Study for the Santa Cruz Valley National Heritage Area*; Frank Eddy and Maurice Cooley, *Cultural and Environmental History of Cienega Valley, Southeastern Arizona* (Tucson: University of Arizona Press, 1983), https://repository.arizona.edu/handle/10150/595449.

15. Michael Stevens, "Archaic and Early Agricultural Period Land Use in the Cienega Valley," *Archaeology Southwest* 15, no. 4 (2001): 3–5, https://www.archaeologysouth west.org/pdf/arch-sw-v15-no4.pdf; Bruce B. Huckle, *Of Marshes and Maize: Preceramic Agricultural Settlement in Cienega Valley, Southeastern Arizona* (Tucson: University of Arizona Press, 1995), https://open.uapress.arizona.edu/projects/of-marshes-and-maize; Conrad J. Bahre, "Land Use History of the Research Ranch, Elgin, Arizona," *Journal of the Arizona Academy of Science* 12, supp. 2 (August 1977), https://www.ltrr.arizona.edu /~sheppard/Heidi/Bahre1977LandUseHistoryAZ.pdf.

16. Rein Vanderpot, "The Mescal Wash Site: A Persistent Place Along Cienega Creek," *Archaeology Southwest* 15, no. 4 (2001): 10–11, https://www.archaeologysouthwest.org /pdf/arch-sw-v15-no4.pdf.

17. George Johnson, "Social Strife May Have Exiled Ancient Indians," *New York Times*, August 20, 1996, https://sites.santafe.edu/~johnson/articles.anasazi.html; "The Hohokam," Arizona Museum of Natural History, https://www.arizonamuseumofnaturalhistory.org /plan-a-visit/mesa-grande/the-hohokam.

18. "The Mysterious Journey of Friar Marcos de Niza," Planetary Science Institute, https://www.psi.edu/about/staff/hartmann/coronado/journeyofmarcosdeniza.html.

19. "Honoring the Life and Legacy of Padre Eusebio Francisco Kino," Kino Historical Society, http://padrekino.com/; "Spanish and Mexican Frontier (1680–1854)," in Mabry, *Feasibility Study for the Santa Cruz Valley National Heritage Area*; John J. Martinez, "Eu-

sebio Kino, S.J.—Not Counting the Cost," S. J. Kino Historical Society, http://padrekino .com/kino-legacy/best-kino-biography/.

20. "The Missions," Padre Kino, http://www.padrekino.org/en/le-missioni/.

21. "Culture History of Southern Arizona: Europeans Arrive," Arizona State Museum, https://statemuseum.arizona.edu/online-exhibit/culture-history-southern-arizona /europeans.

22. D. E. Worcester, "The Spread of Spanish Horses in the Southwest," *New Mexico Historical Review* 19, no. 3 (1944).

23. "Welcome to Ce:wi Duag," Arizona Trail Association, Tohono O'odham Nation, and Coronado National Forest, https://pnts.org/new/wp-content/uploads/2021/12/Welcome -to-Cewi-Duag-Sign.pdf.

24. "Heritage of a Desert Frontier," in Mabry, *Feasibility Study for the Santa Cruz Valley National Heritage Area*; "Culture History of Southern Arizona: Mexican Era," Arizona State Museum, https://statemuseum.arizona.edu/online-exhibit/culture-history -southern-arizona/mexican; "The Spanish Conquistadors and Padres: New Mexico and Arizona, Outposts of Empire," National Park Service, https://www.nps.gov/parkhistory /online_books/explorers/intro4.htm.

25. Diana Hadley, "Landholding Systems and Resource Management in the Sky Island Borderlands," U.S. Forest Service Proceedings RMRS-P-36, 2005, https://www.fs.usda.gov /rm/pubs/rmrs_p036/rmrs_p036_015_025.pdf.

26. Drew VandeCreek, "The Mexican-American War," Northern Illinois University Digital Library, https://digital.lib.niu.edu/illinois/lincoln/topics/mexicanwar; "The Mexican-American War," National Park Service, https://www.nps.gov/places/the-mexican-american -war.htm.

27. "Gadsden Purchase, 1853–54," Office of the Historian, U.S. State Department, https://history.state.gov/milestones/1830-1860/gadsden-purchase.

28. Jim Griffith, preface, in Mabry, *Feasibility Study for the Santa Cruz Valley National Heritage Area*.

29. "Mining Booms," in Mabry, *Feasibility Study for the Santa Cruz Valley National Heritage Area*.

30. "Desert Farming (2000 B.C. to the Present)," in Mabry, *Feasibility Study for the Santa Cruz Valley National Heritage Area*.

31. John Wesley Powell, "Institutions for the Arid Lands," *Century Magazine* 40 (1890): 111–16.

32. "Santa Cruz River: Paradise Lost, Paradise Reborn, Will It Be Lost Again?," Sonoran Institute, https://sonoraninstitute.org/card/santa-cruz-river-success/.

33. "Earth Fissures, Subsidence and Karst in Arizona: Earth Fissures in South-Central Arizona," Arizona Geological Survey, https://azgs.arizona.edu/center-natural-hazards /earth-fissures-subsidence-karst-arizona.

34. "Ranching Traditions (1680 to Present)," in Mabry, *Feasibility Study for the Santa Cruz Valley National Heritage Area*.

35. John Wesley Powell, "The Non-Irrigable Lands of the Arid Region," *Century Magazine* 39, no. 6 (1890).

36. Powell, "Institutions for the Arid Lands."

37. George B. Ruyle, "Rangeland Livestock Production: Developing the Concept of Sustainability on the Santa Rita Experimental Range," presented at Santa Rita Experimental Range: 100 Years (1903 to 2003) of Accomplishments and Contributions, Tucson, October 30–November 1, 2003, https://www.fs.usda.gov/rm/pubs/rmrs_p030/rmrs_p030_034_047.pdf.

38. Jane Wayland Brewster, "The San Rafael Cattle Company: A Pennsylvania Enterprise in Arizona," *Arizona and the West* 8, no. 2 (1966): 133–56, https://www.jstor.org/stable/40167199.

39. "History Overview," Empire Ranch Foundation.

40. "Pima County Leverages Property Tax Revenue to Excel in Capital Improvement Projects and Open Space Acquisition," CRS for Community Resilience, https://floodscience center.org/products/crs-community-resilience/success-stories/pima-county-arizona/; "Floodprone Land Acquisition Program," Pima County, https://www.pima.gov/1684/Floodprone-Land-Acquisition-Program.

41. Connolly and Ledbetter, "Ciénega Creek Natural Preserve."

42. "History Overview," Empire Ranch Foundation; "Empire Ranch History: Gulf American Corporation Ownership, 1970–1975," Empire Ranch Foundation, https://www.empireranchfoundation.org/empire-ranch/empire-ranch-history-1970-1988/gulf-american-corporation-ownership-1970-1975/.

43. "Empire Ranch History: Anamax Ownership, 1975–1988," Empire Ranch Foundation, https://www.empireranchfoundation.org/empire-ranch/empire-ranch-history-1970-1988/anamax-ownership-1975-1988/.

44. Resolution Authorizing the Pima County Flood Control District to Acquire the Flood Prone Portions of the Empire/Cienega Ranches, Pima County Board of Supervisors Resolution No. 1987-FC 29, https://onbase.pima.gov/publicaccess/CL_NextGen_Multi/etc/ft/index.html.

45. D. Dean Bibles, "History of BLM Land Exchanges in Arizona," in *Opportunity and Challenge: The Story of BLM*, https://www.nps.gov/parkhistory/online_books/blm/history/chap5.htm.

46. See D. Dean Bibles, "Repositioning Arizona Lands," presented at The Public Lands During the Remainder of the 20th Century: Planning, Law, and Policy in the Federal Agencies (Summer Conference, June 8–10, 1987), https://scholar.law.colorado.edu/cgi/viewcontent.cgi?article=1015&context=public-lands-during-remainder-planning-law-and-policy-in-federal-land-agencies.

47. Oral Histories of Dean Bibles, Henri Bisson, and Fred Baker, Empire Ranch Foundation, https://www.empireranchfoundation.org/history/dean-bibles-henri-bisson-fred-baker/.

48. Brott, "Celebrating Collaborative Conservation."

49. "Collaboration to Sustain the Cienega Watershed," Cienega Watershed Partnership, http://www.cienega.org/about/our-story/; Adams, "Las Cienegas National Conservation Area"; "Las Cienegas Case Study," Cienega Watershed Partnership, http://www.cienega.org/wp-content/uploads/2016/11/Las-Cienegas-case-study-.pdf.

50. "The Sonoita Valley Planning Partnership: A New Approach to Community Participation in Public Land Management Planning," Creative Cooperation in Resource Management Conference, Tucson, 2000, https://www.hcn.org/issues/190/10072.

51. "Ciénega Creek Natural Preserve," Arizona Heritage Waters, http://www.azheritage waters.nau.edu/loc_cienega.html.

52. See "Tenth Anniversary Celebration of the National Landscape Conservation System," Bureau of Land Management Information Bulletin 2010-43, 2010, https://www.blm .gov/policy/ib-2010-043.

53. Michelle Nijhuis and Oakley Brooks, "Congress Moves on Local Proposals," *High Country News*, November 6, 2000, https://www.govinfo.gov/content/pkg/PLAW-106 publ538/pdf/PLAW-106publ538.pdf.

54. Public Law 106-538: An Act to Establish the Las Cienegas National Conservation Area.

55. "Las Cienegas National Conservation Area in the State of Arizona," *Congressional Record* 146, no. 14 (2000) 21050–55, https://www.govinfo.gov/content/pkg/CRECB-2000 -pt14/html/CRECB-2000-pt14-Pg21050.htm.

56. *Fain Land & Cattle Co. v. Hassell (1990)*, LawPipe Online Legal Research Tool, https://www.lawpipe.com/Arizona/Fain_Land_Cattle_Co_v_Hassell.html.

57. Before *Fain*, the State of Arizona and BLM had identified several land parcels as desirable for exchange. The Arizona congressional delegation realized the need to assist with the needed exchanges. At the request of the delegation, legislation was drafted that would allow the BLM to take state trust lands and pay the State Lands Department with prearranged in lieu federal lands. In November 1988, at the behest of the delegation, Congress passed the Sita Rita Public Land Exchange Act, which provided authority for a large and complex state-BLM land exchange in Arizona and, among other outcomes, established the San Pedro Riparian NCA. The language of the exchange at still provides the secretary of interior the authority to acquire state trust lands via purchase or eminent domain. If there were support by the State for a BLM–trust land exchange, the secretary could secure state trust lands within the NCA by seeking authority for an exchange from Congress.

58. "Approved Las Cienegas Resource Management Plan and Record of Decision," July 2003, Bureau of Land Management Arizona State Office, https://www.cakex.org/sites /default/files/documents/LCROD-WEB.pdf.

59. Jeremy K. Caves, Gitanjali S. Bodner, Karen Simms, Larry A. Fisher, and Tahnee Robertson, "Integrating Collaboration, Adaptive Management, and Scenario Planning: Experiences at Las Cienegas National Conservation Area," *Ecology and Society* 18, no. 3 (2012): 43.

60. Jessica Hitt, Gita Bodner, and Karen Simms, "From Adaptive Management to Climate Adaptation at the Las Cienegas National Conservation Area: Starting Where You Are," Climate Adaptation Knowledge Exchange, November 1, 2011, https://www .cakex.org/case-studies/adaptive-management-climate-adaptation-las-cienegas-national -conservation-area-starting-where-you-are.

61. "Executive Summary: Protection Measures for Certain Lands North of the Sonoita Valley Acquisition Planning District in Pima County, Arizona," Sonoran Institute, 2003, http://www.cienega.org/wp-content/uploads/2016/11/Cienega-Creek-Missing-Link -Study-Executive-Summary-2003.pdf.

62. "Las Cienegas National Conservation Area: Designation and Resource Planning," Cienega Watershed Partnership, http://www.cienega.org/about/our-story/.

63. Byron K. Williams, Robert C. Szaro, and Carl D. Shapiro, *Adaptive Management: The U.S. Department of the Interior Technical Guide* (Washington, D.C.: U.S. Department of the Interior, 2007), https://www.doi.gov/sites/doi.gov/files/uploads/TechGuide -WebOptimized-2.pdf.

64. "Science on the Sonoita Plain Annual Symposium," Cienega Watershed Partnership, http://www.cienega.org/projects/science/sonoita-plain/; Karen Simms, Grant Drennen, Brad Cooper, Gitanjali Bodner, David Gori, *Report on the Biological Planning Process for Livestock Management at Las Cienegas NCA: Fall 2005 Upland Monitoring Results and Adaptive Management by the Bureau of Land Management, Technical Resource Team, and Rangeland Resource Team*, Bureau of Land Management and The Nature Conservancy, May 2006, https://azconservation.org/wp-content/uploads/2021/08/TNCAZ _LasCienegas_Biological_Planning_Process_2005.pdf.

65. "State of the Watershed," Cienega Watershed Partnership, https://azconservation .org/wp-content/uploads/2021/08/TNCAZ_LasCienegas_Biological_Planning_Process _2005.pdf.

66. J. C. Stromberg, "Riparian Mesquite Forests: A Review of Their Ecology, Threats, and Recovery Potential," *Journal of the Arizona-Nevada Academy of Science* 27, no. 1 (1993): 111–24, http://www.jstor.org/stable/40023711.

67. O. W. Van Auken, "Shrub Invasions of North American Semiarid Grasslands," *Annual Review of Ecology and Systemics* 31 (2000): 197–215, https://www.jstor.org/stable /221730; Arizona Game and Fish Department, "Semidesert Grasslands."

68. Daniel George Neary and Jackson McMichael Leonard, "Effects of Fire on Grassland Soils and Water: A Review," Rocky Mountain Research Station, U.S. Forest Service, 2020, https://www.fs.usda.gov/research/treesearch/60165.

69. A. Jay et al., "Chapter 1: Overview" and Patrick Gonzales et al., "Chapter 25: Southwest," in *Fourth National Climate Change Assessment* (Washington, D.C.: U.S. Global Change Research Program, 2018), https://nca2018.globalchange.gov/; "Climate Impacts in the Southwest," U.S. Environmental Protection Agency, https://climatechange.chicago .gov/climate-impacts/climate-impacts-southwest.

70. "Wildlife Corridors," Indiana Department of Natural Resources, Division of Fish and Wildlife, 2004, https://www.in.gov/dnr/fish-and-wildlife/files/HMFSCorridors.pdf; Joshua J. Tewksbury et al., "Corridors Affect Plants, Animals, and Their Interactions in Fragmented Landscapes," *Publications of the National Academy of Sciences* 99, no. 20 (2002): 12923–26, https://www.pnas.org/doi/10.1073/pnas.202242699; R. Ament, R. Callahan, M. McClure, M. Reuling, and G. Tabor, "Wildlife Connectivity: Fundamentals for Conservation Action," Center for Large Landscape Conservation, 2014, https://largelandscapes.org/wp-content /uploads/2019/05/Wildlife-Connectivity-Fundamentals-for-Conservation-Action.pdf.

71. "History of Arizona State Trust Land," Arizona State Land Department, https:// land.az.gov/our-agency-mission/history-trust-land.

72. Hitt, Bodner, and Simms, "From Adaptive Management to Climate Adaptation."

73. James E. Ayres, *Rosemont: The History and Archaeology of Post-1880 Sites in the Rosemont Area, Santa Rita Mountains, Arizona*, Archaeological Series 147, no. 3, report

submitted by Cultural Resource Management Division, Arizona State Museum, University of Arizona, to Anamax Mining Company, 1984, http://www.cienega.org/docs/1984 /Rosemont-History-Archaeology-Post-1880-1984.pdf.

74. "Opposition and Resolutions: Southern Arizona Doesn't Want Another Mine!" Save the Scenic Santa Ritas, https://www.scenicsantaritas.org/opposition/.

75. Tony Davis, "New Rosemont Mine Study Calculates $30B in Economic Benefits," *Arizona Daily Star*, November 29, 2009, https://www.biologicaldiversity.org/news/media -archive/RosemontMine_ArizonaDailyStar_11-29-09.pdf.

76. Thomas Michael Power, *Analyses of Economic Costs of the Proposed Rosemont Copper Project*, report submitted to Coronado National Forest, 2010, https://www.friends -bwca.org/wp-content/uploads/Arizona-Copper-Mining.pdf.

77. "Collaboration to Sustain the Cienega Watershed," Cienega Watershed Partnership.

78. "Science: Water, Wildlife, Plants and Citizen Science," Cienega Watershed Partnership, http://www.cienega.org/projects/education/las-cienegas/science/; "Life and Death After Bullfrogs: Do the Chiricahua Leopard Frogs Have a Chance?," Cienega Watershed Partnership, http://www.cienega.org/2016/11/life-and-death-after-bullfrogs-do-the -chiricahua-leopard-frogs-have-a-chance/.

79. "Restoring Arroyos and Preventing Landscape Erosion," Cienega Watershed Partnership, http://www.cienega.org/projects/conservation-restoration/arroyo/.

80. "Yes! Youth Engaged Stewardship," Cienega Watershed Partnership, http://www .cienega.org/projects/education/yes/.

Chapter 3

1. Griffith et al., "Ecoregions of Arizona."

2. Arizona Commerce Authority, "County Profile for Pima County," https://www.az commerce.com/a/profiles/ViewProfile/12/Pima+County/.

3. U.S. Census Bureau, "Quick Facts, Pima County Arizona," https://www.census.gov /quickfacts/fact/table/pimacountyarizona/LND110210.

4. *Historic Summary of Pima County, September 4, 2001*, report submitted to the Pima County Board of Supervisors, https://content.civicplus.com/api/assets/994307d0-517b -44d0-adf8-fc658f81653f.

5. "The Missions."

6. "Mission Churches of the Sonoran Desert," Through Our Parents' Eyes: History and Culture of Southern Arizona, https://parentseyes.arizona.edu/missions.

7. John G. Douglass and William M. Graves, eds., *New Mexico and the Pimería Alta: The Colonial Period in the American Southwest* (Boulder: University Press of Colorado, 2017), http://read.upcolorado.com/read/new-mexico-and-the-pimeria-alta-the-colonial -period-in-the-american-southwest/section/3f0614ff 8a66-45b1-a121-efa1915ba010; James E. Officer, "Southern Arizona in Hispanic Times," Arizona-Sonora Desert Museum, https://www.desertmuseum.org/members/sonorensis/week9.php.

8. "Founder's Day, Tucson Arizona," Pima County Public Library, https://www.library .pima.gov/content/founders-day-tucson-arizona/; "Culture History of Southern Arizona," Arizona State Museum, https://statemuseum.arizona.edu/online-exhibit/culture-history -southern-arizona/paleo-indian-archaic.

9. "Gadsden Purchase, 1853–1854."

10. William I. Waldrip, "New Mexico During the Civil War," *New Mexico Historical Review* 28, no. 3 (1953), https://digitalrepository.unm.edu/cgi/viewcontent.cgi?article=1799; "HR 357, 37th Congress: A Bill to Provide a Temporary Government for the Territory of Arizona," A Century of Lawmaking for a New Nation: U.S. Congressional Documents and Debates, 1774–1875, Library of Congress, https://memory.loc.gov/cgi-bin/ampage?collId =llhb&fileName=037/llhb037.db&recNum=1985.

11. "Pima County," Pima County Justice Court, September 27, 2000, http://jp.pima.gov /Pages/history/county.htm.

12. *Cultural Landscapes of History in Southern Arizona*, report prepared for the Pima County Board of Supervisors, May 30, 2000.

13. Chuck Huckelberry, "History of Land Use in Pima County," memorandum prepared for the Pima County Board of Supervisors, January 31, 2000, https://prism.lib.asu.edu /items/42680/view.

14. "Central Arizona Water Conservation District (CAWCD)," Arizona State Library Archives and Public Records, https://azlibrary.gov/sla/agency_histories/central-arizona -water-conservation-district-cawcd.

15. Irisita Azary and Michael J. Cohen, *Confounding Water Policy: Voter Representation and Choice in Tucson, Arizona* (yearbook of the Association of Pacific Coast Geographers, 2003), 20–45.

16. David Devine, "Down the Drain," *Tucson Weekly*, January 16, 1997, https://www .tucsonweekly.com/tw/01-16-97/cover.htm.

17. "The Creation and Evolution of the Tucson Mountain District of Saguaro National Park," National Park Service, https://www.epicroadtrips.us/2020/our_ninth_year_in _tucson_off_to_a_good_start/tucson-mountain-park-brief.pdf.

18. "Colossal Cave Mountain Park," National Park Service, https://memory.loc.gov /master/pnp/habshaer/az/az0600/az0658/data/az0658data.pdf.

19. "Catalina State Park," Arizona State Parks, https://azstateparks.com/catalina /explore/park-history.

20. Catalina State Park was originally owned by the State Land Department. After passage of the 1988 Santa Rita Exchange Act, the lease to Catalina Park is now held by the Arizona Parks and Trails Department.

21. *Pima County Regional Flood Control District History Booklet*, report submitted to the Pima County Board of Supervisors, August 7, 2020, https://content.civicplus.com/api /assets/d24de96a-e844-46ca-a466-1b3cba4e4a62.

22. "Empirita Ranch," Pointless Waymarks, July 4, 2020, https://pointlesswaymarks .com/Posts/2020/empirita-ranch-6-18-2020/empirita-ranch-6-18-2020.html.

23. "Empirita Ranch," National Register of Historic Places Registration Form, https:// npgallery.nps.gov/GetAsset/c00ff86f-47e7-4fd8-a925-abb8bbabb5d5.

24. "Colossal Cave Park Historic District: La Posta Quemada Ranch," National Register of Historic Places Registration Form, https://npgallery.nps.gov/GetAsset/2a78ffdd -e3ad-4586-91a6-04ea0f390433.

25. Pima County Administrator's Office, *Protecting Our Land, Water, and Heritage.*

26. Minutes, Pima County Board of Supervisors, April 2, 1985.

27. Pima County Administrator's Office, *Protecting Our Land, Water, and Heritage*.

28. Tony Davis, "A Seminal Sprawl Fight Ends in Compromise," *High Country News*, June 18, 2001, https://www.hcn.org/issues/205/10589.

29. "Welcome to the Historic Canoa Ranch," Pima County Natural Resources, Parks and Recreation, https://storymaps.arcgis.com/stories/b11c30f0d084437989ca713ff6ec2fcc.

30. "Saving the Cactus Ferruginous Pygmy Owl," Center for Biological Diversity, https://www.biologicaldiversity.org/species/birds/cactus_ferruginous_pygmy_owl/index.html.

31. "The Endangered Species Act: Overview and Implementation," Congressional Research Service, updated March 4, 2021, https://sgp.fas.org/crs/misc/R46677.pdf.

32. "Habitat Conservation Plans," U.S. Fish and Wildlife Service, https://www.fws.gov/service/habitat-conservation-plans; Timothy Beatley, "Habitat Conservation Plan: A New Tool to Resolve Land Use Conflicts," Lincoln Institute of Land Policy, https://www.fws.gov/service/habitat-conservation-plans.

33. Resolution of the Board of Supervisors of Pima County, Arizona to Uphold the Endangered Species Act Through Regional Multi-Species Habitat Conservation Planning, Pima County Board of Supervisors Resolution No. 1998-50, https://onbase.pima.gov/publicaccess/CL_NextGen_Multi/api/Document/AesonfzI9ikfgzJyntW6fpdo6HhHIlWl CFbLkA6GYG2ywWtC0Dyzg%C3%81dqivgdCb4frFgUwPGPVhghXOpMXefNP84%3D/.

34. Bruce Babbitt, *Cities in the Wilderness: A New Vision of Land Use in America* (Washington: Island Press, 2005).

35. "County of Orange Natural Communities Conservation Plan/Habitat Conservation Plan," University of California–Irvine Campus Planning and Sustainability, https://planningandsustainability.uci.edu/community/conservation-plan.php.

36. "Multiple Species Conservation Program," County of San Diego Parks and Recreation, https://www.sdparks.org/content/sdparks/en/AboutUs/Plans/MSCP.html.

37. "Timeline of the Sonoran Desert Conservation Plan," Pima County, https://content.civicplus.com/api/assets/da84d923-60fe-4be0-ac29-8b160852ed79.

38. Chuck Huckelberry, "The Sonoran Desert Conservation Plan," 2002, http://www.eebweb.arizona.edu/Courses/Ecol406R_506R/SDCPHuckelberry.pdf.

39. Coalition for Sonoran Desert Protection, "Sonoran Desert Conservation Plan," https://www.sonorandesert.org/learning-more-sonoran-desert-conservation-plan/.

40. Memorandum from County Administrator C. H. Huckelberry to the Pima County Board of Supervisors: Draft Report Sonoran Desert Conservation Plan, October 21, 1998.

41. A Resolution of the Board of Supervisors of Pima County, Arizona to Request Land and Water Conservation Funds to Support the Sonoran Desert Conservation Plan, Pima County Board of Supervisors Resolution No. 1999-247, https://onbase.pima.gov/publicaccess/CL_NextGen_Multi/api/Document/AX9%C3%896IM2xp2b93KgyriWoux Vc7A%C3%89iXXVBlTi50tTRu7roYyZrZ%C3%89Ed5p2r0wY50J2UBPy4XksDR1nXXl 97KIuLFU%3D/.

42. Chuck Huckelberry, "Sonoran Desert Conservation and Comprehensive Land Use Plan," *Sonoran News*, April 2001, https://core.ac.uk/download/pdf/79569839.pdf.

43. Thomas E. Sheridan, "The Sonoran Desert Conservation Plan and Ranch Conservation in Pima County, Arizona," in *Stitching the West Back Together: Conservation*

of Working Landscapes, ed. Susan Charnley, Thomas E. Sheridan, and Gary P. Nabhan (Chicago: University of Chicago Press, 2014).

44. Sheridan, "The Sonoran Desert Conservation Plan."

45. Tony Davis, "Desert Protector Maeveen Behan Dies," *Arizona Daily Star*, November 4, 2009, https://tucson.com/news/local/govt-and-politics/desert-protector-maeveen -behan-dies/article_366c1ba6-e215-55e7-859e-936944b5d4f2.html.

46. *Pima County Multi-species Conservation Plan*, submitted to the Arizona Ecological Services Office of the U.S. Fish and Wildlife Service, Tucson, Arizona, 2016, https:// content.civicplus.com/api/assets/d7a5b8f4-e7cf-49e9-b544-a19aefa11039.

47. Robert J. Steidl, William W. Shaw, and Paul Fromer, "A Science-Based Approach to Regional Conservation Planning," in *The Planner's Guide to Natural Resource Conservation: The Science of Land Development Beyond the Metropolitan Fringe*, ed. Adrian X. Esparza and Guy McPherson (New York: Springer, 2014), https://content.civicplus.com /api/assets/91395f9b-410f-4a97-83a6 d659e0940d81.

48. "Maeveen Marie Behan Conservation Lands System: The First 20 Years (2000– 2021)," Pima County, https://content.civicplus.com/api/assets/38b5839c-81f0-48e3-a74d -56500ea26fe7; "Conservation Lands System," Coalition for Sonoran Desert Protection, https://www.sonorandesert.org/learning-more/conservation-land-system/.

49. Tony Davis, "An End to Tucson's Growth Wars: A Conservation Plan Puts Science Ahead of Politics," *High Country News*, May 1, 2017, https://www.hcn.org/issues/49.7 /an-end-to-tucsons-growth-wars.

50. "About the Conservation Lands System," Pima County Government, https:// oldcms.pima.gov/cms/one.aspx?portalId=169&pageId=53493; "Maeveen Marie Behan Conservation Lands System Regional Policy Plan," Pima County Government, https:// content.civicplus.com/api/assets/e892aad8-22a8-4530-bbe7-0e455a8e3356.

51. "Relationship Between the Multi-Species Conservation Plan and the Conservation Lands System," Pima County, https://content.civicplus.com/api/assets/c6e2e789-6a57 -4e24-b4c2-f599feb1c6cb.

52. "Environmental Element," in *Pima Prospers Comprehensive Plan Initiative*, 2015, https://www.pima.gov/381/34-Environmental-Element.

53. *Multi-species Conservation Plan and Regulatory Streamlining*, report submitted to the Pima County Board of Supervisors, January 19, 2016, https://content.civicplus.com /api/assets/06d4607d-430e-4772-b6da-3667d62418cc.

54. "Record of Decision Pima County Multi-Species Conservation Plan (MSCP) Final Environmental Impact Statement," U.S. Fish and Wildlife Service, May 2016, https://www .fws.gov/sites/default/files/documents/example-record-of-decision-for-environmental -impact-statement.pdf.

55. A Resolution of the Pima County Board of Supervisors, Relating to Conservation and the Environment; Re-affirming the Value of Sonoran Desert Conservation Plan, Recognizing the Critical Role of Maeveen Behan in Developing It, and Re-naming the Conservation Lands System as the "Maeveen Marie Behan Conservation Lands System, Pima County Board of Supervisors Resolution No. 2009-281," https://onbase.pima.gov /publicaccess/CL_NextGen_Multi/etc/ft/index.html.

56. "Riparian Priorities: Sonoran Desert Conservation Plan," memorandum to the Pima County Board of Supervisors, August 21, 2002, https://prism.lib.asu.edu/items /42577/view.

57. David Scalero, "Pantano Jungle Restoration, Cienega Creek Natural Preserve," Pima County Regional Flood Control District, May 19, 2009, https://content.civicplus.com/api /assets/95ddd83a-1995-471d-b4ed-efc358aadc84.

58. "Sonoran Desert Conservation Plan: Riparian Resources," Pima County Government, https://content.civicplus.com/api/assets/a56e671b-ed9f-4495-8d5d-f1aaa1ebc84d.

59. Chuck Huckelberry, "Preserving Ranch Lands in Pima County," memorandum to the Pima County Board of Supervisors, October 12, 2000.

60. Chuck Huckelberry, "Impact of Unregulated Development at the Community and Watershed Level," memorandum to the Pima County Board of Supervisors, https://old cms.pima.gov/UserFiles/Servers/Server_6/File/Government/Office%20of%20Sustain ability%20and%20Conservation/Conservation%20Sciece/sdcp%20reports/Impact-of -Unregulated-Development-at-the-Community-and-Watershed-Level.pdf.

61. Diana Freshwater, Arizona Land and Water Trust, private communication.

62. Chuck Huckelberry, "Mountain Parks and the Sonoran Desert Conservation Plan," memorandum to the Pima County Board of Supervisors, August 3, 1999.

63. "Regional Programming: Pima County," Arizona Department of Transportation, https://azdot.gov/planning/transportation-programming/regional-programming.

64. "Sonoran Desert Wildlife Linkages," Coalition for Sonoran Desert Protection, https:// www.sonorandesert.org/learning-more/wildlife-linkages-2/; "Finding Wildlife Linkages," Coalition for Sonoran Desert Protection, https://www.sonorandesert.org/learning-more /wildlife-linkages-2/finding-wildlife-linkages/.

65. Gloria Gomez, "Pima County RTA Falling Short on Cash, but Largely Meeting Its Goals," *Tucson Weekly*, April 14, 2022, https://www.tucsonweekly.com/TheRange/archives /2022/04/14/pima-county-rta-falling-short-on-cash-but-largely-meeting-its-goals.

66. Chuck Huckelberry, "Cultural Landscapes of Prehistory in Southern Arizona," memorandum presented to the Pima County Board of Supervisors, July 3, 2000.

67. Chuck Huckelberry, "Trails, Rails and Roadways in Pima County," memorandum submitted to the Pima County Board of Supervisors, January 7, 2002.

68. Pima County Administrator's Office, *Protecting Our Land, Water, and Heritage*.

69. "Environmental Education Program," Pima County, https://www.pima.gov/1331 /About-Us.

70. "Environmental Education and Interpretive Programs," Pima County, https://www .pima.gov/1324/Environmental-Education-Interpretive-Pro.

71. "Sonoran Desert Conservation Plan," Pima County, https://www.sonorandesert.org /learning-more/sonoran-desert-conservation-plan/.

72. Chuck Huckelberry, "Summary of Pima County Bond Election Results," memorandum to the Pima County Board of Supervisors, December 14, 2015, https://oldcms.pima .gov/UserFiles/Servers/Server_6/File/Government/Administration/CHHmemosFor%20 Web/December%202015/December%2014,%202015%20-%20Summary%20of%20Pima %20County%20Bond%20Election%20Results.pdf.

73. *Fain Land & Cattle Co. v. Hassell* (1990); *The Art of the Deal: Crafting Smart State Trust Land Exchanges in Arizona*, a Sun Corridor Legacy Program Policy Technical Report Prepared by the Sonoran Institute, February 2011, https://sonoraninstitute.org/files/pdf/art-of-the-deal-crafting-smart-state-trust-land-exchanges-in-arizona-212011.pdf.

Chapter 4

1. Paul R. Fish, Suzanne K. Fish, and John H. Madsen, *Prehistory and Early History of the Malpai Borderlands: Archaeological Synthesis and Recommendations*, General Technical Report RMRS-GTR-176, U.S. Forest Service Rocky Mountain Research Station, September 2006, https://www.fs.usda.gov/rm/pubs/rmrs_gtr176.pdf.

2. "Climate Change in the Southwest: Introduction and Current Climate," National Park Service, https://www.nps.gov/articles/climate-change-in-the-southwest-introduction.htm.

3. Sleeter, Wilson, and Acevedo, "Status and Trends of Land Change."

4. Reggie Fletcher and Wayne A. Robbie, "Historic and Current Conditions of the Southwestern Grasslands," in *Assessment of Grassland Ecosystem Conditions in the Southwestern United States*, ed. Deborah M. Finch, U.S. Forest Service General Technical Report RMRS-GTR-135-Vol.1, January 1, 2004, https://www.fs.usda.gov/rm/pubs/rmrs_gtr135_1/rmrs_gtr135_1_120_129.pdf.

5. John F. Ross, *The Promise of the Grand Canyon: John Wesley Powell's Perilous Journey and His Vision for the American West* (New York: Penguin, 2018).

6. George Hilliard, *A Hundred Years of Horse Tracks: The Story of the Gray Ranch* (Silver City, NM: High-Lonesome, 1996).

7. Nathan Sayre, "The Cattle Boom in Southern Arizona: Toward a Critical Political Ecology," *Journal of the Southwest* 41, no. 2 (Summer 1999): 239–71.

8. Hilliard, *A Hundred Years of Horse Tracks*.

9. Malchus B. Baker Jr., "Hydrology and Watershed Management in Semi-Arid Grasslands," in *The Future of Arid Grasslands: Identifying Issues, Seeking Solutions*, ed. Barbara Tellman, Deborah M. Finch, Carl Edminster, and Robert Hamre, U.S. Forest Service Rocky Mountain Research Station, September 10–13, 1996, https://www.fs.usda.gov/rm/pubs/rmrs_p003/rmrs_p003_158_169.pdf; Carol Raish, "Historic and Contemporary Land Use in Southwestern Grassland Ecosystems," in *Assessment of Grassland Ecosystem Conditions in the Southwestern United States*, ed. Deborah M. Finch, U.S. Forest Service General Technical Report RMRS-GTR-135-Vol.1, January 1, 2004, https://www.fs.usda.gov/rm/pubs/rmrs_gtr135_1/rmrs_gtr135_1_086_119.pdf.

10. Stephen Marshak, *Earth: Portrait of a Planet*, 7th ed. (New York: W. W. Norton, 2022).

11. On May 3, 1887, northern Sonora, Mexico, southeast Arizona, and southwest New Mexico experienced a strong (magnitude 7) earthquake. In its wake, water-table levels throughout the area shifted, dropping in some areas, rising in others. In some areas, once flowing springs dried up, others emerged. The resulting geological changes may have been a contributing factor in causing or accelerating arroyo cutting.

12. "Draft Business Plan for the Sky Island Grasslands," National Fish and Wildlife Foundation, March 24, 2009, https://www.nfwf.org/sites/default/files/skyisland /Documents/Sky_Island_Grass_Biz_Plan.pdf.

13. Heather Schussman and Ed Smith, *Historical Range of Variation for Potential Natural Vegetation Types of the Southwest*, prepared for the U.S. Forest Service, Southwestern Region, by The Nature Conservancy, Tucson, https://www.fs.usda.gov/Internet /FSE_DOCUMENTS/stelprdb5440360.pdf; Junran Li, Sujith Ravi, Guan Wang, R. Scott Van Pelt, Thomas E. Gill, and Joel B. Sankey, "Woody Plant Encroachment of Grasslands and the Reversibility of Shrub Dominance: Erosion, Fire, and Feedback Processes," *Ecosphere*, 2022, https://esajournals.onlinelibrary.wiley.com/doi/epdf/10.1002/ecs2.3949; Timothy E. Paysen, "Fire in Western Shrubland, Woodland, and Grassland Ecosystems," in *Wildland Fire in Ecosystems: Effects of Fire on Flora*, ed. James K. Brown and Jane Kapler Smith, U.S. Forest Service General Technical Report RMRS-GTR-42-vol. 2, 2000, https:// www.fs.usda.gov/psw/publications/4403/Chapter6.pdf.

14. Karen E. Bagne and Deborah M. Finch, *Vulnerability of Species to Climate Change in the Southwest: Threatened, Endangered, and At-Risk Species at Fort Huachuca, Arizona*, U.S. Forest Service Rocky Mountain Research Station General Technical Report RMRS-GTR-302, 2013, https://www.fs.usda.gov/research/treesearch/43616; Megan M. Friggens, Deborah M. Finch, Karen E. Bagne, Sharon J. Coe, and David L. Hawksworth, *Vulnerability of Species to Climate Change in the Southwest: Terrestrial Species of the Middle Rio Grande*, U.S. Forest Service Rocky Mountain Research Station General Technical Report RMRS-GTR-306, July 2013, https://www.fs.usda.gov/rm/pubs/rmrs_gtr306.pdf; "Climate Change in the Southwest: Potential Impacts," National Park Service, https://www.nps.gov /articles/climate-change-in-the-southwest-potential-impacts.htm.

15. Brandon T. Bestelmeyer, Debra P. C. Peters, Steven R. Archer, Dawn M. Browning, Gregory S. Okin, Robert L. Schooley, and Nicholas P. Webb, "The Grassland–Shrubland Regime Shift in the Southwestern United States: Misconceptions and Their Implications for Management," *BioScience* 68, no. 9 (September 2018): 678–90, https://academic.oup.com /bioscience/article/68/9/678/5090179; Carl E. Bock and Jane H. Bock, "Factors Controlling the Structure and Function of Desert Grasslands: A Case Study from Southeastern Arizona," U.S. Forest Service, https://www.fs.usda.gov/rm/pubs/rmrs_p003/rmrs_p003_033_044.pdf.

16. David Williams and Zdravko Baruch, "African Grass Invasion in the Americas: Ecosystem Consequences and the Role of Ecophysiology," *Biological Invasions* 2, no. 2 (June 2000): 123–40, https://www.researchgate.net/publication/225908992_African _Grass_Invasion_in_the_Americas_Ecosystem_Consequences_and_the_Role_of _Ecophysiology; Schussman and Smith, *Historical Range of Variation for Potential Natural Vegetation Types*; "North American Desert Grassland," World Rangeland Learning Experience, https://wrangle.org/ecotype/north-american-desert-grassland.

17. Douglas H. Johnson, *Habitat Fragmentation Effects on Birds in Grasslands: A Critique of Our Knowledge* (U.S. Geological Survey, 2001), https://www.usgs.gov /publications/habitat-fragmentation-effects-birds-grasslands-a-critique-our-knowledge; Jamie Nielson, Kelly Reeves, and Lisa Thomas, "Grasslands of the American Southwest— Disturbance Regimes," National Park Service, 2010, https://www.nps.gov/articles/south west-grasslands-disturbances.htm.

18. David F. Gori and Carolyn A. F. Enquist, *An Assessment of the Spatial Extent and Condition of Grasslands in Central and Southern Arizona, Southwestern New Mexico and Northern Mexico*, prepared by The Nature Conservancy, Arizona Chapter, 2003, https://azconservation.org/wp-content/uploads/2021/08/TNCAZ_Grasslands_Assessment_Report.pdf.

19. Gori et al., "Sky Island Grassland Assessment."

20. Bill McDonald, "The Formation and History of the Malpai Borderlands Group," Malpai Borderlands Group, http://www.malpaiborderlandsgroup.org/?section=26.

21. "Understanding Landscape 15: Malpai Borderlands Case Study," U.S. Natural Resources Conservation Service, 2010, https://www.youtube.com/watch?v=rAiRk6ZcHpY.

22. Joseph Bauman. "'No More Moo by '92' on West Ranges May Be a Simplistic Approach," *Deseret News*, August 1, 1990, https://www.deseret.com/1990/8/2/18874469/no-more-moo-by-92-on-west-ranges-may-be-a-simplistic-approach.

23. Nathan F. Sayre, *Working Wilderness: The Malpai Borderlands Group Story and the Future of the Western Range* (Tucson: Rio Nuevo Press, 2006).

24. Sayre, *Working Wilderness.*

25. "New Life in the Badlands," The Nature Conservancy, October 1, 2015, https://www.nature.org/en-us/magazine/magazine-articles/new-life-in-the-badlands/.

26. Jim Corbett, *Goatwalking: A Guide to Wildland Living* (New York: Viking, 1991).

27. "Private-Public Collaborations in Natural Resource Management: Forging Shared Action Arenas Between Heterogeneous Actors," Center for the Study of Institutional Diversity, Arizona State University, March 30, 2012, https://dlc.dlib.indiana.edu/dlc/bitstream/handle/10535/8062/CSID_WP_2012-001.pdf?sequence=1.

28. "Stewardship with a Vision," Western Landholders Association, 2015, https://www.youtube.com/watch?v=jvYW1dlzVjg.

29. Sayre, "The Cattle Boom in Southern Arizona."

30. "From 'Front Porch' Conversations to an Expanded, Complex Partnership: The Malpai Borderlands Group, Arizona, New Mexico and Mexico," The Nature Conservancy, https://www.conservationgateway.org/ConservationPlanning/partnering/cpc/Documents/CaseStudyMalpai%206.pdf.

31. Ben Brown, "Grassland Management by the Animas Foundation," U.S. Forest Service, https://www.fs.usda.gov/rm/pubs/rmrs_p003/rmrs_p003_248_250.pdf.

32. "Success in New Mexico's Sky Island Country," The Nature Conservancy, https://www.nature.org/en-us/get-involved/how-to-help/places-we-protect/diamond-a-ranch/.

33. "MBG Board of Directors," Malpai Borderlands Group, http://www.malpaiborderlandsgroup.org/?section=25.

34. Stephanie Lynn Gripne, "Grassbanks: Bartering for Conservation," *Rangelands* 27, no. 1 (2005): 24–28; "Malpai Borderlands Partnership: Improving Rangeland and Preserving a Way of Life," Cooperative Conservation America, http://www.cooperativeconservation.org/viewproject.aspx?id=653.

35. Richard Winkler, "Editorial: Malpai Borderlands Group Views on Border Wall," *Herald/Review*, May 19, 2019, https://www.myheraldreview.com/news/malpai-borderlands-group-opposes-border-wall/article_46153290-78e7-11e9-be5c-07f7c894d3fd.html.

36. Randal C. Archibold, "Ranchers Alarmed by Killing Near Border," *New York Times*, April 4, 2010, https://www.nytimes.com/2010/04/05/us/05arizona.html.

37. Richard Winkler, "Malpai Borderlands Group Opposes Border Wall," *Herald/Review*, May 19, 2019, https://www.myheraldreview.com/news/malpai-borderlands-group-opposes-border-wall/article_46153290-78e7-11e9-be5c-07f7c894d3fd.html.

38. Nick Miroff, "Where Trump Border Wall Rises, These Ranchers See Defeat," *Washington Post*, March 6, 2020, https://www.washingtonpost.com/immigration/2020/03/06/where-trumps-border-wall-rises-ranchers-see-scar-range/.

39. Nick Miroff, "See the Animals Caught on Camera Diverting Around Trump's Border Wall," *Washington Post*, March 2, 2020, https://www.washingtonpost.com/graphics/2020/national/amp-stories/animals-at-border-wall/.

40. "Science Advisory Panel," Malpai Borderlands Group, http://www.malpaiborderlandsgroup.org/?section=24; Charles G. Curtin, "Integration of Science and Community-Based Conservation in the Mexico/US Borderlands," *Conservation Biology* 16, no. 4 (August 2002): 880–86, https://www.jstor.org/stable/3061164.

41. Gerald J. Gottfried, Larry S. Allen, Peter L. Warren, Bill McDonald, Ronald J. Bemis, and Carleton B. Edminster, "Private-Public Collaboration to Reintroduce Fire into the Changing Ecosystems of the Southwestern Borderlands Region," *Fire Ecology* 5, no. 1, special issue (2009), https://www.fs.usda.gov/rm/pubs_other/rmrs_2009_gottfried_g001.pdf.

42. Terry Greene Sterling, "'Radical Center' Tries to Shield Ranch Land," *Washington Post*, November 13, 2004, https://www.washingtonpost.com/archive/politics/2004/11/13/radical-center-tries-to-shield-ranch-land/8dd157ec-5600-40c1-9ff7-1fac549ff26d/; Lesli Allison, "Can the Center Hold? Collaborative Conservation Is the Way Out West," Western Landholders Alliance, May 5, 2022, https://onland.westernlandowners.org/2022/directors-letter/can-the-center-hold-collaborative-conservation-is-the-way-out-west/.

Chapter 5

1. Gori et al., "Sky Island Grassland Assessment."

2. "HabiMap Arizona," Arizona Game and Fish Department, https://habimap.azgfd.com/.

3. *Bar X Bar Ranch and Cienega Ranch, Cochise County, Arizona: Protection of a Priority Grassland Landscape, a Report to Accompany an Application to NRCS ACEP-ALE for Bar X Bar Ranch*, Trust for Public Land, February 2021 (provided by Michael Patrick, Trust for Public Land).

4. Marcela Vásquez-León, Colin Thor West, Barbara Wolf, Jane Moody, and Timothy J. Finan, *Vulnerability to Climate Variability in the Farming Sector A Case Study of Groundwater Dependent Agriculture in Southeastern Arizona*, CLIMAS (Climate Assessment for the Southwest) Report Series CL1-02, December 2002, https://prism.lib.asu.edu/_flysystem/fedora/2022-07/pdfcl1-02_1_0.pdf; Noah Gallagher Shannon, "The Water Wars of Arizona," *New York Times*, July 19, 2018, https://www.nytimes.com/2018/07/19/magazine/the-water-wars-of-arizona.html; Ian James and Rob O'Dell, "In Southeastern Arizona, Farms Drill a Half-Mile Deep while Families Pay the Price," *Arizona Republic*, December 5, 2019,

https://www.azcentral.com/in-depth/news/local/arizona-environment/2019/12/05/wells
-drying-up-around-willcox-where-effort-change-groundwater-rules-failed/2357906001/.

5. "Willcox Playa/Cochise Lakes IBA," Arizona Important Bird Area Program, 2011, https://aziba.org/?page_id=712; "Chiricahua Mountain IBA," Arizona Important Bird Area Program, 2011, https://aziba.org/?page_id=330.

6. Kathy Dobie, "An Amateur Rancher Brings the Wastelands of the Southwest Back to Life," *O, The Oprah Magazine*, September 2012, https://www.oprah.com/world/valer -austin-transforming-dead-land-in-mexico.

7. Sayre, *Working Wilderness.*

8. "Local Rancher Working to Protect and Restore Large Sky Islands Grassland Ranch," Trust for Public Land, July 10, 2017, https://www.tpl.org/media-room/local-rancher-work ing-protect-and-restore-large-sky-islands-grassland-ranch; "Arizona Ranch Owner Protects Grasslands and Wildlife Habitat Through a Conservation Easement," New Mexico Land Conservancy, July 20, 2017, https://nmlandconservancy.org/2017/07/20/arizona-ranch -owner-protects-grasslands-and-wildlife-habitat-through-a-conservation-easement/.

9. "Agricultural Conservation Easement Program: ACEP," U.S. Natural Resources Con servation Program, https://www.nrcs.usda.gov/programs-initiatives/acep-agricultural -conservation-easement-program.

10. "Trust for Public Land and Partners Protect Additional 7,800 Acres of Critical Grasslands Near Chiricahua Mountains," Gila Valley Central, August 19, 2022, https:// gilavalleycentral.net/trust-for-public-land-and-partners-protect-additional-7800-acres -of-critical-grasslands-near-chiricahua-mountains/.

11. "Josiah Austin—2020 Arizona Outdoor Hall of Fame," Wildlife for Tomorrow, Oc tober 8, 2020, https://www.wildlifefortomorrow.org/news/2020/10/8/dgm30q4alphmm9 x5ii158dh1076ax2; "Where the Wild Things Are: Arizona's Cienega Ranch," Trust for Pub lic Land, August 17, 2022, https://www.tpl.org/blog/arizonas-cienega-ranch-is-where-the -wild-things-are.

12. "Environmental Quality Incentives Program—EQIP," U.S. Natural Resources Con servation Service, https://www.nrcs.usda.gov/programs-initiatives/eqip-environmental -quality-incentives.

13. Gori et al., "Sky Island Grassland Assessment."

14. "Ecosystem Services from National Grasslands," U.S. Forest Service, https://www .fs.usda.gov/managing-land/national-forests-grasslands/national-grasslands/ecoservices.

15. Fletcher and Robbie, "Historic and Current Conditions of the Southwestern Grasslands."

16. Todd Ontl and Maria Janowiak, "Grassland Carbon Management," U.S. Forest Ser vice Climate Change Resource Center, June 2017, https://www.fs.usda.gov/ccrc/topics /grassland-carbon-management.

17. Kat Kerlin, "Grasslands More Reliable Carbon Sink than Trees: In Wildfire-Prone California, Grasslands a Less Vulnerable Carbon Offset than Forests," University of California–Davis Climate Change, July 9, 2018, https://climatechange.ucdavis.edu/climate /news/grasslands-more-reliable-carbon-sink-than-trees.

18. Gori et al., "Sky Island Grassland Assessment."

19. Andrew Wetzler, "Pollinator and Grassland Declines: A Vicious Cycle?," Natural Resources Defense Council, July 24, 2013, https://www.nrdc.org/bio/andrew-wetzler/pollinator-and-grassland-declines-vicious-cycle.

20. "Pollinators Support Grassland Birds," National Wildlife Federation, August 25, 2017, https://blog.nwf.org/2016/06/pollinators-support-grassland-birds/; Aaron Sexton and Sarah M. Emery, "Grassland Restorations Improve Pollinator Communities: A Meta-analysis," *Journal of Insect Conservation* 24, no. 4 (August 2020): 1–8, https://www.researchgate.net/publication/342486016_Grassland_restorations_improve_pollinator_communities_a_meta-analysis; "Grasslands Worth Millions to Beekeepers, Invaluable to Birds," U.S. Geological Survey, June 7, 2022, https://www.usgs.gov/news/state-news-release/grasslands-worth-millions-beekeepers-invaluable-birds.

21. "Biodiversity Hotspot Defined," Critical Ecosystem Partnership Fund, https://www.cepf.net/our-work/biodiversity-hotspots/hotspots-defined; Leonard F. DeBano, Peter F. Ffolliott, Alfredo Ortega-Rubio, Gerald J. Gottfried, Robert H. Hamre, and Carleton B. Edminster, *Biodiversity and Management of the Madrean Archipelago: The Sky Islands of Southwestern United States and Northwestern Mexico*, U.S. Forest Service Rocky Mountain Forest and Range Experiment Station General Technical Report RM-GTR-264, September 19–23, 1994, https://www.fs.usda.gov/rm/pubs_rm/rm_gtr264.pdf; "Sky Islands," National Park Service, http://home.nps.gov/chir/learn/nature/sky-islands.htm; Aubin Tyler, "In Arizona, a Biodiversity Hot Spot Goes Beyond Science," *Boston Globe*, December 25, 2011, https://www.bostonglobe.com/lifestyle/travel/2011/12/25/the-south western-research-station-delights-scientists-and-guest-naturalists-alike/esQcMaCZOS 2zHIDUlnlR8I/story.html.

22. "What Is a Conservation Easement?," Great Outdoors Colorado, https://goco.org/news/blog/what-is-conservation-easement; "Conservation Easement: A Property Rights Based Tool for Resource Protection," We ConservePA, https://conservationtools.org/guides/19-conservation-easement.

23. "How a Conservation Easement Works—Sample Example of Conservation Easement," Land Conservation Assistance Network, https://www.landcan.org/article/How-a-Conservation-Easement-Works--Sample-example-of-conservation-easement/86; "Land Protection Methods," Arizona Land and Water Trust, https://www.alwt.org/for-landowners/.

Chapter 6

1. "Landmark Study: Human Population Growth, Consumption Has Increased Species Extinctions by More Than 1,000 Times Natural Rate," Center for Biological Diversity, 2014, https://www.biologicaldiversity.org/news/press_releases/2014/extinction-rate-05-29-2014.html; Beth Gavrilles, "Species Going Extinct 1,000 Times Faster than in Pre-Human Times, Study Finds," *UGA Today*, September 17, 2014, https://news.uga.edu/species-extinct-1000-times-faster-than-pre-human-times-0914/; Peter Aldhous, "We Are Killing Species at 1000 Times the Natural Rate," *New Scientist*, May 29, 2014, https://www.newscientist.com/article/dn25645-we-are-killing-species-at-1000-times-the-natural-rate/;

"WWF Report Reveals Staggering Extent of Human Impact on Planet," World Wildlife Fund, October 29, 2018, https://www.worldwildlife.org/press-releases/wwf-report-reveals -staggering-extent-of-human-impact-on-planet.

2. M. Grooten and R. E. A. Almond, eds., *Living Planet Report 2018: Aiming Higher* (World Wildlife Fund, 2018), https://c402277.ssl.cf1.rackcdn.com/publications/1187/files /original/LPR2018_Full_Report_Spreads.pdf?1540487589.

3. *Status of Pollinators in North America* (Washington, D.C.: National Academies Press, 2007), https://nap.nationalacademies.org/read/11761/chapter/2; "Threats to Pollinators," U.S. Fish and Wildlife Service, https://www.fws.gov/initiative/pollinators/threats.

4. "The Recovering America's Wildlife Act Will Help Safeguard Habitats and Biodiversity, Slow Extinction Rates and Secure a Brighter Future for People and Nature," The Nature Conservancy, March 2023. https://www.nature.org/en-us/about-us/who-we-are /how-we-work/policy/recovering-americas-wildlife/; "Habitat Loss," National Wildlife Federation, https://www.nwf.org/Educational-Resources/Wildlife-Guide/Threats-to -Wildlife/Habitat-Loss.

5. "Recovering America's Wildlife Act," National Wildlife Federation, https://www .nwf.org/Our-Work/Wildlife-Conservation/Policy/Recovering-Americas-Wildlife-Act; Jordan E. Rogan and Thomas E. Lacher Jr., "Impacts of Habitat Loss and Fragmentation on Terrestrial Biodiversity," in *Reference Module in Earth Systems and Environmental Sciences* (Amsterdam: Elsevier, 2018); McKinney, Scarlett, and Kemmis, "Large Landscape Conservation."

6. "Ecosystem Services," National Wildlife Federation, https://www.nwf.org /Educational-Resources/Wildlife-Guide/Understanding-Conservation/Ecosystem-Services.

7. "Trends in Water Use in the United States, 1950 to 2015," U.S. Geological Survey Water Science School, June 18, 2018, https://www.usgs.gov/special-topics/water-science -school/science/trends-water-use-united-states-1950-2015.

8. "Groundwater: Our Most Valuable Hidden Resource," The Nature Conservancy, March 13, 2022, https://www.nature.org/en-us/what-we-do/our-insights/perspectives /groundwater-most-valuable-resource/.

9. "Silent Streams? Escalating Endangerment for North American Freshwater and Diadromous Fish," U.S. Geological Survey Coastal and Marine Hazards and Resources Program, 2009, https://www.usgs.gov/programs/cmhrp/news/silent-streams-escalating -endangerment-north-american-freshwater-and-diadromous; *National Rivers and Streams Assessment 2008–2009: A Collaborative Survey*, EPA/841/R-16/007 (Washington, D.C.: Environmental Protection Agency Office of Water and Office of Research and Development, March 2016), https://www.epa.gov/sites/default/files/2016-03/documents /nrsa_0809_march_2_final.pdf; "Ground-Water Depletion Across the Nation," USGS Fact Sheet 103-03, 2003, https://pubs.usgs.gov/fs/fs-103-03/.

10. Niall Clancy, John P. Draper, J. Marshall Wolf, Umarfarooq A. Abdulwahab, Maya C. Pendleton, Soren Brothers, Janice Brahney, Jennifer Weathered, Edd Hamill, and Trisha B. Atwood, "Protecting Endangered Species in the USA Requires Both Public and Private Land Conservation," *Scientific Reports* 10 (2020), article 11925, https://www.nature .com/articles/s41598-020-68780-y; Cara Giaimo, "Endangered Species Get a Huge Bump

When Private Lands Are Brought into the Conservation Mix," *Anthropocene*, July 29, 2020, https://www.anthropocenemagazine.org/2020/07/endangered-species-get-a-huge-bump -when-private-lands-are-brought-into-the-conversation-mix/; Bruce A. Stein, Cameron Scott, and Nancy Benton, "Federal Lands and Endangered Species: The Role of Military and Other Federal Lands in Sustaining Biodiversity," *BioScience* 58, no. 4 (2008): 339–47.

11. *Pima County Multi-species Conservation Plan*, 2016; "Use of Land," in *Pima Prospers Comprehensive Plan Initiative*, 2015, https://content.civicplus.com/api/assets /0aad5f04-63c3-442f-8eb3-d8ff6fb5efc6.

12. "Conserve 30 Percent by 2030: Considerations for an Inclusive, Representative and Resilient Approach," The Nature Conservancy, April 2021.

13. "Terrestrial Resilience Core Concepts," The Nature Conservancy, https://maps.tnc .org/resilientland/.

14. "Biodiversity in Focus: United States Edition," NatureServe, 2023. https://www .natureserve.org/sites/default/files/NatureServe_BiodiversityInFocusReport_medium .pdf; Riley Gonzalez, "The Florida Wildlife Corridor Act: What Is It and Why Does It Matter," University of Florida Thompson Earth Systems Institute, July 24, 2021, https:// www.floridamuseum.ufl.edu/earth-systems/blog/the-florida-wildlife-corridor-act-what -is-it-and-what-changes-will-it-bring/.

15. Pima County Administrator's Office, *Protecting Our Land, Water, and Heritage*.

16. "Edwards Aquifer Protection," The Nature Conservancy, https://www.nature.org /en-us/about-us/where-we-work/united-states/texas/stories-in-texas/edwards-aquifer -protection/; "Edwards Aquifer," Parks and Facilities, San Antonio, https://www.san antonio.gov/ParksAndRec/Parks-Facilities/All-Parks-Facilities/Gardens-Natural-Ar- eas/Edwards-Aquifer.

17. "Land and Water Conservation Fund," U.S. Department of the Interior, https://www .doi.gov/lwcf; "Land and Water Conservation Fund," Bureau of Land Management, https:// www.blm.gov/programs/land-and-water-conservation-fund; "Federal Land Transaction Facilitation Act," Bureau of Land Management, https://www.blm.gov/programs/lands-and -realty/federal-land-transaction-facilitation-act; "Land Acquisition and Realty," U.S. Fish and Wildlife Service, https://www.fws.gov/program/land-acquisition-and-realty.

18. "Sometimes to Save a River, You Have to Buy It," Western Rivers Conservancy, https://www.westernrivers.org/.

19. "Save the Saints," Wildlands Conservancy, https://wildlandsconservancy.org/con servation/savethesaints; Bettina Bosall, "A Quiet Broker of the Wild," *Los Angeles Times*, April 24, 2002, https://www.latimes.com/archives/la-xpm-2002-apr-24-mn-39618-story .html; "Mojave Trails National Monument," Wildlands Conservancy, https://wildlands conservancy.org/conservation/mojavetrailsnm.

20. Andy Lourenzi, "State Trust Lands: Balancing Public Value and Fiduciary Respon- sibility," Lincoln Institute of Land Policy (Cambridge, MA), July 2004, https://www.lincoln inst.edu/publications/articles/state-trust-lands.

21. An Act of Congress on February 24, 1863, created the Arizona Territory and re- served sections 16 and 36 of every township for the benefit of common schools. The Enabling Act of 1910 that allowed the territory to prepare for statehood assigned the

additional sections 2 and 32 for common schools. It also granted 2.35 million acres for other beneficiaries. NB: A section is a 640-acre (1-square-mile) parcel; a township comprises 36 sections.

22. "Federal Land by State 2024: Federal Land Percentage," World Population Review, https://worldpopulationreview.com/state-rankings/federal-land-by-state; "SITLA and Trust Lands Explained," Utah Trust Land Administration, https://trustlands.utah.gov/our-agency/sitla-and-trust-lands-explained/; "State Land Trust," New Mexico Legislative Finance Committee, https://www.nmlegis.gov/Entity/LFC/Documents/Finance_Facts/finance%20facts%20state%20trust%20land.pdf; "Public Access on Trust Land," Colorado State Land Board, https://slb.colorado.gov/public-access; "Agency and Mission," Arizona State Land Department, https://land.az.gov/our-agency-mission.

23. Peter W. Culp, Andy Laurenzi, Cynthia C. Tuell, and Alison Berry, "State Trust Lands in the West: Fiduciary Duty in a Changing Landscape," Lincoln Institute of Land Policy, 2015, https://www.lincolninst.edu/publications/policy-focus-reports/state-trust-lands-in-west-updated-edition.

24. Susan Culp and Joe Marlow, "Conserving State Trust Lands: Strategies for the Intermountain West," Lincoln Institute of Land Policy, 2015, https://www.lincolninst.edu/sites/default/files/pubfiles/conserving-state-trust-lands-full.pdf.

25. *Fain Land & Cattle Co. v. Hassell* (1990).

26. "Conservation Easement: A Property Rights Based Tool"; Jeff Pidot, "Reinventing Conservation Easements," Lincoln Institute of Land Policy, https://www.lincolninst.edu/publications/articles/reinventing-conservation-easements.

27. "Frequently Asked Questions," Land Trust Alliance, https://landtrustalliance.org/take-action/conserve-your-land/frequently-asked-questions.

28. "Conservation Easements," Edwards Aquifer Authority, https://www.edwardsaquifer.org/aquifer-protection/groundwater-protection/conservation-easements/; "Considerations for the Future of the City of San Antonio's Edwards Aquifer Protection Program," Edwards Aquifer Authority, https://www.edwardsaquifer.org/wp-content/uploads/2019/12/CoSA-EAPP-Combined.pdf.

29. "Agricultural Conservation Easement Program."

30. "What Is a Land Trust," Arizona Land and Water Trust, https://www.alwt.org/land-water-conservation/; "Land Protection," Arizona Land and Water Trust, https://www.alwt.org/protection/.

31. The Sentinel Landscapes Partnership, https://sentinellandscapes.org/.

32. Damian Nabil Rawoot, "Conservation Easements in the Madrean Archipelago: Landscape-Scale Strategy or Random Acts of Conservation," master's thesis, University of Arizona, 2017, https://repository.arizona.edu/bitstream/handle/10150/626400/azu_etd_16058_sip1_m.pdf.

33. Peter Elkind, "How Congress Finally Cracked Down on a Massive Tax Scam," *ProPublica*, January 9, 2023, https://www.propublica.org/article/syndicated-conservation-easements-tax-scam-irs-biden.

34. K. King Burnett, John D. Leshy, and Nancy A. McLaughlin, "Building Better Conservation Easements for America the Beautiful," *Harvard Environmental Law Review*,

September 15, 2021, https://harvardelr.com/2021/09/15/building-better-conservation-easements-for-america-the-beautiful/.

35. Babbitt, *Cities in the Wilderness*.

36. "Northwest Forest Plan Overview," U.S. Forest Service, https://www.fs.usda.gov/detail/r6/landmanagement/planning/?cid=fsbdev2_026990.

37. "Conservation Reserve Program," U.S. Farm Service Agency, https://www.fsa.usda.gov/programs-and-services/conservation-programs/conservation-reserve-program/.

38. "Conservation Stewardship Program (CSP)," U.S. Natural Resources Conservation Service, https://www.nrcs.usda.gov/programs-initiatives/csp-conservation-stewardship-program.

39. Caitlin Tan, "USDA Partners with Greater Yellowstone Ecosystem Landowners to Conserve Wildlife Habitat," Wyoming Public Radio, 2022, https://www.wyomingpublicmedia.org/natural-resources-energy/2022-05-23/usda-partners-with-greater-yellowstone-ecosystem-landowners-to-conserve-wildlife-habitat.

40. Vikram Jhawar, "Understanding the Basics of Mitigation Banking," Investopedia, updated January 31, 2022, https://www.investopedia.com/articles/dictionary/031615/understanding-basics-mitigation-banking.asp.

41. *County of San Diego Multiple Species Conservation Program: South County Sub-area Plan Annual Report Year 22*, County of San Diego Parks and Recreation, July 8, 2020, https://www.sdparks.org/content/dam/sdparks/en/pdf/Resource-Management/mscp/MSCP/Documents/2019_MSCP_South%20County_AnnualReport_Final.pdf; "North County Plan—Frequently Asked Questions," San Diego County, https://www.sandiegocounty.gov/pds/mscp/docs/NCPlan_FAQs.pdf.

42. Sarah Farmer, "Payments for Ecosystem Services: Incentives for Landowners to Keep Their Forest as Forest," U.S. Forest Service Southern Station, 2022, https://www.fs.usda.gov/research/srs/products/compasslive/payments-ecosystem-services; D. Evan Mercer, David Cooley, and Katherine Hamilton, "Taking Stock: Payments for Forest Ecosystem Services in the United States," U.S. Forest Service, February 2011, https://www.forest-trends.org/wp-content/uploads/imported/ForestPES_Final.pdf.

43. Emily Fripp, *Payments for Ecosystem Services (PES): A Practical Guide to Assessing the Feasibility of PES Projects* (Bogor, Indonesia: Center for International Forestry Research, 2014).

44. "Grassland CRP," U.S. Farm Service Agency, https://www.fsa.usda.gov/programs-and-services/conservation-programs/crp-grasslands/index.

45. Joshua Howard Goldstein, Carrie K. Presnall, Laura Lopez-Hoffman, Gary Nabhan, Richard Knight, George Ruyle, and Theodore Toombs, "Beef and Beyond: Paying for Ecosystem Services on Western US Rangelands," *Rangelands* 33, no. 5 (January 2010), https://www.researchgate.net/publication/305301966_Beef_and_Beyond_Paying_for_Ecosystem_Services_on_Western_US_Rangelands.

46. "USDA Offers New Forest Management Incentive for Conservation Reserve Program," U.S. Farm Service Agency, January 19, 2021, https://www.fsa.usda.gov/news-room/news-releases/2021/usda-offers-new-forest-management-incentive-for-conservation-reserve-program.

47. David Primozich, *Developing the Willamette Ecosystem Marketplace*, report submitted to the U.S. Environmental Protection Agency, June 30, 2008, http://willamette partnership.org/wp-content/uploads/2014/09/Developing-the-Ecosystem-Credit -Accounting-System.pdf.

48. Irina Prokofieva, "Payments for Ecosystem Services: The Case of Forests," *Current Forestry Reports* 2 (April 26, 2016): 130–42, https://link.springer.com/content/pdf/10 .1007/s40725-016-0037-9.pdf.

49. Leopold, *A Sand County Almanac*, 210–11.

50. Public Law 106-538, An Act to Establish the Las Cienegas National Conservation Area.

51. "Approved Las Cienegas Resource Management Plan and Record of Decision," Bureau of Land Management, Arizona State Office, Tucson Field Office, July 2003, https:// azmemory.azlibrary.gov/nodes/view/201056.

52. Brott, "Celebrating Collaborative Conservation"; Karen Simms, "The Sonoita Valley Planning Partnership: A New Approach to Community Participation in Public Land Management Planning," paper presented at the Creative Cooperation in Resource Management Conference, Tucson, May 2020.

53. Caves et al., "Integrating Collaboration, Adaptive Management, and Scenario Planning."

54. Dean A. Hendrickson and W. L. Minckley, "Cienegas—Vanishing Climax Communities," *Desert Plants* 6, no. 3 (1984), https://www.fs.usda.gov/rm/boise/AWAE/labs /awae_flagstaff/Hot_Topics/ripthreatbib/hendrickson_minckley_cienegas.pdf.

55. "Restoring Arroyos and Preventing Landscape Erosion," Cienega Watershed Partnership, http://www.cienega.org/projects/conservation-restoration/arroyo/.

56. "Cienega Watershed Erosion Management and Restoration Plan," Watershed Management Group, https://lccnetwork.org/sites/default/files/Resources/Cienega%20 Watershed%20Erosion%20Management%20and%20Restoration%20Plan.pdf.

57. "Partnership Helps Conserve Las Cienegas National Conservation Area in Arizona," My Public Lands, https://mypubliclands.tumblr.com/post/73431134414 /partnership-helps-conserve-las-cienegas-national.

58. "Las Cienegas Landscape Restoration Environmental Assessment," Bureau of Land Management, January 2020, https://eplanning.blm.gov/public_projects/nepa/1500108 /20012174/250016558/Las_Cienegas_Draft_EA_508.pdf.

59. "Sky Islands Grassland Restoration," LandScope America, http://www.landscope .org/connect/conservation-projects/project/1753.

60. "Partnership Helps Conserve Las Cienegas."

61. Arizona Game and Fish, "In the Field: Native Fish Introductions in Las Cienegas National Conservation Area," In the Current: Native Aquatic Species Conservation in Arizona, https://inthecurrent.org/itf/native-fish-introductions-las-cienegas-national -conservation-area/.

62. "Prescott Valley Arizona Glassford Hill Pronghorn Capture Success and New Southeastern Arizona Beginnings, January 22–23, 2019," Arizona Antelope Foundation, https://www.azantelope.org/resources/Documents/Final%20Grant%20Report/Final%20 Grant%20Report%2098%20pages.pdf.

63. "Re-establishment of Beaver on the Las Cienegas National Conservation Area," Bureau of Land Management, May 18, 2022, https://eplanning.blm.gov/eplanning -ui/project/2001673/510.

64. "Conservation Action: Land Management," Malpai Borderlands Group, http:// www.malpaiborderlandsgroup.org/?section=22.

65. R. Randall Schumann, comp., *The Malpai Borderlands Project: A Stewardship Approach to Rangeland Management*, U.S. Geological Survey, December 9, 2016, https:// geochange.er.usgs.gov/sw/responses/malpai/.

66. "San Bernardino National Wildlife Reserve," U.S. Fish and Wildlife Service, https:// www.fws.gov/refuge/san-bernardino/about-us.

67. Malpai Borderlands Habitat Conservation Plan Technical Working Group and William Lehman, *Malpai Borderlands Habitat Conservation Plan*, 2008, https://seslibrary.asu .edu/sites/default/files/seslibrary/sources/146/Malapai%20Borderlands%20Conservation %20Plan%20%28Final%29%20-%20reduced.pdf.

68. "Watershed Improvement Project," Malpai Borderlands Group, http://www.malpai borderlandsgroup.org/?section=22.

69. "New Life in the Badlands," The Nature Conservancy, October 1, 2015, https://www .nature.org/en-us/magazine/magazine-articles/new-life-in-the-badlands/.

70. "Landowners and Partners Malpai Borderlands Group and Sky Island Alliance," Stream Dynamics, Inc., https://streamdynamics.us/project/cloverdale-cienega -restoration-project.

71. "The Guadalupe Wildfire," Malpai Borderlands Group, http://www.malpaiborder landsgroup.org/?module=articlemodule&src=51b2303cd296f&action=view_article&id=55.

72. Brandon T. Bestelmeyer, Sheri Spiegal, Rich Winkler, Darren James, Matthew Levi, and Jeb Williamson, "Assessing Sustainability Goals Using Big Data: Collaborative Adaptive Management in the Malpai Borderlands," *Rangeland Ecology and Management* 77 (July 2021): 17–29, https://www.sciencedirect.com/science/article/abs/pii/S1550742421 000312.

73. "Watershed Improvement Project," Malpai Borderlands Group, http://www.malpai borderlandsgroup.org/?module=articlemodule&src=51ec47bca1754&action=view_article &id=45.

74. "Plan for the Recovery of Desert Bighorn Sheep in New Mexico, 2003–2013," New Mexico Department of Game and Fish, August 2003, http://bighorndiseaseinfo.alter vista.org/Bighorn_Disease_Documents/NM_desert_bighorn_recovery_plan_2003-2013 _NMGF_2003.pdf; "Endangered Species," Malpai Borderlands Group, http://www.malpai borderlandsgroup.org/?section=science-and-nature.

75. "San Bernardino Valley Herd Zone," *Pronghorn* 26, no. 3 (2020), https://azantelope .org/resources/Documents/Newsletters/AAF%20Pronghorn%202020%20Q3%20final.pdf.

76. Charles Curtin, *Initial Results of Experimental Studies of Prairie Dogs in Arid Grasslands: Implications for Landscape Conservation and the Importance of Scale*, U.S. Forest Service Proceedings RMRS-P-40, 2006, https://www.fs.usda.gov/rm/pubs/rmrs _p040/rmrs_p040_057_062.pdf.

77. George Zaimes, "Chapter 7: Human Alterations to Riparian Areas," in *Understanding Arizona's Riparian Areas*, ed. George Zaimes (Tucson: University of Arizona Cooperative Extension, 2007), https://extension.arizona.edu/sites/extension.arizona.edu/files/pubs/az1432.pdf.

78. "Restoration of Cienega Creek Bottomlands Cienega Creek Natural Preserve," Pima County Regional Flood Control District and Bureau of Land Management, https://rfcd.pima.gov/wrd/landmgt/cienegapreserve/pdfs/ccnp_bottomlands_restoration_summary.pdf; "Revegetating Abandoned Farmland in the Cienega Creek Natural Preserve, Pima County, Arizona," Pima County, https://content.civicplus.com/api/assets/ddd188fb-d21d-41a2-b02f-eb43cac42991; "Cienega Creek Natural Preserve: Vegetation," Pima County, https://www.pima.gov/1779/Vegetation.

79. David Scalero, "Pantano Jungle Restoration Cienega Creek Natural Preserve," Partners for Fish and Wildlife Program, U.S. Fish and Wildlife Service, May 19, 2009, https://content.civicplus.com/api/assets/95ddd83a-1995-471d-b4ed-efc358aadc84.

80. Chuck Huckelberry, "Bingham Cienega Restoration: Sonoran Desert Conservation Plan," memo to the Pima County Board of Supervisors, October 22, 2001, https://hdl.handle.net/2286/R.I.21387; Erik Rieger, "Restoration at Las Cienegas NCA: Bingham Cienega: Restoring Abandoned Farmland in Arizona's Sonoran Desert," March 17, 2021, https://storymaps.arcgis.com/stories/476eeb82f38b4e00b8d34925f9c537a3.

81. *Santa Cruz River*, special issue, *Sonorensis* 23, no. 1 (Winter 2003), https://www.desertmuseum.org/members/sonorensis/sonorensis2003.pdf.

82. "Santa Cruz River: Paradise Lost, Paradise Reborn, Will It Be Lost Again?," Sonoran Institute, https://sonoraninstitute.org/card/santa-cruz-river-success/.

83. "A Living River: Charting Santa Cruz River Conditions, Downtown Tucson to Marana, 2013–2020," Sonoran Institute, https://sonoraninstitute.org/files/LR-Supplemental-Downtown-Tucson-to-Marana-2013-to-2020.pdf.

84. Pima County Administrator's Office, *Protecting Our Land, Water, and Heritage.*

85. "Our Work: Conservation," Altar Valley Conservation Group, https://altarvalleyconservation.org/our-work/conservation/; "Collaboratives Behind the Scenes: Altar Valley Conservation Alliance," Center for Collaborative Conservation, https://collaborativeconservation.org/2022/11/28/collaboratives-behind-the-scenes-altar-valley-conservation-alliance/.

86. "Projects," Altar Valley Conservation Group, https://altarvalleyconservation.org/our-work/conservation/projects/; "Altar Valley Fire Management Plan," Altar Valley Conservation Alliance, 2008, https://altarvalleyconservation.org/our-work/conservation/projects/altar-valley-fire-management-plan/.

87. "Altar Valley Watershed Plan, 2019–2022," Altar Valley Conservation Alliance, https://altarvalleyconservation.org/our-work/conservation/projects/altar-valley-watershed-plan/.

88. "Sonoran Desert Wildlife Linkages."

89. Pima County Government, *Pima County Multi-species Conservation Plan 2021*, https://content.civicplus.com/api/assets/4ee4250c-ba03-4b96-b74e-53e34c49486f.

90. Henry Brean, "Native Fish Comes Home to Tucson as Part of River Restoration," *Arizona Daily Star*, March 23, 2022, https://tucson.com/news/science/environment /native-fish-comes-home-to-tucson-as-part-of-river-restoration/article_c2904ec4-aa29 -11ec-8603-fb17b0cdd83e.html.

91. "A Year Later and Mission Garden's Topminnow Are Thriving," *Signals*, October 13, 2020, https://www.signalsaz.com/articles/a-year-later-and-mission-gardens-topminnow -are-thriving/.

92. Henry Brean, "Bighorn Fire Prompts Hasty Fish Rescue from Sabino Canyon: Almost 900 Endangered Gila Chubs Were Evacuated to Sites Around Tucson," *Arizona Daily Star*, June 17, 2020, https://tucson.com/news/local/bighorn-fire-prompts-hasty-fish -rescue-from-sabino-canyon/article_395ce6ff-122f-59f6-88cf-958cb14c0c7e.html.

93. Powell, "The Non-Irrigable Lands."

94. "Collaborative Forest Landscape Restoration Program Overview," U.S. Forest Service, https://www.fs.usda.gov/restoration/CFLRP/overview.shtml.

95. Courtney A. Schultz and Theresa Jedd, "The Collaborative Forest Landscape Restoration Program: A History and Overview of the First Projects," *Papers in Natural Resources* 933 (2012), https://digitalcommons.unl.edu/cgi/viewcontent.cgi?article=1942&context =natrespapers.

96. "Application Process Overview and Criteria for Tier 2," U.S. Forest Service, 2022, https://www.fs.usda.gov/restoration/documents/cflrp/2022-app-process-overview -criteria-tier2.docx.

97. "Four Forest Restoration Initiative (4FRI): 4FRI Restoration Strategy," U.S. Forest Service, November 9, 2021, https://www.fs.usda.gov/Internet/FSE_DOCUMENTS /fseprd969259.pdf.

98. *Wyoming Landscape Conservation Initiative 10 Year Anniversary Report, 2007– 2017*, Bureau of Land Management, https://www.blm.gov/sites/default/files/documents /files/WLCI%2010%20Year%20Final%20Web.pdf.

99. "Wyoming Landscape Conservation Initiative Celebrates 10 Years of Impact," Wyoming Game and Fish Department, February 1, 2018, https://wgfd.wyo.gov/News /Wyoming-Landscape-Conservation-Initiative-celebrat.

100. Wyoming Landscape Conservation Initiative, https://www.wlci.gov/.

101. Erica Husse, "An Initiative for Landscape Conservation on Southwest Wyoming," Partnering to Conserve Sagebrush Rangelands, January 30, 2020, https://www.partnersin thesage.com/blog/initiative-for-landscape-conservation-sw-wy.

102. "Facilitating Responsible Development: Habitat Improvements," Wyoming Landscape Conservation Initiative, https://www.wlci.gov/#/Habitat-Improvements.

103. *Wyoming Landscape Conservation Initiative 2018 Annual Report*, Bureau of Land Management, https://www.blm.gov/sites/default/files/documents/files/2018%20WLCI %20Annual%20Report_web.pdf.

104. Bureau of Land Management, "Wyoming Landscape Conservation Initiative—10 Year Anniversary," YouTube, 2018, https://www.youtube.com/watch?v=DWfYObwX3iw.

105. Bureau of Land Management.

106. "Sustaining Large Landscape Conservation Partnerships: Strategies for Success," Sonoran Institute, 2012, https://sonoraninstitute.org/files/pdf/sustaining-large-landscape-conservation-partnerships-strategies-for-success-06012012.pdf.

107. *Economic Impacts of Wyoming Landscape Conservation Initiative Conservation Projects in Wyoming*, U.S. Geological Survey Open-File Report 2019-1135, 2019, https://pubs.usgs.gov/of/2019/1135/ofr20191135.pdf.

108. B. K. Williams, R. C. Szaro, and C. D. Shapiro, *Adaptive Management: The U.S. Department of the Interior Technical Guide* (Washington, D.C.: U.S. Department of the Interior, 2009), https://www.doi.gov/sites/doi.gov/files/migrated/ppa/upload/TechGuide.pdf.

109. "State of the Watershed," Cienega Watershed Partnership, October 5, 2021, http://www.cienega.org/wp-content/uploads/2021/10/SOW_meeting_2021_long-version.pdf.

110. Bestelmeyer et al., "Assessing Sustainability Goals Using Big Data."

111. "Pima County Ecological Monitoring Program," Pima County, https://www.pima.gov/700/Pima-County-Ecological-Monitoring-Progra.

112. *Collaborative Forest Landscape Restoration Program: 5-Year Report, FY 2010–2014*, U.S. Forest Service FS-1047, April 2015, https://www.fs.usda.gov/restoration/documents/cflrp/CFLRP_5-YearReport.pdf.

113. "Is the CFLRP Right for Us?," U.S. Forest Service, https://www.fs.usda.gov/restoration/documents/cflrp/is-cflrp-right-for-us.docx.

114. "Monitoring," Four Forest Restoration Initiative, https://www.fs.usda.gov/main/4fri/monitoring.

115. "Wyoming Landscape Conservation Initiative: Effectiveness Monitoring," U.S. Geological Survey Fort Collins Science Center, October 27, 2016, https://www.usgs.gov/centers/fort-collins-science-center/science/wyoming-landscape-conservation-initiative-effectiveness.

116. Z. H. Bowen et al., *U.S. Geological Survey Science for the Wyoming Landscape Conservation Initiative—2015 Annual Report*, U.S. Geological Survey Open-File Report 2016-1141, 2016, https://www.nrel.colostate.edu/assets/nrel_files/labs/aldridge-lab/publications/ofr20161141Bowenetal2016.WLCI2015.pdf.

117. Kathleen M. Pike, "Climate Control: How Climate Change Impacts Mental Health," *Manhattan Times*, October 9, 2019, https://www.manhattantimesnews.com/climate-controlcontrol-climatico/.

118. Barb Cestero, "Beyond the Hundredth Meeting: A Field Guide to Collaborative Conservation on the West's Public Lands," Sonoran Institute, July 1999, https://sonoraninstitute.org/files/pdf/beyond-the-hundredth-meeting-a-field-guide-to-collaborative-conservation-on-the-wests-public-lands-07011999.pdf.

119. "Partners for Fish and Wildlife," U.S. Fish and Wildlife Service, https://www.fws.gov/program/partners-fish-and-wildlife.

120. Sheldon Alberts, "In Southern Utah, a Restored River Helps Residents and Visitors 'Recharge the Soul,'" Walton Family Foundation, May 14, 2019, https://www.waltonfamilyfoundation.org/stories/environment/in-southern-utah-a-restored-river-helps-residents-and-visitors-recharge-the-soul; Morgan Snyder, "River Recharge Holds Prom-

ise for Water-Stressed Arizona," Walton Family Foundation, January 15, 2019, https://www.waltonfamilyfoundation.org/stories/environment/river-recharge-holds-promise-for-water-stressed-arizona; Sheldon Alberts, "In Parched Arizona, a River's Friend Keeps the Water Flowing," Walton Family Foundation, February 18, 2018, https://www.waltonfamilyfoundation.org/stories/environment/in-parched-arizona-a-rivers-friend-keeps-the-water-flowing.

121. "About the Roundtable on the Crown of the Continent Collaborative," Roundtable on the Crown of the Continent, http://www.crownroundtable.net/; "Regional Conservation Partnership Program (RCPP)," U.S. Natural Resources Conservation Service, https://www.nrcs.usda.gov/programs-initiatives/rcpp-regional-conservation-partnership-program.

122. "Climate Smart Landscape Planning and Design Phase I Report: Approach, Methods and Conservation Design Workshop Results," Landscape Conservation Cooperative Network, https://lccnetwork.org/resource/climate-smart-landscape-planning-and-design-phase-i-report-approach-methods-and.

123. "Collaborative Conservation and Adaptation Strategy Toolbox (CCAST)," Climate Adaptation Knowledge Exchange, http://www.cakex.org/community/directory/organizations/collaborative-conservation-and-adaptation-strategy-toolbox-ccast.

124. "History," Blackfoot Challenge, https://blackfootchallenge.org/history/; "Applegate Partnership and Watershed Council," Applegate Partnership, https://www.applegatepartnership.org/about.

125. "NM Collaborative Zone Grants," Share New Mexico, https://sharenm.org/nm-collaborative-zone-grants/nm-collaborative-zone-grants.

Ending Thoughts

1. E. O. Wilson, *The Diversity of Life* (Cambridge, MA: Harvard University Press, 1992).

2. W. F. Lloyd, *Two Lectures on the Checks to Population* (Oxford: Oxford University Press, 1833).

3. Garrett Hardin, "The Tragedy of the Commons," *Science* 162, no. 3859 (December 13, 1968): 1243–48.

4. Garrett Hardin, "Tragedy of the Commons," Econlib CEE, https://www.econlib.org/library/Enc/TragedyoftheCommons.html.

5. Elinor Ostrom, "Beyond Markets and States: Polycentric Governance of Complex Economic Systems," Nobel Prize in Economics lecture, December 8, 2009.

6. Michelle Nijhuis, "The Miracle of the Commons," *Aeon*, May 4, 2021, https://aeon.co/essays/the-tragedy-of-the-commons-is-a-false-and-dangerous-myth.

7. Powell, "Institutions for the Arid Lands."

8. Powell, "The Non-Irrigable Lands."

9. McKinney, Scarlett, and Kemmis, "Large Landscape Conservation," emphasis added.

INDEX

Note: Page numbers in *italics* refer to illustrative matter.

ABOUT THE AUTHOR

Stephen E. Strom spent forty-five years as a research astronomer after receiving undergraduate and graduate degrees in astronomy from Harvard. He began photographing in 1978 after studying the history of photography and silver and non-silver photography at the University of Arizona. His work has been exhibited widely throughout the United States and is held in several permanent collections, including the Center for Creative Photography and the Boston Museum of Fine Arts.

His photography complements poems and essays in five books published by the University of Arizona Press—*Secrets from the Center of the World, Sonoita Plain, Tséyi' / Deep in the Rock, Earth and Mars: A Reflection, Voices from Bears Ears: Seeking Common Ground on Sacred Land,* and most recently *The Greater San Rafael Swell: Honoring Tradition and Preserving Storied Lands.* His photographs also feature in *Otero Mesa: Preserving America's Wildest Grassland, Death Valley: Painted Light, Tidal Rhythms: Change and Resilience at the End of the Sea, Bears Ears: Views from a Sacred Land, This Desert Hides Nothing,* and *Earth Forms.*